MW00850942

Queer Ecologies

Queer Ecologies

Sex, Nature, Politics, Desire

Edited by Catriona Mortimer-Sandilands
and Bruce Erickson

Indiana University Press ■ BLOOMINGTON AND INDIANAPOLIS

This book is a publication of

Indiana University Press
601 North Morton Street
Bloomington, Indiana 47404-3797 USA

www.iupress.indiana.edu

Telephone orders	800-842-6796
Fax orders	812-855-7931
Orders by e-mail	iuporder@indiana.edu

© 2010 by Indiana University Press
All rights reserved

*No part of this book may be reproduced or utilized in any form
or by any means, electronic or mechanical, including photocopying
and recording, or by any information storage and retrieval system,
without permission in writing from the publisher. The Association
of American University Presses' Resolution on Permissions
constitutes the only exception to this prohibition.*

♾ *The paper used in this publication meets the
minimum requirements of the American National
Standard for Information Sciences—Permanence of Paper
for Printed Library Materials, ANSI Z39.48-1992.*

MANUFACTURED IN THE UNITED STATES OF AMERICA

Library of Congress Cataloging-in-Publication Data

Queer ecologies : sex, nature, politics, desire / edited by Catriona
Mortimer-Sandilands and Bruce Erickson.
    p. cm.
  Includes index.
  ISBN 978-0-253-35483-9 (cloth : alk. paper) — ISBN 978-0-253-
22203-9 (pbk. : alk. paper) 1. Queer theory. 2. Sex. 3. Human
ecology. I. Mortimer-Sandilands, Catriona. II. Erickson, Bruce.
  HQ75.15.Q434 2010
  306.76'601—dc22
                                      2009054117

1 2 3 4 5 15 14 13 12 11 10

For Stacey

For Liz

Whence the setting apart of
"the unnatural" as a specific
dimension in the field of sexuality.

Michel Foucault,
"The Perverse Implantation"

CONTENTS

Part 3 Desiring Nature? Queer Attachments

ACKNOWLEDGMENTS

The editors are deeply grateful to all of the contributors to this volume, each of whom has risen to the challenge of queering his or her ecological position with grace and intelligence. When we came together to discuss the first drafts of our chapters in Toronto in May 2007, it was immediately clear that the whole would be greater than the sum of the parts. For the respectful and insightful dialogue that has so enriched each of our contributions, we thank you all, and especially Brent for his careful and thoughtful note-taking. We are also grateful to the Social Sciences and Humanities Research Council of Canada for its financial support of that initial workshop, without which *Queer Ecologies* would not have come to be.

Thank you to Dee Mortensen at Indiana University Press for her unflagging enthusiasm for the project and her ongoing and patient commitment to its success, to Laura MacLeod for her hard work on so many of its details, and to Carol Kennedy and Nancy Lightfoot for their excellent copyediting. Thank you to Sherri, Stacey, and Hannah for living with one or the other of us throughout the process of organizing, writing, and editing the volume. And thank you to so many of our colleagues in the Faculty of Environmental Studies at York University for understanding that ecology is, indeed, in need of a queering such as this one.

Permission granted by the University of Arizona Press to reprint a revised version of Noël Sturgeon's essay "Penguin Family Values: The Nature of Planetary Environmental Reproductive Justice," as it appeared in *Environmentalism in Popular Culture: Gender, Race, Sexuality, and the Politics of the Natural* (2008), copyright 2008 by the University of Arizona Press.

Queer Ecologies

INTRODUCTION

A Genealogy of Queer Ecologies

CATRIONA MORTIMER-SANDILANDS AND BRUCE ERICKSON

Introduction: Queering Ecology on Brokeback Mountain

In a now-famous scene from Ang Lee's Academy Award winning film *Brokeback Mountain*,[1] characters Ennis Del Mar and Jack Twist have had a bit too much whiskey to drink around the fire at their camp in the Big Horn Mountains of eastern South Dakota and Wyoming, where they are employed by Joe Aguirre in the summer of 1963 to herd and protect his sheep for the grazing season. In the middle of the scene, Ennis drunkenly insists on sleeping outside the tent by the dying fire, but in the middle of the night Jack calls him into the tent and Ennis staggers in. As a brilliant full moon surfs on top of the clouds, Jack reaches over and pulls a sleeping Ennis's arm around him; Ennis wakes and jolts himself away roughly but Jack pursues him and holds onto his jacket. A long second transpires as Jack looks into Ennis's eyes and Ennis meets his gaze, understanding. They have fast, fierce sex, and with no time for so much as a postcoital cigarette, the scene abruptly changes to the next morning, Ennis crawling out of the tent with a visible hangover, cocking his rifle, leaving the campsite without conversation. His next words to Jack are later that day. Rifle still in hand, he sits down beside him and says: "That was a one-shot thing we had going on there." Jack responds: "It's nobody's business but ours." Ennis insists: "You know I ain't queer." Jack agrees: "Me, neither." But that evening, in a warmly lit tent interior, they kiss tenderly and visibly relax into each other's bodies: they may not be queer, but a rose by any other name apparently smells as sweet.

Although a lot more happens in *Brokeback Mountain* that is worthy of comment, notably the contrast between the heterosexual relationships both men develop and the deeply romantic and eventually tragic "high-altitude fucking," to quote Jack, in which the couple engages periodically for the next twenty years, we begin this collection of writings on queer ecologies with that scene because it displays quite dramatically three important junctures at which lgbtq (lesbian/gay/bisexual/transgender/queer) and environmental politics (both defined broadly) intersect.[2] First, Jack and Ennis's shared refusal to name themselves as "queer" is part of an ongoing narrative strategy by which the film distances both men from the taint of urban, effeminate—what Judith Halberstam has called "metronormative"—articulations of gay male identity (2005, 36). Jack and Ennis are cowboys; they know about guns and horses; they eat baked beans and drink whiskey from the bottle rather than having cassoulet with cabernet sauvignon. When Ennis says that he is "not queer," we understand that he means he is not *that* kind of queer: genteel, sensitive, feminine, "gay" in any sense of the word. He is an ordinary white, working-class, masculine-male ranch hand who just happens to have passionate sex and fall in love with an almost equally butch rodeo king.[3] There is nothing queer about it; indeed, their masculine identities are repeatedly confirmed in both this scene and the film as a whole, and the sex unfolds almost *naturally* as part of a deepening, homosocial intimacy that would be as welcome in a camp full of Boy Scouts as it would in a group of urban gay men: indeed, possibly *more* welcome.

Although the politics are not simple and the movie is much commented upon,[4] the point we emphasize is that the presentation of Ennis and Jack in this rural-masculine manner has the effect of "naturalizing" their relationship insofar as their attraction and love can be read as entirely separate and distinct from what have, throughout much of the twentieth century, been presented as "unnatural" or "degenerate" sexualities. We will return to this issue presently; what we stress here is that, for a popular audience, sympathy for and identification with Ennis and Jack's tragic romance is based on the story's effective disarticulation of same-sex love and desire from gay identity, the former of which is presented as natural—masculine, rural, virile—in opposition to the latter's spectral invocation of historical and ongoing discourses of *perversion*. These discourses, as we will suggest below, are an important point of conversation between queer and ecological politics because they reveal the powerful ways in which understandings of nature inform discourses of sexuality, and also the ways in which understandings of sex inform discourses of nature; they are linked, in fact, through a strongly evolutionary narrative that pits the perverse, the polluted and the degenerate against the fit, the healthy, and the natural.

The second queer ecological connection going on in *Brokeback Mountain* is that it is not at all accidental that our sex scene takes place on Brokeback Mountain. Although, as we discover later in the film, even this remote space is not immune to the possibility of heteronormative surveillance, it is clear that, up in the mountains, Jack and Ennis are free to explore their sexual relationship in a way that is simply not possible in the small Wyoming town from which they set out. Wilderness is, in this film, portrayed as a vast field of homoerotic possibility; the two rugged men romp and tumble freely, watched, for the most part, only by rugged mountains. Their desire is both constituted and consummated in a lush hanging river valley surrounded by trees and dramatic, snow-striped peaks; wilderness becomes a "safe" place for outlaw sex, and although there is, later in the film, one sexual encounter between Jack and Ennis in a seedy motel, their ongoing relationship is almost completely located in this one, remote spot.

Clearly, there are relationships between Jack and Ennis's virility and the virility of the wild landscape; the one's masculinity confirms the other's, and both are also affected by their explicit contrast to the claustrophobic and emasculating spaces of domesticity represented by Jack's and Ennis's wives and children.[5] But there is also an interesting subversion of dominant discourses that attach wilderness spaces to performances of *heterosexual* masculinity. As we will discuss below, at least since the early twentieth century, wild spaces have been understood and organized in a way that presents nature—and its personal domination in the guise of hunting, fishing, climbing, and other outdoor activities—as a site for the enactment of a specific heteromasculinity. Particularly in the late nineteenth century, a period that also saw the beginnings of the wilderness preservation and conservation movements, the vast changes that were taking place in North American cities—immigration, urban expansion, industrialization, women's increasing economic independence, and the transformation of the economy from entrepreneurial to corporate capitalism, to name a few factors—created a huge amount of social anxiety, particularly for elite white men. Where once such men could be reasonably confident of their dominance, their power was now called quite radically into question, and outdoor pursuits came to serve as a new space for elite enactments of white male superiority. Again, to cut a long story short, white men came to assert their increasingly heterosexual identities in

[margin annotations: enactment of a specific hetero-masculinity]

[margin annotations: the social anxiety of white men and environmentalism]

the wilderness explicitly against the urban specter of the queer, the immigrant, and the communist, a legion of feminized men who were clearly not of the same manly caliber as the likes of Theodore Roosevelt.[6] This second connection between queer and ecology is thus about the fact that different kinds of nature *spaces* have also come to be overlain with sexual meanings; wilderness areas are highly heterosexualized—increasingly so with the postwar rise of family camping—and urban nature spaces are organized by specific sexual ideals and practices, both in the dominant view and in the many resistances that have taken place to that view.

The third and final connection that is made between queer and ecological politics in that *Brokeback Mountain* scene actually concerns the sheep. Specifically, the presence of the sheep and the resulting fact that Jack and Ennis are *shepherds,* locates the film in a long history of pastoral depictions of nature and landscape and, indeed, an equally long history of pastoral representations of male same-sex eroticism. Beginning with ancient Greek "lyric poetry [such as Theocritus's *Idylls*] depicting the life of shepherds or herdsmen" (Shuttleton 2000, 127), the pastoral tradition emphasizes rural simplicity and, indeed, paints the rustic life of the shepherd in the pasture as a sort of Arcadian, golden age of leisure and erotic play. In ancient Greece and Rome, much of that erotic play was between men, and despite subsequent "homophobic Christian and humanist ethical prescriptions . . . [that] have repeatedly sought to erase or veil pastoral's queer libidinal economies to produce hetero-normative Arcadias" (127), gay scholars and authors (and others) have used this homoerotic literary and artistic tradition to imagine a queer history, a queer space, and indeed a queer nature: the idealized, bucolic "naturalness" of pastoral homoeroticism calls into question the idea that heterosexuality is the only "natural" sex around. Clearly, the portrayal of Jack and Ennis exploring their sexual relationship on a pasture in the mountains, surrounded by sheep and with little else to do (although this pastoral is interrupted by both homophobes and coyotes), ties their story, and the landscape of Brokeback Mountain, to a historical, homoerotic Arcadia,[7] and possibly also to a tradition of representation that resists the normative pairing of nature with *hetero*sexuality.

So there's a lot going on in *Brokeback Mountain* that indicates an ongoing historical, political, spatial, and literary relationship between sex and nature. (Who would have guessed that two "not-queer" white guys fucking among the sheep would be so interesting?) As the film shows us clearly, ideas and practices of nature, including both bodies and landscapes, are located in particular productions of sexuality, and sex is, both historically and in the present, located in particular formations of nature. The critical analysis of these locations and co-productions is what we mean by "queer ecology": there is an ongoing relationship between sex and nature that exists institutionally, discursively, scientifically, spatially, politically, poetically, and ethically, and it is our task to interrogate that relationship in order to arrive at a more nuanced and effective sexual and environmental understanding. Specifically, the task of a queer ecology is to probe the intersections of sex and nature with an eye to developing a sexual politics that more clearly includes considerations of the natural world and its biosocial constitution, and an environmental politics that demonstrates an understanding of the ways in which sexual relations organize and influence both the material world of nature and our perceptions, experiences, and constitutions of that world. Queer, then, is both noun and verb in this project: ours is an ecology that may begin in the experiences and perceptions of non-heterosexual individuals and communities, but is even more importantly one that calls into question heteronormativity itself as part of its advocacy around issues of nature and environment—and vice versa.

Hence this book. The thirteen authors gathered together in the pages of *Queer Ecologies* have all asked important questions at interrelated conjunctures of sex and nature, oriented to probing and challenging the biopolitical knots through which both historical and current relations of sexualities and environments meet and inform one another. Ranging from an analysis of "queer animals" as subjects of environmental and other popular fascination, to a political interrogation of colonial discourses organizing sex (especially sex between men) as an ecological threat, to histories of lesbian and gay creations of natural space, to a consideration of Ellen Meloy's erotic, hybrid nature writing as a specifically ecological future for queer desire, the essays in this collection take up diverse challenges and possibilities posed by the powerful collision of sex and nature. Collectively, we ask: What does it mean that ideas, spaces, and practices designated as "nature" are often so vigorously defended against queers in a society in which that very nature is increasingly degraded and exploited? What do queer interrogations of science, politics, and desire then offer to environmental understanding? And how might a clearer attention to issues of nature and environment—as discourse, as space, as ideal, as practice, as relationship, as potential—inform and enrich queer theory, lgbtq politics, and research into sexuality and society?

In light of the rich range of issues and perspectives included in the following chapters, the role of this introduction is not to cover the same territory in advance. Instead, and beginning with the triad of intersections between histories of sexuality and nature apparent in *Brokeback Mountain,* what we would like to offer is a sort of lightly sketched genealogy of the implicit question posed in the pairing of "queer" with "ecology": What are some of the ways in which the terms have been related, and what kinds of intersection might be specified by their juxtaposition? Specifically, and although there are certainly other ways of conceiving of the histories of this convergence (in particular, we are overlooking a substantial literature on gender and technology that has significantly influenced many of the queer natures appearing in these pages, and also acknowledge the decided Anglo-American-centrism of our introductory account),[8] we suggest that there have been three major areas in which issues of sexuality and nature have been caught up in the same question; these three strands of intersection are what bring us to this collection, even as the essays within it depart from that triad in significant ways. In this introductory essay, then, we will do three things to help narrate the coming-into-being of the project in which we are engaged. First, we will consider some of the historical connections that have been made between discourses of sexuality and nature, focused on the naturalization of particular sexual behaviors in the midst of the rise of evolutionary and sexological thought in the early twentieth century, and also on more recent scientific and critical work on animal sexual relations and environmental change as a sort of evolutionary/ecological practice of "putting sex into discourse." Second, we will explore some ways in which historical and contemporary formations of natural space have been organized by changing understandings and agendas related to sexuality, and in particular, how nature-spaces were and are often designed to regulate sexual activity but with mixed results, including gay, lesbian, and other appropriations of landscapes for a wide variety of queer purposes. Finally, we will document some of the ways queer-identified scholars and others have envisioned a nascent ecology in a variety of literary, philosophical, and pedagogical projects that insist on highlighting, subverting, and transforming heteronormative nature relations. Spanning a wide range of disciplines and locations, these knots of inquiry are key traditions of queer ecological conversation upon which this collection rests.

Histories of Sexuality and Ecology: Un/naturalizing the Queer

As much feminist, queer, and post-Foucauldian scholarship has emphasized, there is nothing especially "natural" about the ways Euro-western societies generally understand sex. As Jeffrey Weeks writes in *Against Nature*, for example, "the fact is . . . that, as Jonathan Katz has [also] said, when we explore the histories of terms like 'heterosexuality' or 'homosexuality' we can only conclude that Nature had very little to do with it" (1991, 88). But that fact has not prevented a whole raft of natures from appearing in biomedical and other discourses of sexuality, and certainly has not prohibited sexual categories, tensions, and assumptions from creeping into environmental and ecological thought. Indeed, the history of sexual understanding, particularly (qua Foucault) with the modern advent of a *scientia sexualis* emphasizing systematic sexual knowledge and proliferating a host of naturalizing sexual discourses linking individual sexual practice and experience with reproductive biology, is full of nature-talk, and nature-talk, including in its contemporary environmental forms, is full of sex. *reproductive biology versus individual sexual practice*

Historically, the rise of evolutionary thought in Charles Darwin's wake generally coincided with the rise of sexological thought in Richard von Krafft-Ebing's: new forms of biological and environmental knowledge jostled with new ideas about sex, and their commingling has had lasting results. In *The History of Sexuality, Volume 1* (1978), Foucault argues that the regulation of sexuality in modernity has been organized through two important discursive constellations: a biology of population and a medicine of sex. Although he understands these modes of biopolitical knowledge to be logically separate and distinct, it remains the case that the historical origins of modern understandings of sex, sexuality, sexual identity, and sexual orientation are grounded in biological discourses that are heavily influenced by evolutionary thought, and conversely, that evolutionary thought is supported by modern understandings of sex as an internal and essential category, and also by notions of natural sexuality from which nonreproductive sexualities are understood as deviant. *science as a tool to establish certain sexual practices has normative behavior*

Consider one trajectory as an example of this convergence. Darwin's ideas on sexual selection, detailed especially in *The Descent of Man* (1871), focused on the ways in which competition occurred among males and among females of the same species in order to choose the "best" reproductive partner; although for Darwin certain traits clearly evolved as a result of natural selection (making the organism most able to survive its environment), other traits evolved from sexual selection (making the organism most attractive to reproductive partners of the same species). *Descent* details a huge range of activities and attributes, from nest building and tail feathers in birds to spear making and beards in human males, that found new prominence and significance as elements in a system of selection; sex became a matter of fitness, and individual attributes could now be evaluated based on their apparent adaptiveness to an organism's reproductive capacity. Indeed, although natural and sexual selection are different processes, in their co-relation as "selection," as modes of species adaptation, there was in Darwin a link between an organism's relationships to its environment and its sexual relations.

Foucault has argued that the very category of "the homosexual" was a creation of this Victorian period, a naturalizing move in such institutions as sexology and medicine in which sex came to be understood not as a set of acts but as a state of internal being (in this case, a deviant one), an "implantation of perversion" that had the effect of retroactively crafting heterosexuality as equally internal and constitutive: a question of one's nature. As he notes, modern medical institutions moved us from a regulation of sexual acts to an organization and "treatment" of sexual identities; where once there may have been women who had sex with women (to the extent that that particular conception was allowed to exist, which by many accounts it was not in the Victorian period), now there were formal bearers of sexual categories—"gender inverts," "tribades," and "lesbians"— whose sexual activities with other women could be linked to some basic biological fault. In short, in the early twentieth century, sexuality became naturalized; an individual's sexual desires were recoded as expressions of an inherent sexual condition, and that condition was understood in strongly biologized terms.

Evolutionary thinking (some of it only very loosely related to Darwin) gave this new series of sexualized "beings" an even greater narrative force. Not only was reproductive sexuality obviously necessary to the survival of the species, but individual moments of sexual and gendered behavior and physiognomy could now be tied to stories of evolutionary advantage and disadvantage (one neo-Darwinian teleology seems to be that if a trait exists it must be adaptive, and if that trait is gendered or sexualized then that adaptation must be sexually selected). Nature thus entered sex in powerful ways; although Darwin would likely cringe at some of the uses to which evolutionary thought has been put, with the popularization of his work came an increasing naturalization of sexual politics. For sexologist Havelock Ellis, for example, evolutionary narrative provided a way of explaining the existence of a diverse range of sexual phenomena, from modesty to masturbation to homosexuality. In his massive *Studies in the Psychology of Sex* ([1905] 1936), he combined biological with social Darwinism in a highly influential treatise on "sexual inversion," a term he used "to indicate that the sexual impulse is *organically and innately* turned toward individuals of the same sex" ([1905] 1936, 4, emphasis added).[9] Homosexuals became "natural." Interestingly, for Ellis, the fact that inversion was congenital allowed it to be morally neutral; as a "fact of nature" it was, in fact, *part* of the narrative of evolution rather than its aberration. Predating Bruce Bagemihl's theory of "biological exuberance" by almost one hundred years, Ellis wrote: "One might be tempted to expect that homosexual practices would be encouraged whenever it was necessary to keep down the population" (9).

But the naturalization and attendant moral neutrality of homosexuality were hotly contested by thinkers who were—also inspired by evolutionary ideas—committed to the idea of sexual perversion as a form of biosocial degeneracy, including Krafft-Ebing himself. As we will see below, some of these thinkers offered environmental causes for the appearance of homosexual degeneracy, including the emasculations caused by urbanization and industrialization: homosexuality, here, was a congenital *disease*, a threat to the fitness of the evolving human species rather than a simple abnormality, as Ellis would have it. As Dana Seitler (2004) narrates elegantly, competing physiognomic theories vied for prominence at the time, using what now appears to be an utterly arbitrary selection of physical traits to form "groups" of degenerates, whose physical peculiarities were taken as obvious indicators of their perversion, variously throwbacks to a "less evolved" state or, as degeneracy theories would have it, damaged or diseased cases caused by environmental or social mistake or decline. It is also worth noting, as does Magubane (2003), that these experimental forms of physical/environmental measurement were part of a larger emergence of scientific racism, in which different "races" were characterized by distinct physical characteristics as part of a colonial project of intellectual as well as economic dominance (sexual narratives intersected with and supported many of these racist stories, and both Darwin and Ellis use examples from "primitive" peoples to substantiate their evolutionary views). As with homosexuality, the application of evolutionary narratives to the explanation of race was fraught with difficulty: in particular, the ongoing tendency to equate reproductive fitness with the possession of those characteristics that happened to be (in their own minds, at least) associated with white, upper-class, western heterosexual men was certainly at play in many of the evolutionary and sexological accounts of the time.[10]

This rather self-congratulatory white heteronormativity was at play not only in the categorization of human bodies and sexualities; it was also amply present in the post-Darwinian development of evolutionary thought, especially that trajectory concerned with theories of sexual selection. Specifically, as heterosexuality came to be understood as a natural state of being (with nature understood, here, as a biological imperative against which deviant sexualities could be condemned as unnatural), theories of sexual selection had an increasingly difficult time coming to terms with the presence of same-sex but apparently sex-related activities and behaviors among the nonhuman species upon which so much of their evolutionary evidence rested. In a 1912 reconsideration of evolutionary theory, for example, Delage considers the presence of same-sex (potentially) erotic behaviors in certain animal species a bit of a perplexity for the theory of sexual selection: "The dancing swarms of many kinds of insects are found to be composed of males alone and no females are near enough to see" (1912, 103). As Jennifer Terry has documented extensively, reproductive sexual penetration is nonetheless a master-narrative in many evolutionary accounts, in which "nonreproductive behaviours have been seen as linked to the establishment of social relations, including cooperation and hierarchies, and have been interpreted not in terms of pleasure and desire but as signals of dominance, submission, reciprocity, and competition and an assumed struggle for survival" (2000, 154). In some cases, the assumption of heterosexuality has overridden otherwise pretty clear expressions of same-sex *sex,* requiring long and complicated explanations about, say, social hierarchy among primate females in order to bring the story back to the central issue of heterosexual copulation. "To many biologists and ethologists," writes Terry, "the problems presented by nonreproductive sexual behaviour have to do mainly with how it thwarts, disturbs, or, in the best light, merely supplements heterosexual reproduction" (154).

Although sexual selection is certainly not the only thing going on in evolutionary thought, and although one could argue that a robust understanding of *natural* selection could easily include diverse forms of sexual pleasure as a dimension of a given species' relations to its environments, it remains the case that heterosexuality also appears as a defining adaptive capacity in much ecological thought. In this model, heterosexual reproduction is the only form of sexual activity leading directly to the continuation of a species from one generation to the next; thus, logically, other sexual activities may turn out to be aberrant as a result of environmental transformations that exert their toxic effects on at-risk species by interfering with their reproductive capacities (as with the "effeminization" of bald eagles in the Great Lakes). If the ability of a species to survive in its environment is tied to its reproductive fitness, then "healthy" environments are those in which such heterosexual activity is seen to be flourishing; if the environment is not optimal, then the effects may be experienced sexually, and can be seen most clearly in dysfunctional sexual biology or behavior such as homoeroticism. Clearly, this reasoning is not entirely sound, guided more by heteronormative assumptions than by a complex understanding of the diverse social relations of sexuality occurring in various animal species and environments. But it has had unfortunate consequences. In one case, well-meaning ecologists, convinced of the evolutionary pathology of same-sex sexual behavior, argued that the widespread presence of female homoerotic activity among seagulls in a particular location must be evidence of some major environmental catastrophe (Silverstone 2000). As it turns out, it wasn't: the world is apparently full of lesbian gulls. But this kind of "repro-centric" environmental position remains dominant; it has even been used to argue that the increasing prominence of transgendered individuals (human and other) is clear evidence of environmental contamination.[11] However much one might want to be able to pinpoint animal indicators of pollution or other environmental change, the *assumption* that gender dimorphic heterosexuality is the only natural sexual form is clearly not an appropriate benchmark for ecological research. It is clearly not the case that all sex leads to reproduction, for humans and other animals alike, yet the presence of nonreproductive sexual activities is frequently read as a sign of ecological decline: another twist on degeneracy theory. Indeed, the sexual blind spot in environmentalism is extensive: even in arguments about the environmental destruction caused by human population growth, the invisibility of anything like sexual diversity demonstrates that the paradigm of natural heterosexuality overrides the obvious existence of plenty of nonreproductive sexual options that might be more ecologically appropriate under the circumstances. (Bagemihl's [1999] "biological exuberance" notwithstanding, this option has not been taken seriously by proponents of sustainable development.)

Evolutionary thought has, of course, moved considerably away from some of the cruder teleologies noted above (many would argue that they were never present in Darwin to begin with), and the sleights of narrative hand by which nonreproductive sexual acts are rendered necessarily irrelevant, secondary, or degenerate in relation to reproductive sex have been challenged in many ways. Although this introduction is not the place to catalogue emergent perspectives in evolutionary theory, it is worth noting that several recent texts have responded to repro-centrism and extensively catalogued the existence of same-sex sexual activities in a wide variety of animal species, most prominently Bruce Bagemihl's *Biological Exuberance*

(1999), Joan Roughgarden's *Evolution's Rainbow* (2004), and Paul Vasey and Volker Sommer's *Homosexual Behaviour in Animals* (2006). To these significant texts, Myra Hird's important article "Naturally Queer" adds this summative insight: "Sexual 'difference' might be culturally signifi-cant, but [as nonlinear biology shows] this term obscures the much more prevalent sex diversity among living matter" (2004, 86), which includes a diversity of asexual modes of reproduction as well as several multi-gen-dered ones that appear to defy dominant, dimorphic accounts of sexual reproduction altogether. Indeed, in her 2006 "Animal Transex," she goes even further, arguing that "we need to resist the temptation to name cer-tain species as queer . . . [and] consider how we might understand trans in humans, say, from a bacterial perspective" (2006, 45). The interplay of sociocultural understandings of queer with organismic sexual multiplicity is important, as Elizabeth Wilson insists, "because it renders the human, cultural and social guises of queer less familiar and more captivated by biological and social forces" (quoted in Hird 2006, 45, but note also the complex politics of representation and voyeurism, as discussed in Chris [2006] and also by Alaimo, Bell, and Sturgeon in this volume).

Queer Environments: The Sexual Politics of Natural Spaces

For a second intersection between sexuality and nature, we move to a consideration of the politics of natural *space* and the ways in which devel-oping sexual politics, institutions, and practices have had an effect on the organization and regulation of nature as a socially produced set of places, and vice versa. In parallel with the ways that environmental science and related fields of knowledge have been shaped by heteronormativity—and in intersection with them, through discourses of health and degeneracy— modern nature-spaces have been deeply influenced by institutions and practices that have assumed and imposed particular sexual relations on the landscape. In turn, particular kinds of natures have been cultivated in order to produce and promote particular forms of sexual subjectiv-ity. Both historically and in the present, then, sexual politics has had a distinctly environmental-spatial dimension, and landscapes have been organized to produce and promote (and prohibit) particular kinds of sexual identity and practice.

One of the most obvious sites in which heteronormativity has influ-enced ideas and practices of natural space is in parks, both wilderness and urban, not least because parks are publicly designated "nature" spaces and thus subject to more formal attention—and environmentally inflected moral regulation—than other sites of human interaction in and with the natural environment. Indeed, it is worth noting that parks emerged *as* public institutions in much the same time period as the above-noted articulation of evolution and degeneracy: the naturalization of (apparently fragile) heterosexuality in the midst of a perceived proliferation of deviant sexual types and expressions began, in the mid- to late-nineteenth century, to create social anxiety about the state of white European masculinity, and the parks movement was heavily influenced by a desire to shore it up. In particular, anxiety was leveled at cities, and urbanization, industrialization, and environmental contamination (not to mention immigration) were held to blame for the social, moral, and even physical "decline" of the population said to be occurring at the time—as evidenced, apparently, by the increased visibility of homosexual activity in cities. Gay men were at the center of this anxious articulation. In part as a result of the idea that homosexuality was a sort of (creeping) illness, medical thinkers of the late nineteenth century came to believe that the environmental conditions of large urban centers actually *cultivated* the homosexuality that people were (they thought, increasingly) seeing; as Peter Boag writes, "medical experts associated 'American' homosexuality with the city, in part because of the urban center's heavily immigrant population, but especially because of its environmental conditions. Pollution, tainted foods, and even the fast-paced nature of urban life 'induced' it" (2003b, 49). An array of explanations was offered for this supposed urban degeneration: the idea that the work men did in cities no longer brought them into close and honorable contact with nature; the completely inaccurate and highly racist belief that homosexuality was associated with immigrant populations; and the growing idea that homosexuality might, as a form of biological degeneracy, have environmental causes.

Parks were a curative response; with clear biopolitical overtones, they were created in part as places in which heterosexual masculinity could be performed and solidified away from the dramatic upheavals of American social and economic transformation, a restoration of the dominant social body through rigorous, health-giving recreation. As numerous authors have pointed out, beginning in the late-nineteenth century challenges to white, heteromasculine privilege in the form of (for example) women's increasing economic independence, the restructuring of urban employment, the rapidly changing racial and ethnic politics of large cities, and the changing nature of sociality caused by the reorganization of patriarchal family relations under capitalism created a lot of public anxiety for the urban bourgeoisie (see D'Emilio 1983).[12] To state it rather baldly, white men's economic supremacy was under threat, and with it many of the traditional anchors of discursive white masculine privilege. As Kimmel (2005) has pointed out, for example, a shift occurred in this period toward an increased corporealization of male power, a greater emphasis on the body and physical strength as signs and sources of male power. Theodore Roosevelt is the poster-boy for this transition: raised as a bookish child and politically rejected in his youth, he reinvented himself as a strapping, virile, and muscular man whose physical prowess came to be equated with and stand for his political strength. For our argument, it is no accident that Roosevelt found his body in the western wilderness of the United States; against the corporeally and even mentally enervating influences of civilization and urbanity, Roosevelt needed an elite and remote recreational space in order to reinvent and reassure his masculinity against the (effeminizing, changing) eastern city. Indeed, Haraway (1989) links the emergence of this Rooseveltian masculinity with the emergent taxonomic knowledge on display at the American Museum of Natural History. The corporealization of masculinity was clearly tied to the naturalization of heterosexuality, and primate taxidermy and display offered another material practice through which this emerging connection was established and made part of public discourse.

"Wilderness" was thus an important site for the cultivation of hetero-masculinity in several ways in this period (as, in many respects, it still is). Most importantly for our argument, perhaps, the rise of a preservationist movement in North America was a direct response to public concern with the declining nature of/in cities; combined with the rise of a public discourse of urban emasculation, the perception of a dwindling number of wild spaces in the continental United States came to be a focal point for urban anxieties about the loss of national character, coded as male (homosocial, *not* homosexual). Wilderness spaces such as parks came to be valued as sites to be preserved away from the corrupting influences of urban industrial modernity, and in particular, as places where new ideals of whiteness, masculinity, and virility could be explored away from the influence of emancipated women, immigrants, and degenerate homosexuals. The early parks movement was thus born partly from a desire to facilitate recreational practices that would restore threatened masculine virtues. Of course, this desire was also planted in the assumption that cities were sites of the particular moral degeneracy associated with homosexuality.

The joint construction of sexuality and nature is quite complex in this period; although we are not able pursue the idea here, it is also tied to modern ideas of race and nation in both the United States and Canada (see Erickson 2003). There are, however, two sets of ideas to pull out. First, there is the assumption that homosexuality is a product of the *urban,* and that rural and wilderness spaces are thus somehow free from the taint of homoerotic activity. Nothing, in fact, could be further from the truth. At the end of the nineteenth century and well into the twentieth, the western wilderness was a space heavily dominated by communities of men. These men—prospectors, cowboys, ranchers, foresters—frequently engaged in homosexual activity. Indeed, if sexologist Alfred Kinsey's research was correct, there was in the nineteenth century *more* same-sex sexual activity among men in the remote wilderness than there was in the cities. As Boag documents extensively in his work on the regulation of homosexuality in the U.S. Pacific Northwest (2003a), homosocial sites such as logging camps and fishing operations included complex networks of sexual activity among men, and it was even the case that some urban men would leave the city in search of them.

Prior to the establishment and popularization of medical discourses establishing same-sex attachments as matters of biology and identity, such men were not understood as "homosexuals." To quote Kinsey, "these are men who have faced the rigors of nature in the wild. . . . Such a background breeds the attitude that sex is sex, irrespective of the nature of the partner with whom the relation is had" (in Boag 2003a, 52). It was not until homosexuality became coded as an inherent identity/condition that it came to be understood as a form of degeneracy and located in the artificiality of cities. Certainly, the increasing concentration of single male workers in some cities, and the rapid transformation of family relationships more generally, made it possible for interested men to find homoerotic contacts and/or social networks of men working in increasingly clerical occupations. Port cities such as New York, San Francisco, and Vancouver became very important places for homosexual men to carve out spaces for their fledgling sexual communities. But it was the growing *visibility* of these communities, and the increasing association of homosexuality with degeneracy, that tied the homosexual to the urban, *not* necessarily some quantitatively greater homoerotic presence (even though one must certainly acknowledge that urban conditions have allowed many aspects of gay male and lesbian culture to flourish, and that visibility has taken a particular shape as a result). The point is that the implantation of perversion was a distinctly urban phenomenon, and the fact of the proliferation of sexual possibilities in developing cities shaped the emergence of homosexuality as unnatural; emerging proto-environmental critiques of the destructive artificiality of cities were thus instrumental in shaping ideas about the artificiality of gay men in particular (although these ideas were effectively contested, as we will describe below).

Lesbian history offers a slightly different inflection on these articulations of nature and sex. As noted above, inverts and tribades became objects of intense and pathologizing medical scrutiny at about the same time as urbanization and economic transformation made it genuinely possible for (middle-class) women to achieve economic independence from men—meaning that sexual and other intimate relations between women became both visible and a threat.[13] As Carroll Smith-Rosenberg documents (1985), in the developing conception of invert pathology, "unwholesome environments" made it possible for inverts to make advances on other women, especially (for Havelock Ellis, at least) on women who were not inverts but who might be predisposed to weakness for their advances. Such environments were ones that fostered women's interactions independent of men: colleges and boarding schools, clubs, and political organizations. In terms of nature, then, on the one hand, women were encouraged to engage in supposedly wholesome activities, including recreational nature pursuits; the boys' scouting movement was not opposed to the inclusion of girls, for example, even though it meant the encouragement of women's friendships (perhaps because it strongly encouraged such activities as part of a woman's cultivation of domestic competence, tying women's nature-experiences directly back into patriarchal families). On the other hand, this inclusion was fragile and confined to a sort of domestic environmental border zone, in which (white) women were understood as bastions of effeminizing civilization in an essentially male wilderness. Lesbians could stand only as abominations in relation to this masculine ideal, and stories of women taking up gender-bending positions as male adventurers thrill in the double transgression involved: unnatural acts in nature.[14]

More recently, the pervasive assumption that gay and lesbian communities are essentially urban has had the lasting effect of erasing the ongoing presence of rural gay men and lesbians whose lives might not look much like white, metronormative, male-dominated Christopher Street: *Queer as Folk* and *The L-Word* could not have been set in Wisconsin or Saskatchewan, not because there are no gay men or lesbians in rural communities (see Bell and Valentine 1995b, Howard 1999, Kramer 1995, Osborne and Spurlin1996, Riordan 1996, and Wilson 2000), but because gay and lesbian identity-production has been tied to particular urban formations as the spaces most authentically suited to the creation and expression of true gay and lesbian sexual culture. Indeed, as Kath Weston (1995) has pointed out, the movement from rural to urban space has become symbolically overloaded in "coming-out" stories. Although it is certainly historically the case that migration of gay men and lesbians to particular urban areas has contributed to queer visibility, and thus to community vitality, the concomitant erasure of rural gay and lesbian possibilities has *contributed* to their ongoing flight from rural and suburban communities, to the ghettoization of queer culture as inherently and only urban, and to the widespread assumption that country spaces are inherently hostile to anything other than monogamous heterosexuality (and possibly polygyny). One cannot ignore violence perpetrated against gay men, lesbians, transgender and queer-identified individuals in rural settings, as it is certainly the case that homophobia is alive and well and living down on the farm: rural Christian conservatives in Oregon and Colorado nearly got homophobic ballot measures passed in their states in 1992 (which would, as Hogan describes in her chapter, have effectively criminalized public discussion of homosexuality in Oregon), and more recently have openly admitted the homophobic rationale behind the successful (although contested) 2008 "Unmarried Couple Adoption Ban" in Arkansas. But it is still clear that urban spaces are often *more* dangerous than rural ones and that systematic homophobic violence needs to be understood as a phenomenon with distinctly urban dimensions. The idea that natural spaces are always already hostile to gay men and lesbians, complete with the image of the homophobe lurking behind the trees, has the unfortunate status of being a self-fulfilling prophesy (see Bell 1997a, Filemyr 1997, and Romesburg 2007).

These spatial-sexual processes have also affected the spaces of *nature,* not only in formal and designated natures, but also across socionatural environments more broadly. On the one end of the spectrum, and most obviously, we see the physical concentration of gay men and lesbians in particular urban neighborhoods and their creation of distinct social, commercial, and recreational (including sexual) natures; in different cities in different ways, distinct patterns of gay and lesbian community *organize* urban nature in particular ways. As John Binnie and Gill Valentine write in their review of literatures in queer geography (1999), these "gay landscapes" (e.g., Manuel Castells's San Francisco [1983] and Tamar Rothenberg's Park Slope, New York [1995]) include both formal and informal institutions, and particular communities secure queer space in different ways, including occupations and organizations of the physical setting itself. As David Bell notes (1995, 1997b), for example, public sex is not only a form of physical occupation but also a practice of intimate citizenship, one that, we would argue, often demands and creates particular kinds of public nature to accommodate and facilitate it (see van Lieshout 1997). In this case, a particular sexual sociality shapes physical nature-spaces—parks, ravines, paths, empty lots—as part of a public challenge to heteronormativity, and perhaps especially to the official heteronormativity of designated nature-space.

These heteronormative attempts to regulate sex in urban areas—including the ongoing active (and actively contested) prohibition of public homosexual activity—have also had lasting effects on urban environments. It is important to note that the urban parks movement was also a response to discourses of degeneracy, and public green spaces were promoted by a gamut of social reformers intent on improving the health and virtue of, in particular, the urban working class. In cities as well, the idea of park-nature as a space for the disciplined cultivation of virtue had an important sexual component. For their creators, following the lead of prolific landscape architect Frederick Law Olmsted, urban parks were "for the people": parks were developed inside cities (e.g., Central Park, Mount Royal Park, and the Emerald Necklace—all Olmsted's) to give urban inhabitants a public green space in which to gather and recreate. Certain kinds of activities were explicitly designed into these landscapes. For example, given the attachment of moral fitness to physical fitness demonstrated by organizations such as the Boy Scouts, sporting facilities such as ball fields were prominent in urban park development. In addition, there was a clear sense in Olmsted's designs that parks were places to see and be seen; they were sites for public spectacle of a particular kind, including the conspicuous display of middle-class respectability and wealth. Parks were places for the public cultivation of morally upstanding citizens; they were thus advocated as sites of regulated sexual contact, in which courting heterosexual couples could "tryst" in an open space that was both morally uplifting and, given its visibility, highly disciplined. As Gordon Brent Ingram writes:

> Many of the city centre parks in North America and Europe were first established or were redesigned in the late nineteenth century with an emphasis on the public promenade, the male gaze, suppression of public sexual contact, and team sports as a means to lift up working-class morality. Such public parks have usually been programmed for what are sometimes conspicuous displays of heterosexual desire, courtship, and conquest. (1997b, 102)

The design of urban parks, then, included an agenda of discouraging expressions of sexuality other than those formally sanctioned in the public eye; morally and physically sanctioned heterosexual courtship was, in turn, built into the landscape with the strategic placement of such visibly pair-appropriate facilities as benches to punctuate the romantic stroll, open-walled gazebos, and wide "lover's lanes" that provided for plenty of long-range visibility along straight corridors through the trees.

The heterosexist spatiality of cities and urban spaces is, as texts such as Bell and Valentine's *Mapping Desire* (1995a) and Ingram, Bouthillette, and Retter's *Queers in Space* (1997) document (and challenge), an increasingly public issue. (Petra Doan [2007] adds important transgender perspectives to literatures on the public contestation of urban space.) Less publicized, however, is the fact that heterosexism in rural landscapes has physically shaped what *rural* nature looks like—beyond the mere fact that the existence of parks, recreational and rural natures is directly marked with heterosexism.[15] For one small example, think about public campgrounds. Particularly during and after the 1950s with the rise of the postwar auto-recreation culture (and the desire to get women to "return" to heterosexual domesticity after the war), camping was reinvented as a (car-based) family activity rather than an inherently rugged and masculine one (see Cerullo and Ewen 1984). In this era of heterosexualization, many camping facilities were created with an intentional design to resemble suburban cul-de-sacs—each campsite clearly designed for one nuclear family—and all camping occurring in designated "private" spaces away from "public" recreational activities such as swimming, hiking, and climbing (Hermer 2002). Trees were cut down in a pattern that screened campsites from one another, but not from the roadway or path, so that the rangers or wardens could still see in and make sure nothing illegal or immoral was taking place.

For a second and earlier example, consider Boag's analysis of the settlement of much of the state of Oregon. As he notes, in the mid-nineteenth century, the Donation Land Act (DLA) encouraged a heterosexual pattern of colonization because of the way land was allotted to settlers. "A white male who was twenty-one or older . . . received a 160-acre parcel and an additional 160 acres for his wife" (2003b, 47). Women were not eligible for allotments as single people, and it was clearly in the advantage of men to have the two parcels, so "very young girls suddenly became marriageable and were soon wives" (Johanson, quoted in Boag 2003b, 47). Because of the comparatively large size of these allotments and the popularity of the program, not only did the DLA encourage heterosexual marriage along with the settlement of the west, but it imposed a monolithic culture of single heterosexual family-sized lots on the land, with significant effects on the economic and environmental history of the region from nuclear family farming patterns, the inhibition of town development, and increased forestation.

As a result of the association of degenerate queers with cities, and rural and wilderness landscapes with men and/or heterosexual (Jeffersonian, agrarian) families, the idea that nature is a primary place in which to develop moral and physical fitness has had a lasting effect: as Roosevelt has already shown us, bodies are also key spaces for the spatial production of sex and nature. In the deployment of wilderness in the nineteenth century toward masculine identification, and also in the cultivation of visible heterosexual courtship rituals in urban spaces, it is clear that bodies have been organized to interact with nature-spaces in a particularly disciplined and heterosexualized manner. One more example adds a further dimension. As Bryant Simon's research has demonstrated, in the United States, the Great Depression and World War II were also periods of hotly contested masculinity, and wilderness—this time, as a workplace—was deployed to develop the male body as disciplined nature-object. Here, organizations such as the Civilian Conservation Corps provided unemployed young men with physically and morally healthy work in the wilderness. At apparent risk of degeneracy in cities—the twin specters, here, of homosexuality and communism—such men were located in camps far from urban centers and, between 1933 and 1942, strenuously "installed 89,000 miles of telephone line, built 126,000 miles of roads and trails, constructed millions of erosion control dams, planted 1.3 billion trees, erected 3,470 water towers, and spent over 6 million hours fighting forest fires" (Simon 2003, 80–81). All of these developments were markers of a national desire for a particular kind of man as much as they were about the infrastructural needs of particular landscapes: probably more so. But they also left a clear imprint on the landscape; many of these large infrastructural projects paved the way for postwar suburban and exurban development, in addition to road travel, hydroelectric generation, and forest conservation.

With capitalist globalization, a new host of spatial relations joining queer with ecology has emerged. Some of these conjoinings center on collisions of tourism with indigenous and other non-Western cultures and spaces, including gay and lesbian niche tourism as well as sex tourism that, in some cases, makes use of historical pastoral conventions to paint an exotic and sexualized (often Oriental) other (Altman 2000). Others involve the contestation of Western sexual categories by diverse sexual minorities whose lives, bodies, and natures are not nearly captured by even the proliferating initials in the acronym "lgbtq" (Oswin 2007); as Gosine (2005a, 2005b) has documented, such contestations include challenges to international institutions and discourses of environment and development, not least because of strongly sexualized understandings of population and "good" environmental citizenship within the international development community. Still others make use of postcolonial theory to challenge the intersections of sex and nature in both historical and more recent imperialist practice, and indicate how culturally specific dominant Western ideas of sex and space turn out to be, both individually and together (see Cruz-Malavé and Manalansan 2002 and Spurlin 2006). Although these cross-cultural, transnational, and postcolonial investigations are only just beginning, they certainly highlight the fragility and specificity of the articulations of sex, bodies, and natures that are under consideration in this volume (for wider discussion of cross-cultural corporeal and sexual plurality, see Herdt 1996 and Nanda 2000).

Queering Ecological Politics

The final intersection we would like to explore in this introduction concerns the articulation of sexuality and nature as a form of eco-sexual *resistance*. Although, as apparent in the above discussions, resistances have been with us all along, it is worth specifically considering, again in a loosely genealogical way, a history of queer ecological attempts to confront and transform the kinds of ecologically implicated heteronormativity that we have begun to document here. This anthology may depart in significant ways from the trajectories thus far taken by nascent queer ecological critiques, but it is still part of a tradition of resistance that should be acknowledged here.

That said, if we were to judge from televisions shows such as *Queer as Folk* and *The L-Word*, we would hardly nominate gay men and lesbians as such as the world's best nature stewards. Quite the opposite, in fact: gay culture, in the mainstream, is extraordinarily tied to lifestyle consumerism, particularly for white urban gay men but also increasingly for urban "lifestyle" lesbians as well. As Andil Gosine has written, "gay men, the story goes, shop. Urban gay men live in chic condominium apartments, buy a lot of hair and body care products, [and] have great taste in cars, clothes, and interior design" (2001, 35). Although one might be tempted to celebrate in these popular shows the general public's apparently increased acceptance of gay so-called lifestyles, we offer that only a very narrow band of gayness—that portion tied to the fetishistic exchange of aesthetic commodities—ends up being at all "acceptable." Gay men and lesbians are OK not because they are queer, but because they are exemplary consumers in a society that judges all people by their ability to consume. Note that working-class queer folk, lower-income or anti-aesthetic lesbians, and older, sicker, or even HIV-positive gay men are not the ideal subjects of *Queer as Folk*. Not only is this band of British/North American "acceptance" of queer culture thus very narrow, but the continuing mainstream political process by which gay men and lesbians strive to be "accepted" in consumer society limits the full scope of political potential in gay, lesbian, bi, transgender, and other queer-identified communities. To quote Tony Kushner, "It's entirely conceivable that we will one day live miserably in a thoroughly ravaged world in which lesbians and gay men can marry and serve openly in the army and that's it" (in Gosine 2001, 35).

Our argument is thus that we should reorient our politics and take on something like a queer ecological perspective, a transgressive and historically relevant critique of dominant pairings of nature and environment with heteronormativity and homophobia, in order to outline possibilities responsive to these relations and, equally, explicitly critical of the continued organization of dominant metrosexualities through an environmentally disastrous (and often ethically void) lifestyle consumerism. Here, we are advocating a position not only of queering ecology, but of greening queer politics. The extension of queer into ecology is not, then, simply a question of making nature more welcome to gay inhabitation; it is also an invitation to open queer theory to ecological possibilities, and to thus produce a queering of ecocultural relations along the lines of Halberstam's queering of space: "in opposition to the institutions of family, heterosexuality, and reproduction . . . according to other logics of location, movement and identification" (2005, 1). Queer ecology suggests, then, a new practice of ecological knowledges, spaces, and politics that places central attention on challenging hetero-ecologies from the perspective of non-normative sexual and gender positions.

This critical project is not entirely new. Gay men, lesbians, and others identified as "against nature" have historically used ideas of nature, natural spaces, and ecological practices as sites of resistance and exploration. In literature alone, one can find numerous examples of authors who have self-consciously deployed dominant nature discourses in the service of queer possibilities, who have brought conventions of nature writing to celebrate sexual diversity, who have taken dominant narratives of nature to task to create space for non-heterosexual possibilities, and who have written in new ways to reflect their views of the commingling of queer and ecological possibilities. In other realms, one can see gay, lesbian, bi, trans-gender, and queer-identified individuals and communities insisting, in different ways, on the opening of nature spaces and ecological knowledges to sexually diverse—and sexually critical—possibilities. And most overtly, several recent works of environmental thought have carefully explored the ecological potentials of queer theory and practice, not only challenging the heteronormativity of mainstream environmental ethics and politics but offering new modes of theorizing human/more-than-human relation-ships. This section offers a few examples of these queer possibilities.

As noted above, pastoralism is a literary tradition with a decidedly queer history. As David Halperin (1983) and Byrne Fone (1983) have de-scribed, ancient bucolic poetry contained a range of sexual acts, desires, and preferences, and subsequent romantic reinventions of pastoral con-ventions have, despite homophobic attempts to the contrary, continued to include male homoeroticism as a central facet of the pastoral depiction of nature as a site for innocent, corporeal plenitude. In this pastoral literary tradition—which also meandered into the work of such writers as Walt Whitman and Henry David Thoreau, both highly recognizable figures in environmental history and literature—contemporary gay critics empha-size that natural settings have been important sites for the exploration of male homosexuality *as* a natural practice. Rural spaces in particular have served, in a wide range of literatures, as places of freedom for male homoerotic encounters (famously, in Forster's *Maurice* [1971], which was not published until after his death). In addition, *because* of the association of nature with ideas of innocence and authenticity, gay male writers have been able to use pastoral literary conventions as a way of making an argu-ment for the authenticity of homosexuality. This "homophile pastoralism," as Shuttleton emphasizes, not only has been used by such writers as André Gide to make political claims for gay equality on the basis of the natural-ness of homosexuality, but also has been used to challenge the very idea of the naturalness of *heterosexuality*. In Shuttleton's reading, Gide (in his ([1920] 1952) novel *Corydon*) tells a pastoral story in which shepherds not only engage in same-sex love but muse, together, on the mysteries of mak-ing love to girls. The young shepherd is a typical pastoral figure; he is close to nature in his daily work, and is also largely in the company of other young men, with whom he engages not only in the immediate pleasures of the flesh but also in the reflective dialogue associated with the young men's passage from a state of natural, youthful innocence to socialized manhood. What is key, here, is that same-sex passion is associated with that natural innocence, and opposite-sex eroticism is the thing that needs to be *learned* in order to enter the adult social order. What we have, here, is a "reverse discourse" that pairs nature with the homoerotic, and artificiality with the heteroerotic; against an assumption of natural heterosexuality, Gide actually positions heterosexuality as a normative practice *into* which the young shepherds must be disciplined. As Shuttleton writes, "Gide launches a trangressively counter-intuitive argument that it is this compulsory heterosexuality which is constructed and inauthentic since it needs to be taught and culturally maintained" (2000, 134).[16]

Along similar lines, some lesbian authors have also used pastoral literary traditions to develop a reverse discourse that argues for the naturalness of women's same-sex love relationships and/or the congenital equality of lesbians. These "lesbian pastoral" literatures have a history that extends well back into the nineteenth century, for example into the writings of such authors as Sarah Orne Jewett, for whom the institution of romantic friendship between women (as portrayed particularly in her novel *Deephaven*) was a privileged site from which to stage an exploration of natural environments. Most prominently, though, Radclyffe Hall actively deployed neo-pastoral conventions in her important novel *The Well of Loneliness* (1928). In *The Well*, Hall paints a portrait of her sexual invert protagonist, Stephen Gordon, as a quintessentially natural figure by locating her firmly in the homosocial male rituals of the English landed gentry. Stephen's moral credentials are iteratively established in the novel as she participates in, and succeeds brilliantly at, riding and hunting (which she later rejects as cruel to the fox), as she demonstrates fairness and kindness in relation to animals and the landscape more broadly, and as she develops a romantically steeped commitment to stewarding the landscape that she will inherit. She can't, and doesn't, because she is an invert and not a "girl" and can't be both *and* the inheritor of her aristocratic nature; Hall underscores, however, that the *fact* that she can't is a matter of injustice, not degeneracy, and that the "congenital nature" of the invert (Ellis writes the opening commentary) is, perhaps, even more noble and natural than that of the ordinary heterosexual.[17]

But the pastoral is not the only literary form through which queer-identified authors have sought to engage and challenge relations between sexuality and nature. As Jonathan Dollimore demonstrates brilliantly (1991), Gide's and Hall's naturalizations of desire (among others) can be counterposed to the aesthetic of Oscar Wilde, for whom "insubordinate inversions" of ideas of nature and authenticity tied aesthetic to sexual transgressions in significant (and, for Wilde, personally risky) ways. His disruptions of conservative, Victorian articulations of sex, nature, and nation "subverted the essentialist categories of identity which kept morality in place" (68), and indeed, his plays on surface and artifice called into question the entire project of articulating sexual identity with "deep" nature in any authentic way. Along similar lines, Stacy Alaimo (1999) reads a range of historical and contemporary feminist texts for the ways in which they engage, in varied ways, both natured discourses (including evolutionary thought) and natural environments. Among the works she discusses is Jane Rule's (1964) novel *Desert of the Heart,* which Alaimo reads as intentionally *anti*-pastoral in that it rejects a celebratory idea of lesbian connection to nature and instead plays with a complex tension between an idea of nature as discursive *constraint* on lesbian sexuality and an idea of nature as a physical space that can both incite and represent lesbian desire. Dianne Chisholm similarly underscores the transgressive diversity of queer appropriations and rewritings of space, in this case, with a focus on urban spaces. Engaging the work of Walter Benjamin, she reads such authors as Samuel Delany as configuring specifically queer occupations and transformations of urban spaces, in which queer space "demarcates a practice, production, and performance of space beyond just the mere habitation of built and fixed structures . . . and designates an appropriation of space for bodily, especially sexual, pleasures" (2005, 10).

From Whitman and Thoreau to Gloria Anzaldúa and Jamaica Kincaid, many other works of literature have engaged sex and nature in significant and innovative ways and could be offered up to queer ecological reading (there are several examples of such reading included in this volume, ranging from Adrienne Rich to Derek Jarman); just as "nature" has been involved in complex ways in the organization and regulation of sexual knowledges, spaces, and practices, so too have writers challenged and worked with these involvements in order to queer them. To name one particularly self-conscious example, Eli Clare's memoir *Exile and Pride* (1999) takes on the task of queering nature through a series of connected essays about his experiences growing up as a dyke (his term) in a rural Oregon logging community and his move into urban queer and environmental politics; these reflections are cross-cut with stories about his disability (cerebral palsy) and history of sexual abuse, and they centrally concern the ways in which his corporeal, class, and sexual experiences challenge not only dominant understandings of naturalized sexuality but also mainstream gay/lesbian and environmental politics (including both pastoralism and romanticism). The violences of his past in sexual and ecological conjuncture add up to a complex reading of the present: "My queer body: I spent my childhood, a tomboy not sure of my girlness, queer without a name for my queerness. I cut firewood on clearcuts, swam in the river, ran the beaches at Battle Rock and Cape Blanco. When I found dykes, fell in love for the first time, came into a political queer community, I felt as if I had found home again" (10). And: "In writing about the backwoods and the rural, white, working-class culture found there, I am not being nostalgic, reaching backward toward a re-creation of the past. Rather I am reaching toward my bones" (11). And: "The mountain will never be home" (12).[18]

Neither are queer ecological resistances confined to the literary. As suggested in an earlier section, gay men and lesbians have not only engaged and transformed environmental discourses, but have also resisted and shaped natural environments themselves. For example, despite the attempts of park planners to discourage it, many gay men have made use of public urban green spaces as sites for both individual sexual contact and community-oriented activism. Ironically, exactly *in* the parks that were frequently designed to discourage homosexual activity, men have found and created a form of sexual community that, it could be argued, borrows pastoral elements that pair nature and homoeroticism in quite a transgressive way. There are at least two important elements to consider. In the first place, what is significant about public sex in parks is that it is *public*, meaning that it overtly challenges heteronormative understandings of what is appropriate behavior for public, natural spaces. Here, we must remember that public parks are *disciplinary* spaces, in which a very narrow band of activities is sanctioned, practiced, and experienced; only certain kinds of nature experience are officially allowed. In this context, one can consider public gay sex as a sort of *democratization* of natural space, in which different communities can experience the park in their own ways, and in which a wider range of natural experiences thus comes to be possible. As Grube recounts a sexual encounter in Queen's Park, Toronto: "I stayed there because I loved storms, love to see nature in its violence. . . . We enjoyed ourselves so much, and of course the rain had swept in and we were all wet, and all those soggy clothes to put on. But it was joyous. . . . I love wild, spontaneous moments like that where . . . it just goes crazy and it's wild" (1997, 134–35). Clearly, wild sex in a public park in a thunderstorm is a far cry from the prim courtship rituals embodied in Olmsted's formal promenades. While park sex remains controversial, it seems that gay men's—and lesbians' and others'[19]—re-appropriations of these socionatural spaces fosters an alternative and critical awareness of urban nature. Such awareness has, in some instances, galvanized gay communities to take environmental action; to give one example, shortly after the 1969 Stonewall riots in New York, a popular cruising area in Queens, Kew Gardens, was destroyed by extensive tree cutting. "Within a week . . . there were public actions showing conscious visibility, and the first gay liberationist environmental group, Trees for Queens, was formed to restore the park" (Ingram, 1997a, 47).

As several essays in Rachel Stein's collection *New Perspectives on Environmental Justice* (2004) demonstrate—several of which are penned by contributors to the current volume—this tradition of sexual/ecological politics can be conceived as a form of sexual environmental justice, not least because more mainstream framings of environmental issues tend to ignore the homophobic and heterosexist relations that provide the social context for many environmental issues. Nancy Unger (2004), for example, documents a rich history of sexed and sexual articulations of environmental justice and also documents the specific heterosexism of the backlash against Rachel Carson upon the publication of *Silent Spring.* Giovanna Di Chiro (2004) points to the sexual politics of the environmental genome project. Katie Hogan (2004) outlines the strong environmental justice narratives that appear in contemporary gay mystery fiction. And Noël Sturgeon (2004) unpacks recent environmental popular culture for children, revealing there both heterosexist and profoundly racist conventions. As Stein herself notes in the book's introduction, beginning an understanding of environmental politics with issues of race, gender, and sexuality expands the understanding of what "counts" as an environmental issue; viewed as a site of articulation between ecological and social concerns, the environment, from a queer, feminist, and anti-racist perspective, comes to be understood as "where we live, work, play and worship" (2004, 1), a field open to a variety of intersectional analyses between sexual and environmental politics.

Gay men, lesbians, and other queer-identified groups and individuals have, in fact, created a variety of different spatial-political relationships to natural environments. Gay cruising areas in cities disrupt dominant understandings of public/private natures in acts of sexual appropriation, to be sure, but there have also been many other attempts to figure gay and lesbian community against the grain in suburban and rural natures as well. In the early twentieth century and influenced by strongly pastoral sentiments, English gay activist and utopian socialist Edward Carpenter was strongly committed to a rural socialist project of vegetarianism, voluntary simplicity, and manual agricultural labor; he also considered rural natures suitable places for what he called the "Uranian" temperament (indeed, it was a visit to Carpenter that inspired Forster to write

Maurice).[20] In the United States, and influenced by more recreational than socialist desires, as Esther Newton documents in her historical work on the gay resort at Cherry Grove, Fire Island, the barrier island landscape both allowed and fostered a queer, pre-Stonewall community "between escape and nesting, between voluntary exile and the longing to belong. . . . This resort, whose isolation from the mainland was the condition for its existence, is where gay people were able, not only in one way but in many, to achieve American ideals. It is also where an intrepid minority of heterosexuals adapted to and came to enjoy living in a gay-defined summer world" (1993, 7–8).

And perhaps informed by more overtly environmental ideals, back-to-the-land movements of both lesbians and gay men began in the 1970s and continue into the present. Communities such as the Womanshare Collective in southern Oregon were founded on the idea of rural nature as a privileged set of spaces in which women could find, "in the healing beauty of nature," "a safe space to live, to work, to help create the women's culture [they] dreamed of" (quoted in Sandilands 2002, 137). These "wimmin's lands" had complex ecological goals, ranging from opening rural landscapes to women by transforming heterosexual relations of property ownership, to withdrawing the land from patriarchal-capitalist agricultural production and reproduction, to symbolically reinscribing the land with lesbian erotic presence, to creating a distinct lesbian "public sphere" founded on both lesbian separatist and overtly ecological concerns (see also Kleiner 2003).[21] While many of these communities have disappeared, others are still there (as Unger's chapter in this volume attests) as examples of what it looks like to live intentionally as a lesbian environmentalist. To quote one long-term resident: "Women's land, lesbian land . . . [is] land that women have purchased and are living on [as lesbians]. It is intended to serve lesbians, not only the ones who live here, and it is intended to be lesbian land evermore. . . . And moving to the country stretches who a lesbian is" (Sandilands 2002, 142).[22] According to Scott Herring, it can also stretch the definition of who a fag is: as demonstrated in the early years of the journal *RFD* (*Radical Faerie Digest*), rural gay men challenged the increasing metronormativity of gay politics by building what he calls a "critical rusticity" that offered "an intersectional opportunity to geographically, corporeally and aesthetically inhabit non-normative sexuality that offers new possibilities for the sexually marginalized outside the metropolis as well as inside it" (2007, 346). Related to the interconnected networks of lesbian separatist communities (including journals of their own such as *Maize*), the "faggot separatism" that the journal promoted throughout the 1970s imagined a rural, queer public sphere in which ideas of nature, agriculture, stewardship, and human-animal relations could be challenged and rethought against and among the experiences of sexual minorities.

Finally, in the realm of environmental philosophy and politics, there have been concerted attempts to articulate formally a queer ecological position. Beginning with a special issue in 1994 of the Canadian environmental studies journal *Undercurrents* entitled "Queer/Nature," several works have appeared offering a range of theorizations of the relationship between sexual and ecological politics. Perhaps the best known of these works is Greta Gaard's article "Toward a Queer Ecofeminism" (1997), in which she explores the historical, philosophical, and religious roots of what she understands as a strong relationship between the oppression of queers and the domination of nature. Specifically, she examines, using a broadly ecofeminist framework of analysis, how "Western culture's devaluation of the erotic parallels its devaluations of women and of nature" (115) and understands that "queers are feminized, animalized, eroticized and naturalized in a culture that devalues women, animals, nature, and sexuality" (119). One of the most valuable insights to come out of Gaard's work is her emphasis on "erotophobia" as a key link between heterosexism and ecological degradation, as it opens the door to a consideration of environmentalism *as* a sexual politics, as a form of aesthetic and corporeal struggle against the disciplinary logics of heteropatriarchal capitalism; this connection has been taken up and refined by subsequent authors such as Lee and Dow (2001), and extended into other realms of environmental thought such as environmental education (Russell, Sarick, and Kennelly 2002). More phenomenologically inclined thinkers such as Elizabeth Grosz (1995, 2005) have also explored, beginning from the corporeal materiality of bodies and their interactions and agencies, ethical and political possibilities arising from sexual and erotic encounters with the more-than-human world, a queering that operates at the level of polymorphous bodies and pleasures as well as (or instead of) identities and discourses. As Grosz writes, "feminist, queer and other struggles around sexuality and pleasure may find their struggles are strengthened . . . [if] they acknowledge the pre-personal forces at work in the activities of sexed bodies, institutions and social practices" (2005, 195; see also Alaimo and Hekman 2008 and Sandilands 2001, 2004a).

To return almost full circle to the beginning of this genealogy, Ladelle McWhorter's wonderful philosophical and personal account of bodies and pleasures (1999) insists on a problematization of sexual (and other) corporeality that includes both the human body and the more-than-human world in its imagination. She outlines a dominant, modern understanding of sovereign or managerial bodies, in which relations of corporeal subjection offer up the flesh of the less powerful to, for example, the expert guidance of others (in which one can see, for example, homosexual nature explained and guided by sexology and evolutionary theory): "Those deemed deviant on any developmental scale are rightfully subject to those who are not deviant and who have the expertise to redirect development to bring it back into accord with the ideal norm" (160). In response, she argues—using both Foucault and tomatoes—for an appreciation of *deviation* as the basis of both a sexual and an ecological politics. "What is good is that accidents can happen and new things can emerge. . . . What is good is that the world remain ever open to deviation" (164). This kind of philosophical articulation, while beginning in a critical analysis of heteronormativity and sexual oppression, moves out into a wide-ranging exploration of what it might mean to "queer" a whole range of environmental philosophies, practices, and institutions.

Cognizant of the work of ecofeminist theorists and activists such as Sturgeon who point to the ongoing need to understand nature as a site of specifically *political* contestation (1997), we note that both queer and environmental activists have long since insisted that the redrawing of conceptual boundaries is intimately linked to the transformation of material practices involving both human and more-than-human natures. Although there are many other lines of political flight that we might have considered, this genealogy has suggested that "queering ecology" involves the opening up of environmental understanding to explicitly non-heterosexual forms of relationship, experience, and imagination as a way of transforming entrenched sexual and natural practices toward simultaneously queer and environmental ends. The essays included in this collection draw on a range of queer and ecological theories in order to do so, but they share this fundamental supposition: scrutinizing and politicizing the intersections between sex and nature not only opens environmentalism to a wider understanding of justice, but also deploys the anti-heteronormative insistences of queer politics to potentially more biophilic ends than has been generally imagined.

Queer Ecologies: Sex, Nature, Politics, Desire

The essays in this anthology draw from, but are not confined by, these different genealogical currents of queer/ecological intersection. Thus, the book is organized into three sections that, we feel, reflect potential sites for further theorizing queer ecologies, and although these sections clearly overlap the genealogical avenues mentioned above, they also overflow them in what we hope are productive ways. The three sections consist of important themes of conversation at the intersection of sexuality and nature: investigations of the "sexuality" of nature, the intersections between queer and ecological inflections of bio/politics (including spatial politics), and the queering of environmental affect, ethics, and desire.

AGAINST NATURE? QUEER SEX, QUEER ANIMALITY

In part 1, each of the four authors examines how sexual natures are produced through the concepts of animal and human, nature and culture. This debate has recently received a significant amount of popular attention, perhaps because, as Alaimo records in her chapter, the intimacy of humans and domestic animals has made the plurality of animal sexualities one of those "open secrets" that we all know. Bagemihl, Roughgarden, and Vasey and Sommer, among others, have clearly illustrated the astounding difference in sexual practices through the evolutionary chain, including dolphins, macaques, feral cats, and pink flamingos (John Waters vindicated!). Clearly this body of scientific research illustrates the mistaken accusation of queer acts as being against nature, a theme that is taken up in more than one contribution to this volume. Nonhuman same-sex acts, as both Bell and Alaimo argue, point us directly to the definition of nature and culture, for at the very least they change how we see the natural life of animals, and perhaps they also make us question the possibility of explaining nature as separate from culture. As these essays also demonstrate, Haraway's reworking of nature and culture is a key trajectory for queer ecological thinking: "Cyborg unities," she tells us, "are monstrous and illegitimate" (1991, 154). They question the distinction between animal and human and carve out a space to rethink the possibilities of inhabiting the material world at the end of the twentieth century. Drawing the complexities of these relationships into the twenty-first century, most recently with the help of her dogs, Haraway argues for a consideration of neither nature nor culture, but naturecultures as the interaction between the two.

While queer subjects have recently found support in the biological sphere, the opposition between nature and culture has more often been a hindrance, and the accusation of being against nature still holds much cultural power in religious and political spheres. Yet, instead of reclaiming the naturalness of queer activity, the authors in this section directly challenge the split between nature and culture upon which charges of being against nature rely. The chapters illustrate the multiple ways that social subjects (both human animal subjects and nonhuman animal subjects) carry these concepts in our daily lives, from the politics of animal and human reproduction to the acceptance of social diversity as strength. Taking up Haraway's call to investigate the space of illegitimate natures, these queer ecologies balance between legitimizing queer behavior (it is, after all, a profound part of life all over the planet) and delegitimizing the binary constructions of sexuality and animality that have informed scientific and cultural discussions of sex.

While Bagemihl invokes the biological exuberance of nature to illustrate just how limiting, and patently heterosexist, dominant scientific lenses are—just how much culture has infringed upon getting at the real life of animals—Alaimo recasts this excess in broader terms. The queerness of animals, Alaimo suggests in chapter 1, "Eluding Capture: The Science, Culture and Pleasure of 'Queer' Animals," also clearly illustrates the unassimilability of sexual diversity. The multiple, even astonishing, modes of sexual behavior amongst animals can inspire a challenge to the nature/culture dualism by eluding representation (as she confesses, "Who knew?"). The standard reductionist terrain of science works very imperfectly here, and Alaimo shows how this imperfection opens up the social and political options for a green queer theory of pleasure. Released from its biologically determined frames, pleasure takes up possibilities that force us to reconsider our notions of human and animal.

The acceptance of queer animals as a place of public debate hinges upon the broad public acceptance of diversity as beneficial to social groups. Yet when the rationale behind celebrating such diversity is questioned, as McWhorter remarks in chapter 2, often it is linked to a biologized understanding of the strength of a species: the more diverse the species, the more resistant it is to external threats or disease or disaster. In "Enemy of the Species," McWhorter forces us to examine the genealogy of this discourse of diversity, arguing that inherent within the biologically amorphous concept of species are those internal threats that impact the overall strength of the species. Historically, queers have been placed as part of this internal threat, along with people of color, people with disabilities, and chronically ill people. Given this lineage, any attempt to argue for sexual diversity as a biological asset of the species needs to challenge the ontological position of the species in our discussions.

Exploring the privileged position given to reproduction in discussions of animals and nature, Sturgeon (chapter 3) stretches out the threads that link together notions of family, reproduction, and nature. From the Right's celebration of the documentary *The March of the Penguins* to the rather minor and conciliatory place that indigenous peoples of the Arctic have been given in discussions of global warming, Sturgeon illustrates the central normalizing position that heterosexual reproductive nuclear families have taken in popular discussions of the changing global environment. By examining these constructions of family through a reproductive justice lens, we can see how the material relationships are often excluded from the clichéd trope that we "belong to the same family." Penguins, as the children's book *And Tango Makes Three* will tell us, do not have only opposite-sex relationships, and their modes of reproduction, intimately integrated into the Antarctic environment, do not map neatly onto human sexual family patterns. Yet the privileging of Western family units of reproduction (which are closely aligned to Western modes of production) dominates popular discussions of both penguins and ecological change: Al Gore's most dramatic slide (aided by the use of a cherry picker) shows growing population as the major threat to a stable climate.

By intertwining stories of the sex performance group Fuck for Forests, queer animals, and the nudist movement, in chapter 4 Bell highlights the often contradictory ways in which nature and culture are mobilized through discourses of sexuality. Whereas Fuck for Forests sees cultural infringements upon nature in the context of both sex and nature, naturists take pains to separate culture from nature, represented in the nonsexual spaces to be nude. The recent literature on queer animals utilizes nature, in the form of queer animal sex, as a challenge to the cultural production of a heterosexist evolutionary format, whereby survival equals heterosexual reproduction. The diverse positions ascribed to nature and culture in these three lenses illustrate the dynamic of Haraway's naturecultures, a recognition of the necessarily intertwined relationship of nature and culture. Illustrating this commingling, Bell's stories of sexual natures highlight how naturecultures are themselves often very queer.

GREEN, PINK, AND PUBLIC: QUEERING ENVIRONMENTAL POLITICS

Part 2 explores the practices of queer ecology that have taken root in different times and spaces. If a motherly Lois Gibbs and a fatherly David Suzuki are the fantasy champions of environmentalism, these chapters look beyond the heterosexual family unit to find a broader potential for environmental and queer politics. Specifically, the authors here illustrate not just the ideological nature of the environmental family unit, but also the productive use of the intersections between sex and nature as sites of political engagement. Working against a metronormative stereotype of gay life as inherently consumerist, many queer activists have taken up the connections between nature and sexuality as a critique of the normalized subject positions (pink or green) that consumer subjectivity offers. While queer activists are struggling through the commodification of gay lifestyle in Calvin Klein ads, televisions shows such as *Queer as Folk* and *The L-Word,* and the marketing of gay and lesbian festivals (such as metropolitan Pride events or the Gay Games), environmentalists are faced with the crisis of green consumerism as it threatens to take the winds from the sails built up against consumer waste (Floyd 1998, Gosine 2001). The tensions between consumer politics and pink and green activism are broad and terminally unresolved, but they point to the increasing power of capital to territorialize moments of resistance. The dynamics of queer environmental politics, as the chapters in this section illustrate, offer places for both environmental and queer activists to counter the normalized subjectivities offered by mainstream political choices.

From sisterhood movements to toxic neighborhood tours, the authors in this section offer alternatives to the encroaching politics of normalized subjectivity by illustrating the coalitional possibilities of queer ecological questions. Yet these coalitions do not always fit easily together, and queer ecology involves a necessary critique of the heteronormativity and whiteness of environmental politics. Sexuality, gender, and race, as can been seen in discourses of reproduction, overpopulation, wilderness conservation, and gentrification, are as significant factors within environmental change as the supposedly straightforward processes of ecology. The trouble with wilderness, as William Cronon's landmark (1996) piece suggests, is that it presents a political agenda based upon our image of wilderness, a dated, racist, gendered, and sexualized wilderness. The task of clarifying a new politic in which Gibbs, Suzuki, and other political activists will not be typecast expectantly into the heterosexual family unit deals with building new understandings of the spaces of environmental practice.

The rather unfortunate and not always subtly racist analysis of overpopulation that haunts much American environmentalism—most recently, as both Gosine and Sturgeon note, in Gore's documentary *An Inconvenient Truth*—holds within it a longstanding revulsion against what Gosine illustrates as "the sex of others." Malthusian politics, he argues in chapter 5, links up with homophobic discourses about gay male sex through a concern for the public safety of a national culture. The genealogies of overpopulation and the criminalizing of sexual acts between men find common links in the anxieties of national space. Using colonial history to show how nationalism is established through racialized heterosexuality, Gosine demonstrates how sex between men and non-white sex have been cast as dangers to nature, making them threats to public safety. Thus, a queer ecological framework not only would offer a possibility of coalitions between racial and sexual inequities, but also would necessarily provide an analysis of the contemporaneous development of race, sexuality, and nature through each other.

The recognition of queer ecologies is built upon the understanding that these alternative cultures of nature have been ongoing throughout both the environmental movement and gay and lesbian history. In chapter 6, Unger documents some of these practices that have played an important role within the construction of lesbian space in the United States. Starting with the bohemian freedom offered to black lesbians in Harlem and moving through the white rural lesbian retreat community of Cherry Grove, the back-to-the-land movement in Oregon, the Pagoda womynspace in Florida, and the proliferation of women's festivals such as the Michigan Women's Festival, to the recent experiences of Alapine Village, Unger argues that the alternative spaces were and are influenced by the environments around them. Not only that, though: these spaces provided examples of alternative environments that address the sexism, homophobia, and violence that have been adopted within larger environmental movements.

While environmental justice groups have long argued that the claim of the natural is a particular normalizing discourse, it is still often used as a rallying cry around which mainstream environmental problems are mobilized. In chapter 7, Di Chiro examines how the threat to presumably natural gender patterns has been the central organizing principle around recent activism on toxic pollution. Media and activists focus on the specific disruptions to hegemonic ideas of masculinity, femininity, and heterosexuality, taking issue with the size of alligator penises and the presence of intersex fish in particular environments. Without dismissing the absolute need to address the accumulation of toxic chemicals in the worlds we inhabit, Di Chiro shows how the misplaced concern over abnormal sexual difference apparent in several works by influential toxic activists tends to produce a heterosexist and transphobic hysteria instead of focusing on serious health problems, including breast, ovarian, and testicular cancer, immune system breakdown, diabetes, and heart disease. By acknowledging the politics of normalcy that operates within these toxic discourses, Di Chiro shows the possibility of a truly coalitional politics that embraces a wide variety of subjects and biological positions while maintaining a critical perspective on the changing materialities of our bodies and environments.

Addressing the productive politics of coalition building, something that has long been a topic within both queer and environmental politics, Hogan demonstrates in chapter 8 how a queer ecological politics contests the use of nature to establish social hierarchies. Using Joseph Hansen's detective novel *Nightwork* and Heather MacDonald's film *Ballot Measure 9* as examples of coalition politics, Hogan's chapter exposes the ideological production of queers as against nature. In its discussion of the Oregon Citizens' Alliance's ballot initiative to drastically restrict the rights of gay and lesbians, *Ballot Measure 9* targets how the frame of nature is mobilized to portray queers as perverse and unnatural. *Nightwork* similarly contests "against nature" discourses to show that, rather than queers being a threat to nature and society, it is rather homophobia and capitalism that are toxic. To confront the politics of the naturalization of nature, these texts both develop a coalitional politics that address the complex racial, economic, and sexual dynamics that can help challenge "the ways in which nature and the natural are used to condemn, control, and stigmatize communities and groups."

For Ingram, the concern for the political consequences of queer space is one of the benefits of using queer theory in conjunction with landscape ecology. By queering the social and natural sciences within the field of landscape ecology, Ingram argues that queer ecologies can provide a useful material analysis to historical and emerging patterns in queer life. Using the production of Vancouver's West End as a specific, gay-positive neighborhood, chapter 9 illustrates the changing dynamics of political and spatial interests in the area and challenges urban discourses of gay enclaves as "ghettoes." The West End, often seen as a place of urban eroticization, tells a complicated story of economic interests pairing with both some specific queer subjectivities at the expense of others, and with the larger queer community at the expense of racial and economic minorities. By using a conceptual framework articulated in the pairing of queer urban history with landscape ecology, Ingram argues that these patterns of coalition and contradiction can be analyzed to provide us with a better description of the urban experience of queer subjectivities, along with a deeper vision of the modes of urban eroticization for which we should be looking.

DESIRING NATURE? QUEER ATTACHMENTS

In his discussion of the queer politics of Michel Foucault, Halperin argues that queer theorizing produces possibilities to counter the "paucity of choices" for ways that we can become "infinitely more susceptible to pleasures" (1995, 81). This question is no doubt the one that Ennis and Jack are attempting to deal with on the shoulders of Brokeback, and it is a question that has arisen in a surprising number of places. While fist-fucking and S/M are Foucault's (and Halperin's) models, we can also see this expansion of pleasure in, say, Jean-Pierre Jeunet's 2001 film *Amélie,* in which Audrey Tautou's character finds solace in the touch of seeds and beans as an expression of her frustration with traditional heterosexuality, or even in Rachel Carson's long-term romantic friendship with Dorothy Freeman (Carson 1995; see also Grosz 1995). Queer ecology allows us to understand the links provided by queer theory to understand that our pleasures are not merely between humans, but are expanded and significantly shaped by the production of nature and space around us.

Asking questions of what is desired in and through nature necessarily tours us through the politics of sexuality, mobilized through scientific, national, or literary codes. But like much else that goes on in the name of nature, desire is always surpassing the frames established for it, and a queer politics of desire allows us to become open to what exists beyond the discursive frameworks that have been established for these experiences. As Grosz argues, one of the tasks of queer politics is to "embrace the openness, to welcome unknown readings, new claims, provocative analyses—to make things happen, to shift fixed positions, to transform our everyday expectations and habitual conceptual schemas" (1995, 174). A similar openness to excess is found within much ecological writing, where the phenomenological interaction with the expanse of that which is beyond the human is reason enough for inquisitive openness to new pleasures. This desire for experience is at the heart of Annie Dillard's *Pilgrim at Tinker Creek* (1974), the style and desire of which is queered in the work of Ellen Meloy, examined in this volume by Chisholm. The possibilities of queer desire for nature offer not just moments of pleasure, but, as the authors in this section illustrate, moments in which we can make the necessary connections between the policing of sexuality and the increasing destruction of nonhuman life. Queer attachments work both to celebrate the excess of life and to politicize the sites at which this excess is eradicated.

Exploring the potency of poetry to challenge naturalizations of heterosexuality, in chapter 10, "The Place, Promised, That Has Not Yet Been," Stein draws upon the work of Adrienne Rich and Minnie Bruce Pratt to illustrate lesbian responses to the positioning of lesbian eroticism as a "crime against nature." Both Rich and Pratt deploy intimate descriptions of natural landscape paired with lesbian homoeroticism to embed forbidden desire in spaces that have been appropriated by homophobic regulation. Where Rich explores complex questions of identity, including sexuality, as they are embedded in natural landscapes, Pratt explicitly tackles crime-against-nature discourse, particularly as it appears in the U.S. anti-sodomy laws that saw her separated from her children. Both authors use the erotics developed between nature and poet to illustrate both lesbian love and the violence inherent in the naturalization of hierarchical social relationships. Indeed, in Pratt's and Rich's poetry, the crime against nature is enforced heterosexuality, not erotic same-sex desire.

Ecological texts mix with national spaces, and often those texts work to naturalize a sexual relationship within the national imagination of its citizens. Erickson's chapter 11, "fucking close to water," takes as its starting point a comic articulation of Canadian identity, "a Canadian is someone who knows how to make love in a canoe," and interrogates how the sexual identity mobilized by the canoe hides the naturalization of a nation built upon colonial soil. The citizenship idealized in this statement not only hides a heterosexuality connected intimately to nation and nature, but also presupposes the nation as a natural entity. As a leisured craft that was adopted from indigenous peoples, the canoe represents a particularly salient place to interrogate not merely the heterosexual politics of the nation, but also the ways the sexual politics are dependent upon the colonial assumption of superiority held by the state. Tomson Highway's novel *The Kiss of the Fur Queen* illustrates the destructive impact of colonial heterosexual institutions upon two Cree brothers, and requires us to think about the nation without assuming its continued existence.

It is part of the circumstances of queer relations of and to nature, given the devastating impact on both constellations that occur daily, that significant energy must be directed toward documenting, resisting, and, indeed, living through periods of loss. Yet, as Mortimer-Sandilands shows in chapter 12, "Melancholy Natures, Queer Ecologies," the impact of loss upon queer ecologies need not be immobilizing. Using recent reformulations of Freud's theory of melancholy, she argues that public acknowledgments of loss offer queer ecological activists a language in which to resist a commodification of nature that removes the specificity of nature, including the possibility of grieving for individual elements and instances of nature. Modern environmental concern is motivated by a need to mourn lost objects, but rarely is the value of what is lost recognized; instead there is a mad scramble to find replacements, replicating through the commodity form the same relations of ecological destruction that created the loss in the first place. Using the work of Jan Zita Grover and Derek Jarman, writers who connect ecological devastation to their personal experiences of working and living with AIDS, Mortimer-Sandilands asks us to dwell on what has been lost and recognize the value of devastated landscapes instead of fetishizing the about-to-be-absences of more "pristine" nature.

Connections, assemblages, and becomings form central concerns for many queer and nature writers, and the possibilities offered by nature for models and metaphors are truly quite limitless. Chisholm, in her "Biophilia, Creative Involution, and the Ecological Future of Queer Desire" (chapter 13), takes nature writer Ellen Meloy as her guide to the rewriting of E. O. Wilson's "biophilia," the connections between human and animal. While not connected to lgbtq politics specifically, Meloy's musing on the desire of nature and the desire for nature radically resituate contemporary understandings of biological and sexual desire. Chisholm pairs Meloy with Deleuze and Guattari to show to how Meloy's "biophiliac" tendencies situate becomings as a possible queer ecological position. In this way, the chapter speaks to how cutting-edge ecological thinking understands queer desire to be the quintessential life force, since it is precisely queer desire that creates the experimental, co-adaptive, symbiotic, and nonreproductive interspecies couplings that become evolution.

In sum, all thirteen contributions to *Queer Ecologies* both draw on and stretch the boundaries of the queer ecological imaginings apparent in previous works in, for example, science studies, environmental history, queer geography, ecocriticism, and queer theory. Embodying profound epistemological revisions as well as philosophical, political, and aesthetic challenges to hegemonic pairings of sex and nature, the volume points to an ecology that embraces deviation and strangeness as a necessary part of biophilia, sexual pleasure and transgression as foundational to environmental ethics and politics, and resistance to heteronormativity as part and parcel of ecological science and green strategy alike. Against the commodification of nature as resource and as spectacle, and also against the fetishization of lgbtq consumerist lifestyles, *Queer Ecologies* argues for a perspective based on the mobilization of queer perspectives and politics against "against nature" toward radical ecological ends.

1. Early versions of parts of this introduction previously appeared in Mortimer-Sandilands (2005). *Brokeback Mountain* won the 2006 Academy Awards for Best Director, Best Adapted Screenplay, and Best Score. The film is based on the short story "Brokeback Mountain" by E. Annie Proulx in *Close Range* (1999).

2. There are various versions of this abbreviation in current usage—glbt, lgbttq, etc. We have, in this volume, retained each author's individual choice.

3. Although we do not have space to explore this point here, Jack is actually a bit more "gay" than Ennis, and this characterization is quite important. Jack allows himself to dream of the two men sharing a life and a future together; Ennis cannot or will not. Jack eventually pursues other men; Ennis does not. Jack is killed, possibly as a result of homophobic violence; Ennis is not. At the end of the day, the film does not leave much space open for positive expressions of gay identification, let alone same-sex relationships. And as Kathleen Chamberlain and Victoria Somogyi (2006) point out, while the opening of the film in 1963 could be read as an accurate portrayal of the absence of public representations of gay male community at the time, the fact that the film also ends, in the mid-1980s, with no change to that absence erases the entire history of the post-Stonewall emergence of gay men and lesbians into public life and unwittingly reinforces the story in which rural places are only and always dangerous places for queers.

4. For a selection of critical perspectives on the film, see the Fall 2006 issue of *Intertexts* (Lubbock) and the Spring 2007 issue of *Film Quarterly*.

5. There are ways in which both Jack and Ennis are *imperfectly* virile in the heteromasculine mode, especially in their class positions, which leave Jack married to a woman who approves of his death and Ennis living in a trailer afraid to talk to his daughter. We consider also that their unsuitability for heterosexuality effectively de-naturalizes it: their "natural" masculinity is expressed together in the wilderness, and institutionalized heterosexuality is clearly an effeminized and unnatural space in which both men suffocate (and Jack dies). There are many notes of misogyny, here, that are also apparent in other instances of the gay pastoral.

6. Roosevelt haunts *Brokeback Mountain:* he went to nearly the same region that Ennis is from to remake himself in light of accusations that he was effeminate.

7. Although there are clear differences between Wyoming and Arcadia, both physically and economically.

8. Donna Haraway's work (e.g., 1991) is an important place from which to consider the potential of feminist science and technology studies to "queer" nature. Literatures on non-Western sexualities and their relations to non-Western creations of nature clearly reveal other kinds of queer ecologies in addition to resistances to the Anglo-American ones on which we generally rely here; see Pflugfelder (1999).

9. Ellis distinguished congenital homosexuality from "pseudohomosexuality," which he considered to be socially produced in such places as schools (and thus preventable, as he details in the conclusion to the work).

10. There have, of course, been many critical challenges to evolutionary theory, sexual selection, and the obvious abuses some sociobiologists and evolutionary psychologists have perpetrated on Darwin's work. For a selection of such challenges, see Gowalty (1997).

11. TransAdvocate.org (http://www.antijen.org/transadvocate/index.html) claims to be a website "dedicated to exploring the relationship between our environment and gender." It notes, for example, that "although little research is available directly linking transsexualism to exposure to endocrine disrupting chemicals, a wide array of evidence indicates a relationship, including sexual developmental effects found in

wildlife, corroborating animal laboratory studies, and to a more limited extent, human studies." Nancy Langston (2003) considers this research carefully and thoroughly, but manages still to assert essential dimorphism as necessary to sexual and gender health. Although the effect of endocrine disruption on human (and other animal) health is a serious issue, the line of research is profoundly flawed in several ways, not least its reduction of transgender identities to biological questions and its equation of sexual health with sexual difference.

12. These different processes occurred unevenly and under specific geographical, political, and cultural conditions. Recent historical studies are rich with detail about the particular ways in which gay and lesbian communities shaped and were shaped by particular cities; see, for example, Chauncey (1994) and Kennedy and Davis (1994).

13. Although it is clear that women had a variety of sexual relations with one another in other historical periods (not to mention other places), one view is that (white, upper-class) women's "romantic friendships" were not much of a threat to patriarchal family forms until the late nineteenth century, were generally invisible, and were, when considered at all, understood as natural relationships for women because they were not read as sexual. They were thus also, as Sandilands (2004b) has documented, relationships through which *women* could experience nature homosocially (and sometimes even homoerotically).

14. The performance art of the Lesbian National Parks and Services (a.k.a. the "Lesbian Rangers," Shawna Dempsey and Lorri Millan) takes aim at exactly these lesbophobic discourses, and especially at the complete invisibility of lesbians in dominant wilderness discourses. Dempsey and Millan not only perform a caricatured and hyper-visible lesbian sexuality "in" and "as" nature, but also, as rangers, take on the authority of the park itself to *enforce* lesbian visibility. See Dempsey and Millan (2002), and also Sandilands (2004c).

15. Although the examples used in this introduction are primarily North American, Little and Panelli (2007) explicitly raise the question of nature and sexuality in the Australian Outback and explore the ways heterosexist expectations and practices directly shape perceptions of nature. There is a growing literature on nature and sexuality in Australia that also includes Waitt and Gorman-Murray (2008).

16. Shuttleton also offers a strong critical reading of *Maurice*, which, he argues, rewrites elements of the pastoral toward a "homoeroticised backwoods" (2000, 138).

17. As Shuttleton demonstrates, pastoralism is—even in its queer deployments— often highly problematic: it "may be a homoerotic genre, but is nevertheless constructs identities within existing, often exploitive, hierarchies of social class, gender and ethnicity" (2000, 129). Along similar lines, Bobby Noble (2004) is critical of Hall's particular invocation of class and nation in her naturalization of inversion.

18. Clare has also written an interesting essay (2004) in which he explores both the physicality and the metaphoricity of the "stone" in stone butch.

19. See Ingram's conversation with Pat Califia on the culture of public sex in the South of Market Area in San Francisco in Ingram, Bouthillette, and Retter (1997, 177–96).

20. See Carpenter (1908). Sheila Rowbotham's (2008) biography of Carpenter is a must-read, as it documents not only Carpenter's extraordinary social influence (he met and wrote about Forster, and also Whitman and John Addington Symonds), but also his social context. He appears, through her, as an iconoclast, but a very intelligent one.

21. Many lesbian separatists held environmental concerns central to their politics. For example, Sally Miller Gearhart's 1979 novel *The Wanderground* envisions a world in which women, freed from oppressive male influence, are able to live

together in polygynous sexual relationships in a rural world that is carefully separate from destructive, male-dominated cities. In that woman-centered world, women are better able to find both rich erotic and social relations to one another, and rich social and erotic relations to their natural environments, which are actively prevented in heterosexual, patriarchal societies. Thus, the novel argues—in a sort of radical feminist pastoral—that heterosexuality is not natural, and that it is destructive both to women and to nature; here, we have a narrative that reverses the idea that homosexuality is an urban illness, and instead argues that *heterosexism* is the urban, anti-nature ill to which lesbians must respond.

22. We have to point out a delicious irony. The state of Oregon contains a particularly high concentration of separatist wimmin's lands. As indicated earlier, that state, in the nineteenth century, was particularly heterosexually organized because of the DLA's privileging of heterosexual families in its allotment practices. Because this land allotment strategy had, among other things, the long-term effect of discouraging town development, in the late twentieth century we see, even on the interstate corridor, very sparse settlement and comparatively low land prices. Both of these factors helped to create an ideal environment for lesbian intentional communities.

REFERENCES

Alaimo, Stacy. 1999. *Undomesticated Ground: Recasting Nature as Feminist Space.* Ithaca, N.Y.: Cornell University Press.

Alaimo, Stacy, and Susan Hekman, eds. 2008. *Material Feminisms.* Bloomington: Indiana University Press.

Altman, Dennis. 2000. Marginality on the Tropic. In *De-Centring Sexualities: Politics and Representation beyond the Metropolis,* ed. Richard Phillips, Diane Watt, and David Shuttleton, 37–48. London: Routledge.

Bagemihl, Bruce. 1999. *Biological Exuberance: Animal Homosexuality and Natural Diversity.* New York: St. Martin's Press.

Bell, David. 1995. Perverse Dynamics and the Transformation of Intimacy. In *Mapping Desire: Geographies of Sexualities,* ed. David Bell and Gill Valentine, 304–17. London: Routledge.

———. 1997a. Anti-Idyll: Rural Horror. In *Contested Countryside Cultures: Otherness, Marginalisation and Rurality,* ed. Paul Cloke and Jo Little, 94–108. London: Routledge.

———. 1997b. One-Handed Geographies: An Archaeology of Public Sex. In *Queers in Space: Communities\Public Places\Sites of Resistance,* ed. Gordon Brent Ingram, Anne-Marie Bouthillette, and Yolanda Retter, 81–87. Seattle, Wash.: Bay Press.

Bell, David, and Gill Valentine, eds. 1995a. *Mapping Desire: Geographies of Sexualities.* London: Routledge.

———. 1995b. Queer Country: Rural Lesbian and Gay Lives. *Journal of Rural Sociology* 11: 113–22.

Binnie, John, and Gill Valentine. 1999. Geographies of Sexuality: A Review of Progress. *Progress in Human Geography* 23.2: 175–87.

Boag, Peter. 2003a. *Same-Sex Affairs: Constructing and Controlling Homosexuality in the Pacific Northwest.* Berkeley and Los Angeles: University of California Press.

———. 2003b. Thinking Like Mount Rushmore: Sexuality and Gender in the Republican Landscape. In *Seeing Nature Through Gender*, ed. Virginia Scharff, 40–59. Lawrence: University Press of Kansas.

Carpenter, Edward. 1908. *The Intermediate Sex: A Study of Some Transitional Types of Men and Women*. London: Allen and Unwin.

Carson, Rachel. 1995. *Always, Rachel: The Letters of Rachel Carson and Dorothy Freeman, 1952–1964*. Ed. Martha Freeman. Boston, Mass.: Beacon Press.

Castells, Manuel. 1983. *The City and the Grassroots: A Cross Cultural Theory of Urban Social Movements*. London: E. Arnold.

Cerullo, Margaret, and Phyllis Ewen. 1984. The American Family Goes Camping: Gender, Family and the Politics of Space. *Antipode* 16.3: 35–46.

Chamberlain, Kathleen, and Victoria Somogyi. 2006. "You Know I Ain't Queer": *Brokeback Mountain* as the Not-Gay Cowboy Movie. *Intertexts* (Lubbock) 10.2: 129–44, 195–96.

Chauncey, George. 1994. *Gay New York: A Social and Cultural History of Male Homosexuality in New York City, 1890–1970*. New York: Basic Books.

Chisholm, Dianne. 2005. *Queer Constellations: Subcultural Space in the Wake of the City*. Minneapolis: University of Minnesota Press.

Chris, Cynthia. 2006. *Watching Wildlife*. Minneapolis: University of Minnesota Press.

Clare, Eli. 1999. *Exile and Pride: Disability, Queerness and Liberation*. Cambridge, Mass.: South End Press.

———. 2004. Neither Stone nor Wing. In *From the Inside Out: Radical Gender Transformation, FTM and Beyond*, ed. Morty Diamond, 147–54. San Francisco, Calif.: Manic D Press.

Cronon, William. 1996. The Trouble with Wilderness, or Getting Back to the Wrong Nature. *Environmental History* 1.1: 7–28.

Cruz-Malavé, Arnaldo, and Martin Manalansan, eds. 2002. *Queer Globalizations: Citizenship and the Afterlife of Colonialism*. New York: New York University Press.

Darwin, Charles. 1871. *The Descent of Man and Selection in Relation to Sex*. London: John Murray.

Delage, Yves. 1912. *The Theories of Evolution*. London: Frank Palmer.

D'Emilio, John. 1983. Capitalism and Gay Identity. In *Powers of Desire: The Politics of Sexuality*, ed. Ann Snitow, Christopher Stansell, and Sharon Thompson, 100–113. New York: Monthly Review Press.

Dempsey, Shawna, and Lorri Millan. 2002. Video. *Lesbian National Parks and Services: A Force of Nature*. Winnipeg, Manitoba: Video Pool Media Arts Centre.

Di Chiro, Giovanna. 2004. Producing "Roundup-Ready®" Communities? Human Genome Research and Environmental Justice Policy. In *New Perspectives on Environmental Justice: Gender, Sexuality and Activism*, ed. Rachel Stein, 139–60. New Brunswick, N.J.: Rutgers University Press.

Dillard, Annie. 1974. *Pilgrim at Tinker Creek*. New York: Harper and Row.

Doan, Petra. 2007. Queers in the American City: Transgendered Perceptions of Urban Space. *Gender, Place and Culture* 14.1: 57–74.

Dollimore, Jonathan. 1991. *Sexual Dissidence: Augustine to Wilde, Freud to Foucault*. Oxford, U.K.: Clarendon Press.

Ellis, Havelock. [1905]1936. *Studies in the Psychology of Sex*. Vol. 1, part 4, *Sexual Inversion*. New York: Random House.

Erickson, Bruce. 2003. Colonial Climbs of Mount Trudeau: Thinking Masculinity through the Homosocial. *TOPIA: Canadian Journal of Cultural Studies* 9: 67–82.

Filemyr, Ann. 1997. Going Outdoors and Other Dangerous Expeditions. *Frontiers: A Journal of Women Studies* 18.2: 160–77.

Floyd, Kevin. 1998. Making History: Marxism, Queer Theory, and Contradiction in the Future of American Studies. *Cultural Critique* 40: 167–201.

Fone, Byrne R. S. 1983. This Other Eden: Arcadia and the Homosexual Imagination. *Journal of Homosexuality* 8.3–4: 13–34.

Forster, E. M. 1971. *Maurice*. Toronto, Ontario: MacMillan.

Foucault, Michel. 1978. *The History of Sexuality. Volume 1: An Introduction*. New York: Vintage Books.

Gaard, Greta. 1997. Toward a Queer Ecofeminism. *Hypatia* 12.1: 114–37.

Gearhart, Sally Miller. 1979. *The Wanderground: Stories of the Hill Women*. Watertown, Mass.: Persephone Press.

Gide, André. [1920] 1952. *Corydon: Four Socratic Dialogues*. London: Secker and Warburg.

Gosine, Andil. 2001. Pink Greens: Ecoqueers Organize in Toronto. *Alternatives* 27.3: 35–36.

———. 2005a. *Sex for Pleasure, Rights to Participation, and Alternatives to AIDS: Placing Sexual Minorities and/or Dissidents in Development*. Institute of Development Studies Working Paper 228.

———. 2005b. Stumbling into Sexualities: International Discourse Discovers Dissident Desire. *Canadian Woman Studies* 24.2–3: 59–64.

Gowalty, Patricia Adair, ed. 1997. *Feminism and Evolutionary Biology: Boundaries, Intersections, and Frontiers*. New York: Chapman and Hall.

Grosz, Elizabeth. 1995. *Space, Time and Perversion: Essays on the Politics of Bodies*. New York: Routledge.

———. 2005. *Time Travels: Feminism, Nature, Power*. Durham, N.C.: Duke University Press.

Grube, John. 1997. "No More Shit": The Struggle for Democratic Gay Space in Toronto. In *Queers in Space: Communities\Public Places\Sites of Resistance*, ed. Gordon Brent Ingram, Anne-Marie Bouthillette, and Yolanda Retter, 127–45. Seattle, Wash.: Bay Press.

Halberstam, Judith. 2005. *In a Queer Time and Place: Transgender Bodies, Subcultural Lives*. New York: New York University Press.

Hall, Radclyffe. 1981 (1928). *The Well of Loneliness*. New York: Avon Books.

Halperin, David. 1983. *Before Pastoral: Theocritus and the Ancient Tradition of Bucolic Poetry*. New Haven, Conn.: Yale University Press.

———. 1995. *Saint Foucault: Towards a Gay Hagiography*. New York: Oxford University Press.

Haraway, Donna. 1989. *Primate Visions: Gender, Race, and Nation in the World of Modern Science*. New York: Routledge.

———. 1991. *Simians, Cyborgs and Women*. New York: Routledge.

Herdt, Gilbert, ed. 1996. *Third Sex, Third Gender: Beyond Sexual Dimorphism in Culture and History*. New York: Zone Books.

Hermer, Joe. 2002. *Regulating Eden: The Nature of Order in North American Parks*. Toronto, Ontario: University of Toronto Press.

Herring, Scott. 2007. Out of the Closets, Into the Woods: *RFD*, Country Women, and the Post-Stonewall Emergence of Queer Anti-Urbanism. *American Quarterly* 59.2: 341–72.

Hird, Myra. 2004. Naturally Queer. *Feminist Theory* 5.1: 85–89.

———. 2006. Animal Transex. *Australian Feminist Studies* 21.46: 35–50.

Hogan, Katie. 2004. Detecting Toxic Environments: Gay Mystery as Environmental Justice. In *New Perspectives on Environmental Justice: Gender, Sexuality and Activism*, ed. Rachel Stein, 249–61. New Brunswick, N.J.: Rutgers University Press.

Howard, John. 1999. *Men Like That: A Southern Queer History*. Chicago: University of Chicago Press.

Ingram, Gordon Brent. 1997a. Marginality and the Landscape of Erotic Alien(n) ations. In *Queers in Space: Communities\Public Places\Sites of Resistance*, ed. Gordon Brent Ingram, Anne-Marie Bouthillette, and Yolanda Retter, 25–52. Seattle, Wash.: Bay Press.

———. 1997b. "Open" Space as Strategic Queer Sites. In *Queers in Space: Communities\Public Places\Sites of Resistance*, ed. Gordon Brent Ingram, Anne-Marie Bouthillette, and Yolanda Retter, 95–125. Seattle, Wash.: Bay Press.

Ingram, Gordon Brent, Anne-Marie Bouthillette, and Yolanda Retter, eds. 1997. *Queers in Space: Communities\Public Places\Sites of Resistance*. Seattle, Wash.: Bay Press.

Jeunet, Jean-Pierre, dir. 2001. Motion picture. *Amélie (Le Fabuleux Destin d'Amélie Poulain)*. UGC and Miramax Films.

Kennedy, Elizabeth Lapovsky, and Madeleine Davis. 1994. *Boots of Leather, Slippers of Gold: The History of a Lesbian Community*. New York: Penguin Books.

Kimmel, Michael. 2005. *Manhood in America: A Cultural History*. New York: Oxford University Press.

Kleiner, Catherine. 2003. Nature's Lovers: The Erotics of Lesbian Land Communities in Oregon, 1974–1984. In *Seeing Nature Through Gender*, ed. Virginia Scharff, 242–62. Lawrence: University Press of Kansas.

Kramer, Jerry Lee. 1995. Bachelor Farmers and Spinsters: Gay and Lesbian Identities and Communities in Rural North Dakota. In *Mapping Desire: Geographies of Sexualities*, ed. David Bell and Gill Valentine, 200–213. London: Routledge.

Langston, Nancy. 2003. Gender Transformed: Endocrine Disruptors in the Environment. In *Seeing Nature Through Gender*, ed. Virginia Scharff, 129–66. Lawrence: University Press of Kansas.

Lee, Ang, dir. 2006. Motion picture. *Brokeback Mountain*. Paramount Pictures.

Lee, Wendy Lynne, and Laura M. Dow. 2001. Queering Ecological Feminism: Erotophobia, Commodification, and Lesbian Identity. *Ethics and the Environment* 6.2: 2–21.

Little, Jo, and Ruth Panelli. 2007. "Outback" Romance? A Reading of Nature and Heterosexuality in Rural Australia. *Sociologica Ruralis* 47.3: 173–88.

Magubane, Zine. 2003. Simians, Savages, Skulls and Sex: Science and Colonial Militarism in Nineteenth Century South Africa. In *Race, Nature and the Politics of Difference*, ed. Donald S. Moore, Jake Kosek, and Anand Pandian, 99–121. Durham, N.C.: Duke University Press.

McWhorter, Ladelle. 1999. *Bodies and Pleasures: Foucault and the Politics of Sexual Normalization*. Bloomington: Indiana University Press.

Mortimer-Sandilands, Catriona. 2005. Unnatural Passions? Toward a Queer Ecology. *Invisible Culture 9*. http://www.rochester.edu/in_visible_culture/Issue_9/title9.html.

Nanda, Serena. 2000. *Gender Diversity: Crosscultural Variations*. Long Grove, Ill.: Waveland Press.

Newton, Esther. 1993. *Cherry Grove, Fire Island: Sixty Years in America's First Gay and Lesbian Town*. Boston, Mass.: Beacon Press.

Noble, Jean Bobby. 2004. *Masculinities without Men: Female Masculinity in Twentieth Century Fictions*. Vancouver: University of British Columbia Press.

Osborne, Karen Lee, and William J. Spurlin, eds. 1996. *Reclaiming the Heartland: Lesbian and Gay Voices from the Midwest.* Minneapolis: University of Minnesota Press.

Oswin, Natalie. 2007. The End of Queer (as We Knew It): Globalization and the Making of a Gay-Friendly South Africa. *Gender, Place and Culture* 14.1: 93–110.

Pflugfelder, Gregory M. 1999. *Cartographies of Desire: Male-Male Sexuality in Japanese Discourse, 1600–1950.* Berkeley and Los Angeles: University of California Press.

Proulx, E. Annie. 1999. *Close Range: Wyoming Stories.* New York: Charles Scribner.

Riordan, Michael. 1996. *Out Our Way: Gay and Lesbian Life in the Country.* Toronto, Ontario: Between the Lines Press.

Romesburg, Don. 2007. Camping Out with Ray Bourbon: Female Impersonators and Queer Dread of Wide Open Spaces. *Reconstruction: Studies in Contemporary Culture* 7:2. http://reconstruction.eserver.org/072/romesburg.shtml.

Rothenberg, Tamar. 1995. And She Told Two Friends: Lesbians Creating Urban Social Space. In *Mapping Desire: Geographies of Sexualities,* ed. David Bell and Gill Valentine, 165–81. London: Routledge.

Roughgarden, Joan. 2004. *Evolution's Rainbow: Diversity, Gender, and Sexuality in Nature and People.* Berkeley and Los Angeles: University of California Press.

Rowbotham, Sheila. 2008. *Edward Carpenter: A Life of Liberty and Love.* London: Verso.

Rule, Jane. 1964. *Desert of the Heart.* Toronto, Ontario: Macmillan.

Russell, Constance L., Tema Sarick, and Jacqueline Kennelly. 2002. Queering Environmental Education. *Canadian Journal of Environmental Education* 7.1: 54–66.

Sandilands, Catriona. 2001. Desiring Nature, Queering Ethics: Adventures in Erotogenic Environments. *Environmental Ethics* 23.2: 169–88.

———. 2002. Lesbian Separatist Communities and the Experience of Nature: Toward a Queer Ecology. *Organization and Environment* 15.2: 131–63.

———. 2004a. Eco Homo: Queering the Ecological Body Politic. *Social Philosophy Today* 19: 17–39.

———. 2004b. The Importance of Reading Queerly: Jewett's *Deephaven* as Feminist Ecology. *Interdisciplinary Studies in Literature and the Environment* 11.2: 57–77.

———. 2004c. Where the Mountain Men Meet the Lesbian Rangers: Gender, Nation and Nature in the Rocky Mountain Parks. In *This Elusive Land: Women and the Canadian Environment,* ed. Melody Hessing, Rebecca Raglon, and Catriona Sandilands, 142–62. Vancouver: University of British Columbia Press.

Scharff, Virginia, ed. *Seeing Nature through Gender.* Lawrence: University Press of Kansas.

Seitler, Dana. 2004. Queer Physiognomies: Or, How Many Ways Can We Do the History of Sexuality? *Criticism* 46.1: 71–102.

Shuttleton, David. 2000. The Queer Politics of Gay Pastoral. In *De-Centring Sexualities: Politics and Representation Beyond the Metropolis,* ed. Richard Phillips, Diane Watt, and David Shuttleton, 125–46. London: Routledge.

Silverstone, Martin. 2000. The Case of the Lesbian Gulls. *Equinox* 110: 6.

Simon, Bryant. 2003. "New Men in Body and Soul": The Civilian Conservation Corps and the Transformation of Male Bodies and the Body Politic. In *Seeing Nature through Gender,* ed. Virginia Scharff, 80–102. Lawrence: University Press of Kansas.

Smith-Rosenberg, Carroll. 1985. *Disorderly Conduct: Visions of Gender in Victorian America.* New York: Alfred A. Knopf.

Spurlin, William J. 2006. *Imperialism within the Margins: Queer Representation and the Politics of Culture in Southern Africa.* New York: Palgrave.

Stein, Rachel, ed. 2004. *New Perspectives on Environmental Justice: Gender, Sexuality and Activism.* New Brunswick, N.J.: Rutgers University Press.

Sturgeon, Noël. 1997. *Ecofeminist Natures: Race, Gender, Feminist Theory and Political Action.* New York: Routledge.

———. 2004. "The Power is Yours, Planeteers!" Race, Gender and Sexuality in Children's Environmental Popular Culture. In *New Perspectives on Environmental Justice: Gender, Sexuality and Activism,* ed. Rachel Stein, 262–76. New Brunswick, N.J.: Rutgers University Press.

Terry, Jennifer. 2000. "Unnatural Acts" in Nature: The Scientific Fascination with Queer Animals. *GLQ: A Journal of Lesbian and Gay Studies* 6.2: 151–93.

Unger, Nancy. 2004. Women, Sexuality and Environmental Justice in American History. In *New Perspectives on Environmental Justice: Gender, Sexuality and Activism,* ed. Rachel Stein, 45–62. New Brunswick, N.J.: Rutgers University Press.

van Lieshout, Maurice. 1997. Leather Nights in the Woods: Locating Male Homosexuality and Sadomasochism in a Dutch Highway Rest Area. In *Queers in Space: Communities|Public Places|Sites of Resistance,* ed. Gordon Brent Ingram, Anne-Marie Bouthillette, and Yolanda Retter, 339–55. Seattle, Wash.: Bay Press.

Vasey, Paul, and Volker Sommer, eds. 2006. *Homosexual Behaviour in Animals: An Evolutionary Perspective.* Cambridge: Cambridge University Press.

Waitt, Gordon, and Andrew Gorman-Murray. 2008. Camp in the Country: Re-negotiating Sexuality and Gender through a Rural Lesbian and Gay Festival. *Journal of Tourism and Cultural Change* 6.3: 185–207.

Weeks, Jeffrey. 1991. *Against Nature: Essays on History, Sexuality and Identity.* London: Rivers Oram Press.

Weston, Kath. 1995. Get Thee to a Big City: Sexual Imagination and the Great Gay Migration. *GLQ: A Journal of Lesbian and Gay Studies* 2: 253–77.

Wilson, Angelia R. 2000. Getting Your Kicks on Route 66! Stories of Gay and Lesbian Life in Rural America, c. 1950–1970. In *De-Centring Sexualities: Politics and Representation Beyond the Metropolis,* ed. Richard Phillips, Diane Watt, and David Shuttleton. 199–216. London: Routledge.

Against Nature?
Queer Sex, Queer Animality

CHAPTER 1

Eluding Capture: The Science, Culture, and Pleasure of "Queer" Animals

STACY ALAIMO

We're Deer. We're Queer. Get Used to It. A new exhibit in Norway
outs the animal kingdom.
                                        —Alisa Opar

Biological Exuberance is, above all, an affirmation of life's vitality
and infinite possibilities: a worldview that is at once primordial
and futuristic, in which gender is kaleidoscopic, sexualities are
multiple, and the categories of male and female are fluid and
transmutable. A world, in short, exactly like the one we inhabit.
                                        —Bruce Bagemihl

[W]e are acting with the best intentions in the world, we want
to add reality to scientific objects, but, inevitably, through a sort
of tragic bias, we seem always to be subtracting some bit from
it. Like a clumsy waiter setting plates on a slanted table, every
nice dish slides down and crashes on the ground. Why can we
never discover the same stubbornness, the same solid realism by
bringing out the obviously webby, "thingy" qualities of matters
of concern?
                                        —Bruno Latour

"Nature" and the "natural" have long been waged against homosexuals, as well as women, people of color, and indigenous peoples. Just as the
pernicious histories of Social Darwinism, colonialism, primitivism, and
other forms of scientifically infused racism have incited indispensable critiques of the intermingling of "race" and nature,[1] much queer theory has
bracketed, expelled, or distanced the volatile categories of nature and the
natural, situating queer desire within an entirely social, and very human,
habitat. This now compulsory sort of segregation of queer from nature is
hardly appealing to those who seek queer green places, or, in other words,

an environmentalism allied with gay affirmation, and a gay politics that is also environmentalist. Moreover, the question of whether nonhuman nature can be queer provokes larger questions within interdisciplinary theory regarding the relations between discourse and materiality, human and more-than-human worlds, as well as between cultural theory and science. In short, we need more robust, complex ways of productively engaging with materiality—ways that account for the diversity and "exuberance" of a multitude of naturecultures, ways that can engage with science as well as science studies. Queer animals—"matters of concern" for queer, green, human cultures—may foster such formulations.

Recent popular science books, such as Bruce Bagemihl's monumental *Biological Exuberance: Animal Homosexuality and Natural Diversity* (1999) and Joan Roughgarden's *Evolution's Rainbow: Diversity, Gender, and Sexuality in Nature and People* (2004), as well as the work of Myra J. Hird, present possibilities for radically rethinking nature as queer, by documenting the vast range of same-sex acts, same-sex childrearing pairs, intersex animals, multiple "genders," "transvestism," and transsexuality existing throughout the more-than-human world. Bagemihl's 750-page volume, two-thirds of which is "A Wondrous Bestiary" of "Portraits of Homosexual, Bisexual, and Transgendered Wildlife," astounds with its vast compilation of species "in which same sex activities have been scientifically documented" (1999, 265). Bagemihl restricts himself to mammals and birds, but even so, he discusses nearly three hundred species and "more than two centuries of scientific research" (1999, 1–2). Rich not only with scientific data, but also with photos, illustrations, and charts, Bagemihl's exhaustively researched volume renders any sense of normative heterosexuality within nature an absurd impossibility. Joan Roughgarden's book, *Evolution's Rainbow: Diversity, Gender, and Sexuality in Nature and People* (2004), which consists of three sections, "Animal Rainbows," "Human Rainbows," and "Cultural Rainbows," paints an expanse of sexual diversity across both animal and human worlds. In October 2006, the Naturhistorisk Museum in Oslo, Norway, opened "the first-ever museum exhibition dedicated to gay animals." "Against Nature?" sought to "reject the all too well known argument that homosexual behavior is a crime against nature" by displaying species known to engage in homosexual acts. The exhibit "outs" these animals by telling a "fascinating story of the animals' secret life . . . by means of models, photos, texts, and specimens" (Against Nature 2007). Ironically, the patriarchal diorama of the early twentieth century that served, as Donna Haraway argues, as a "prophylactic" against "decadence" (1990, 26), is followed by

FIGURE 1.1. "Gay Animals: Swans," from "Against Nature?" exhibit, Per E. Aas, Natural History Museum, University of Oslo, Norway.

an exhibition that unveils sexual diversity in the world of animals. Queer animals have also gained notoriety with the controversy over a German zoo's plan "to test the sexual orientation of six male penguins which have displayed homosexual traits" and set them up with female penguins because they want "the rare Humboldt penguins to breed" (Gay Outrage 2005). After the public outcry, zoo director Heike Kueke reassured people that they would not forcibly break up the homosexual penguin couples, saying, "Everyone can live here as they please" (*Ananova* 2005). *Dr. Tatiana's Sex Advice to All Creation: The Definitive Guide to the Evolutionary Biology of Sex,* includes a letter from a manatee worried that their son "keeps kissing other males," signed "Don't Want No Homo in the Florida Keys." Dr. Tatiana replies: "It's not your son who needs straightening out. It's you. Some Homosexual activity is common for animals of all kinds" (Judson 2003, 143). More surprising, perhaps, the television sex show host Dr. Susan Block, with her explicit website replete with porn videos and sex toys, promotes a peaceful philosophy of "ethical hedonism," based on "the Bonobo Way." "The Bonobo Way," which includes a great deal of "lesbian" sex, "supports the repression of violence and the free, exuberant, erotic, raunchy, loving, peaceful, adventurous, consensual expression of pleasure" (Block 2007).[2]

According to the website for the "Against Nature?" exhibit (2007), "Homosexuality has been observed in most vertebrate groups, and also from insects, spiders, crustaceans, octopi and parasitic worms. The phenomenon has been reported from more than 1,500 animal species, and is well documented for 500 of them, but the real extent is probably much higher" (Against Nature 2007). Notwithstanding the sheer delight of dwelling within a queer bestiary that supplants the dusty, heteronormative Book of Nature, the recognition of the sexual diversity of animals has several significant benefits. Most obviously, scientific accounts of queer animals insist that heteronormativity has damaged and diminished scientific knowledge in biology, anthropology, and other fields. Roughgarden charges that "the scientific silence on homosexuality in animals amounts to a cover-up, deliberate or not," thus scientists "are professionally responsible for refuting claims that homosexuality is unnatural" (2004, 128). Bruce Bagemihl (1999) and Myra J. Hird (2004b) document how the majority of scientists have ignored, refused to acknowledge, closeted, or explained away their observations of same-sex behavior in animals, for fear of risking their reputations, scholarly credibility, academic positions, or heterosexual identity. Most notably, Bagemihl includes a candid reflection of biologist Valerius Geist, who "still cringe[s] at the memory of seeing old D-ram mount S-ram repeatedly": "I called these actions of the rams *aggrosexual* behavior, for to state that the males had evolved a homosexual society was emotionally beyond me. To conceive of those magnificent beasts as 'queers'—Oh God!" (Bagemihl 1999, 107). A queer-science-studies stance parallel to that of feminist empiricism would insist that the critique and eradication of heteronormative bias will result in a better, more accurate account of the world—simply getting the facts (not-so) straight. Although Margaret Cuonzo warns of the possibility for homosexist, anthropocentric, "or even egocentric" bias in accounts of queer animals (2003, 231), these possibilities seem highly unlikely given the pervasive heteronormativity not only in science, but in the wider culture.[3] Moreover, as Catriona Mortimer-Sandilands argues, citing the case in which ecologists assumed that the lesbian behavior of seagulls "must be evidence of some major environmental catastrophe" (and it wasn't), "the assumption that heterosexuality is the only natural sexual form is clearly not an appropriate benchmark for ecological research" (2005). In short, environmental sciences require better accounts of the sexual diversity of natural creatures; otherwise heteronormative bias may render it even more difficult to understand the effects of various toxicants. Giovanna Di Chiro's essay in this collection demonstrates the vital need for environmental sciences and environmental politics that are not propelled by homophobia or misogyny. Endocrine disruptors alone demand an extraordinarily complex and nuanced understanding of the "mangling" (in Pickering's [1995] terms) of environmental science, health, and politics, with misogyny, homophobia, and other cultural forces.

From a cultural studies perspective that focuses on discursive contestation, it is easy to see queer animals as countering the pernicious and persistent articulation of homosexuality with what is unnatural. The multitude of examples given by Bagemihl (1999) and Roughgarden (2004), not to mention the explicit photos and illustrations, strongly articulate "queer" with "animal," making sexual diversity part of a larger biodiversity. This cultural studies model of political-discursive contestation, however, may, by definition, bracket all that which is not purely discursive—ironically, of course, the animals themselves—and thus limit the possibilities for imagining a queer ethics and politics that is also environmentalist. (This difficulty is part of a larger problem within cultural theory of finding ways of allowing matter to matter.) But even within the paradigm of discursive contestation, trouble arises, since the normative meanings of nature and the natural have long coexisted with their inverse: nature as blank, dumb, or even debased materiality. In other words, if conservatives are hell-bent on damning homosexuals, they will, no doubt, simply see all this queer animal sex as shocking depravity and consign those of us who are already outside of the Family of Man to the howling wilderness of bestial perversions. No doubt the rather sweet-looking illustrations of say, female hedgehog "courtship" and cunnilingus included in Bagemihl's book, which would delight many a gay-affirmative viewer, would disgust others (Bagemihl 1999, 471).

Rather than simply toss queer animals into the ring of public opinion to battle the still pervasive sense that homosexuality is unnatural, we need to embrace the possibilities for the sexual diversity of animal behavior to help us continue to transform our most basic sense of what nature and culture mean. For many cultural critics, who fear that any engagement with nature, science, or materiality is too perilous to pursue, queer animals are segregated into a universe of irrelevance. But it is possible, I think, to look to queer animals, not as a moral model or embodiment of some static universal law, but in order to find, in this astounding biological exuberance, a sense of vast diversity, deviance (in the way that Ladelle McWhorter [1999] recasts the term),[4] and a proliferation of astonishing differences that make nonsense of biological reductionism. Moreover, it is crucial that we see animals not as genetically driven machines but as creatures embedded within and creating other "worlds" or naturecultures, as Haraway (2003) puts it.

Epistemology of the Zoological Closet

Eve Sedgwick's paradigm of the "open secret" captures the way in which nonhuman animals have been fixed within a zoological closet: many people have witnessed some sort of same-sex activity between animals and yet still imagine the natural world as unrelentingly straight. Such determined ignorance emerges from a heteronormative epistemology. As Sedgwick explains, ignorance—as well as knowledge—has power: "These ignorances, far from being pieces of the originary dark, are produced by and correspond to particular knowledges and circulate as part of particular regimes of truth" (1990, 8). Decades ago, when my brother was young, my mother bought him a pair of hamsters. Fearing we would be overrun by a proliferation of tiny mammals, she chose two females. My brother was baffled and my mother stunned to discover the spectacle of their seemingly nonstop oral sex. Despite this family memory, I must admit that I was rather astonished by Hird's, Roughgarden's, and Bagemihl's accounts of the enormous variety of sexual diversity throughout the nonhuman world. Who knew? This sense of astonishment, as I will discuss, below, can rouse a queer-green, ethical/epistemological/aesthetic response, even as it may be implicated in regimes of closeted knowledges.

The sexual diversity of animals, I contend, matters. Predominant modes of social theory, however, which still assume a radical separation of nature and culture, tend to minimize the significance of queer animals. Just as most feminist theory has engaged in a "flight from nature" (see Alaimo 2000), most cultural critics have cast out queer animals from the field of cultural relevance. Jonathan Marks, for example, in *What it Means to Be 98% Chimpanzee: Apes, People, and Their Genes* (2002) takes his place in a long line of people who have attempted to clearly demarcate human from animal by seizing upon some key difference: "One of the outstanding hallmarks of human evolution is the extent to which our species has divorced sexuality from reproduction. Most sexuality in other primates is directly associated with reproduction" (2002, 110). Just as language, tool use, and other supposed keys to the Human Kingdom have been usurped by evidence of similar accomplishments across a range of species, the deluge of evidence of same-sex sex among animals collapses this claim. Marks, however, contends that the female "same-sex genital stimulation" of the bonobo is exceptional, arguing that "virtually all primates are sexually active principally as a reproductive activity" (111). Paul Vasey's extensive studies of Japanese macaques, discussed below, as well as the accounts of hundreds of other species that engage in same-sex pleasures, counter Marks's assertion. More generally, however, Marks criticizes the way in which we, as humans, look to other primates, especially chimps, as the key to understanding our "true" selves: "They are us, minus something. They are supposed to be our pure biology, unfettered by the trappings of civilization and its discontents. They are humans without humanity. They are nature without culture" (165). On this point, Marks offers a demystifying critique, especially of the way in which the cultural framework of the scientists may be mistaken as "a contribution of the chimps, rather than for our own input" (ibid.). Even as it is useful to expose the popular pursuit of seeking the primal truth of the human within the animal, and even as it is likewise important to wrestle with the thorny epistemological problems that animal ethology poses, I would argue that it is also crucial to critique the narrow evolutionary narrative of progress inherent in the notion that "they" are "nature without culture." Nonhuman animals are also cultural creatures, with their own sometimes complex systems of (often nonreproductive) sex. The overall effect of Marks's debunking—when unaccompanied by any attempt to formulate productive ways of engaging with scientific accounts of animals—is to banish animals to a wilderness of irrelevance, where they serve as the backdrop for the erection of human achievement.

Jennifer Terry offers an incisive discursive critique of "the scientific fascination with queer animals," in which "animals provide models for scientists seeking to determine a biological substrate of sexual orientation" (2000, 152). She exposes how "reproductive sexuality provides the master narrative in studies of animal sexuality and tethers queer animal behavior to the aim of defining reproduction as the ultimate goal of sexual encounters" (154). Drawing on Haraway's work, Terry begins her essay by stating that "animals help us tell stories about ourselves, especially when it comes to matters of sexuality" (151). She concludes by arguing that the "creatures that populate the narrative space called 'nature' are key characters in scientific tales about the past, present, and future. Various tellings of these tales are possible, but they are always shaped by historical, disciplinary, and larger cultural contexts" (185). Terry illuminates such contexts in a useful way throughout the essay. This mode of critique, however, framed as it is by the emphasis on "narrative space," cages animal sexual practices within human stories. Although Terry draws heavily on Haraway, Haraway herself, especially in her most recent work, seems wary of modes of cultural critique that bracket the materiality and the significance of the nonhuman: "Dogs, in their historical complexity, matter here. Dogs are not an alibi for other themes; dogs are fleshly material-semiotic presences in the body of technoscience. Dogs are not surrogates for theory; they are not here just to think with. They are here to live with" (2003, 5). Even as Haraway executed one of the most dazzlingly complex and multidimensional scientific/cultural critiques in her 1990 masterpiece *Primate Visions,* she insisted that the "primates themselves—monkeys, apes, and people—all have some kind of 'authorship'" (1990, 8). Her work on primates and dogs, especially, demonstrates this sort of commitment to them—to the world—even as she admits "how science 'gets at' the world remains far from resolved" (1990, 8). I do not have the space here to explore the debates in science studies regarding these broader epistemological questions. I contend, however, that we need models capacious enough to include both cultural critique and a commitment to uncovering material realities and agencies.[5]

Cynthia Chris, in *Watching Wildlife,* exposes the heteronormativity of wildlife films, explaining that most "wildlife films posit heterosexual mate selection as not only typical but inevitable and without exception" (Chris 2006, 156). Even the show *Wild and Weird—Wild Sex,* "downplays—even avoids—same-sex behaviors in the cavalcade of animal sexualities it frames as varied" (157). Despite her analysis of the heteronormativity of the wildlife genre, however, Chris ultimately warns against celebrating queer animals:

> Evidence of same-sex behaviors among animals and genetic influences on homosexuality among humans is used as ammunition in battles waged over gay rights for which advocates might be better off relying on other discourses through which civil rights are claimed. Such evidence remains inconclusive, uneasily generalizable across species, subject to wildly divergent interpretations, and likely to fail the endeavor of understanding animal behavior on its own terms. (165)

Chris's conflation here of animal sexual behavior with "genetic influences on homosexuality among humans" is disturbing, in that it assumes that if animals do something, they do it because of genetic programming. The extent to which any sexual orientation could possibly be influenced by genetic factors is a question that is entirely separate from the sexual diversity of animals. Rather than assuming that the "genetic human" is the thing that is equivalent to animality, it would be much more accurate to think of animal sex as both cultural and material, and genetics as much more of a dynamic process, inextricably interwoven with organism and environment.[6] While Chris would rather have us "rely on other discourses," in part because the evidence for queer animals is "uneasily generalizable across species and subject to wildly divergent interpretations," I will argue below that this very sense of being not generalizable is what makes accounts of animal sexual diversity so potent. They highlight a staggering expanse of sexual diversity in nonhuman creatures that is the very stuff of a vaster biodiversity. Environmentalists and queers can engage with accounts of the sexual diversity of animals, allowing them to complicate, challenge, enrich, and transform our conceptions of nature, culture, sex, gender, and other fundamental categories.

Roger N. Lancaster in *The Trouble with Nature: Sex in Science and Popular Culture* wades through "a toxic waste dump of ideas" hoping to "discover sophisticated new biological perspectives on sex and sexuality" but encountering instead "the same old reductivism warmed over" (2003, xi). He argues that the "attempts at supposedly 'queering' science . . . consolidate an astonishingly *heteronormative* conception of human nature" (29). While he presents incisive critiques of heteronormativity and scientific reductivism, many of his arguments endorse a strict nature/culture opposition. Such an opposition, of course, underwrites the very reductivism that he supposedly opposes.[7] For example, he argues that "society, bonding, hierarchy, slavery, rape, and harem" are "concepts, relations, and activities characteristic of humans" and implies that "facts of nature" and "facts of culture" should remain utterly separate (61). While "slavery, rape, and harem" leap out as all-too-human in terminology, there is certainly solid evidence for "society, bonding, [and] hierarchy" within many animal species.[8] Lancaster advocates that we "reject the naturalized regime of heteronormativity in its totality" in order to be "finished with the idea of normal bodies once and for all" (31). Ironically, even as Lancaster's book casts scientific accounts of nature as nothing but "trouble," the surprising range of sexual diversity within nonhuman animals could actually foster Lancaster's utopian dream. Even Lancaster himself becomes momentarily seduced by Bagemihl's book, which he warns is "anthropomorphic" and "fetishistic," a collection of "charms and talismans of a coming science that would at least be progressive once again" (114).

When nature and culture are segregated within different disciplinary universes, detrimental oppositions result, in which animal sex is reduced to a purely reproductive function and in which human sexuality—in its opulent range of manifestations—becomes, implicitly, at least, another transcendent human achievement that places us above the brute mating behaviors of nonhuman creatures. Rather than continuing to pose nature/culture dualisms that closet queer animals as well as animal cultures, and rather than attempting to locate the truth of human sexuality within the already written book of nature, we can think of queer desire as part of an emergent universe of a multitude of naturecultures.

Pursuing Pleasures, Creating Cultures

Human-animal dualisms, which reduce animal sex to a mechanical act of instinct or genetic determinism, should be supplanted with models of naturecultures (Haraway 2003), in which sexual activity is always indivisibly material and social.[9] Interestingly, unlike much of the scholarship in the humanities, many scientific accounts of animal sex do not reduce it to mechanistic forces or genetically determined instinct. Sex, in nonhumans as well as humans, is partly a learned, social behavior, embedded within and contributing to particular material-social environments. Kristin Field and Thomas Waite, for example, begin their study of male guppies with the following premise: "On a longer timescale, social environment and 'learned sexuality' can have dramatic effects on the expression of species-typical sexual behavior" (Field and Waite 2004, 1381; Woodson [2002], cited in Field and Waite [2004]). In terms of environmental ethics and politics, it is crucial to acknowledge animals as cultural beings, enmeshed in social organizations, acting, interacting, and communicating. An understanding of animal cultures critiques the ideology of nature as resource, blank slate for cultural inscription, or brute, mechanistic force. Lest we imagine that the view of animal-as-machine without feelings, sentience, or value vanished with Descartes, Werner Herzog's comments in *Grizzly Man* (2005) that tag a particular bear as Treadwell's "murderer" at the same time they announce that the "blank stare" of the bear betrays the bear's dreadful vacuity remind us that the demonization and mechanization of animals persists. Even as sexual activity has been assumed to be a biological drive, the recognition of the sheer astonishing diversity of animal "sex-gender systems" (Rubin 1975), provokes us to understand animals as "cultural" beings. Bagemihl himself argues that it is "meaningful to speak of the 'culture' of homosexuality in animals, since the extent and range of variation that is found (between individuals or populations or species) exceeds that provided by genetic programming and begins to enter the realm of individual habits, learned behaviors, and even community-wide 'traditions'" (1999, 45). Myra J. Hird concurs, arguing that "it is no longer feasible to maintain that only humans have culture: there are as many cultures as there are species with cultural behavior because each species is neurophysiologically unique" (2004b, 93).

The pursuit of pleasure may itself be a dynamic force within some animal cultures. Two of the most prominent markers of culture, in fact—tool use and language—have arisen, for some animals, as modes of sexual pleasuring. Drawing on the research of Susan Savage-Rumbaugh, which began in the 1970s, Bagemihl describes the "'lexicon' of about a dozen hand and arm gestures—each with a specific meaning" that bonobos use to "initiate sexual activity and negotiate various body positions with a partner (of the same or opposite sex)" (1999, 66). He includes a chart illustrating these hand movements and translating them into commands such as "Approach" or "Move Your Genitals Around" (67). Bagemihl argues that among primates, humans included, "as sexual interactions become more variable, sexual communication systems become more sophisticated." He concludes, that "it is possible, therefore, that sexuality—particularly the fluidity associated with nonreproductive sexual practices—played a significant role in the origin and development of human language" (69). Bagemihl's claim for the influence of sexuality on the development of tools is equally bold. Citing examples of how many primates not only use, but manufacture, objects to aid with masturbation, Bagemihl claims that "the pursuit of sexual pleasure may have contributed, in some measure, to our own heritage as creatures whose tool-using practices are among the most polymorphous of any primate"(71). Bagemihl's arguments are compelling, and certainly subvert the grand narratives of the Origins of Man, which lay claim to tool making and language as exclusively human. His claim, however, may still be problematic, in that there is a sense in which nonhuman sexual practices become significant because of their role within linear narratives that culminate in the development of the human. But only a slight shift here is needed to read these examples of tool use and language development as part of particular animal naturecultures in which the pursuit of sexual pleasure is one of the most quintessentially "cultural" sorts of activities. Indeed, it is difficult not to be impressed with the creativity, skill, tenacity, and resourcefulness of a female bonnet macaque who "invented some relatively sophisticated techniques of tool manufacture, regularly employing five specific methods to create or modify natural objects for insertion into her vagina":

> For example, she stripped dry eucalyptus leaves of their foliage
> with her fingers or teeth and then broke the midrib into a piece less

than half an inch long. She also slit dry acacia leaves in half length-wise (using only a single half) and fashioned short sticks by breaking longer ones into several pieces or detaching portions of a branch. Implements were also vigorously rubbed with her fingers or between her palms prior to being inserted into her vagina, and twigs, leaves, or grass blades were occasionally used unmodified. (70–71)

An artist at work. It is tempting to read this account through Roger N. Lancaster's notion of desire: "This desire is on the side of poetry, in the original and literal sense of the word: *poiesis*, 'production,' as in the making of things and the world. Not an object at all, desire is what makes objects possible" (2003, 266). Even as Lancaster places desire "squarely within a social purview" (266), elaborating an ultra-human sort of sexuality that is all culture and no nature, the tool-making, language-creating, culturally embedded, pleasurable practices of nonhuman animals invade this ostensibly human terrain, muddying the terms.

Whereas many cultural critics cast animal sex into the separate sphere of nature, many scientific accounts of queer animal sex have rendered them too cultural, so as to render them not sexual. Indeed, Block's philosophy of the ethical hedonism of the bonobo is indicative of a general understanding, in the wider culture, that the "reason" bonobos have so much sex, including same-sex sex, is to reduce social conflicts. Such explanations may well make all that mounting seem like just another chore. Whereas Block celebrates the eroticism of the bonobos, many scientific accounts of same-sex genital activities emphasize their social functions in such a way as to define them as anything other than sex. As Vasey and his colleagues explain, much same-sex sexual behavior has been interpreted as "socio-sexual," meaning "sexual in terms of their external form, but . . . enacted to mediate some sort of adaptive social goal or breeding strategy" (Vasey 2004b, 399). Take, for example, the 1998 textbook *Primate Sexuality,* by Alan F. Dixon. The chapter "Sociosexual Behavior and Homosexuality" begins by making it clear that what might look like same-sex sex among nonhuman primates is merely "motor patterns": "The form and functions of sociosexual patterns vary between species, but the important point is that motor patterns normally associated with sex are sometimes incorporated into the nonsexual sphere of social communications" (147). In order to claim that these "motor patterns" are not sex, he places "sex" in a sphere entirely separate from "social communications," a strange segregation for either hetero or homo sexual relations.[10] Obviously, as Vasey explains, "sexual motivation and social function are not mutually exclusive" (Vasey

2004a, 351). Social function, then, often closets same-sex animal sex by black-boxing pleasure and elevating the social into an abstract and disembodied calculus. The gleeful-erotic illustrations appearing in Dixon's textbook, however, counter the reduction of these activities to mechanistic motor patterns by depicting several entirely different same-sex primate mounts, that—to a less mechanistically constrained eye—suggest such things as desire, effort, playfulness, pleasure—and sex.

Within this landscape of Byzantine heteronormativity, scientists who do suggest that same-sex genital activity may be something like sex often do so tentatively. M. K. Shearer and L. S. Katz state that female goats "may mount other females to obtain sexual stimulation. To the observer, there appears to be a hedonistic component associated with the body pressure and motions involved while mounting" (2006, 36). Vasey must put forth a strong case to even begin to claim that the sexual behavior between female Japanese macaques is, in fact, sexual:

> Despite over 40 years of intensive research in populations in which females engage in same-sex mounting and courtship . . . there is not a single study in existence demonstrating any sort of sociosexual function for these behaviors. Rather, all the available evidence indicates that female-female mounting and courtship are not sociosexual behaviors. Female Japanese macaques do not use same-sex mounting and courtship to attract male sexual partners, impede reproduction by same-sex competitors (Gouzoules and Goy, 1983; Vasey, 1995), form alliances, foster social relationships outside consortships (Vasey, 1996), communicate about dominance relationships (Vasey, Faroud, Duckworth, and Kovacovsky; 1998), obtain alloparental care (Vasey, 1998), reduce social tension associated with incipient aggression (Vasey et al., 1998), practice for heterosexual activity (i.e. female-male mounting), or reconcile conflicts. (Vasey 2004b, 399)

Clearly, same-sex activity between animals is considered not-sex until proven otherwise. All possibilities for its existence—other than pleasure— must be ruled out before it can be understood as sex.[11] The predominant scientific framework, oddly, parallels the mainstream environmentalist conception of nature that Sandilands critiques as "both actively de-eroticized and monolithically heterosexual" (Sandilands 2001, 176).[12] As Sandilands explains, drawing upon the work of Greta Gaard, "[e]rotophobia is clearly linked to the regulation of sexual diversity; normative heterosexuality, especially in its links to science and nature, has the effect of regulating and instrumentalizing sexuality, linking it to truth and evolutionary health rather than to pleasure and fulfillment (2001, 180). Queer animals may play a part, then, in helping us question "eco-sexual normativity" through asserting "polymorphous sexualities and multiple natures" (Sandilands 1999, 92–93). Queer animals may also foster an ontology in which pleasure and eroticism are neither the result of genetically determined biological drives nor tools in cultural machinations, but are creative forces simultaneously emergent within and affecting a multitude of naturecultures. Pleasure, in this sense, may be understood within Karen Barad's notion of performativity as "materialist, naturalist, and posthumanist," "that allows matter its due as an active participant in the world's becoming, its ongoing 'intra-activity'" (2003, 803).

Eluding Capture

A universe of differing naturecultures, propelled by the pursuit of pleasure as well as other forces, can hardly serve as a foundation for biological reductionism, gender essentialism, heteronormativity, or models of human exceptionalism. The multitude of utterly different models of courtship, sexual activity, childrearing arrangements, gender, transsexualism, and transvestism that Bagemihl and Roughgarden document portray animal lifeworlds that cannot be understood in reductionist ways. Myra J. Hird argues that biology "provides a wealth of evidence to confound static notions of sexual difference" (2004a, 85). Her exuberant essay encourages us to imagine *"The Joy of Sex* for plants, fungi, and bacteria. Schizophyllum, for instance, has more than 28,000 sexes. And sex among these promiscuous mushrooms is literally a 'touch-and-go' event, leading Laidman to conclude that for fungi there are 'so many genders, so little time'" (86). Hird presents a convincing case for embracing queer natures as the quintessential boundary transgressors, rather than assuming that "living and non-living matter" is "the stubborn, inert 'outside' to transgressive potential" (85). She concludes her piece by noting that since "gay parenting, lesbianism, homosexuality, sex-changing, and other behaviors in animals are prevalent in living matter, [i]t is at least curious that queer theory does not devote more space to the abundant queer behavior of most of the living matter on this planet" (88).

Indeed, animal sex may de-sediment intransigent cultural categories, beginning with heteronormativity, though not ending there. For example, Vasey and his colleagues, in an investigation of female-female mounting behavior, conclude that "[f]emale mounting in Japanese macaques is not a defective counterpart to male mounting. There is no evidence that females were attempting to execute male mounts, but failing to do so" (Vasey et al. 2006, 127). Rather, the female mounting is "female-typical," exhibiting a strikingly different repertoire of movements (126). The macaques may remind us of Judith Butler's argument that homosexuality is not an imitation of heterosexuality, and Jeanne Hamming's argument that the dildo is not "a representation of a penis," but instead, a "post-gender, nonphallic signifier" (Hamming 2001, 330). Vasey himself argues that his study "raises the much broader issue of what constitutes male or female behavior," since it makes little sense to characterize mounting as "male" when "females, in certain populations, engage in this behavior so frequently, and do so in a female-typical manner" (Vasey et al. 2006, 127). Most feminist theory distinguishes between sex and gender, positing "gender" as a cultural, and thus solely human construct. Roughgarden, on the other hand, sees gender in nonhuman animals, defining it as "the appearance, behavior, and lived history of a sexed body" (2004, 27). She notes that "many species have three or more genders" (28), such as the white-throated sparrow, which has "four genders, two male, and two female." These genders are distinguished by either a white stripe or a tan stripe, which correspond to aggressive and territorial versus accommodating behaviors. As far as sex goes, 90 percent of the breeding involves a tan-striped bird (of either sex) with a white-striped bird (of either sex) (9). Haraway's call to see animals as other worlds, replete with "significant otherness" (2003, 25) resounds when trying to make sense of the multitude of animal cultures that just don't fit within human—even feminist, even queer—models. Just as animal sex (and gender) may complicate the foundations of feminist theory, animal practices may also denaturalize familiar categories and assumptions in queer theory and gay cultures. For one thing, nearly all the animal species, as well as individual animals, that have been documented as engaging in same-sex relations also engage in heterosexual sex, meaning that "universalizing" models of sexuality work better for most nonhuman animals than "minoritizing" models. The queer animals I've been referring to, as a convenient shorthand, are queer in a multitude of ways, but rarely do any of them correspond to early-twenty-first-century categories of gay or lesbian. Roughgarden explains that most male bighorn sheep live in "homosexual societies," courting and copulating with other males, via anal penetration. It is the nonhomosexual males who are considered "aberrant": "The few males who do not participate in homosexual activity have been labeled 'effeminate' males. . . . They differ from 'normal males' by living with the ewes rather than joining all-male groups. These males do not dominate females, are less aggressive overall, and adopt a couched, female urination posture. These males refuse mounting by other males" (2004, 138). As Roughgarden contends, these sheep challenge gay/straight categories: "The 'normal' macho bighorn sheep has full-fledged anal sex with other males. The 'aberrant' ram is the one who is straight—the lack of interest in homosexuality is considered pathological" (138). Inevitably, in an attempt to understand the remarkable differences in animal cultures, most accounts draw upon human categories and terms. Even as she critiques the "biased vocabulary" of scientists, Roughgarden uses many terms lifted too unproblematically from twentieth-century American culture, such as "domestic violence" and "divorce," which flattens and distorts the significant otherness of animal cultures.

Interestingly, both Roughgarden and Bagemihl argue that many non-Western cultures have a greater knowledge of and appreciation for the sexual diversity of the nonhuman world. Roughgarden, for example, notes that in the South Sea Islands of Vanuatu, pigs have "been bred for their intersex expressions": "Among the people of Sakao, seven distinct genders are named, ranging from those with the most egg-related external genitalia to those with the most sperm-related external genitalia" (2004, 37). Similarly, Bagemihl contends that contemporary theoretical accounts of sexual diversity pale next to both the scientific accounts of animal sexuality and the knowledge systems of particular indigenous groups who recognize animal sexual diversity:

> The animal world—right now, here on earth—is brimming with countless gender variations and shimmering sexual possibilities: entire lizard species that consist only of females who reproduce by virgin birth and also have sex with each other; or some multigendered society of the Ruff, with four distinct categories of male birds, some of whom court and mate with one another; or female Spotted Hyenas and Bears who copulate and give birth through their "penile" clitorides, and male Greater Rheas who possess "vaginal" phalluses (like the females of their species) and raise young in two-father families; or the vibrant transsexualities of coral reef fish, and the dazzling intersexualities of gyandromorphs and chimeras. In their quest for "postmodern" patterns of gender and sexuality, human beings are simply catching up with the species that have preceded us in evolving sexual and gender diversity—and aboriginal cultures have long recognized this. (1999, 260–61)

Despite the scientific aim to make sense of the world, to categorize, to map, to find causal relations, many who write about sexual diversity in nonhuman animals are struck with the sense that the remarkable variance regarding sex, gender, reproduction, and childrearing among animals defies our modes of categorization, even explodes our sense of being able to make sense of it all. These epiphanic moments of wonder ignite an epistemological-ethical sense in which, suddenly, the world is not only more queer than one could have imagined,[13] but more surprisingly itself, meaning that it confounds our categories and systems of understanding. In other words, queer animals elude perfect modes of capture. In Andrew Pickering's model, science is "an evolving field of human and material agencies reciprocally engaged in a play of resistance and accommodation in which the former seeks to capture the latter" (1995, 23). Paradoxically, this model allows us to value scientific accounts of sexual diversity in nonhuman animals, in the sense that these accounts are accounting for something—something more than a (human) social construction—and yet, it also encourages an epistemological-ethical stance that recognizes the inadequacy of human knowledge systems to ever fully account for the natural world.

By eluding perfect modes of capture, queer animals dramatize emergent worlds of desire, action, agency, and interactivity that can never be reduced to a background or resource against which the human defines himself. Haraway, defining her term "companion species," explains: "There are no pre-constituted subjects and objects, and no single sources, unitary actors, or final ends. . . . A bestiary of agencies, kinds of relatings, and scores of time trump the imaginings of even the most baroque cosmologists" (2003, 6). Such responses emanate from a queer, green, place, in which pleasure, desire, and the proliferation of differing lifeworlds and interactions provoke intense, ethical, reactions. As Brian Massumi argues, "intensity is the unassimilable" because, "structure is the place where nothing ever happens, that explanatory heaven in which all eventual permutations are prefigured in a self consistent set of invariant generative rules" (2002, 27). Many responses to sexual diversity in nonhuman creatures emanate this sort of intensity of the unassimilable. Volker Sommer, for example, concludes his epilogue to *Homosexual Behavior in Animals: An Evolutionary Perspective,* by asking: "Is the diversity of sexual behavior that we can observe in nature anything other than mindbogglingly beautiful?" (2006, 370). In a review of Bagemihl's book, Duane Jeffery comments that "nature's inventiveness far outruns our meager ability to categorize her productions," adding that "the sheer inventiveness—

exuberance—of nature overwhelms" (2005, 72). Roughgarden, herself a transgender woman and ecologist, notes that in writing her book she "found more diversity than [she] had ever dreamed existed," calling her book the "gee-whiz of vertebrate diversity" (2004, 2), an expression that captures the reader's response as much as the book's content. Bagemihl carefully wraps up his "labor of love" with layers of wonderment. We first encounter the poem "Snow" by Louis MacNeice (which includes the line "World is crazier and more of it than we think"), then two lines from e. e. cummings—"hugest whole creation may be less/incalculable than a single kiss"—both of which stand as epigraphs to the entire volume, then an epigraph by Einstein for the introduction: "The most beautiful thing we can experience is the mysterious. It is the source of all true art and science. He to whom this emotion is a stranger, who can no longer pause to wonder and stand rapt in awe, is as good as dead: his eyes are closed" (Bagemihl 1999, 1). A grand, two-page map of "The World of Animal Homosexuality," on the second and third pages of the introduction, invites us to see the earth as an entirely different place, one populated with a multitude of queer sexualities. Unlike Latour's clumsy waiter whose "nice dishes" crash to the ground, Bagemihl wishes to deliver "'the facts' about animal behavior'" as well "captur[ing] some of their 'poetry'": "In addition to being interesting from a purely scientific standpoint, these phenomena are also capable of inspiring our deepest feelings of wonder, and our most profound sense of awe" (1999, 6). Such wonder and awe, may, I hope, help foster queer-green ethics, politics, practices, and places.

NOTES

I am grateful to Bruce Erickson and Catriona Mortimer-Sandilands for inviting me to contribute to this exciting project. Many thanks to all the participants in the Queer Ecologies workshop for their comments on this essay. Special thanks to David Bell for the Barbara Ehrenreich article, and to Jeanne Hamming for her comments and support.

1. For more on race and nature see Moore, Kosek, and Pandian (2003). See the essays in this volume by McWhorter and Gosine for more on the relations among race, nature, and sex. Dana Seitler documents the emergence of sexual "perversity" as interconnected with other categories: "the construction of perversity appears as part of a story in which race, gender, physical deformation, sexuality, and many other bodily forms and practices emerge in ontologically and epistemologically interdependent ways" (2004, 74).

2. Susan Block is not the only one inspired by bonobo sex. Barbara Ehrenreich,

in a piece entitled, "Let Me Be a Bonobo," predicts a "surge in trans-species people, who will eagerly go over to the side of the chimps." She explains that another "reason to make the human-to-ape transition is the sex": "Bonobos, genetically as close to humans as larger chimpanzees, use sex much as we use handshakes—as a form of greeting between individuals in any gender combination" (Ehrenreich 2007, x). Kelpie Wilson's science fiction novel *Primal Tears* features a half-bonobo, half-human protagonist named "Sage" (2005). Interestingly, the same sort of alliance between sexual freedom and environmentalism that Susan Block promotes becomes a problem in the novel when some of Sage's fans transform her "Rainbow Clubs"—which are intended to promote the protection of endangered bonobos—into sex clubs.

3. Cuonzo also refers to the "'other minds' problem," questioning whether, say, the illustrations in Bagemihl's book, "pictures of animals in what looks like sexual activity," are, in fact, sex: "But how do we know that these behaviors are what they seem to be?" (2003, 230). While it is epistemologically and ethically useful to underscore the limits of human knowledge, it is just as problematic—if not perverse—to then conclude that because we cannot, absolutely, know these behaviors "are" sex, then they are not. Certainly, heterosex between animals is not held up to such a high standard of "proof." Cuonzo's skepticism seems a perfect example of how cultural critics are much better (in Latour's terms) at "subtracting reality."

4. McWhorter's brilliant recasting of deviance articulates sexual deviance with evolutionary deviation, resulting in a formulation that generates a queer green ethics: "It was deviation in development that produced this grove, this landscape, this living planet. What is good is that the world remain ever open to deviation" (1999, 164).

5. See the essays within *Material Feminisms* (Alaimo and Hekman 2008) for a range of approaches that combine postmodernism, poststructuralism, and social construction with a commitment to productively engaging with the materiality of human bodies and more-than-human natures and environments. Hekman and I argue that a paradigm shift is underway in which the linguistic turn that has dominated humanities scholarship is being transformed by theories that engage with material forces. Hekman's essay "Constructing the Ballast: An Ontology for Feminism" (2008) provides an excellent map of four different "settlements" in contemporary theory in which this new paradigm is emerging.

6. See, for example, Evelyn Fox-Keller's critique of genetic determinism in *The Century of the Gene* (2002). Another striking counterpoint to genetic determinism would be Ronnie Zoe Hawkins's contention that "the message of the genome is the opposite of biological determinism: our primate biology provides us with a tremendous amount of behavioral flexibility, while our social and cultural environments are often in the role of maintaining practices that have become maladaptive" (2002, 60–61).

7. See Lynda Birke's discussion of how most critiques of biological determinism apply only to humans, which means that they not only ignore the behavior of other animals but also rely upon a strict human/animal dichotomy (1994, 110–30).

8. My facile division of this terminology raises larger epistemological and ethical questions regarding the discourses for animal sex. Terms that seem too anthropomorphic disrespect the differences of various nonhuman creatures. Terms that seem too anti-anthropomorphic shore up the human/animal divide, casting animals as mechanistic creatures of instinct or genetic determinism. Clearly there is no way out of this dilemma; our terms are strands within these webs of meaning, relation, and effect.

9. One aspect of the new materialism in science studies, or of "material feminisms" (see Alaimo and Hekman 2008), is an openness to the transgressive, progressive potential for theoretical engagements with materiality. Myra J. Hird puts it

succinctly in "Naturally Queer": "We may no longer be certain that it is nature that remains static and culture that evinces limitless malleability" (2004a, 88). Roughgarden states: "Biology need not be a purveyor of essentialism, of rigid universals. Biology need not limit our potential" (2004, 180). In *Undomesticated Ground,* I discuss a range of women writers, from the late nineteenth century to the present, who challenge the conception of nature as a ground of fixed essences, rigid sexual difference, and already apparent norms, values, and prohibitions (Alaimo 2000, 17).

10. Frans de Waal writes that some "authors and scientists are so ill at ease [with the bonobo's sexuality] that they talk in riddles. . . . It's like listening to a gathering of bakers who have decided to drop the word 'bread' from their vocabulary, making for incredibly circumlocutory exchanges. The sexiness of bonobos is often downplayed by counting only copulations between adults of the opposite sex. But this really leaves out most of what is going on in their daily lives. It is a curious omission, given that the 'sex' label normally refers to any deliberate contact involving the genitals, including petting and oral stimulation" (2005, 93).

11. Similarly, Cynthia Chris argues that within television wildlife shows homosexuality is "not a natural act to be understood on its own terms, but a phase of foreplay prior to the real reproductive deal, an assertion of power, or an experience though which one risks subordination. Pleasure for these creatures, is strictly on the rocks" (2006, 165).

12. Queer animals may disrupt the prevalent marketing of nature as the quintessentially wholesome (straight) family recreational site. Just as I always wonder, every time I teach Whitman's "Song of Myself," what decades of school children (and their teachers) thought about that blatant homosexual moment within the poem, I wonder how dolphin-tour operators respond to the question, "What are they doing?!" when, say, a group of male dolphins, penises very much in plain sight, rub against each other in a frenzy of pleasure, right next to the tour boat. Oh, to have access to an archive of these conversations!

13. The reference alludes to the J. B. S. Haldane quote "The Universe is not only queerer than we suppose, it is queerer than we can suppose," which Bagemihl, Hird, and Lancaster all use as an epigraph.

REFERENCES

Against Nature? An Exhibition on Animal Homosexuality. 2007. Naturhistorisk museum, Oslo Norway. http://www.nhm.uio.no/besokende/skiftende-utstillinger/againstnature/index-eng.html.

Alaimo, Stacy. 2000. *Undomesticated Ground: Recasting Nature as Feminist Space.* Ithaca, N.Y.: Cornell University Press.

Alaimo, Stacy, and Susan J. Hekman, eds. 2008. *Material Feminisms.* Bloomington: Indiana University Press.

Ananova. 2005. Penguins Can Stay Gay. http://www.ananova.com/news/story/sm_1284769.html.

Bagemihl, Bruce. 1999. *Biological Exuberance: Animal Homosexuality and Natural Diversity.* New York: St. Martin's Press.

Barad, Karen. 1998. Getting Real: Technoscientific Practices and the Materialization of Reality. *differences: a Journal of Feminist Cultural Studies* 10.2: 87–128.

———. 2003. Posthumanist Performativity: Toward an Understanding of How Matter Comes to Matter. *Signs: Journal of Women in Culture and Society* 28.3: 801–31.

Birke, Lynda. 1994. *Feminism, Animals, and Science: The Naming of the Shrew.* Buckingham, U.K.: Open University Press.

Block, Susan. 2007. The Bonobo Way. http://www.blockbonobofoundation.org/.

Chris, Cynthia. 2006. *Watching Wildlife.* Minneapolis: University of Minnesota Press.

Cuonzo, Margaret. 2003. Queer Nature, Circular Science. In *Science and Other Cultures: Issues in Philosophy of Science and Technology,* ed. Robert Figueroa and Sandra Harding, 221–33. New York: Routledge.

De Waal, Frans. 2005. *Our Inner Ape: A Leading Primatologist Explains Why We Are Who We Are.* New York: Riverhead Books.

Dixon, Alan F. 1998. *Primate Sexuality: Comparative Studies of the Prosimians, Monkeys, Apes, and Human Beings.* Oxford, U.K.: Oxford University Press.

Ehrenreich, Barbara. 2007. Let Me Be a Bonobo. *Guardian,* Thursday, May 10, 32.

Field, Kristin L., and Thomas A. Waite. 2004. Absence of Female Conspecifics Induces Homosexual Behavior in Male Guppies. *Animal Behavior* 68: 1381–89.

Fox-Keller, Evelyn. 2002. *The Century of the Gene.* Cambridge, Mass.: Harvard University Press.

Gay Outrage over Penguin Sex Test. 2005. *BBC News.* http://news.bbc.co.uk/2/hi/europe/4264913.stm, February 14.

Gouzoules, H. and Robert W. Goy. 1983. Physiological and social influences on mounting behavior of troop-living female monkeys (*Macaca fuscata*). *American Journal of Primatology* 5.1: 39–49.

Hamming, Jeanne. 2001. Dildonics, Dykes and the Detachable Masculine. *European Journal of Women's Studies* 8.3: 329–41.

Haraway, Donna J. 1990. *Primate Visions: Gender, Race, and Nature in the World of Modern Science.* New York: Routledge.

———. 2003. *The Companion Species Manifesto: Dogs, People, and Significant Otherness.* Chicago: Prickly Paradigm Press.

Hawkins, Ronnie Zoe. 2002. Seeing Ourselves as Primates. *Ethics and the Environment* 7.2: 60–103.

Hekman, Susan. 2008. Constructing the Ballast: An Ontology for Feminism. In *Material Feminisms,* ed. Stacy Alaimo and Susan Hekman, 85–119. Bloomington: Indiana University Press.

Herzog, Werner, dir. 2005. Motion picture. *Grizzly Man.* Lions Gate Entertainment.

Hird, Myra J. 2004a. Naturally Queer. *Feminist Theory* 5.1: 85–89.

———. 2004b. *Sex, Gender and Science.* New York: Palgrave.

Jeffrey, Duane. 2005. Review of Joan Roughgarden's *Evolution's Rainbow. Politics and the Life Sciences* 23.2 (10 November): 71–77.

Judson, Olivia. 2003. *Dr. Tatiana's Sex Advice to All Creation: The Definitive Guide to the Evolutionary Biology of Sex.* New York: Vintage Books.

Lancaster, Roger N. 2003. *The Trouble with Nature: Sex in Science and Popular Culture.* Berkeley and Los Angeles: University of California Press.

Latour, Bruno. 2004. Why Has Critique Run Out of Steam? From Matters of Fact to Matters of Concern. *Critical Inquiry* 30: 225–48.

Marks, Jonathan. 2002. *What it Means to Be 98% Chimpanzee: Apes, People, and Their Genes.* Berkeley and Los Angeles: University of California Press.

Massumi, Brian. 2002. *Parables for the Virtual: Movement, Affect, Sensation.* Durham, N.C.: Duke University Press.

McWhorter, Ladelle. 1999. *Bodies and Pleasures: Foucault and the Politics of Sexual Normalization.* Bloomington: Indiana University Press.

Moore, Donald S., Jake Kosek, and Anand Pandian, eds. 2003. *Race, Nature, and the Politics of Difference.* Durham, N.C.: Duke University Press.

Mortimer-Sandilands, Catriona. 2005. Unnatural Passions? Notes Toward a Queer Ecology. *Invisible Culture* 9. http://www.rochester.edu/in_visible_culture/Issue_9/title9.html.

Opar, Alisa. 2006. We're Deer. We're Queer. Get Used to It: A New Exhibit in Norway Outs the Animal Kingdom. *Plenty Magazine: Environmental News and Commentary,* October 25.

Pickering, Andrew. 1995. *The Mangle of Practice: Time, Agency, and Science.* Chicago: University of Chicago Press.

Roughgarden, Joan. 2004. *Evolution's Rainbow: Diversity, Gender, and Sexuality in Nature and People.* Berkeley and Los Angeles: University of California Press.

Rubin, Gayle. 1975. The Traffic of Women: Notes on the "Political Economy" of Sex. In *Toward an Anthropology of Woman,* ed. Rayna Reiter, 157–85, 198–200. New York: Monthly Review Press.

Sandilands, Catriona. 1999. Sex at the Limits. In *Discourses of the Environment,* ed. Eric Darier, 79–94. Oxford, U.K.: Blackwell.

———. 2001. Desiring Nature, Queering Ethics: Adventures in Erotogenic Environments. *Environmental Ethics* 23.2: 169–88.

Sedgwick, Eve Kosofsky. 1990. *Epistemology of the Closet.* Berkeley and Los Angeles: University of California Press.

Seitler, Dana. 2004. Queer Physiognomies; Or, How Many Ways Can We Do the History of Sexuality? *Criticism* 46: 71–102.

Shearer, Meagan K., and Larry S. Katz. 2006. Female-Female Mounting among Goats Stimulates Sexual Performance in Males. *Hormones and Behavior* 50: 33–37.

Sommer, Volker. 2006. Against Nature?! An Epilogue about Animal Sex and the Moral Dimension. In *Homosexual Behaviour in Animals: An Evolutionary Perspective,* ed. Paul Vasey and Volker Sommer, 365–71. Cambridge: Cambridge University Press.

Terry, Jennifer. 2000. "Unnatural Acts" in Nature: The Scientific Fascination with Queer Animals. *GLQ* 6.2: 151–93.

Vasey, Paul L. 2004a. Pre- and Postconflict Interactions between Female Japanese Macaques during Homosexual Consortships. *International Journal of Comparative Psychology* 17: 351–59.

———. 2004b. Sex Differences in Sexual Partner Acquisition, Retention, and Harassment during Female Homosexual Consortships in Japanese Macaques. *American Journal of Primatology* 64: 397–409.

Vasey, Paul L., Afra Foroud, Nadine Duckworth, and Stefani D. Kovacovsky. 2006. Male-Female and Female-Female Mounting in Japanese Macaques: A Comparative Study of Posture and Movement. *Archives of Sexual Behavior* 35.2: 117–29.

Wilson, Kelpie. 2005. *Primal Tears.* Berkeley, Calif.: Frog Limited.

Woodson, J. C. 2002. Including "Learned Sexuality" in the Organization of Sexual Behavior. *Neuroscience and Biobehavioral Reviews* (Jan. 26): 69–80.

CHAPTER 2

Enemy of the Species

LADELLE M^cWHORTER

For at least a decade, a common strategy for promoting acceptance of racial, ethnic, and religious minorities in many corporate and educational institutions has been to insist that diversity in any population is superior to homogeneity. Homogeneity, it is said, tends toward stagnation. If the "population" is a work team, for example, advocates of diversity suggest that homogeneity of perspective is likely to equal redundancy of ideas and approaches—in other words, impoverished creativity leading to reduced productivity. If the population is a student body, advocates suggest that homogeneity of background and social position is likely to result in re-inforcement of received opinions rather than educational challenge and advancement. Diversity, then, is a crucial factor in healthy development; it is a stimulus to improvement and a defense against the stupidity of unquestioned routine.

Some advocates for lgbtq inclusion in corporate and educational institutions have claimed the same benefits for sexual diversity and diversity of gender expression. Steven Keyes, vice president for compensation, benefits, and human resources policy at Nationwide Insurance, explains, "Having a corporate culture that embraces diversity improves the productivity of our associates, helps the company recruit the best talent and makes Nationwide more competitive in the insurance and financial services industry" (Keyes 2007). In my home university, the University of Richmond, lgbtq and allied groups have spent years petitioning for inclusion in the institution's ongoing "diversity initiative" in the hope of receiving recognition, material support for programming, and protection from discrimination and harassment. Institutions such as mine consider diversity valuable, so the most obvious way to persuade institutional elites to accept and protect queer people is to present ourselves as representatives of a form of diversity, sexual diversity.

The value of diversity of whatever sort is not self-evident, however. Value depends upon empirical conditions and institutional goals. Nevertheless, opponents of this or that group's inclusion rarely attack the value of diversity per se; instead, they insist that the group or institution under scrutiny has enough diversity already or that other principles—efficiency or speed or standard measures of merit—outweigh diversity's importance in a given situation. But why? Why not bring the value of diversity itself into question? Why does diversity as a concept have such political currency and force?

The reason that diversity's value so often goes unchallenged, I believe, is that behind this sociological notion of diversity lies a biological principle that lends the sociological notion much of its persuasive power even when not explicitly invoked: genetic diversity is a species' shield against extinction during environmental upheaval and a resource for its evolutionary advancement.[1] If all individuals in the population are alike genetically, everyone is vulnerable to disease or predation in exactly the same ways. A single catastrophe could wipe out the entire line.

Environmentalists warn of this danger constantly. If, for example, all the corn plants in all the fields for millions of square miles are clones of one parent plant, any genetic susceptibility that parent plant had is replicated in all its daughters, so one virus could kill them all. Genetic diversity allows for the possibility that not all the plants would be vulnerable to the same degree, so some would likely survive to perpetuate their species. Simultaneously, as this example also shows, genetic diversity enables evolutionary development. After introduction of a virus fatal to many corn plants, the remaining plants would constitute a gene pool slightly different from the one that existed before. The species, thus, would have adapted to a changed environment, namely, one including the new virus. Sometimes such adaptations are direct results of catastrophe, as in this example, but they can also result from mutations that give some organisms an advantage over others of their own species; individuals bearing the mutated genes produce more offspring, which eventually edge out their non-mutant cousins in the gene pool. Thus the species evolves.

In short, genetic variation promotes species survival through adaptation across generations. From the perspective of "the species," then, genetic variation (at least to some degree) is a good thing. When this principle crosses out of biology and into public discourse, it lends value to diversity of morphology and diversity of outlook as well as diversity of genotype. From the perspective of "the human community," one might say, racial, ethnic, religious, and other forms of diversity are likewise a good thing. They make society more adaptable by increasing the chances that some members of it will understand the problems we face and see solutions even if other members do not. They prevent intellectual, artistic, and institutional stagnation. They serve as resources for society as it evolves.

As Michel Foucault reminds us, however, everything is dangerous; if we make any political use of concepts imported from other disciplinary regimes or even other political movements, they may bear along with them elements of those regimes or movements that we would rather not countenance or further. One consequence of the importation of genetic diversity's value into queer politics, I fear, is that we may inadvertently reinforce concepts of *species* that underwrite discourses that historically have condemned sexual variation (and a great deal else besides, such as interracial heterosexuality). Human diversity is of value genetically, after all, only insofar as species preservation and adaptation are valued managerial goals. Historically, those positioned to manage human populations and human evolution were the ones to define the key terms—such as "human" and "species"—and they did so in ways many queer activists would likely find objectionable.

The term "species" acquired its scientific meaning in the late eighteenth century in the work of naturalist Georges-Louis Leclerc, Comte de Buffon. But the concept has never been free of controversy. It suffered through contentious transformations in the nineteenth century (including debates over whether Negroes and Indians were *Homo sapiens* or not), only to be destabilized again in the wake of Charles Darwin's work. It underwent revisions in the early twentieth century but became increasingly problematic as that century drew to a close—even while massive amounts of tax money were poured into species-specific genome research. Politically charged from its scientific inception, the concept of *species* has often brought great harm to both racial and sexual minorities over the past two hundred years.

Much discrimination against sexual minorities throughout the twentieth century was the result of theories expounded by sexologists—especially physicians, psychiatrists, and criminologists—whose studies of "sexual deviance" produced popular images of homosexual and transgendered people as menacing degenerates who were due no respect, "therapies" that destroyed many people's health and lives, and public-hygiene policies intended to eliminate or exploit sexual subcultures. Early on, much of this occurred in the context of Race Hygiene and Race Betterment movements, which were to a great extent species movements predicated on the idea that *Homo sapiens* must be purged of deviance and thus preserved and enabled to evolve. Queer people—like dark-skinned (savage) people, disabled (defective) people, chronically ill (weak, feeble) people, and so on—were degenerates who might contaminate the bodies and bloodlines of the evolutionary avant-garde and thus derail *Homo sapiens'* biological advance. Therefore, these people were held to be, literally, biological enemies of the human species, pollutants and pathogens whose very presence posed a physical and possibly mortal threat not only to individuals but to the species as a whole. In many quarters the harm continues even today; sexology's and scientific racism's intellectual descendents still insist that queer people and other out-groups are, in various ways, enemies of the human species. When queer people and our advocates are drawn into public discourse on these terms, we defend sexual diversity as an integral aspect of the species—a natural variation rather than a "cancer," an evolutionary asset rather than a sterile dead end. But the terms themselves are not challenged. As a result, the assumptions that the species is ontologically real and that it is morally prior to all else remain unquestioned. But those assumptions are worth questioning—philosophically and politically. This essay's task is to initiate that project.

Origin of the Species Concept

Ernst Mayr, hailed at his death at the age of one hundred in February of 2005 as the greatest evolutionary biologist of the twentieth century,[2] was also a philosopher and historian of the biological sciences and was deeply interested in the history of the concept of *species* as well as in the evolution of species themselves. In a classic 1963 essay, Mayr asserts that, historically, there are three fundamental meanings of the word *species* in relation to the natural world.[3] First is the Platonic understanding of species as unchanging types. Individuals, on this view, are more or less imperfect instantiations of a type; their imperfections account for the differences among individuals of the same species. The species is the durable and thus real entity and is the proper object of natural philosophy and, later, of natural history. Linnaeus—Carl von Linné, the eighteenth-century Swedish naturalist who developed the system of classification of beings into genera and species still used in modified form today—believed in the existence of real species in this Platonic sense and devised his taxonomy in order to delineate them. On this view, two house cats may differ in size and color, for example, but they are simply imperfect tokens of the same type, two instantiations of the same species, which transcends as well as informs them. A second meaning of the term "species," according to Mayr, is that put forth in the medieval period by the nominalist Occam, who claimed that the concepts of species taxa, like all universal or class concepts, are abstractions derived from our experience of a number of seemingly similar individuals. There is no real entity, the species feline, to which all house cats belong; there are only individual cats and the class term "cat," to which humans conventionally attach conceptual and metaphysical significance.

Neither of these concepts of *species* is satisfactory, Mayr claims. On the one hand, the real world surely does contain something more than the unrelated particulars of the nominalist; cats really are related to each other in some way that accounts for their very real anatomical and functional similarities. But, on the other hand, empirical scientists have little use for the transcendent and thus intangible categories of the Platonic realist; the Platonic form Catness has no place in natural history. Thus, practicing natural historians and biologists in the modern period needed and gradually developed a more satisfactory definition for the term "species," which Mayr expounded in 1942 in *Systematics and the Origin of Species* and refined in several subsequent essays, a definition known as the biological species concept. According to Mayr's classic formulation, "species are groups of interbreeding natural populations that are reproductively isolated from other such groups" (1992, 17).

Mayr was the first to acknowledge that, while he formulated the biological species concept, he did not create it ex nihilo. He credits Buffon with the idea that species can be distinguished empirically—as opposed to metaphysically—by reference to their interfertility or lack thereof. Buffon held that two classes of living entity can be considered distinct species if cross-breeding either (1) is impossible, (2) is sterile, or (3) produces offspring who are themselves sterile. In nature, morphological dissimilarity renders cross-breeding impractical if not impossible in the vast majority of cases. Stallions do not pollinate apple blossoms, for obvious reasons, and conifers do not impregnate sows. In practice, therefore, the question of species difference rarely arose in the natural history of the eighteenth century. The question had real importance only where morphological similarity made sexual contact appear possible, as in varieties of birds, dogs and wolves, and some domesticated herbivores. Buffon's assertion enabled establishment of conceptual boundaries that were empirically grounded. Horses and asses are distinct species despite morphological similarities, Buffon held, because cross-breeding, where fertile, results consistently in sterile hybrids, namely, mules.

From a twentieth-century perspective, Mayr, who spent much of the 1930s and 1940s integrating biology with genetics, found Buffon's account of species boundaries more than merely practical and empirically warranted; he found it positively prescient, because it pointed to what Mayr and other geneticists believed was a fact crucial to the evolution of life, namely that species comprise distinct gene pools, species are genetic populations. Horses and asses are not members of one species, because while there may be some genetic mixing in a few individuals (mules), across the two populations there is no intergenerational gene flow. This is the understanding of species most of us were taught in school; it is the one to which we implicitly appeal when arguing that sexual diversity is of benefit to the human species. What most of us were not taught in school is how controversial this conception of species was and still is. The next two sections of this paper will examine that controversy in both its historical and its contemporary manifestations.

Species' Troubled Past

In fact the conceptual line of descent from Buffon to Mayr is not as direct and unbroken as Mayr implies. While Buffon's assertion that species identification is a matter of interfertility did win general acceptance by the nineteenth century, it did not settle the questions of either the essential nature or the origin of species. Like Occam, Buffon was a nominalist who viewed species taxa as concepts only, not as the names of natural kinds. In nature, he believed, there were only individuals, not classes or genera.[4] He did not believe species had essential natures; thus his descriptive claims were not attempts at definition in that sense. And the question of species' origins was not one that greatly exercised most eighteenth-century naturalists, even those who believed taxa were real natural entities, because most assumed divine creation and at least relative fixity.[5] In the nineteenth century, however, as theological assumptions lost ground in scientific circles and the intellectual impact of the new discipline of geology began to be felt, the questions of the nature and origin of species became increasingly urgent as well as controversial.

Nowhere did that controversy rage more heatedly than in the United States, with its "peculiar institution" of chattel slavery. In the 1830s, the American abolition movement grew to become an organized political force and began pressuring Congress to abolish human bondage, contending that it was simply wrong to enslave fellow human beings, no matter what benefits to society might result and no matter what racial differences might exist in intelligence, strength, health, or ability. Never before had slavery's proponents been put on the defensive as they were from 1832 until slavery's demise in 1863. Old justifications for slavery—such as the biblical story of the curse of Ham and the case for the institution's economic benefits—no longer carried weight. Different, more timely rationales were needed. Slavery's defenders turned to science. Negroes were simply not fellow human beings, they argued, for Negroes and Caucasians were in fact distinct species. Whether that argument was plausible turned, in part, on the definition assigned to the term "species."

Among the principal parties to the scientific debate were naturalist John Bachman of Charleston, South Carolina; physician Josiah Nott of Mobile, Alabama; Samuel G. Morton, world-renowned anatomist and professor of medicine in Philadelphia; and Harvard botanist Louis Agassiz, who arrived in the United States from Switzerland in 1846. In 1851 Nott, the most vocal of slavery's scientific proponents, backed up his polygenist contentions with reference to English biologist James Cowles Prichard's definition:

> The meaning attached to the term *Species* in natural history is very definite and intelligible. It includes *only* the following conditions, namely, *separate origin and distinctness of races, evinced by a constant transmission of some character peculiarity of organization.* A race of animals or of plants marked by any peculiar character which it has ever constantly displayed, is termed a species; and two races are considered specifically different, if they are distinguished from each other by some characteristic which the one cannot be supposed to have acquired or the other to have lost, through any known operation of physical causes; for we are thence led to conclude, that tribes thus distinguished have not descended from the same original stock. (Nott 2005, 128–52)[6]

As long as species were simply groups of living beings distinguished by morphological characters, Nott believed that he could safely claim—drawing on the work (and considerable prestige) of Samuel Morton, who had found significant racial differences in cranial capacity—that Caucasians, Negroes, and American Indians were separate species.

In defense of monogeny (the theory that humanity is one unitary species), Bachman offered his own definition: "Species we define as those individuals resembling each other in dentition and general structure.

In wild animals as a general rule they must approach the same size; but both in wild and domesticated animals they must have the same duration of life, the same period of utro-gestation, the same average number of progeny, the same habits and instincts, in a word, they belong to one stock that produce fertile offspring by association" (2005, 220).[7] In defense of this definition—which includes the idea of interfertility, unlike the definition Nott cited—Bachman quotes Cuvier, Decandole, Edwards and Comte, and Martin.[8]

People of mixed race were common in the United States in the nineteenth century. Who could doubt that racial crosses were fertile? As long as Buffon's criterion of interfertility stood, it seemed that human beings were all of one species. The interfertility criterion was the single biggest obstacle to scientific acceptance of polygeny, as Nott well knew. Thus, he knew also that he had either to dislodge Buffon or to prove, contrary to empirical evidence, that racial crosses were not really fertile in the required sense after all.

Josiah Nott was not a timid man. In 1843, just four years after publication of Morton's massive study *Crania Americana,* Nott argued that "Mulattoes" (crosses between Negroes and Caucasians) were sterile hybrids like mules and thus that Negroes and Caucasians met Buffon's requirement and qualified as two distinct species. Having worked for fifteen years as a physician to many Negroes (he served the wealthy families of Mobile, so he also treated their slaves), Nott claimed to have observed not only morphological differences between blacks and whites but also peculiarities in "Mulattoes" that rendered them less healthy, shorter-lived, and less fertile than either Negroes or Caucasians. In particular, he had observed that "mulatto women are particularly delicate—are subject to many chronic diseases, and especially derangement of the catamenia, prolapsus uteri, leucorrhoea, and other diseases peculiar to females." They are also "bad breeders and bad nurses—many of them do not conceive at all—most are subject to abortions, and a large portion of their children die at an early age" (1843, 253). Each successive generation of "Mulattoes" is weaker and less able to procreate until, by the fourth, the line inevitably dies out.

By thus bending Buffon's criterion somewhat—progressively lessened fecundity rather than absolute sterility in the offspring of a cross-racial pairing—and by offering anecdotal evidence rather than a systematic study, Nott made it appear that racial crosses met the definition of hybrid and, therefore, that Negroes and Caucasians could legitimately be considered different species. Morton, who had not yet taken a position on the issue, congratulated Nott on his masterful handling of the problem. Thereafter, the two maintained a firm friendship.

On the strength of this, or similarly altered definitions of species, between 1846 and 1850 most respected scientists in the United States converted to polygeny. Morton publicly espoused the doctrine by 1851. Agassiz had done so privately since 1847 and in 1850 made a public declaration at the meetings of the American Society for the Advancement of Science in Charleston (Horsman 1987, 104, 115). Taken together, these men formed what is now known as the American School of Anthropology. Their crowning achievement as a group was the publication in 1854 of the enormously influential compendium *Types of Mankind,* edited by Nott and Egyptologist George Gliddon. That book, along with Morton's morphological studies, was cited as scientific support in arguments for racial slavery and then for racial segregation through the rest of the nineteenth century.

Thus was the concept *species* refashioned to serve as a tool for perpetuating racial oppression. But we should not assume that this largely cynical process of refashioning was also a process of politicizing a concept that had been apolitical before. Concepts, Foucault tells us, are for cutting.[9] They are never merely benign representations of a natural arrangement. The concept *species* was neither politically nor morally neutral before polygenists turned it against Native and African Americans and their white allies. *Species* could be made to function oppressively to separate whites from blacks because—as the nominalist Buffon acknowledged— it was already a tool for marking separations in nature's heterogeneous continuities in the interest of prevailing human practices.

In 1859 *The Origin of Species* appeared. The theory of natural selection that Darwin propounded in that book reopened the debate over the definition of "species"[10] (if, indeed, it had ever been closed).[11] Some maintained—as did Darwin himself[12]—that the concept was practically meaningless, given the inevitability of evolution. There are no eternally fixed types, nor are there eternally distinct lines of descent. All life on earth, no matter how morphologically or functionally distinct at present, conceivably could be traced back to a single germ line. But biologists still needed some way to mark the very real differences and similarities between synchronically existing organisms, and the term "species" had a history to recommend it for the purpose. So the question was: How much difference (and difference of what sort) was sufficient to justify calling a group of organisms a species distinct to others in its vicinity and, now, distinct to its own ancestors? Despite the title of his book, however, as

Ernst Mayr points out, Darwin never gave a scientific account of what came to be called speciation (Mayr 1992, 15). He argued convincingly that species must change over time, but he did not say when change amounts to the birth of a new species. In short, he never answered the question of the origin of species.

Regardless of the gaps in Darwin's theory, however, it quickly took hold in the scientific world and in educated circles more generally. Its consonance with prevailing notions of technological, intellectual, and moral progress frequently resulted in conflation of evolutionary modification with evolutionary advancement. Although the theory of natural selection was non-teleological, even Darwin himself sometimes spoke of adaptation as improvement, as if species were on a path to perfection, as if there were an ultimate standard against which their present state could be measured and evaluated.

Natural selection, enthusiastic adherents agreed, was responsible for some amazing feats. Not only had it produced millions of plants and animals remarkable for their physiological adaptations to their environment, but it had even produced one animal able to vary its environment by conscious decision. Natural selection had produced the rational animal *Homo sapiens*, and *Homo sapiens* had produced something called "civilization." Civilization was a biological developmental outcome, a species character (to use the language of natural history). Evolution had produced human beings of superior intellect and moral feeling, and these biological traits had enabled the development of modern technology and civil society.

Of course, enthusiasts acknowledged, this process was incomplete. Many members of the species were inadequately adapted to the radically changed environment. Some groups—Africans, Pacific Islanders, indigenous peoples of North and South America—had never evolved sufficiently to produce a civilization, European and North American theorists believed, so it was unlikely they could adapt to its demands. But even among the higher races, there were individuals who could not adapt—criminals, idiots, the mad, the degenerate, the chronically ill. Like the lower races, these individuals were weaklings that natural selection must eliminate.

If it were allowed to. As the nineteenth century drew to a close and the new century commenced, fear began to settle over the Caucasian elite. Natural selection had brought the human species far, true enough. But was it still operating? Was humanity still evolving, or was that very civilization that evolution had produced circumventing the evolutionary process? After all, modern technology made it possible to save lives that otherwise would have been lost, allowing people with inferior traits to mature and reproduce. And modern morality, so often expressing itself in charity toward the weak and defective, similarly enabled the inferior to procreate. Many feared that human evolution had stalled. Worse still, the process could even reverse itself. Humanity's evolutionary avant-garde might find itself swamped by the rising tide of inferiority that its own intelligence and generosity had made possible. Civilization could be lost as humanity devolved once again into savagery.

A number of theorists in the first two decades of the twentieth century warned of these dire possibilities. One of the most influential was Madison Grant, a New York attorney and conservationist who co-founded the Save-the-Redwoods League and the Bronx Zoo and was instrumental in establishing Glacier and Denali National Parks. Civilization, Grant insisted, had evolved only under the harshest of environmental conditions, where human beings were forced to either innovate, reason, cooperate, and plan ahead or die. "The climatic conditions must have been such as to impose a rigid elimination of defectives through the agency of hard winters and the necessity of industry and foresight in providing the year's food clothing and shelter during the short summer," he wrote in 1916. "Such demands on energy, if long continued, would produce a strong, virile, and self-contained race" (Grant 1916, 152–53). In Paleolithic times these conditions obtained, Grant believed, along the coasts of the Baltic Sea. The race that was thus created gradually migrated northwestward to become the peoples known as the Nordics or Teutons. As they advanced in technological competence and overwhelmed less intelligent and less fit races, they spread farther, crossing first the North Sea to populate the British Isles—and in the process to become the Anglo-Saxons—and then eventually crossing the Atlantic to become the Anglo-Americans. The evolutionary avant-garde of the twentieth century were, therefore, the New England blue-bloodlines to which Grant himself belonged.

And the rising tide of inferiority was everybody else. Civilization could be saved only if that tide was stemmed, and that would require virile Anglo-Saxon resolve. "Mistaken regard for what are believed to be divine laws and a sentimental belief in the sanctity of human life, tend to prevent both the elimination of defect in infants and the sterilization of such adults as are themselves of no value to the community. The laws of nature require the obliteration of the unfit" (Grant 1916, 44–45). Aid to the poor, weak, and disabled was out of the question. Instead, Grant advocated sterilization for the criminal, diseased, insane, and other weaklings and also for those he termed "worthless race types," by which he meant Jews, blacks, and indigenous peoples. Negroes in particular were objectionable.

"Negroes have demonstrated throughout recorded time that they are a stationary species, and that they do not possess the potential of progress or initiative from within" (66). By whatever means necessary, they should be kept apart from Nordics and prevented from corrupting Nordic bloodlines. Furthermore, immigration should be seriously curtailed to prevent Jews and Catholics from eastern and southern Europe—members of the Mediterranean and Alpine races as distinct to the Nordic—from entering the United States.[13] "Either the races must be kept apart by artificial devices of this sort, or else they ultimately amalgamate, and in the offspring the more generalized or lower type prevails" (193).

Grant's friend Lothrop Stoddard wholeheartedly agreed. "The admission of aliens should, indeed, be regarded just as solemnly as the begetting of children, for the racial effect is essentially the same," he wrote in 1920. "Immigration is thus, from the racial standpoint, a form of procreation, and like the more immediate form of procreation it may be either the greatest blessing or the greatest curse" (Stoddard 1925, 252). Immigration from every continent except Europe would be an unmitigated curse, Stoddard believed, and the only Europeans who should be allowed in were those who were of Nordic stock and free of defect and disease.

In 1917, these extremely well known and influential men and their allies in such organizations as the Immigration Restriction League (a group of prominent Harvard alumni), the American Breeders' Association (later the American Genetics Association), and the Association of Medical Superintendents of American Institutions for the Insane (later the American Psychiatric Association) won passage of an immigration restriction bill that went far beyond measures already in place. The new law instituted literacy tests, caps on total numbers of immigrants, national quotas, and denial of entry on the basis of a condition called "constitutional psychopathy." Three decades after publication of Krafft-Ebing's *Psychopathia Sexualis,* sexual inversion was held to be a form of psychopathy—a nondelusional insanity—so the new law effectively screened out anyone who did not conform to prevailing gender norms or who admitted to homosexual desire. Further, any immigrant who, during the first five years of residence in the United States, committed a crime or showed signs of any allegedly hereditary physical or mental defect, including sexual inversion, could be deported.

Inferior people could not be allowed into the United States.[14] This obviously included Africans and Asians, who had been barred from entry by a series of immigration laws enacted over the past two decades, as had lunatics, disabled people, people with any of a list of diseases, and those who could not afford to pay the head tax.[15] In 1917, for overtly eugenic reasons, Congress barred people who were feebleminded, morally degenerate, or sexually suspect as well. But they were not satisfied. In 1924 they reduced the number of people who could immigrate to the United States to an annual total of 150,000, apportioned by the percentage of resident immigrants from each nation as counted in the 1890 census—pointedly before the massive influx from Poland, Hungary, Russia, and Italy. Thus the Immigration Restriction Act of 1924 made the United States the most exclusive country in the world. Its provisions, developed in the name of racial purity and preservation of (Nordic) civilization, remained in effect well past the middle of the twentieth century.

The Anglo-Saxon race was the bearer of the genes that produced civilization. It could not allow those genes to be swamped by what Stoddard called the "rising tide of color" from outside the country. Neither could it allow those genes to be swamped by degenerate, feebleminded defectives in inner cities and rural shanties. Just as the tide must be forced back with the dikes of immigration restriction, it must be stemmed from within by a set of laws and policies designed to segregate the unfit and, where necessary, ensure their sterility. The dikes of racial segregation had to be strengthened. Likewise, the dikes of intellectual and moral segregation had to be set in place and maintained. In the 1910s many state governments undertook population surveys to determine the extent of the "menace of the feebleminded" and to make provisions to confine them in sex-segregated institutions and farm colonies.

The introduction of the Simon-Binet IQ test in 1912 made identification of the intellectually unfit quick and easy. Public schools became the screening ground, and many states enacted laws requiring pupils who scored in the imbecile range (mental age three to seven years) to be placed in segregated classes until adolescence, at which time they were to be institutionalized.[16] Eugenic psychologist Henry Goddard modified the test—originated in France by Theodore Simon and Alfred Binet—to include a grade of feeblemindedness beyond the imbecile. Goddard classified individuals with a test-measured mental age of eight to twelve years as morons and advocated their segregation as well. Most states adopted his position. Additionally, many individuals were classified as moral imbeciles, people with normal cognitive capacity but defective moral judgment. Without a tool to identify such people, officials relied on testimony about habits and actions to determine the presence of moral defect. Women who had children out of wedlock were automatically so classified, but any deviation from heterosexuality and prescribed gender roles could earn a person the label of moral imbecile in addition to the label of degenerate, lunatic, or psychopath.

Hundreds of thousands were locked up for life as a result of these efforts to offset the perceived threat to natural selection and the evolution of the human species. But still the tides of inferiority rose. Clearly if civilization was to survive and advance, those who were most evolved must turn its technologies to the task of eliminating once and for all the defective genes that threatened to swamp their own. More or less quietly, eugenically alert physicians had been sterilizing defectives in prisons, hospitals, and asylums since the 1880s, and the practice had grown with the introduction of the techniques of vasectomy and salpingectomy in the late 1890s. In 1927 the U.S. Supreme Court endorsed these eugenic practices with Chief Justice Oliver Wendell Holmes's declaration in *Buck v. Bell*:

> We have seen more than once that the public welfare may call upon the best citizens for their lives. It would be strange if it could not call upon those who already sap the strength of the State for these lesser sacrifices, often not felt to be such by those concerned, in order to prevent our being swamped with incompetence. It is better for all the world, if instead of waiting to execute degenerate offspring for crime, or to let them starve for their imbecility, society can prevent those who are manifestly unfit from continuing their kind. (quoted in Bruinius 2006, 21)

By 1972, the number of Americans legally sterilized without their consent would reach 65,000.[17] Thus were the enemies of the species eliminated and *Homo sapiens*' evolutionary advance safeguarded and ensured.

Adolf Hitler learned a great deal from American eugenicists, particularly about involuntary sterilization. In fact, the Nazis based their 1934 involuntary sterilization law on the Model Eugenical Sterilization Law drafted by American biologist Harry Laughlin in 1922 . Laughlin, director of Cold Spring Harbor's Eugenic Records Office, called for the sterilization of at least 10 percent of the U.S. population, all those he deemed "socially inadequate"; his model law applied to people who were:

> (1) Feeble-minded; (2) Insane, (including the psychopathic); (3) Criminalistic (including the delinquent and wayward); (4) Epileptic; (5) Inebriate (including drug-habitués): (6) Diseased (including the tuberculous, the syphilitic, the leprous, and others with chronic infections and legally segregable diseases): (7) Blind (including those with seriously impaired vision); (8) Deaf (including those with seri-

ously impaired hearing): (9) Deformed (including the crippled); and (10) Dependent (including orphans, ne-er-do-wells, the homeless, tramps and paupers) (section B(b)). (Laughlin, 1976 [1922])

By 1934 nearly thirty U.S. states had enacted such laws, although few went as far as Laughlin's model. The Canadian provinces of Alberta and British Columbia had such laws as well, as did the countries of Denmark and Finland, the Canton of Vaud in Switzerland, and the state of Vera Cruz in Mexico.[18] The Nazis, the Anglo-Saxons' Teutonic cousins, had some serious eugenic catching up to do.

Of course, such programs are always more efficiently managed in a dictatorship, so the Nazi eugenic sterilization campaign proceeded apace, commanding the admiration of American advocates such as Laughlin, his Cold Spring Harbor colleague Charles Davenport, and Paul Popenoe, executive director of the Human Betterment Foundation and co-author, with Ezra Gosney, of *Sterilization for Human Betterment,* a 1929 report on the results of 6,000 sterilizations performed in California. By 1937, the Nazis had managed to sterilize approximately 250,000 Germans. Soon thereafter they dispensed with the generational delay and began to eliminate defectives outright through eugenic "euthanasia."

Although no North American government ever enacted a policy of eugenic killing, the specter of euthanasia always haunted the eugenics movement. Given the principles and assumptions that animated it, adherents could not help but consider the possibility. In an address to the Medical Association of the State of Alabama in April 1936, William Partlow, medical superintendent of the state home for the feebleminded, reminded his audience:

> Until medical science improved social, public health and sanitary conditions, nature's survival of the fittest defended the human race against the dangers of degeneracy. Now that under the present order of a humane world, the weak are preserved as well as the strong, if we are to continue as a virile, upstanding race in body and mind, eugenics demands its share of study and attention or euthanasia may become a necessity. (Partlow 1936, 12)

The previous year, Partlow and his allies had failed in an attempt to broaden Alabama's 1919 sterilization law, and he was determined not to lose the fight in the next legislative session.

Alabama's law was the weakest in the country, applying only to residents of the state home for the feebleminded and only upon their discharge. Since few were discharged, few were sterilized. Unlike many other states, Alabama did not authorize sterilization for the mentally ill or for incorrigibles in prisons and reformatories. Partlow wanted to change that. His proposed law would have authorized a three-man committee to sterilize "any sexual pervert, Sadist, homosexualist, Masochist, Sodomist, or any other grave form of sexual perversion or any prisoner who has twice been convicted of rape" or thrice imprisoned for any offense (Larson 1995, 140). Those designated for sterilization would have no right of judicial review; all decisions were to be made by physicians and public health officers.

The bill had passed the state legislature and seemed destined for enactment when Governor Bibb Graves unexpectedly vetoed it. In response, the legislature passed a second bill identical in scope but with provision for appeal. Graves vetoed that. Salpingectomy was known to result in complications and death in some cases, he observed; it was morally wrong to expose patients to such a risk for reasons that had nothing to do with improving their own health. Historian Edward Larson speculates, however, that Graves had some other reasons as well.

Partlow's colleague Dr. J. N. Baker had testified before the state legislature during the debate. "With bated breath," he had proclaimed, "the entire civilized world is watching the bold experiment in mass sterilization recently launched in Germany." Not only would the population be purified and strengthened, but the Germans would realize a huge savings in tax money as a result of this "bold experiment," Baker predicted. He was confident that the Nazis had the right idea. But many of Governor Graves's constituents saw things differently. Graves received a number of letters suggesting that many citizens viewed the sterilization bill as, in the words of one writer, "an attempt to Hitleresque Alabama." Another constituent wrote, "In my judgment the great rank and file of the country people of Alabama do not want this law; they do not want Alabama, as they term it, Hitlerized" (Larson 1995, 145). Eugenicists such as Baker and Partlow may have been looking to Germany for inspiration in the mid-1930s, but many others were looking at Germany in horror.[19]

Partlow, Baker, and others pushed for broadened sterilization authority for another ten years, but as the policies of the Nazi regime became more widely understood in the United States, such measures lost their appeal. The eugenics movement lowered its profile and changed its tactics. Frederick Osborn, a driving force in the transformation of eugenics through mid-century, warned eugenicists against casting their program of species improvement in narrowly racial terms. "It would be unwise for eugenists to impute superiorities or inferiorities of a biological nature to social classes, to regional groups, or to races as a whole," he wrote in 1937.

> Scientists are not at all sure that any races or social classes in this country are above or below others in biological capacity for developing socially valuable qualities. But they are sure that even if there are differences between the average biological capacities of such groups, they are small compared to the much greater differences existing between individuals. Eugenics should therefore operate on a basis of individual selection. A program of selection of the best individuals and the best family stock, from every race and socio-economic class, will have wide scientific support. (1937, 106)

Osborn enlarged upon this position in his 1940 book *Preface to Eugenics,* maintaining that eugenics is only viable in a democracy where individuals are respected:

> The eugenics ideal recognizes that each human being is by his heredity unique. This uniqueness, which pervades every cell in his body, justifies respect for the individual. . . . Eugenics, in asserting the uniqueness of the individual, supplements the American ideal of respect for the individual. Eugenics in a democracy seeks not to breed men to a single type, but to raise the average level of human variations, reducing variations tending toward poor health, low intelligence, and anti-social character, and increasing variations at the highest levels of activity. (1940, 296–97)

Racists—like Hitler—seek to breed a single type of person; they seek conformity to one phenotypic ideal. But, ultimately, breeding programs of that sort are dysgenic, because they do not select for the variations that will really enable the human species to advance—strength, vitality, high intelligence, and socially valuable conduct. We must renounce naïve, phenotypic racism, Osborn argued; we must concentrate on eliminating inferior genotypes and cultivating superior genotypes wherever they are found. The future good of the species depends on minimizing abnormality and defect.[20]

The Species and Modern Genetics

It is commonly believed that eugenics died with Hitler and that those who clung to the project of creating a master race or purifying humanity of the so-called socially inadequate were totally marginalized after World War II. Modern genetics stepped in, corrected the scientific misperceptions that had powered the race purification movement at the turn of the century, and by the 1930s thoroughly discredited eugenics as a pseudoscience. But the historical facts are a little less straightforward and far less reassuring.

The science that Frederick Osborn appealed to in 1937 was not the science of eugenics. It was the science of genetics, the science practiced by men such as Thomas Hunt Morgan, Theodosius Dobzhansky, and Ernst Mayr. And when he claimed scientific support for his eugenic position, he knew what he was talking about. The project of eliminating defect and abnormality through managed breeding was embraced by many geneticists, even while race-based discrimination was opposed. The preface to Osborn's 1968 book *The Future of Human Heredity* was written by Ernst Mayr's colleague Theodosius Dobzhansky, arguably the second greatest geneticist of the twentieth century if Mayr is the first. In it Dobzhansky acknowledged that "zealous proponents" had hindered the acceptance of eugenics as a practice. "And yet," he maintained, "eugenics has a sound core. The real problem which mankind will not be able to evade indefinitely is where the evolutionary process is taking man, and where man himself wishes to go. Mr. Osborn has for several decades been the clear-sighted leader of the eugenical movement in America, who strove to make the substance of eugenics scientific and its name respectable again" (in Osborn, 1968, vi).[21] Geneticists of the highest rank did not reject eugenics during or after World War II. Purged of its animosity toward various racial groups, eugenics was not only accepted but championed. Meanwhile, immigration quotas and restrictions remained in place. Classification of people as defective on the basis of IQ tests, diagnoses such as sexual psychopathy, and transgender behavior continued and resulted in institutionalization of thousands of people, many of whom were subjected to treatments such as aversion therapy, lobotomy, clitoridectomy, and physical or chemical castration. Eugenic arguments and ideals had created a network of institutional power that held all forms of physical or behavioral difference suspect and that overtly endeavored to stamp out all deviation from the narrowly defined heterosexual norm. Outrage against the Nazi regime did nothing to quell this systematic violence against sexual and gender deviation. In fact, sexual and gender deviants were routinely removed from the breeding population, deprived of civil rights, subjected in some cases to what might well be termed torture, and exploited in medical experiments for at least another quarter century.

It could be argued that this was all simply a mistake, much as the previous reliance on racial phenotypes as indicators of genetic inferiority had been a mistake. Science is a self-correcting enterprise, we might say optimistically; eventually scientists recognize their mistaken beliefs and abandon them. Just as scientifically honest eugenicists learned that Negroes, Asians, and various other racial groups were not genetically inferior to Caucasians, modern geneticists will learn that homosexuals and transgendered people are not genetically inferior to straights. Science will eventually prove that, on the contrary, sexual diversity persists because it contributes to our species' health, strength, and prospects for survival. Indeed, geneticist Dean Hamer has already advanced arguments along these lines (Hamer and Copeland 1994, chapter 8).

But before we place our bets on this strategy, we need to look more closely at the concepts such arguments rely on. Just what is a species in modern genetic discourse? Let us recall Mayr's definition: "Species are groups of interbreeding natural populations that are reproductively isolated from other such groups" (1992, 17). This definition seems both plausible and benign in its familiarity. Mayr claims a venerable heritage for it, and it enjoyed widespread scientific acceptance for much of the twentieth century. But it was never uncontested, and by 1970 it was seriously challenged on several scientific fronts.[22] Subsequent critique was so serious and so destabilizing that at present there is no generally agreed upon scientific definition of "species."[23] Hence, any attempt to argue either that queer people are enemies of the human species or that we are important contributors to it must falter for lack of a clear referent for one of its key terms. That in itself is reason to avoid making such arguments and to criticize our political adversaries when they do. But there is another reason to avoid resting pro-queer arguments on the concept of species, a reason embedded in the history of the twentieth-century controversy within biology over Ernst Mayr's definition.

No concept is without its political charge, as was said above. Mayr's definition is no exception. Conceived in the 1930s, it was a product of its time, just as the opposition to it that arose in the 1970s was a product of its time. Because these were times of great hostility toward sexual and gender deviance, we cannot ignore the possibility—indeed the likelihood—that these still current if contested definitions reflect and even perhaps foster and perpetuate that hostility.

Mayr's definition is all about sex—all about who has sex with whom. A species consists of a collection of individuals who do or could have fertile sexual contact with one another. A species is thus a population that shares a single "gene pool." Current combinations of DNA as they exist in the individual members of the population can be reshuffled through sexual reproduction to create a new population of individuals, the next generation, but the gene pool itself remains intact.[24] Evolution affects not the individuals but the gene pool through processes such as mutation and genetic drift; natural selection acts on the pool to eliminate some genotypes. Over time the gene pool alters. But as long as it remains isolated from other gene pools, the successive populations are one evolving species distinct to all others.

It may be hard to see either political influence or political motivation in Mayr's talk of populations and pools. The problems begin to emerge, however, when Mayr turns to discussion of speciation. In order to become and remain a "good species" (Mayr's phrase) rather than a mere variety, a gene pool must dam itself off from alien gene flows. A species-in-the-making (a variety in the process of becoming a "good species") must evolve what Dobzhansky (1935) had termed "reproductive isolating mechanisms";[25] it must erect barriers to fertile sexual contact with neighboring varieties. Barriers might include such mechanisms as a slightly different estrus or hibernation or migration cycle, different courtship behaviors or mating calls, or a different physical basis for sexual selection. These mechanisms would preclude gene flow from parent or sibling populations and give the developing species a chance to establish a separate gene pool. Thus, descriptions of species taxa crucially involve descriptions of their reproductive isolating mechanisms, and a true or good species is one whose mechanisms actually do prevent gene flow from outside the population.

This definition has a variety of empirical difficulties, as biologists have untiringly pointed out over the years. For example, some biologists object to it because it renders asexual organisms non-specific. It may also count morphologically distinct groups—such as red and black oaks—as one species; hence it does not square with standard taxonomic speciation.[26] It also makes identification of extinct species difficult by undermining morphology as a reliable indicator of speciation. But one of the most serious criticisms of the definition was raised by Hugh E. H. Paterson in 1976 (Paterson 1993). Everyone agrees, Paterson says, that speciation can occur when one species is split into two geographically separated areas for a long time. Different environments will select for different alleles until the two groups are genetically and probably morphologically distinct. This is called speciation in allopatry. But can speciation occur in sympatry—that is, can one species become two distinct species within the same environment? Yes, say Dobzhansky and Mayr, because a subset of the species can evolve reproductive isolating mechanisms that dam off the gene flow from the parent species. Once these are in place, we have two gene pools and so two species. No, says Paterson, because the processes of natural selection would never favor any trait that made most offspring of the developing subgroup sterile. Reproductive isolating mechanisms simply cannot evolve, he maintains, at least not as essential components of the process of speciation in sympatry. If they do evolve, they are incidental to the operation of natural selection in favor of other adaptive traits.[27]

Furthermore, by making reproductive isolation an essential feature of speciation, adherents of the biological species concept import a kind of teleology into the theory of natural selection. Nature *wants* diversity of species, they imply, because, as Dobzhansky puts it, "the living world has deployed itself to master a progressively greater range of environments and ways of living" (quoted in Paterson 1993, 100). Speciation is life's way of colonizing new environments in a drive to conquer the planet. Paterson views this as an illegitimate assumption in a scientific theory. Life has no aims, he maintains. Nature does not select for diversity per se; it selects for fecundity, the opposite of sterility; diversity (the isolation of distinct gene pools) occurs as a side effect. Thus it will not do to make intersterility an essential component of the definition of species.

My concern here, however, is not with the biological species concept's biological value but with its political investments and sources. It is clearly a reflection of a society in which Jim Crow racism was in full force, preoccupation with miscegenation was pervasive, and fears of hereditary degeneracy abounded. Racial segregation and immigration restriction, as well as eugenic institutionalization and sterilization of the unfit, were all about damming the gene flow from suspect segments of the larger population in order to isolate the (straight, white, middle-class) subpopulation reproductively to produce a good species exclusive of—to use the language of the day—Negroes, Asiatics, defectives, and perverts. The process of speciation as Mayr and Dobzhansky describe it is, precisely, the project of twentieth-century eugenics. Even their fluid metaphors are taken from the prevailing eugenic discourse: Stoddard's image of the rising tide of color swamping the vessels of Nordic germ plasm is not far in the background, and his repeated calls for dikes to protect the Nordic race from contamination by its presumed inferiors might have been the prototype for the very concept of reproductive isolating mechanisms staving off foreign gene flows. There is nothing particularly fluid about DNA. Twentieth-century geneticists' ubiquitous use of water metaphors—flows, pools, and the like—was not descriptive; it was evocative of the eugenic discourses out of which genetics grew and to which it remained attached. Eugenicists were trying to create a new (super)human species by managing sexual behavior and restricting sexual contact; geneticists thus imagined that all new species were created that way. Far from abandoning eugenics in the 1940s, geneticists raised the basic principles of eugenic practice to the status of natural law.

It is not surprising that, seen in this light, Mayr's biological species concept came under fire in the 1970s, at precisely the same time that Jim Crow racism was collapsing and activists were pressing for deinstitutionalization and reclassification of various types of "mental defectives." Many objections were then raised against Mayr's definition of species and the premier biological status of Dobzhansky's isolating mechanisms, yet these brilliant geneticists and many of their colleagues still favored their beleaguered sexual definition. Indeed, in 1970 Dobzhansky reasserted it: "Species are systems of populations: the gene exchange between these systems is limited or prevented by a reproductive isolating mechanism or perhaps by a combination of such mechanisms" (quoted in Templeton 1992 160–61). In 1985, Paterson asked whence this insistence. He gave a sociological answer: "[T]his favor might stem from deep-seated biases in our Western cultural background." It might be traced to religious belief, he suggested, but he also pointed out the biases embedded in language. "In English, notice how approbative are words such as pure, purebred, thoroughbred, and how pejorative are those like mongrel, bastard, halfbreed, and hybrid. Such cultural biases, which act subtly, almost subliminally, through the vocabulary and imagery of languages, might well predispose the unwary to favor ideas like that of 'isolating mechanisms' with the role of 'protecting the integrity of species.'" He went on to note, "When Dobzhansky introduced the isolation concept in 1937, it was accepted almost without resistance. This acceptance is in sharp contrast to the usual opposition that greets new ideas (cf. Kuhn 1970), and could well have been due to these cultural predisposing factors" (Paterson 1992, 144–45).[28] In 1937, it was common sense: The way to produce a new species was to isolate it reproductively from the larger population. By 1985, however, it was common sense no longer. But what was?

Many alternatives to Mayr's biological species concept were put forward. In the introduction to his 1992 anthology on the subject, Marc Ereshefsky counts more than twenty definitions of "species" current and offers eight for consideration in the debate his book represents.[29] One of those is Paterson's, called the Recognition Concept. According to Paterson, a species is "that most inclusive population of individual biparental organisms which share a common fertilization system" (Paterson 1992, 149). The fertilization system is what establishes a delineated gene pool, or a field for gene recombination. It is a positive, not a negative, phenomenon; its function is to enable reproduction rather than to prohibit it. "Successful fertilization in even the simplest of unicellular eukaryotes requires the assistance of a series of adaptations which constitute what might be called the fertilization system of the organism" (146). These adaptations may include motility and endocrine periodicity. But especially important on Paterson's view is the system of signals by which organisms identify an "appropriate mating partner" (148). These signals differ greatly in different organisms. They may be chemical, aural, or behavioral. But in each case, membership in a species is determined by whether an organism is able to recognize and respond to a signal from an appropriate potential mate. Paterson adds, parenthetically, "'Appropriate' here implies no more than an individual of opposite sex drawn from the same 'field for gene recombination'" (148). We thus shift our attention away from protecting the species from genetic corruption through rigidly policed segregation to maintaining the species through heterosexual courtship.

By the 1980s, at least for those scientists who accepted Paterson's Recognition Concept, the definition of "species" essentially involved gendered heterosexual behavior. Paterson quotes R. A. Fisher to reinforce his point: "The grossest blunder in sexual preference, which can be conceived of an animal making, would be to mate with a species different from its own and with which the hybrids are infertile or, the mixture of instincts and other attributes appropriate to different courses of life, at so serious a disadvantage as to leave no descendants" (quoted in Paterson 1993, 2). To choose a mate with whom one could not possibly have fertile sex is a terrible error against which natural selection must safeguard. Individuals "deviant in one or more of the steps comprising the SMRS [species mate recognition system] are less likely to be recognized as mates by conspecifics. The more deviant an individual is, the lower its selective advantage" (Paterson 1993, 65–66). Through natural selection, deviantly gendered or sexed organisms must die off, rendering gendered heterosexuality a stable feature of normal members of any species. This is the essential truth about species and the natural way of things.

Of course not all biologists accept Paterson's view. His definition is influential, but not hegemonic.[30] Nevertheless, its currency should give us pause as we consider biology as a resource for valuing the lives of non-heterosexual and transgendered people.

Queer Political Options

To return to the question that served as the impetus for this long discussion, then, should queer people use arguments based on the presumed value of diversity in our political endeavors? I hope I have demonstrated that this is a much more complex question than one might suppose and thus that any answer is likely also to be complex, as well as very specific to a given empirical situation. There are real dangers involved in making arguments from analogy to scientific principles. In this case one danger is that of failure, because the scientific principle at issue is not well defined and so not securely warranted. Another danger is that of success, because the scientific principle at issue may carry with it a whole history of connections and meanings that may not serve queer interests and purposes in the long run. A major lesson to be learned from this look at the history of the concept *species* is that science has not demonstrated that it merits the authority often given it to decide social, political, and moral questions. At its best, science is an important tool and component in the process of making such decisions, not a final arbiter. In many cases, we do better to question the authority—and in some cases the validity—of the science used against us rather than to embrace scientific concepts and values uncritically.

If sexual and gender diversity are valuable in human society, they are so regardless of their value for species preservation or evolution. Arguments for their value need not rely on arguments for the value of genetic diversity. But that means we actually have to *make* the arguments for their value in various contexts explicitly and not simply by way of vague gestures toward current quasi-scientific "common sense." Exactly what is good about sexual and gender diversity? If we have no ready answers, then we better not make the assertion in the first place. What we can do in the meantime, however, is force opponents of our inclusion in social institutions and civil society to explain why they believe uniformity of sexuality and gender are valuable or why diversity of sexuality and gender are bad. And when they base their arguments on evolution and preservation of the species, we can be ready to counter them—because they clearly do not know what they are talking about.

NOTES

1. Donna Haraway notes this contemporary conflation of cultural and genetic diversity (1997).

2. Kevin de Queiroz called Mayr "almost certainly the greatest of all biologists" (de Queiroz 2005, 261). E. O. Wilson goes a step further, placing Mayr in the company of Einstein: "Ernst Mayr, one of the 20th century's greatest scientists and a principal author of the modern theory of evolution, passed away on February 3, 2005, at the age of 100" (Wilson 2005, v).

3. There are, of course, a number of meanings of the term in other contexts such as mathematics, metallurgy, grammar, and shipping. Mayr is interested only in the meanings that have played some role in natural science (Mayr 1992, 15–25).

4. "The more we increase the number of divisions in the productions of nature, the closer we shall approach to the true," Buffon wrote, "since nothing really exists in nature except individuals, and since genera, orders, and classes exist only in our imagination" (quoted in Foucault 1970, 146–47).

5. If not absolute fixity, then at least fixity with reference to the species' original location in the Great Chain of Being. For a discussion of this, see Foucault (1970, esp. 150–60).

6. Nott does not give a reference for the passage from Prichard.

7. This essay was originally published in 1855 and is a rebuttal of Nott's attack and a critique of Agassiz.

8. These all occur on page 219 of Bachman (2005). Cuvier: "We are under the necessity of admitting the *existence of certain forms* which have perpetuated themselves from the beginning of the world, without exceeding the limits first prescribed. All the individuals belonging to one of these forms constitute a species." Decandole: "We unite under the designation of species all those individuals who mutually bear to each other so close a resemblance as to allow of our supposing that they may have proceeded originally from a single being or a single pair." Edwards and Comte: "The name species is applied to an assemblage of individuals which bear a strong resemblance to each other, and which are perpetuated with the same essential qualities." Martin: "Species are fixed and permanent forms of being, exhibiting indeed certain modes of variation, of which they may be more or less susceptible; but maintaining throughout those modifications, a sameness of structural essentials transmitted from generation to generation, and never lost by the influence of causes, which otherwise produce obvious effects."

9. Foucault writes, "[K]nowledge is not made for understanding; it is made for cutting" (1977, 154).

10. For some discussion of this event in this intellectual context, see Haller (1970, 1319–29).

11. According to Robert J. O'Hara, it hadn't. "The species problem has never once dropped from sight in the long history of systematics" (1993, 231).

12. For an interesting discussion of Darwin's rhetorical strategy, see Beatty (1992, 227–46).

13. Between 1889 and 1914, 80% of newcomers in the United States were from southern and eastern Europe. Between 1900 and 1910, six million came from Austria-Hungary, Spain, Italy, and Russia: Italy—285,000, Austria-Hungary—338,000, and the Russian Empire—250,000 (Dowbiggin 1997, 193).

14. Neither could they be allowed into Canada. By 1911 Canada was the fastest-growing country in the world, with a population jump over the previous decade of

43%. Canada soon began limiting immigration along the same eugenic lines as the United States. By 1923 they effectively barred Asians and Africans (McLaren 1990, 47, 55–56).

15. In great part to protect American labor interests, Chinese immigration had been ended in the late nineteenth century. Physically and mentally defective people, unaccompanied children under seventeen, and prostitutes were barred in 1907. It is unknown how many Canadians were legally sterilized. Records in Alberta indicate 2,822, but records in British Columbia have been lost. McLaren believes that only a few hundred people were sterilized in British Columbia, meaning fewer than 4,000 legal sterilizations occurred in Canada (McLaren 1990, 159–60).

16. Those who scored in the infant to two years range were called idiots. Many of them were already institutionalized, and few were in public schools. Officials considered them far less dangerous than imbeciles because they were incapable of committing most crimes and highly unlikely to procreate. They were not considered much of a menace to society, except insofar as they might descend into poverty and have to be maintained at public expense.

17. Figures vary in the literature, but Philip Reilly (1991), seems to have made the most careful study and is the most frequently cited authority on the subject. This is his figure.

18. For this list as well as a list of U.S. state laws, see Landman (1933, 403). Landman gives a list of twenty-seven states. South Carolina enacted its law after his article appeared but before the Nazis enacted theirs. Georgia was the last U.S. state to enact an involuntary sterilization law, which it did in 1937.

19. The sequence of events is discussed in the context of a much more in-depth analysis of the U.S. eugenics movement in McWhorter (2009), chapter 5, especially pp. 222–31.

20. It is very important to note that the eugenic turn Osborn advocated was from selection of racial to selection of familial stock. The best families, not the best races, would be supported, while the worst would be slated for extermination. Over the course of the 1950s and 1960s, this familial selection got reinterpreted as a pro-family practice, and eugenic programs (including involuntary sterilization) were rearticulated as pro-family measures. In *Racism and Sexual Oppression in Anglo-America,* I argue that much of the late-twentieth-century pro-family movement is rooted in the eugenics movement (which was in turn rooted in scientific racism). Its purpose is not to support the interests of families; its purpose is to support the interests of families thought likely to produce children with certain valued characteristics and to condemn and disrupt families thought likely to produce delinquents, defectives, and perverts. Unfortunately there is not space to elaborate on those historical connections here. For discussions of so-called pro-family movements and their links with nationalism, etc., I refer the reader to other essays in this volume, especially Sturgeon and Gosine.

21. Dunn and Dobzhansky write: "It would obviously be to the advantage of society if the distribution of human genes could be controlled or modified in such a way that the good ones would increase and the bad ones would decrease" (Dunn and Dobzhansky, 1946, 62–64). They go on to discuss sterilization as one means of accomplishing this, although they neither condone nor condemn the practice. In the same book, however, they decisively condemn selection on the basis of race, in stark contrast to their apparently morally neutral look at sterilization to eliminate familial defect.

22. The first major salvo was Robert R. Sokal and Theodore J. Crovello's 1970 article, "The Biological Concept of Species: A Critical Evaluation," which is reprinted in

Ereshefsky (1992). They conclude that "the biological species is an arbitrary category, which may be useful in given situations but is not a fundamental unit of evolution" (50).

23. According to de Queiroz (2005), by the late 1990s the biological literature contained dozens of proposed alternatives to Mayr's biological species concept.

24. Dunn and Dobzhansky give a simple explanation for this phenomenon in the appendix to chapter 4 of their 1946 book.

25. He introduced this concept in a paper in 1935 entitled "A Critique of the Species Concept in Biology." He treated the issue at much greater length in his 1937 book *Genetics and the Origin of Species* (Paterson 1993).

26. For examples of concerns about asexual entities, see Ehrlich and Raven (1992, 57–67), and Templeton (1992, 159–83). For a discussion of oak tree differentiation, see Van Valen (1992, 69–77).

27. Paterson sees this criticism as crucially involving a distinction between function and effect. For a discussion of this distinction, see Lambert (1995, 238–59).

28. This essay was originally published in 1985.

29. De Queiroz (2005, 245) counts at least twenty-four in circulation by 2005.

30. For an in-depth discussion of Paterson's views, see his 1993 book. For critical discussion see Templeton (1992, 159–83), and Lambert and Spencer (1995). The Lambert and Spencer volume contains twenty essays "brought together as a pragmatic and analytic tribute to the ideas of Hugh Paterson" (ix), according to P. H. Greenwood, the author of its foreword.

REFERENCES

Bachman, John. 2005. An Examination of the Characteristics of Genera and Species as Applicable to the Doctrine of the Unity of the Human Race. In *Race, Hybridity, and Miscegenation, Vol. 1: Josiah Nott and the Question of Hybridity,* ed. R. Bernasconi and K. Dotson, 214–37. Bristol, U.K.: Thoemmes Continuum.

Beatty, John. 1992. Speaking of Species: Darwin's Strategy. In *The Units of Evolution: Essays on the Nature of Species,* ed. M. Ereshefsky, 227–46. Cambridge, Mass.: MIT Press.

Bruinius, Harry. 2006. *Better for All the World: The Secret History of Forced Sterilization and America's Quest for Racial Purity.* New York: Knopf.

de Queiroz, Kevin. 2005. Ernst Mayr and the Modern Concept of Species. In *Systematics and the Origins of Species: On Ernst Mayr's 100th Anniversary,* ed. J. Hey, W. Fitch, and F. J. Ayala, 243–61. Washington, D.C.: National Academic Press.

Dobzhansky, Theodosius. 1935. A Critique of the Species Concept in Biology. *Philosophy of Science* 2.3: 344–55.

Dowbiggan, Ian Robert. 1997. *Keeping America Sane: Psychiatry and Eugenics in the United States and Canada, 1880–1940.* Ithaca, N.Y.: Cornell University Press.

Dunn, L. C., and Theodosius Dobzhansky. 1946. *Heredity, Race, and Society.* New York: Penguin Books.

Ehrlich, Paul R., and Peter H. Raven. 1992. Differentiation of Populations. In *The Units of Evolution: Essays on the Nature of Species,* ed. Marc Ereshefsky, 57–68. Cambridge, Mass.: MIT Press.

Ereshefsky, Marc. 1992. Introduction. In *The Units of Evolution: Essays on the Nature of Species,* ed. Marc Ereshefsky, xiii–xvi. Cambridge, Mass.: MIT Press.

Foucault, Michel. 1970. *The Order of Things: An Archeology of the Human Sciences.* New York: Vintage.

———. 1977. Nietzsche, Genealogy, History. In *Language, Counter-memory, Practice: Selected Essays and Interviews,* ed. D. F. Bouchard, 139–64. Ithaca, N.Y.: Cornell University Press.

Grant, Madison. 1916. *The Passing of the Great Race, or the Racial Basis of European History.* New York: Charles Scribner's Sons.

Haller, John S., Jr. 1970. The Species Problem: Nineteenth-Century Concepts of Racial Inferiority in the Origin of Man Controversy. *American Anthropologist* 72: 1319–29.

Hamer, Dean, and Peter Copeland. 1994. *The Science of Desire: The Search for the Gay Gene and the Biology of Behavior.* New York: Simon and Schuster.

Haraway, Donna, 1997. *Modest_Witness@Second_Millennium, FemaleMale©_Meets_OncoMouse™.* New York: Routledge.

Horsman, Reginald. 1987. *Josiah Nott of Mobile: Southerner, Physician, and Racial Theorist.* Baton Rouge, La.: Louisiana State University Press.

Keyes, Steven. 2007. Statements of Support for the Employment Non-Discrimination Act. *Human Rights Campaign.* http://www.hrc.org/

Kuhn, Thomas S. 1970. *The Structure of Scientific Revolutions.* Chicago: University of Chicago Press.

Lambert, David M. 1995. Biological Function: Two Forms of Explanation. In *Speciation and the Recognition Concept: Theory and Application,* ed. D. M. Lambert and H. G. Spencer, 238–59. Baltimore, Md.: Johns Hopkins University Press.

Lambert, David M., and Hamish G. Spencer, eds. 1995. *Speciation and the Recognition Concept: Theory and Application.* Baltimore, Md.: Johns Hopkins University Press

Landman, J. H. 1933. The Human Sterilization Movement. *Journal of Criminal Law and Criminology (1931–1951)* 24.2: 400–408.

Larson, Edward J. 1995. *Sex, Race, and Science: Eugenics in the Deep South.* Baltimore, Md.: Johns Hopkins University Press.

Laughlin, Harry. 1976. Modern Eugenical Sterilization Law. In *Eugenics Then and Now,* ed. C. J. Bajema, 138–52. Stroudsburg, Pa.: Dowden, Hutchinson and Ross.

Mayr, Ernst. 1992. Species Concepts and Their Application. In *The Units of Evolution: Essays on the Nature of Species,* ed. M. Ereshefsky, 15–26. Cambridge, Mass.: MIT Press.

McLaren, Angus. 1990. *Our Own Master Race: Eugenics in Canada, 1895–1945.* Ithaca, N.Y.: Cornell University Press.

McWhorter, Ladelle. 2009. *Racism and Sexual Oppression in Anglo-America: A Genealogy.* Bloomington: Indiana University Press.

Nott, Josiah. 1843. The Mulatto a Hybrid—Probable Extermination of the Two Races if the Whites and Blacks Are Allowed to Intermarry. *American Journal of the Medical Sciences* (July): 252–56.

———. 2005. Diversity of the Human Race. In *Race, Hybridity, and Miscegenation,* Vol. 1: *Josiah Nott and the Question of Hybridity,* ed. R. Bernasconi and K. Dotson, 128–52. Bristol, U.K.: Thoemmes Continuum.

O'Hara, Robert J. 1993. Systematic Generalization, Historical Fate, and the Species Problem. *Systematic Biology* 42.3: 231–46.

Osborn, Frederick. 1937. Implications of the New Studies of Population and Psychology for the Development of Eugenic Philosophy. *Eugenical News* 22.6: 104–107.

———. 1940. *Preface to Eugenics.* New York: Harper and Brothers.

———. 1968. *The Future of Human Heredity: An Introduction to Eugenics in Modern Society.* New York: Weybright and Talley.

Partlow, William D. 1936. A Debt the World Owes Medical Science. *Journal of Medical Association of the State of Alabama* 6.1 (July): 6–12.

Paterson, Hugh E. H. 1992. The Recognition Concept of Species. In *The Units of Evolution: Essays on the Nature of Species,* ed. M. Ereshefsky, 139–58. Cambridge, Mass.: MIT Press.

———. 1993. *Evolution and the Recognition Concept of Species: Collected Writings,* ed. S. F. McEvey. Baltimore, Md.: Johns Hopkins University Press.

Reilly, Philip. 1991. *The Surgical Solution: A History of Involuntary Sterilization in the United States.* Baltimore, Md.: Johns Hopkins University Press.

Sokal, Robert R., and Theodore J. Crovello. [1970] 1992. The Biological Concept of Species: A Critical Evaluation. In *The Units of Evolution: Essays on the Nature of Species,* ed. M. Ereshefsky, 27–56. Cambridge, Mass.: MIT Press.

Stoddard, Lothrop. 1925. *The Rising Tide of Color against White World-Supremacy.* New York: Charles Scribner's Sons.

Templeton, Alan R. 1992. The Meaning of Species and Speciation: A Genetic Perspective. In *The Units of Evolution: Essays on the Nature of Species,* ed. M. Ereshefsky, 159–86. Cambridge, Mass.: MIT Press.

Van Valen, Leigh. 1992. Ecological Species, Multispecies, and Oaks. In *The Units of Evolution: Essays on the Nature of Species,* ed. M. Ereshefsky, 69–78. Cambridge, Mass,: MIT Press.

Wilson, E. O. 2005. Preface. In *Systematics and the Origins of Species: On Ernst Mayr's 100th Anniversary,* ed. J. Hey, W. Fitch, and F. J. Ayala, v–vi. Washington, D.C.: National Academic Press.

CHAPTER 3

Penguin Family Values: The Nature of Planetary Environmental Reproductive Justice

NOËL STURGEON

In 2005, a nature documentary entitled *The March of the Penguins* was a surprise hit, winning an Academy Award in 2006 for best documentary. The beautifully filmed story of the improbable but gorgeous Antarctic Emperor penguins and their incredible effort to produce and nurture their babies was a tale of terrific difficulties overcome with amazing persistence. In an interesting twist, and to the astonishment of the director, Luc Jacquet, right-wing fundamentalist Christians in the United States adopted the film as an inspiring example of monogamy, traditional Christian family values, and intelligent design. At around the same time, apparently unbeknownst to right-wing fundamentalist Christians, penguins had become a symbol of the naturalness of gay marriage.

Meanwhile, in other political and cultural discourses, penguins (along with polar bears) became popular symbols of what we would lose to global warming. Relatively invisible in the public cultural arena, in contrast, were the growing and unequal effects of the pollution of our atmosphere on marginalized human beings such as indigenous peoples in the Arctic regions, who are struggling to preserve their cultures and societies in the face of rapid climate change. Instead of attention to these issues, penguins have become the newest terrain on which to fight culture wars over human reproduction, while at the same time they have become the latest environmentalist icons. What is the connection between these popular cultural trends? Does it matter in terms of environmental consequences what kind of familial and sexual arrangements we make?

The Nature of Reproduction

As I have argued elsewhere, familial and sexual arrangements are clearly important to environmental issues (Sturgeon 1994). Reproduction (including questions of sexuality as well as gender and race) is an important political issue in our culture, a contested topic in almost every arena of our life. Here, I propose a broader notion of reproduction than customary, using the term "environmental reproductive justice" as a way of connecting environmental issues with social justice issues. In doing so, I am building on the insights of feminists, especially feminists of color and Global South feminists, who have argued for the term "reproductive justice" as opposed to "reproductive rights." "Reproductive justice" refers to more than the mainstream concept of "reproductive rights" (e.g., access to abortion, birth control, the morning-after pill, etc.); it attempts to address the need to access the means of supporting and nurturing children (e.g., childcare, health care, prenatal care, freedom from coerced sterilization, healthy environments, clean air, food, and water, adequate housing, etc.), not just the need to allow individual women to control whether or not they become pregnant. The critique of the narrower term "reproductive rights" was made by feminists of color, poor feminists, and Global South feminists of the emphasis by more privileged feminists on "reproductive choice" and should be recognized as part of the effort to develop a global feminist environmental justice analysis (Silliman and King 1999; Silliman et al. 2004; Smith 2005). Giovanna Di Chiro (2008) argues for a similar perspective, conceptualizing reproduction as necessarily about the intertwined reproduction of the environment, communities, and individuals, which she calls "living environmentalism." Di Chiro shows how women environmental justice activists consistently challenge a division between reproductive issues and environmental issues in their efforts to sustain healthy communities and control the means of social reproduction.

It is important to try to think differently and clearly about these interrelated questions. But how we reproduce—whether we are reproducing people, families, cultures, societies, and/or the planet—is politicized in several layered and contradictory ways. Ironically, given the extreme consequences of certain human models of reproduction for the environment, appeals to the "natural" are one of the standard ways this politicization of reproduction is obscured. And embedded in contemporary appeals to the natural status of reproduction are deep attachments to political positions with serious economic and environmental consequences: to dominance of the Global North over the Global South, to sexism, to heterosexism, and to unfettered exploitation of environmental resources by corporations and social elites. Those attachments need to be brought out and analyzed for us to be able to properly understand and to critically examine present political discourses around reproduction, including those of environmental activists. And yet, gender and sexuality are often ignored as part of explanatory schemes used to analyze contemporary political and economic arrangements.

For example, Thomas Frank, in his book *What's the Matter with Kansas?* perceptively explores the contradiction embedded in the recent right-wing dominance of U.S. politics, examining the reasons far-right conservatives have been able to mobilize lower-income people on their side even though the political and economic policies working-class people are asked to support are contrary to their own class interests (Frank 2004). Though his analysis is insightful in many ways, he still pays little or no attention to the way in which changes in gender roles and reproductive labor have been an essential part of this story. Though Frank does not note this, the wedge issues that he portrays being used to whip up feelings of anger, oppression, and fear among those who support the extreme right wing—abortion, "vulgarity" in popular culture, homosexuality, family values, and so on—are all centrally about beleaguered gender expectations, driven by changes in economic practices in a globalizing economy. Thus, the recent right-wing coalition that has done so much damage to environmental agendas has been deeply driven by issues of gender and sexuality.

In short, the politics of gender are often both the politics of reproduction and the politics of production—the intertwined ways that people produce more people, manage bringing up children, figure out how to do the work at home at the same time as the work that brings in a paycheck, decide how and where to buy food, clothing, shelter, and transportation, take care of elders, and create and maintain all of the social institutions that surround this work. And all of this is central to whether or not our ways of living cause environmental degradation. The politics of reproduction—of people, families, economies, and environments—centers around gendered arrangements of work and sexuality, and recognizing this politics is important in coming up with solutions to social and environmental problems, let alone in resisting manipulative political discourses.

Furthermore, these social arrangements are heteronormative; they are naturalized by assumptions about human relationships—sexual, affective, generational, economic and institutional—that assume as a foundation a particular family form, embedded within a romance plot involving narrow views of male and female attraction, differentiated gender and work roles, and unequal power relations. Yet, we are encouraged to think of these sexual/social arrangements as "only" personal, a matter of individual choice (in the liberal version) or of natural/divine determination (in the conservative version). To the contrary, such a heteronormative, patriarchal foundation is not just about family and personal relationships, but also structures understandings and consent to matters of citizenship, market relations, nationhood, and foreign policy. As Lauren Berlant and Michael Warner have put it:

> Heterosexual culture achieves much of its metacultural intelligibility through the ideologies and institutions of intimacy. . . . First, its conventional spaces presuppose a structural differentiation of "personal life" from work, politics and the public sphere. Second, the normativity of heterosexual culture links intimacy only to the institutions of personal life, making them the privileged institutions of social reproduction, the accumulation and transfer of capital, and self-development. . . . Intimate life is the endlessly cited elsewhere of political public discourse, a promised haven that distracts citizens from the unequal conditions of their political and economic lives, consoles them for the damaged humanity of mass society, and shames them for any divergence between their lives and the intimate sphere that is alleged to be simple personhood. (1998, 553)

Though one could argue that such a use of intimacy to evade the realities of unequal social and economic arrangements could be based on any form of sexual relationship, this argument would miss the way in which present social and economic structures are based on a tight insistence on the connection between normative heterosexuality (in other words, socially sanctioned, limited versions of only some kinds of heterosexual behaviors, intimacies, and relationships) and "acceptable," natural, reproduction.

Heterosexist arguments commonly conceptualize human sexuality as strictly binary (homosexuality vs. heterosexuality; "opposites attract"; "men are from Mars, women are from Venus"), and normative (heterosexuality is assumed to be better—more natural, more moral, more normal, more wholesome, better for parenting children). Such assumptions structure social institutions in such a way that heterosexuality is privileged: not simply heterosexual sexual practices, but dominant notions about what a family should look like; who should do the domestic work; how women and men should look, act, and behave; and how life should be maintained (producing what is called heteronormativity). The assumption that heterosexuality is the only form of sexuality that is biologically reproductive underlies heterosexism and gives it its persuasive force. Normative heterosexuality is seen as natural and therefore right *because* it is a form of sexuality that is reproductive. But more closely examined, this logic is not persuasive; sex is not simply about human reproduction in the sense of having babies. After all, given contemporary reproductive technologies and practices, as well as the fact that sexual desire is far more complex and motivated by far more than the potential for pregnancy, actual heterosexual sex is not so closely connected to reproduction as these arguments about its naturalness want us to believe. Otherwise, no heterosexual would have sex unless s/he intended to conceive a child, and no heterosexual would have any kind of sex other than sex that would produce a child. Rather, these heterosexist arguments are usually about preserving and reproducing particular forms of family, social power, and economic practice.

For example, one could argue that the importance of the "pro-life, pro-family" perspective on reproductive rights issues is not just motivated by a desire to prevent abortions, but is also centrally about the reproduction of a certain historically and culturally specific idealized family form: a father who is the authority; a mother who is the helpmate and chief childcare provider; and several children living in a framework that is Christian, religious, patriarchal, heterosexual, nationalistic, U.S., and nuclear—that is, right-wing. As Roger N. Lancaster argues: "The family is to act as a miniature welfare state, modulating consumption, curbing excess desires, improvising child care, and providing social security—in the absence of a Keynesian or social-democratic regulatory state . . . it is the dreamworld conveyed in the . . . 'serious' media . . . where the conservative variant of the neoliberal utopia is attributed to the biologically fixed 'nature' of desire" (2003, 336).

One of the fears mobilized to support opposition to reproductive rights, emphasized especially in anti-abortion rhetoric, is the fear that allowing women (especially young women) to decide about their own sexuality and pregnancies flies in the face of what are seen as normal, natural relationships of control and decision making underlying what is believed to be a normal, natural family structure (often articulated as a worry about the apparent reduction of "parental rights" or "fathers' rights" entailed in women's access to abortion). This fear also concurrently appeals to an underlying racism and classism that wants to prevent women of color and poor women in particular from having access to choices and support for their own reproductive decisions, and thus forming other kinds of families than the kind imagined to be the model blessed by the (right-wing) Christian God. Thus, a central belief of right-wing Christians (and some other conservative religious perspectives) is that the heterosexual, patriarchal family is divinely created. But there is a close relationship between God and Nature in the logic of this position, because the other foundational assumption is that such a family is also the only normal and natural one. In fact, it is this slide between and among "normal," "natural," and "divine" that allows right-wing Christian arguments to sound persuasive to a broader public that may be less invested in this specific religious-based family structure but that may remain uncritical of such implied connections between this family form and nature (a dynamic clearly in play in the public debate over gay marriage).

What Lancaster (as well as many other feminist and queer theorists commenting on the use of essentialist ideas of nature to legitimate a conservative form of family values) overlooks is that this particular family form, especially when located within a suburban, consumer economy dependent on extremes of global inequality, might be an important origin of our present environmental problems—and also that environmental health is centrally important to reproduction as well as production. When such heteronormative family forms are bound up in environmentally dangerous social and economic practices, we have a situation in which we are promoting environmental damage by naturalizing heteronormative patriarchy, preventing us from imagining and putting in place alternative ways of living more lightly on the earth. In the present U.S. context, the suburban American family that is most frequently portrayed in our popular culture and our political arguments as natural depends on women's unpaid domestic labor, particularly in the areas of childcare and eldercare; the use of nonrenewable fuel-intensive transportation such as cars and long-distance shipping of consumer products; and the promotion of women as "shoppers" who buy all of their food, clothes, and consumer goods in stores that are involved in globalized production and distribution chains dependent on the exploitation of the labor of the poor, often in the Global South, and often women. Painting particular reproductive arrangements as natural in one way or another is an important tool to control political debates about these reproductive and productive arrangements. The burden that is implicitly placed on the Western suburban heteronormative family form to guarantee human survival in the face of environmental degradation of the biosphere is based on a dangerous contradiction. Thus, resisting and/or critically evaluating claims to the natural is an essential method of enabling people to consciously create better, more environmentally sound, and more socially just arrangements of work and life.

This chapter examines the relationship among heterosexist, patriarchal, and colonialist discourses about the family and reproduction, including those found in environmentalist rhetoric. Though I will focus on how discourses of the natural are deployed in popular culture depictions of hetero- and homosexuality, as well as depictions of overpopulation, these cases are only two examples of popular cultural discourses about reproduction that depend on problematic assumptions about what is natural and that can lead us astray in trying to solve political, economic, and environmental problems. The overall point I wish to make is that reproduction is a materialist and a planetary issue—that is, all reproduction comes with consequences for the global environment, economies, and social practices. If we take the term "reproduction" in its broadest sense, what are the socioeconomic and sociopolitical arrangements best suited for successful and sustainable reproduction, on the biological, social, and environmental levels? What happens to our understanding of reproductive politics if we take a wider view, always thinking about the environmental consequences of those social, economic, and political practices we presently engage in? What happens if we refuse to separate human fertility and the fertility of the earth, not by promoting an ancient pagan set of practices and beliefs, but by examining the reciprocal relationship between the reproductive capacities of humans and what gets called "the environment" (i.e., animals, plants, nature)? For instance, what are the reproductive consequences of toxic environments for human mothers and fathers?[1] And how is the effort to find sustainable and just practices of living with planetary implications challenged by the forces of economic globalization, changing gender roles, militarism, natural resource depletion, and environmental pollution? I try to answer partially some of these questions by exploring various stories about reproduction found (or conversely, made invisible) in contemporary popular culture, in an attempt to think about how our accepted ideas about the nature of babies, families, marriage, populations, genes, and parenting intertwine with and influence our understanding of environmental issues, or what might be called planetary reproduction, an approach that could be labeled environmental reproductive justice.

Penguin Family Values: Sexuality in Nature

I'll start with competing popular versions of what might be called "penguin family values," that is, the use of the sexual and mating habits of penguins as tokens in the culture wars over the naturalness of hetero-sexuality or homosexuality. As I mentioned at the start, the 2005 nature documentary, *The March of the Penguins,* drew a surprise fan base: right-wing fundamentalist Christian evangelicals. According to the *New York Times,* some conservative religious ministries encouraged their families to attend *The March of the Penguins* together and to write about their spiritual responses according to prompts provided by their pastor. The conservative film critic and radio host Michael Medved was quoted as say-ing: "[*The March of the Penguins*] passionately affirms traditional norms like monogamy, sacrifice and child rearing. . . . This is the first movie [tra-ditional Christian audiences] have enjoyed since *The Passion of the Christ.* This is *The Passion of the Penguins*" (quoted in J. Miller 2006).

Particularly odd about this promotion of the penguin family as the ideal Christian family was the equal gender division of labor depicted in the film. Though conservative Christians claim traditional family values involve a complementary appreciation of women's work and men's work, each having a valued and necessary place in the family, the patriarchal framework of the husband acting as Christ to the wife as his domestic helpmate belies true equality.[2] Unlike the idealized patriarchal division of labor that fundamentalist Christians espouse, the division of domestic labor by the penguins is not complementary but rather more strictly equal. After the egg is hatched, the male penguin takes care of it by balancing it on his feet, while the female penguin is the first of the pair to make the arduous seventy-mile trek back to the water to get food for the baby chick. When the females return, the males transfer the now-hatched chick to them for care, feeding, and warmth while they make their trek to the ocean in turn. Both leave to forage for food and both care for offspring. This ar-rangement is very unlike the historically specific (beginning in the 1950s) white middle-class suburban division of labor by gender so frequently thought of as "traditional" by U.S. conservatives, in which the man is the breadwinner and the woman the domestic worker. Interestingly, the pen-guin's domestic arrangement is closer to the arrangement required by the transformation of the economy by globalization and modernization in the 1990s, a transformation that has caused real anxiety in the U.S. working and middle classes and prompted a conservative backlash against feminist promotion of domestic and economic equality that conservatives believe is undermining family values (Coontz 1992; May 1988).

One possible way to understand the right-wing Christian fondness for the penguin's arrangement of sharing domestic labor, so unlike what they usually promote, is the effect of the heroic way the males are portrayed, daddies suffering collectively to protect their young against the brutal cold and blinding snowstorms. Clearly, this is how patriarchs should protect their families, with complete commitment and at risk to themselves. The female penguins in the movie, though also sacrificing their health and well-being for their babies, somehow aren't as moving in their long arduous walk as the huddled mass of penguin dads toughing it out together through the Arctic night; neither is the females' equally long wait for the males to return an important part of the narrative. Such a heroic portrayal may also be a way of unconsciously taking out the sting of the material reality that, under the conditions of postindustrial global capitalism, women are often co-breadwinners, and men may have to do more domestic labor to keep the family going. Another aspect that might have been attractive to social conservatives is the way the film closely connects romance (or desire) with the goal of having children and giving birth, avoiding the messy reality of polymorphous human sexuality. In doing so, *The March of the Penguins* is following a standard anthropomorphic script of television nature shows, in which animal mating and reproduction is consistently represented as a metaphor for human heteronormative romance and nuclear families (Mitman 1999; Wilson 1992).

What really made this adoption of penguins as promoters of a moral majority so ironic, however, was the already iconic status of penguins as devoted gay couples and parents. The bonding of same-sex penguin pairs, it turns out, not only is fairly common but was actually enjoying an unprecedented amount of publicity in the two years just before the film arrived. In fact, as several letter writers to the *New York Times* pointed out in their response to the article about penguin conservatism,[3] the disjuncture between these two popularized images of penguins just showed how radically separated from each other are communities of gay people and communities of right-wing religious conservatives: if the Christian fundamentalists had just bothered to Google "gay penguins" or even "penguins," they would have immediately encountered a number of gay penguin sites, including the story of Roy and Silo, the Central Park Zoo gay penguin couple about whom a children's book was written, and the saga of the gay penguin community at a German zoo. They should have been prepared by the popularity of the penguin as a symbolic saboteur of Christian conservatism; if so, they wouldn't have been so surprised and outraged by the liberal tolerant moral of the children's film *Happy Feet* (dir. George Miller, 2006). It's worth taking a little closer look at each of these cultural phenomena to see how discourses of the natural are flexibly used in the culture wars around sexuality.

Roy and Silo were two penguins who lived at the Central Park Zoo, and who were deeply bonded to one another. As is often the case, because penguin genitalia are not obviously sex-differentiated, the keepers did not know that the pair was same-sex until they noticed that an egg was never produced. Upon closer examination (necessitating, most likely, a DNA test to distinguish sex), the keepers discovered that Silo and Roy were both male. Though the couple went through all the usual courting displays, sexual activity, and nest-building behaviors, they were missing an essential element of their reproductive ambitions: an egg. The zookeepers decided to help them out by providing them with another penguin's egg (it's not clear what arrangement was made with the surrogate mother). Roy and Silo successfully raised their egg into a healthy chick, named Tango. The couple and their baby were celebrities in the Central Park Zoo, and became a tourist stop on many gay (and straight) people's visits to New York City. This charming penguin family romance was memorialized in the children's book *And Tango Makes Three* (Parnell and Richardson 2005). The book proposes the moral that all kinds of families, and all kinds of reproductive methods, are equally valuable as long as love, stability, and nurturing are involved. As a back-cover blurb of *And Tango Makes Three* by well-known openly gay actor Harvey Fierstein says: "This wonderful story of devotion is heartwarming proof that Mother Nature knows best." The assertion that love and parenting naturally—indeed, biologically— come in both heterosex and same-sex forms was a moral lesson based on nature that enraged many right-wing religious homophobes. Right-wing religious activists in a number of U.S. communities sought to keep *And Tango Makes Three* out of libraries and schools.[4] Roy and Silo's story and the publication of the book were not just innocent and diversionary stories, but were also cultural tokens of the political contest around gay marriage and gay parental and adoption rights. For human beings, the Central Park penguins were made into a living symbol of the naturalness and success of gay marriage and, depending on one's position in this contest, were celebrated or excoriated by humans as a result.

Of course, *And Tango Makes Three* did not cover the continuing saga of Roy and Silo's relationship. After raising Tango, the couple eventually broke up, and Silo became sexually involved with a female penguin named Scrappy. Some of New York's gay community took it hard that the apparently committed relationship of Silo and Roy was not as solid as they had hoped. Given the powerful legitimating force in the United States of the idea of nature underlying what is acceptable in human behavior, these cultural contests were about serious, material issues, particularly for gay, lesbian, bisexual, and transgendered people's lives. For queer activists involved in struggling against right-wing attacks on their communities and families, the relationship of the gay penguins served as welcome proof of the natural nature of same-sex love, romance, parenting, and domestic stability. In their lives, threatened by heteronormative institutions that, far from protecting their relationships (and the property accumulation and parental obligations stemming from them), were openly hostile to them, the symbol of the gay penguins was not a trivial thing. Presumably, they were therefore relieved when, in another twist of the story, Silo abandoned the female penguin, Scrappy, and returned to Roy. Whether or not Silo was really gay or was instead bisexual might be a matter for human gossip columns (and possible fodder for the complicated debates around bisexual identity and definitions of gayness), but since as far as we can tell, penguin society has little interest in the nuances of sexual identity politics, we can presume that none of the penguins was particularly concerned with the goings-on in the love triangle of Roy, Silo, and Scrappy.

The saga of the German penguins shows similar human political and emotional investments in the durability and naturalness of same-sex penguin pairs. In February 2005, it was announced that of the five pairs of Humboldt penguins at the Bremerhaven Zoo in Bremen, three were same-sex pairs, all males (lesbian penguins, though they exist in nature and in captivity, seem invisible in these stories, perhaps because examining tuxedo-wearing birds who were female would raise questions of cross-dressing that would complicate the morality tales). As in the Central Park story, the Bremerhaven zookeepers noticed the same-sex pairings only because of their lack of reproductive success. Rather than attempt adoption of eggs to realize all zoos' mission of promoting reproduction among their animals, the Bremerhaven strategy was to bring in four female penguins from a Swedish zoo (*Ananova* 2005a). The announcement of this program to introduce "foreign females" to seduce and break up the gay male penguin pairs outraged the German gay community, a community with a history of strong sensitivity to the implication of the extermination of gay people and the prevention of their reproductive capacities. Demonstrations outside the penguin cages against "the organised and forced harassment through female seductresses," to quote one of the German activists, produced a policy reversal on the part of the zoo, which flew the Swedish female penguins home unrequited (*Ananova* 2005b). As Heike Kueke, director of the zoo, said in explaining the policy reversal, "Everyone can live here as they please" (ibid.). Bremerhaven's gay penguins were thus protected from the incursions of heteronormative reproductive agendas, adding along the way a bit of nationalist pride to the underlying symbolism of the naturalness of homosexuality.

Ironically, though both the gay community and the religious right have been invested in the symbolic importance of penguin monogamy and long-term pair bonding, an assumption of the permanence of penguin bonds appears to be problematic in terms of actual penguin behavior. Penguin sexuality, it turns out, is quite variable, with breeding behaviors based on both homosexual and heterosexual pairs, trios, quartets, and single parents. Among all species of penguins, partners frequently break up and choose another mate after a season or two of reproductive pairing, though some, such as the Humboldt penguin, frequently form very long-term, multi-year bonds. Penguin family values may include monogamy, but usually only if it is serial, and it doesn't seem to matter too much to the penguins if it is same-sex or hetero-sex monogamy (Bagemihl 1999).

Arguments from the natural about sexuality, of whatever kind, especially when one uses penguins as one's touchstone, turn out to be pretty slippery (Haraway 1995; see also Alaimo and Bell in this volume). In general, the sexual practices of animals are so variable that little can be proved about human sexuality using animal examples, though it is a common narrative in popular culture. Furthermore, as Roger Lancaster points out, though there might appear to be short-term advantages to arguing that gayness is biological, inherent, and therefore natural and immutable, there are serious dangers in using these arguments. Not only do arguments from nature about sexuality play into the logic of conservative versions of the family as well as biological determinism, but they carry very dangerous possibilities for many people:

> At best, then, the new innatist claims [i.e., that homosexuality is genetically determined] carve out a protected niche for homosexual exceptionalism. At worst, they reify the prevailing logic of heterosexual metaphysics and thus actively contribute to the reproduction of an exclusionary homophobic—and sexist—environment. For gays can only be gay "by nature" in a "nature" that already discloses men and women whose deepest instincts and desires are also different "by nature." In the resulting sexual imaginary, biologically engineered "real" men are always in hot pursuit of "real" women, who always play coy. In such a paradigm, every conventional gender norm, down to the last stereotype, is attributed to a fixed, immutable biology. Men do better at math and science because of that thing in the brain. Women are better at housework and childcare because

of their hormones. Men are aggressive and women are nurturing because we are hunters and gatherers in our heart of hearts. And gay men are gay because they inherited a genetic defect, which caused something to go wrong in that thing in the brain. It's normal. It's natural. It's just the way men are and women are.

Norms reified; men and women trapped in their "natures"; a radical division of gay people from straight people, of queer sex from normal sex, of our experiences from theirs. . . . One scarcely has to imagine extreme scenarios to see that this is not good for gay people. Or for straight people, either. (2003, 280)

Finally, as I have stated before, in both pro-heterosexist and pro-gay cases, arguing for the naturalness and superiority of the U.S. nuclear family form ignores its implications in environmental problems. But this does not prevent penguin family values from playing a role in environmentalist popular culture.

Environmentalist Penguins Fight Back

In fact, if one were worried not about what Emperor penguins might symbolize for human sexual mores, but about the penguins' own reproductive health, one would focus not on their domestic, political, or sexual arrangements, but on the important relationship between their biology and their environment: their adaptation to their particular environmental niche.[5] Emperor penguins are supremely and exactly suited to the particularities of their challenging Antarctic climate, and the method of protecting their eggs and raising their chicks that so thrills both the Christian right and gay penguin supporters is the only way that they have managed to maintain their population and continue their reproductive cycles. Whether this adaptation demonstrates an intelligent design or not could no doubt be a point of debate, depending on whether one admires the amazing feat of the survival of the penguins in such a demanding climate or whether one would want to argue that a truly intelligent designer would have provided a more secure and sensible warm spot for the penguin's egg other than balancing it on two very hard and wobbly feet. Nevertheless, to see the Emperor penguin as just a survivor is to miss a central part of its existence: that it is matched in specific and fairly inflexible ways to its particular environment. The Emperor penguin is not a survivor but an integral element of its environment, existing nowhere else but the Antarctic. This element of integration with and dependence upon environmental particularities is something we are comfortable with when thinking about animals, but not when we are thinking about human societies, because our dominant frameworks see us as separate from and in control of nature.

What focusing narrowly on mating habits as political signifiers misses is the undeniable fact that the penguin's Antarctic environment is rapidly changing because of the warming trend called global climate change. The southern polar ice is melting at a rate faster than at any other time in the geological record. For the Emperor penguin, this means a longer and longer walk to find ice thick enough to support the huddled penguins for the length of time needed for the birth and raising of the penguin offspring. This imminent threat to the existence of the Emperor penguins as a species is the unspoken backdrop to *The March of the Penguins*, as director Luc Jacquet admits. The director and the producers deliberately refrained from mentioning global warming in the movie, as they were worried about giving the movie a "political" message (J. Miller 2006). But they clearly did hope the movie would raise people's consciousness about the beauty and value of the penguins, so that when discussion of their status as a newly endangered species became more well known, people would have sympathy for these special animals and be interested in saving them.

Indeed, the movie does seem to have produced a widespread attachment to the image of the penguin as a symbol of good and beauty, especially when portrayed as under environmental threat. For example, Al Gore's documentary on global warming, *An Inconvenient Truth* (2006), covers the crisis of the melting Antarctic ice at length. Interestingly, though his movie never refers to the Emperor penguins at all (using the more common icon of the polar bear as an endangered animal), those marketing *An Inconvenient Truth* chose an image for an ad in the *New York Times* that could easily have been from *The March of the Penguins*. The ad shows a line of Emperor penguins on their long march, making a clear connection to the other award-winning documentary and counting on the public's affection for the penguins to increase their concern about global climate change. The caption for the ad says, "We're all on thin ice."[6] Another consciousness-raising documentary on global warming, Tom Brokaw's (2006) Discovery Channel documentary *Global Warming: What You Need to Know*, likewise uses images of Antarctic penguins to drive home the danger of the melting polar ice. The good feelings produced by portraying penguins as the ultimate in natural families and moral behavior are manipulated into environmental concerns by stressing the endangered status of the penguins. This also leads to a rise of the use of penguins in advertising of the period. As pointed out in an article in the *New York Times* on the increasing use of penguins in various marketing venues:

> "There's obviously something about these little guys that is leading advertisers to think it says something about us as consumers to associate ourselves with penguins," said Michael Megalli, a partner at Group 1066, a corporate identity consulting company in New York. One theory Mr. Megalli offered is what he called "the Al Gore thing"—that is, "we want to reassure ourselves penguins will have a place in a world with global warming." (Elliot 2007)

Similarly, a 2008 Ad Council promotion for the organization Earth Share shows a family of Emperor penguins (with a large parent watching over three smaller penguins) on a grassy expanse, under the caption: "How can you help protect the prairie and the penguin?" as though penguins and prairies could ever be found in the same place. Once again, penguins are removed from their singular habitat and constructed as a human-like family (Emperor penguins have only one chick at a time) in order to appeal to a desire to protect "the prairies and the penguins and the planet."

This use of penguins as symbols of good family morals endangered by human-caused environmental problems appears again in the movie *Happy Feet* (2006). In this 2006 Academy Award–winning animated children's movie, an Emperor penguin community is held together by their ability and reverence for singing. Each penguin, in an individualistic twist improbable in a species that has almost no visible differentiation (including, as mentioned above, little obvious sexual difference), must find its own "heartsong." The heartsong not only defines each penguin as a singular being but also is essential to enabling the penguin to find his or her one single true love and therefore to breed successfully, another popular cultural version of romanticized monogamous heterosexuality determined by nature. The hero of the film, the boy penguin Mumble, cannot sing, however—though he can dance, an ability that is treated with horror and shame by his parents, peers, and elders. Like homosexuality, his desire to dance not only is different, but threatens to consign him to a life of infertile relationships with other outcasts, because without a heartsong, he will not attract a differently sexed mate. In this case, the outcasts Mumble befriends are another species of penguin, a small band of male Chinstrap penguins he meets. Interestingly enough, the five male Chinstrap penguins are marked by their "Latino" accents, quite different from the dominant "white" accents of Mumble's family (though his father has a "Southern" accent that could be read as "black," his name, Elvis, reassures us that Mumble does not come from an interracial family—his mother, Norma Jean, is clearly meant to be "white"). Though this new interracial family of men takes Mumbles in, their constant jokes about females ease any possible concerns about sexual undercurrents in their robust homo-sociality. Thus, references to homosexuality are frequent in the film, but always flavored with the kind of liberal tolerance covering over ultimate rejection that is a thin veneer for heterosexist anxiety. For example, when the tribal chieftain of the Chinstraps, voiced by Robin Williams, com-mands: "Turn to the penguin next to you, and give him a great big hug," two of the male penguins show a homophobic anxiety meant to be even more humorous because of the "Mexican" accents: "Wha-chu hugging me for?" "He tol me too." "Get away!" "Nah, you liiike it!"

When Mumble's difference is blamed for the decreasing availability of fish that is causing a famine for the Emperor penguin society, he is cast out by the high priests and vows to find the cause of the food scarcity, which turns out to be overharvesting by human fishing corporations. By the end of the movie, Mumble's penguin charm, along with his dancing ability, has mobilized human beings to stop overfishing. His love of his commu-nity, his success in bringing back the fish, and his over-the-top dancing also destroy his community's intolerance of difference. Not incidentally, Mumble ultimately wins over the (female) love of his life and ends up in a happy, heterosexual, and successfully reproductive nuclear family. The reliance on symbols of naturalness to uphold messages of inclusion thus carries significant dangers of assimilation to a norm one might not wish for, particularly in terms of environmental impacts of certain family forms. Queer families turn out to be just the same as straight families. Everyone can dance *and* sing, so there is no reason to question specific family forms. They're determined by nature.

That the resolution of all of Mumble's problems seems to require the restoration of his natural status as the head of a heterosexual family under-mines the message of inclusion around sexuality quite a bit, but this fact didn't prevent Christian conservatives from being outraged at the barely disguised attack of the movie on their positive interpretation of *The March of the Penguins* (Medved 2006). An example of this reaction, from very close to home for me, was an editorial in my local daily, the *Moscow-Pullman Daily News*. The writer, Ed Iverson, railed against *Happy Feet* as "one of the most blatant agenda pieces I have ever had to sit through . . . pure piffle, drivel and swill." He claims that the movie takes direct aim at Christian conservatism and pictures it as responsible for environmental evils as well as racism, sexism, and homophobia: "We know that the culprits [who cause the overfishing] are stand-ins for Western civilization because as hero and friends arrive at the scene of the destruction, the view that leaps onto the screen is a Christian church, cross and graveyard included" (Iverson 2006). Iverson is the librarian for a extremist Christian college called St. Andrews, whose leader is infamous for his stated belief that homosexuality is the cause of AIDS and that American slavery was a Christian system that was benevolent for black people, so one should not be surprised at his elision here between "Western civilization" and far-right Christianity.

But even beyond the extremism of certain very conservative positions such as Medved's and Iverson's, the influences of *The March of the Penguins* and of *Happy Feet* have combined to promote penguins as popular symbols that conflate heterosexist family ideals with the need to resist environmental threats. Cashing in on the popularity and specific connection made between normality, healthy and happy families, and penguins, Roche Pharmaceuticals contracted with the copyright holders of *Happy Feet* to produce an ad campaign. A Roche ad depicting a mother penguin from *Happy Feet* protecting a baby penguin, uses the caption: "It's flu season: protect your family like never before."

There is no question that real, as opposed to symbolic, penguins are in fact endangered by human-caused environmental problems. Penguin reproduction, for individuals and for species, is closely dependent on systems of planetary reproduction, including global climate systems. Currently, those systems are set on a course of rapid warming by the carbon and methane emissions produced by human industrialization, air pollution, and factory farming practices, economic practices not unrelated to the high-consuming, decentralized formation of the U.S. nuclear family structure. Seeing the penguins as representative of natural human family forms, whether hetero- or homosexual, completely misses the actual nature of the penguin's reproductive system, which is interfused with the Antarctic environment. The lesson of the penguins is not a lesson in intelligent design or in patriarchal heroics or in the naturalness of gay marriage; rather, it should be a lesson in the ways in which human social reproduction is interrelated with and dependent upon environments both regional and planetary, and vice versa.

Deconstructing Polar Opposites: Endangered Peoples, Endangered Cultures, Endangered Natures

It is interesting that in the face of this popular cultural emphasis on the negative environmental effects of climate change on animal reproduction and hence survival, there is little mention of *people's* reproduction and survival; where this issue appears, it often only stresses problematic ideas about particular people's supposed over-reproduction. Missing from the popular culture arena, for the most part, is any attention to the immediate threat to numerous groups of people especially vulnerable to climate change by reason of geography, poverty, or political discrimination. The use of a group of people as a symbol of endangered species is uncomfortable for the authors of popular culture (as it should be), partly because it calls up questions of unequal responsibility and unequal consequences that are difficult to deal with in the arena of popular culture as entertainment. Both recent global warming documentaries mentioned above, Gore's and Brokaw's, use images of penguins and polar bears to dramatize the consequences of melting polar ice, but neither mentions the impact of climate change on Arctic indigenous peoples, one of the groups of people already most seriously impacted by climate change. I juxtapose this story with the story of the Emperor penguins with trepidation, since indigenous people are not penguins, and endangered tribal cultures are not endangered species. Seeing indigenous people as endangered species and thus equating them with animals is dangerous because such depictions can be racist.[7] Such a parallel re-enacts the questionable trope of the "disappearing Indian," a dominant narrative that discounts and obscures the struggle of real indigenous peoples to exist and successfully transform their cultures strategically for survival. Arctic indigenous tribes may be threatened by climate change, but they are resilient and experienced in resisting threats to their people. As Chickaloon Grand Chief Gary Harrison says in *Through Arctic Eyes* (2005), a movie documenting the effects of climate change on Arctic indigenous people: "We've adapted in the past, which is why we are still here."

Yet as a story about the environmental politics of reproduction, the ways in which cultural reproduction needs to be valued as much as biological reproduction, the relation of planetary reproduction to human reproduction, and the need to comprehend human beings as embedded in environmental systems on which they are dependent, the experience of the indigenous peoples of the Arctic region needs to be more widely known.[8] As many sources note, because of the rigors of survival in Arctic areas, Arctic native peoples are necessarily close to an environment that is particularly sensitive to the effects of climate change, a region tied to the global ecological system in so many intricate ways that changes in the Arctic have worldwide consequences.

Rather than seeing themselves as an endangered species, vulnerable and helpless, Arctic First Nations have been politically active in publicizing the problem of global climate change and suggesting solutions for many years before other people paid attention to the issue.[9] They have known that the threats they face to their culture and livelihoods are early warnings for the threats people around the world will face. Patricia Cochran, former chairperson of the Inuit Circumpolar Council, points out the worldwide implications of what Arctic First Peoples are experiencing now: "All of this will have a profound impact on the viability of indigenous cultures throughout the North, and further afield. Everything is connected in nature; what happens in Alaska will affect all other places of the world as a cascading effect, as scientists call it, will occur" (Cochran 2007).

I learned something about what the indigenous Arctic peoples are facing during an event sponsored by the Smithsonian in Washington, D.C., in October 2005. As part of a celebration of all things Arctic, which spotlighted its excellent collection of Arctic art and animals and publicized its support of research on the Arctic, the Smithsonian Museum organized a panel primarily of Yu'pik people on the topic of global warming and its effect on their lives and their land. Between the morning and afternoon performances of Native Arctic dancers, who drummed and sang under the watchful eye of the preserved African elephant in the main lobby, an audience gathered in the auditorium to listen to the panel, whose title was based on a indigenous description of the crisis: "The Earth Is Moving Faster Now" (Krupnik and Jolly 2002).

The title referred to the fact that global climate change has had a measurable impact on the lives of these indigenous people for a number of years. Over 8 percent of the sea ice has melted, with severe consequences for marine life, caribou herds (because migration patterns are disrupted), and coastal villages (because sea ice creates a buffer for coastal settlements against large waves). Increased thunderstorms and lightning cause more forest fires. Dangerous levels of UV radiation cause increased incidence of skin cancer and damage to eyesight. Ecological stress and disruption to traditional plant and animal food sources force a turn to a diet of store-bought foods that cause diabetes (Krupnik and Jolly 2002; Mercredi 2005).

On the Smithsonian panel, Cristina Alava, a Yu'pik elder and teacher, spoke about the difficulty of bringing back edible meat from long distance hunting trips if the weather continued to warm. As the permafrost melts earlier and freezes later, it becomes very difficult to transport meat over the softened tundra and to keep the large carcasses cold enough so they don't rot before getting to the hunters' families. Orville Huntington, an

Athabascan employee of the U.S. Fish and Wildlife Service, showed slides of the ice retreating and talked about the "silence of the moose" in the region, as their seasonal travels are disrupted by the changing climate. Huntington emphasized the depth and complexity of indigenous knowledge about the area, and the possibility of losing this knowledge along with the animals and the ice. Harry Brower Jr., a indigenous whaler, scientist, and subsistence hunter, also spoke about the ways in which subsistence living is part of cultural survival and an important method for keeping the world in balance. Other panelists echoed this theme, describing the Yu'pik understanding of the way in which the environment is part of a larger universe with moral and cultural aspects that are maintained by the practices of indigenous peoples who have lived on the land for thousands of years.

One of the striking aspects of the discourse of the panelists was their insistence on speaking as knowledgeable experts based on their own cultural expertise, their beliefs and experience as indigenous people, even when they mentioned along the way that some of them had degrees in biology and wildlife management and/or worked in the fields of education and literacy. It was crucially important for them to try to get across to the audience that their knowledge arose from their way of life, which similarly was embedded in the environment, and that this interdependence of cultural identity, expert knowledge, land, and animal existence was at the brink of extermination from global warming. In contrast, the white scientists who introduced and commented on the panel consistently referred to the indigenous panelists as community members and artisans, rather than scientists and researchers, undercutting their status as experts. The point the indigenous panelists were making, however, was that the extensive knowledge they had about sustainable practices, whether it was supported by scientific expertise or traditional experience, was knowledge that arose from a particular way of life, one that needed to be respected and maintained. It was not knowledge gained from the mystical identity of being Ecological Indians, but was rather sophisticated information needed now by all those, indigenous or not, trying to understand and redress climate change. In contrast, the panelists implied, an industrialized and consumer economy's dependencies on nonrenewable fuels, emission-producing technologies, mobility, and manufactured goods were not just unsustainable, but gave those who lived in these ways false understandings of the way material, life-sustaining practices worked. Material practices of reproduction and production have epistemological implications; that is, they affect what we know and how we know it. We are all, like the penguins, suited or not suited to particular ecological contexts, and living without respect for those contexts has consequences. Worse, from the perspective of the indigenous panelists, global capitalist industrialized ways of living and (not) knowing threaten the existing knowledge base needed to live in sustainable ways, not least because the cultural existence of indigenous people is threatened.

The worst example of white condescension and willful misapprehension of the point being made by these indigenous experts was the introduction to the event by a retired white Alaskan politician. While acknowledging the likelihood that indigenous Arctic cultures are being irreversibly changed by global climate change, he referred admiringly to the idea that an ice sculpture is made more beautiful because it is transient and proudly pointed out that the state of Alaska had made computers available to tribal villages in order to allow native artisans to more effectively sell their crafts in a global economy. From his point of view, this was a sufficient way to preserve Native Alaskan culture in the face of what he clearly accepted as the inevitable "transience" of their existence and their way of life due to global climate change and the requirements of a global economy.

Randel Hansen (2005) calls this situation the "ethnocide via climate change of Arctic indigenous communities." How do we think about this situation as these processes accelerate so that, within a generation, these indigenous communities may not survive? Is this natural? What kind of environmental politics can encompass the threat to both Emperor penguins and Alaskan Natives from global climate change? The disjuncture between the politics of species preservation and the politics of environmental justice presents a barrier to thinking through the relation between these looming disasters. For instance, in *An Inconvenient Truth,* there is a lengthy discussion of the consequences of the melting of the northern and southern polar ice. There is no mention at all of the consequences of this drastic change on Arctic indigenous peoples. Instead, there is a wrenching depiction of an animated polar bear trying unsuccessfully to get onto a melting ice floe in a vast, iceless sea. Yet the ecologies of the polar bear and of the Arctic indigenous peoples are interrelated, and surely both are worth concern and intervention. They are also ecologies interrelated with industrialized ecologies. The reproduction of industrialized economic systems, particular by the United States and other Western countries, has consequences for planetary ecological workings on a global scale as well as on the scale of communities, families, and species, determining the ability of animals, families, and cultures to reproduce in healthy and sustainable ways.

In a point relevant to my earlier discussion of the penguins, we should understand family structure in these indigenous communities as arising from interrelationships among animals, land, and economic practices. Family does not float free in nuclear groupings of two adults (heterosexual or not) and two children, independent of the consequences of their material practices, whether they are industrialized or hunter-gatherers. The idea that families either are separate from or purely reflect a romanticized or anthropomorphized nature is an illusion, whether they are Western or indigenous or any other kind of family. So the point is not that we all have to or should replicate the family structures of Arctic indigenous peoples (which are varied), but we might try, as environmentalists, feminists, and gay activists, to be cognizant of the material interrelationships produced by particular familial forms so that we can choose responsible ways of living, producing, consuming, and reproducing on our planet. Romanticizing indigenous people, or ignoring the technological and ecological underpinnings of all ways of living, are different forms of racism, both of which can make ecological ethnocide invisible.

Too Many People, Too Few Penguins

The silence around issues of environmental reproductive justice and the preference for an environmentalism that values "pure" nature is apparent throughout Gore's film, especially in its reliance on the moribund politics of overpopulation. Though Gore does point out that the industrialized Western economies, particularly the United States, are the biggest culprits in terms of harmful greenhouse gas emissions, his narrative proceeds for the most part as though all U.S. citizens are equally responsible as individuals for problematic ways of using fossil fuels. He does mention the support by Exxon Mobil for the disinformation campaign that has undermined scientific warnings about the dangers of global warming, but Gore's is a very mild version of an environmental justice analysis that would stress the ways in which social inequalities and corporate domination of political processes, rather than separate individual consumer decisions (less about choice than people believe, as they operate within complex economic systems), are driving the creation and maintenance of environmental problems.

Instead, Gore's scariest and most visually arresting image of the cause of global warming is a steeply rising population curve, the one slide of his slideshow that requires him to mount a moving vertical platform to follow its rapid and inexorable growth. Slides depicting the disasters already caused by global warming show black people devastated by Hurricane Katrina and brown people fleeing flooding caused by monsoons. Thus, the reproduction of the planet is presented as most threatened by the reproduction of people, especially particular people of color, those that are overpopulating the planet. In most popular discussions of the causes of increasing global warming, those in the Global South (who have yet to industrialize) are the ones portrayed as likely to push us over the brink. China, in particular, is often held out as a threat to reining in global climate change, as it is the largest Global South country to industrialize, and is beginning voraciously to use the oil, gas, and coal technologies that produce most greenhouse emissions. The Gore film is careful not to demonize the Chinese, but to show them as struggling with the implications of their growing dependence on nonrenewable fuels, which is indeed consequential for stopping global warming. For instance, he points out that the Chinese have better automobile emission standards than does the United States. But because of the context he offers, the Chinese are still presented as the symbol of the upcoming threat presented by the combination of overpopulation and increasing industrial emissions. Ironically, this overpopulation is presented as natural, and no explanations are offered for it. No recognition is made of the possibility that the Chinese, and other so-called developing countries, may be able to choose different patterns of consumption, different family forms, support for the empowerment of women that is the only reliable way to control birth rates, and different ways of production that are environmentally sound, and that do not fit the pattern of a natural evolution toward an industrialized consumer economy, presented as progress.

Gore's film, with its relative sensitivity to the possibility of demonizing Global South peoples and its recognition of the responsibility of the United States and the role of corporate greed, is one of the better examples of mainstream environmentalism's approach to the topic of overpopulation. But its reliance on this trope as part of the explanation unfortunately legitimates other, less sensitive or outright racist versions of environmentalist arguments about overpopulation. As the Committee on Women, Population, and the Environment notes, since the early 1990s a disturbing political climate has developed in which older population-control rhetoric, undermined in its effectiveness by international women's and anti-racist movements, has been revived under the rubric of "environment and security," a paradigm in which intra- and interstate conflict is explained by overpopulation producing "resource scarcity" and environmental degradation (Gosine 2005; Silliman and King 1999).

This trend is borne out by examples such as Gore's film, in which human reproduction (especially that of the poor, immigrants, and people in the Global South), is depicted as a major environmental problem, as in those environmentalist arguments that overpopulation is a serious threat to the earth, such that some environmentalists argue against having children at all. In most popular culture versions of this argument, the reproduction of the "Others'" (i.e., people in the Global South's) population is portrayed as the central problem, both environmentally (especially in terms of energy use) and socially (because of the struggles in the Global South with AIDS, armed conflict, poverty, and famine). The reproduction of "our" (developed industrial societies) population, however, despite the vastly greater amount of resources consumed, the reliance of the economy on the exploitation of Global South resources and labor, and the political domination of other countries by the Global North, is made invisible by this way of thinking about the problem of overpopulation, especially when coupled with the promotion of the suburban nuclear family in environmentalist popular culture.

For example, a former board member of the Sierra Club, John Tanton, has since the 1970s built a set of anti-immigration organizations (including founding the Federation for American Immigration Reform) that are virulently racist at the same time as they support organizations (such as Population-Environment Balance) that claim that immigrants and overpopulation are the source of environmental problems. In the environmentalist discourse blaming overpopulation for environmental problems, the reproductive capacities of poor brown women are portrayed both as natural, in the sense of uncontrollable and inevitable, and as unnatural, in the sense of damaging the health of the environment. In some of this discourse, through a perverse kind of putative feminism, one of the qualities that constitute these families' backwardness is the assumption that they are patriarchal structures that restrict women's rights and prevent women from engaging in family planning that would bring down their birth rates. Though patriarchal power within families may indeed prevent women from controlling their own reproductive capacities, this analysis ignores international family planning policies such as imposed by the United States until very recently that insisted on prioritizing abstinence-only programs rather than birth control, and that did not provide educational, health, political, and legal support for women when they did become pregnant.

Once again, we return to the question of just what kind of family forms, embedded in what kind of power relations and economic processes, are best for the interrelated survival of people, animals, and the planet. The discourse of overpopulation presents as problematic large extended families, primarily agricultural, often depicted as "pre-modern" and patriarchal, without critically analyzing the global regimes that produce poverty, encourage large families, impose moralistic and impractical sexual attitudes such as abstinence, and prevent women from gaining political rights and independence. When these global regimes also are primarily responsible for climate change that results in drought, desertification, and crop failure, not to mention the militarism and conflict that produce internal displacement and destroy ecologies, it is outrageous to portray overpopulation in the Global South as the main cause of environmental problems. Gosine argues, after rehearsing the long history of a connection between environmentalist emphasis on overpopulation and racist attitudes toward nonwhite and Global South peoples:

> When environmentalists sound warnings about overpopulation, they are usually expressing fears over the reproduction of (poor) nonwhite people, not of white people, whose populations in all Western countries are in decline (but whose consumption habits generally are not). Calls for educational fixes to inform "populations" about why they should want to bear fewer children advance an imperialist cultural agenda that demands that nonwhite people adopt the cultural, social and economic practices and systems of organization dominant in Western countries (e.g., the prototypical nuclear family), while blaming the foolishness of Third World men and women (since the solution is Western education) for environmental degradation. (2005, 80–81)

Environmental Justice Family Values

Given the issues I have raised about discourses about overpopulation, about the use of penguins to symbolize environmentalist and family values simultaneously, and about narratives that make invisible the plight of Arctic native peoples, what kind of rhetoric should environmentalists use to bring people to their side? One thing they probably should not do is depict environmentalism as a heteronormative family romance. Such rhetoric obscures the need to put pressure on corporations to change their labor practices—including health care, childcare, pay equity, and global labor practices (all, I would argue, important to real family values)—

as part of an environmentalist agenda. In sidestepping these issues, the environmentalist family romance runs the risk of undermining people's willingness to recognize the ways in which families built on Global North consumerism may need to change their understandings of their relationship with the natural world, and thus their practices of living and working, a critical stance that also requires challenging heterosexist norms. Examples of these family romance plots abound, from both corporate and environmentalist sources. From the corporate angle, for instance, a 2007 television ad by Phillips for its energy-saving light bulb "Ecotone" shows a baby on a melting ice floe in the midst of giant threatening icebergs; as the camera zooms in on the baby's frightened eye, the eye becomes the light bulb, and the baby is miraculously transported to the safety of mother's backpack and father's protection as the white nuclear family strolls through a park.

An environmentalist example is a 2006 ad for the Sea World/Busch Gardens Conservation Fund, which brings together many of the motifs discussed in this essay. Starting with the sun rising on a wild world, followed by wildebeests and gazelles gamboling in herds, the ad first focuses on two lion cubs. "Sisters," the caption pronounces, as we sigh in appreciation of the cute and cuddly cubs. Then we are shown dolphins playing in the sea, leaping above the ocean. "Cousins," says the ad. A frilled lizard, its distinctive bonnet-like membrane spread widely, rushes toward the camera with comical aggression. "Little Brother," says the ad (assuming that we know that all little brothers are adorable brats). Next we see two bighorn rams, colliding in fierce challenge. "In-Laws," says the caption, naturalizing the clichéd sitcom plot of fighting in-laws. A Chinstrap penguin appears, a baby bird protected on its feet. "Father," says the ad, proving that once again, as *The March of the Penguins* shows, those penguins are really great dads. Then the camera pans rapidly outward from the Antarctic continent, like reversing Google Earth, pulling far enough out to see Earth seen from space.[10] "Mother Earth," says the caption, making a common and problematic move that results in the feminization of the planet. "We all belong to the same family," says the penultimate frame of the ad, and while the caption is replaced by the mission of the Conservation Fund ("Research, Protection, Rehabilitation, Education"), the earth floats beautifully in space, magically free of all the conflict, power, inequality, and policy failure that actually undermine effective environmentalism. The ad closes on a picture of a mountain lake, with the Sea World/Busch Gardens Conservation

Fund logo superimposed on it, and the caption "Conservation: It's in our nature."

Do we really all "belong to the same family"? Is conservation "in our nature"? What does this mean for understanding our environmental problems? What kind of family is environmentally sustainable, and how can we encourage such considerations? If corporations such as Roche and Phillips and environmentalists such as the Conservation Fund use the same narrative frames and images of nature that legitimate heterosexist, white, middle-class nuclear families, how will we develop a useful critique of that family form's complicity in environmental problems? If the family we think of as natural and normal is white, Western, heterosexual, and middle-class, how will we raise consciousness and concern about indigenous and Global South families, many of which suffer more severely from environmental problems today? The rhetoric of penguin family values limits us to the same ideas of what is natural that are promoted by those institutions and corporations that cause environmental destruction. To value nature and to correct social inequalities, we might want to shake off these normative ideas about nature, to see it as more dynamic, more interrelated with human practices, more agentive, and more complicated than we can if we rely solely on these dominant stories about nature. Haraway's term "naturecultures" is designed for just this kind of conceptual understanding of the relation between nature and culture, nature and human, human and animal, and human and machine (Haraway 2004).

The importance of seeing reproduction in a planetary environmental justice context involves conceptualizing reproduction as an environmental issue that crucially rests on realities of human nature in ways not usually entertained. For example, one essential aspect of human nature that we need to recognize and seriously consider, in my view, is our ability to change our biology, to construct terrestrial environments, and to collectively choose (hopefully, not coercively impose) what kind of social arrangements are most productive, sustainable, and pleasurable. To me, the most important characteristic of human nature is this ability to change and control one's environment, precisely *not* to be determined by one's biology or one's genes (or one's deity, but that is perhaps another matter). Recognizing this natural human capacity, I propose, is the only perspective that is the responsible one, for it requires us to be accountable for the societies we support, the lives we live, the resources we use. If we recognize this characteristic as one essential aspect of being a biological human, it does not follow that humans are therefore in control of every aspect of the world, however, or have a right to construct whatever environments we choose (Bird 1987, Cuomo 1997, Merchant 2004, Warren 2000). We are not outside the earth looking down upon it. Instead, we are inside specific biosystems and complex relationships with other biological entities; we impact and are impacted by the interrelationships of those entities. Responsibility to these ecological niches, networks, and dynamics can be brought into view only if we understand ourselves as animals among other animals, with varied sexualities, complicated family relationships, complex political systems, and multiple desires. Perhaps we are peculiar animals with astounding abilities, but we are still part of an interconnected world and thus answerable to it.

NOTES

This chapter was written for this anthology prior to its publication in Sturgeon, *Environmentalism in Popular Culture: Gender, Race, Sexuality, and the Politics of the Natural* (2009), in which it appears, with slight differences, as chapter 5. Thanks to the University of Arizona Press for permission to include it here. And heartfelt thanks to all the participants in the Queer Ecologies workshop for their excellent feedback (fairy penguins unite!), with special appreciation to Cate Mortimer-Sandilands and Bruce Erickson for their support. Thanks also to Nishant Shahani for his insightful suggestions, and to Hart Sturgeon-Reed for his technical assistance with retrieving and capturing photos, films, and ads, and for his T-shirt's motto, "One by one, the penguins steal my sanity."

1. Though I won't concentrate on these discourses here, outside of the Christian right, many writers, bloggers, TV commentators, and movie scriptwriters portray human reproduction as determined by genetic forces beyond our control, a kind of discourse that often results in rationalizing sexist practices claimed to be underlying unfair economic competition, masculinist violence, social inequality, heterosexist dominance, and/or military conflicts. Too frequently, portraying genetics as a determining aspect of people's lives becomes an unthinking way of justifying unequal social arrangements as natural and inevitable. For example, popular genetic science discourse is frequently resorted to in a superficial way in order to claim that competition and violence are the driving forces behind reproductive success. The human male's drive to spread his genes, to dominate a given territory, and to successfully reproduce is depicted as a natural imperative; thus it might seem normal and inevitable that men would be more adulterous, less willing to take on domestic chores (sometimes articulated as a resistance to "commitment"), or comfortable with sexually exploitative attitudes toward women. Furthermore, links between these supposed evolutionary instincts and the reoccurrence of complicated social phenomena such as wars, economic colonialism, and male supremacy are assumed in the popular sphere to be obvious and thus phenomena that are impossible to eradicate. In actual scientific discourse, whether or not there are causal relationships between individual social behaviors and genetic makeup, let alone causal relationships between complex forms

of collective action and genetic factors, is intensely debated and deeply contested; any such claims by responsible scientists tend to be narrowly applied. Yet this scientific caution does not stop various agents of popular culture from presenting stories of genetic determinism as scientific truths.

2. For an example of how fundamentalist Christians describe the proper relationship between husband and wife, see ChristianAnswers.net 2006.

3. See letters by Michael Shober, Gitta Zomorodi, and Rick White, in "About That March" in the Science Times letters section of the *New York Times*, Tuesday, September 20, 2005, D4.

4. Attempts either to remove *And Tango Makes Three* from libraries or to move it from children's fiction to areas of the libraries less likely for children to go to on their own were made in Illinois, Missouri, Georgia, Tennessee, North Carolina, Iowa, and Wisconsin. See Huh 2006.

5. In an article by Hillary Mayell (2005), several scientists point out the ways in which anthropomorphizing penguin mating and sexual behavior as love produces misleading understandings of penguin behavior. But, as marine biologist Gerald Kooyman states in this article: "Simplifying some aspects of the penguins' life story makes it more accessible to the general public." What I would point out is that this particular form of heteronormative romanticizing is not just simplifying, but conveys a heteronormative ideology.

6. Ad for *An Inconvenient Truth,* in the *New York Times,* Saturday, June 17, 2006, A23.

7. For an important discussion of the racist and heterosexist implications of the use of the concept of species, see McWhorter's chapter in this volume.

8. The main groups of Alaskan aboriginal peoples are Athabascan, Aleut, Alutiiq, Tlingit/Haida, Inupiaq, and Yup'ik. Athabascans live in the central-eastern part of Alaska. The Aleut (not their name but the Russian label for the people) and the Alutiiq live along the Aleutian Archipelago to the southwest. The closely related Haida and Tlingit nations live in southeasteran Alaska, southwestern Yukon, and northwestern British Columbia. The Inupiaq live in the northern Alaskan interior and the Seward Peninsula. The Yu'pik, or Yupiit, live in western Alaska, along the Bering Sea Coast and inland, as well as on St. Lawrence Island, which is forty miles from the Siberian Coast, home to the Siberian Yu'pik in what is now Russia. Other Arctic First Peoples include the Sami, indigenous to what is now Scandinavia and Greenland (who also have an immigrant presence in the Alaskan area, along with their reindeer), the Canadian Inuit, the Inuvialit of western Canada, and the Kalaaiit, or Greenlanders. Reliant on fishing and hunting, particularly of caribou, elk, moose, whale, and seal, Arctic indigenous peoples have histories of living off their land extending at least as far back as 400 BC. Extensive knowledge of animal behavior and weather patterns were essential to their survival for this long period of time (Chaussonet 1995).

9. Because of the transnational context of their tribal lands, Arctic indigenous political activism spans a number of national locations and has been present in the international arena for some time. See the work of the Inuit Circumpolar Conference (www.inuitcircumpolar.com) and the Circumpolar Conservation Union (www.circumpolar.org). In December 2005, the Inuit Circumpolar Conference submitted a petition to the Inter-American Human Rights Commission saying that the United States was denying the Arctic indigenous peoples their human rights by refusing to halt greenhouse gas emissions (Crowley and Fenge 2005). The petition was denied.

10. For a discussion of the problems with the environmentalist use of the earth-seen-from-space image, see Garb (1990) and Sturgeon (2009).

REFERENCES

Ananova. 2005a. Zoo Tempts Penguins to Go Straight. http://www.ananova.com/news/story/sm_1275591.html.

———. 2005b. Penguins Can Stay Gay. http://www.ananova.com/news/story/sm_1284769.html.

Bagemihl, Bruce. 1999. *Biological Exuberance: Animal Homosexuality and Natural Diversity.* New York: St. Martin's Press.

Berlant, Lauren. 1997. *The Queen of America Goes to Washington City.* Durham, N.C.: Duke University Press.

Berlant, Lauren, and Michael Warner. 1998. Sex in Public. *Critical Inquiry* 24: 547–66.

Bird, Elizabeth. 1987. The Social Construction of Nature: Theoretical Approaches to the History of Environmental Problems. *Environmental Review* 11.4: 255–64.

Brokaw, Tom, dir. 2006. *Global Warming: What You Need to Know.* Discovery Channel. (Aired July 16, 9:00 PM).

Chaussonet, Valerie. 1995. *Crossroads Alaska.* Washington, D.C.: Arctic Studies Center, Smithsonian.

ChristianAnswers.net. 2006. Should Christians Support Women's Liberation Movements? http://www.christiananswers.net/q-eden/edn-f003.htm106.

Cochran, Patricia. 2007. Arctic Natives Left Out in the Cold. *BBC News,* January 4. http://news.bbc.co.uk/2/hi/science/nature/6230731.stm.

Colborn, Theo, Dianne Dumanoski, and John Peterson Myers. 1997. *Our Stolen Future: Are We Threatening our Fertility, Intelligence and Survival?* New York: Plume A Penguin Group.

Coontz, Stephanie. 1992. *The Way We Never Were: American Families and the Nostalgia Trap.* New York: Basic Books.

Crowley, Paul, and Terry Fenge. 2005. Inuit Petition Inter-American Commission on Human Rights to Oppose Climate Change Caused by the United States of America. *Inuit Circumpolar Council.* http://www.inuitcircumpolar.com/index.php?ID=316&Lang=En.

Cuomo, Christine. 1998. *Feminism and Ecological Communities: An Ethic of Flourishing.* New York: Routledge.

Di Chiro, Giovanna. 2008. Living Environmentalisms: Coalition Politics, Social Reproduction, and Environmental Justice. *Environmental Politics* 17.2: 276–98.

Edelman, Lee. 2004. *No Future: Queer Theory and the Death Drive.* Durham, N.C.: Duke University Press.

Elliot, Stuart 2007. A Procession of Penguins Arrives on Madison Avenue. *New York Times,* January 10. http://www.nytimes.com/2007/01/10/business/media/10adco.html?ex=1184043600&en=efcbe26c4bea35f0&ei=5087&mkt=bizphoto.

Frank, Thomas. 2004. *What's the Matter with Kansas?* New York: Henry Holt.

Garb, Yaakov. 1990. Perspective or Escape? Ecofeminist Musings on Contemporary Earth Imagery. In *Reweaving the World: The Emergence of Ecofeminism,* ed. Irene Diamond and Gloria Feman Orenstein, 264–78. San Francisco: Sierra Club Books.

Gosine, Andil. 2005. Dying Planet, Deadly People: "Race"-Sex Anxieties and Alternative Globalizations. *Social Justice* 32.4: 69–86.

Guggenheim, Davis, dir. 2006. Motion picture. *An Inconvenient Truth.* Lawrence Bender Productions.

Hansen, Randel. 2005. The Future is Now: Arcs of Globalization, Indigenous Communities, and Climate Change. Paper Presented at the Annual Meeting of the American Studies Association, November 4–7, Washington, D.C.

Haraway, Donna. 1995. Otherworldly Conversations, Terran Topics, Local Terms. In *Biopolitics: A Feminist and Ecological Reader on Biotechnology*, ed. Vandana Shiva and Ingunn Moser, 62–92. London: Zed Books.

———. 2004. Cyborgs to Companion Species: Reconfiguring Kinship in Technoscience. In *The Haraway Reader*, 298–320. New York: Routledge.

Huh, Nam Y. 2006. Schools Chief Bans Book on Penguins. *Boston Globe*, December 20. http://www.boston.com/news/nation/articles/2006/12/20/ schools_chief _bans_book_on_penguins.

Iverson, Ed. 2006. Opinion. *Moscow-Pullman Daily News*, December 2–3, Weekend Edition, 7D.

Jacquet, Luc, dir. 2005. Motion picture. *The March of the Penguins*. Bonne Pioche Productions.

Krupnik, Igor, and Dyanna Jolly, eds. 2002. *The Earth is Faster Now: Indigenous Observations of Arctic Environmental Change*. Washington, D.C.: Arctic Research Consortium of the United States.

Lancaster, Roger N. 2003. *The Trouble with Nature: Sex in Science and Popular Culture*. Berkeley: University of California Press.

May, Elaine Tyler. 1988. *Homeward Bound: American Families in the Cold War Era*. New York: Basic Books.

Mayell, Hillary. 2005. *March of the Penguins*: Too Lovey-dovey to be True? *National Geographic News*, August 19. http://news.nationalgeographic.com/ news/2005/08/ 0819_050819_march_penguins.html.

Medved, Michael. 2006. Don't be Misled by Crappy Feet! *The Michael Medved Show, Townhall.com*, November 17. http://michaelmedved.townhall.com/blog/ g/5094f586-fed7-4cf4-872c-d20b94c78024.

Merchant, Carolyn. 2004. *Reinventing Eden: The Fate of Nature in Western Culture*. New York: Routledge.

Mercredi, Tookie, dir. 2005. Motion picture. *Through Arctic Eyes: Athabascan Observations on Climate Change*. Arctic Athabascan Council.

Miller, George, dir. 2006. Motion picture. *Happy Feet*. Kingdom Feature Productions.

Miller, Jonathan. 2006. March of the Conservatives: Penguin Film as Political Fodder. *New York Times*, September 13, D2

Mitman, Gregg. 1999. *Reel Nature: America's Romance with Wildlife on Film*. Cambridge, Mass.: Harvard University Press.

Parnell, Peter, and Justin Richardson. 2005. *And Tango Makes Three*. New York: Simon and Schuster Children's Publishing.

Silliman, Jael, and Ynestra King, eds. 1999. *Dangerous Intersections: Feminist Perspectives on Population, Environment, and Development*. Boston, Mass.: South End Press.

Silliman, Jael, et al. 2004. *Undivided Rights: Women of Color Organize for Reproductive Justice*. Boston, Mass.: South End Press.

Smith, Andrea. 2005. *Conquest: Sexual Violence and American Indian Genocide*. Boston, Mass.: South End Press.

SPLC. 2002. The Puppeteer. *Intelligence Report*. Southern Poverty Law Center, Summer. http://www.splcenter.org/intel/intelreport/article.jsp?pid=180.

Sturgeon, Noël. 1994. The Power is Yours, Planeteers! Race, Gender, and Sexuality in Children's Environmental Popular Culture. In *New Perspectives on Environmental Justice: Gender, Sexuality and Activism*, ed. Rachel Stein, 262–76. New Brunswick, N.J.: Rutgers University Press.

——. 2009. *Environmentalism in Popular Culture: Gender, Race, Sexuality, and the Politics of the Natural.* Tucson: University of Arizona Press.

Warren, Karen J. (2000). *Ecofeminist Philosophy: A Western Perspective on What It Is and Why It Matters.* Oxford, U.K.: Rowman & Littlefield.

Wilson, Alexander. 1992. *The Culture of Nature: North American Landscape from Disney to the Exxon Valdez.* Cambridge, Mass.: Blackwell.

CHAPTER 4

Queernaturecultures

DAVID BELL

In this chapter, I want to think about what Jeffrey Weeks (1991, 86) calls "the nature of our sexual natures" by considering three particular articulations of the nature of sex and the sex of nature: eco-porn, queer animals, and naturism. In so doing, my aim is to use these lenses to think through the broader articulations of sex and nature, or "nature loving," that the chosen examples simultaneously reaffirm and unsettle, drawing on Donna Haraway's (2003) discussion of "naturecultures"—of the impossibility of uncoupling "nature" from "culture," and of the need to find new ways to think about and talk about the multiple and heterogeneous associations and "queer confederacies" that are produced here through attempts to lay claim on nature as an uncontestable realm of sexual truth.

In so doing, my aim is to make a modest contribution to the interdisciplinary endeavor that as yet bears no coherent name, but that is captured in this book's title, and others such as Giffney and Hird's (2008) *Queering the Non/Human*. This work marks an important intervention in queer theory, science studies, environmentalism, philosophy, and ethics and, as Giffney and Hird note, brings together the humanities, social sciences, and natural sciences. Now, this is going to always be an uneasy coming-together, since the intellectual heritages of these different sites of knowledge production have shown increasing differentiation from each other. I should know: I work in a school of geography, where my natural science colleagues would largely scoff at the notion of queer ecologies while working hard on projects concerned with ecological science. It frequently seems to me that the traffic between these disciplines could be a lot more vigorous, and I hope that this chapter, like others in the book, is suggestive of the productive potential for thinking a subject like nature in as many different ways as possible. In what follows, I will discuss my three chosen sites for such nature-talk, and then stitch together some common threads in a discussion.

Welcome, Nature Lover!

In July 2004, at an outdoor music festival in Kristiansand, Norway, Leona Johansson and Tommy Hol Ellingsen appeared on stage with a band called The Cumshots. After delivering a short speech about the destruction of the rainforest, the couple stripped and had sex on stage while the band played on. Arrested and charged with public nudity and indecent behavior, the pair relocated to Berlin, Germany, rather than face jail. From there they continue their project of connecting sex and nature.

Ellingsen and Johansson run and front a not-for-profit organization called Fuck For Forests (FFF), which stages public sex acts that are photographed or videoed and then shown via their subscription website in exchange for donations to ecological projects.[1] Through this site, FFF articulates an explicit link between sex politics and ecopolitics:

> Our goal is to save nature, but it is also important to show the beauty of natural sex and sexuality. We believe that through a better relationship to our spiritual and sexual body, we can change the reality around us. . . . We believe that humanity's bad relationship to sexuality has a lot in common with the destroying of nature. Sexuality is a beautiful part of nature. . . . Sexuality and nature is [sic] connected. We are basically here because of sex. But open sexuality is often looked down upon as something dirty and strange. We felt sexuality was treated like nature, with disrespect. So why not use pure, open-minded sexuality to put focus on this unnatural way of treating this planet? (FFF 2007)

FFF's embodied ecopolitics is thus aligned with earlier political uses of sexed bodies, where the supposed naturalness of sex provides a platform for nature-centered activism—the utopian pastoralism evoked in Walt Whitman and lived out by Edward Carpenter, lesbian separatist communes, and radical faeries, stretching ambivalently up to *Brokeback Mountain* and to practices such as dogging (Bell 2006a, Herring 2006, Shuttleton 2000). The staging of nature-loving through sex acts framed in "natural settings" by FFF at once repoliticizes public sex and also renaturalizes it through fucking *in* as well as *for* forests. In choosing natural settings, then, FFF also connects to cultures of public sex in "the wild," where the setting confirms the naturalness of sex but also the publicness of nature. There are two key variants of this equation: (1) those in which nature itself is "the public," the approving wilderness that affirms sex acts considered taboo by human society, whose prying eyes and laws cannot reach into the wild (I will return to ideas of a more-than-human public later; see also Fone 1983); and (2) as in the case of FFF, a political publicness that needs human eyes and laws in order to make its point. Here is a scene from the FFF site, described by San Francisco online journalist Gregory Dicum:

> Tommy and Leona are having sex on a tree stump in the middle of a Norwegian clear-cut. . . . A few minutes earlier, Leona and Tommy stood at the same spot lecturing about the evils of industrial forestry. But now they're moaning in feral ecstasy, overcoming the powerful negativity of the place—the broken branches and dried-out logs—with the juices of the life force itself. (Dicum 2005)

As FFF's website says, the group don't consider itself exhibitionist, though "it is possible to experience quite exciting moments with public sex if you know somebody is watching." Of course, in another sense FFF depends entirely on people watching: its fund-raising comes from subscribers paying to view both footage of the two main members and other images donated by like minds. The sex-positive stance of eco-porn unsettles the standard critique of the porn industry by instating an ethical objective and by drawing on what Ruth Barcan (2004) calls a "reality porn" ethic and aesthetic, one that stresses "real" bodies and "real" sex as an antidote to scripted, airbrushed, commercial porn. Barcan describes the flourishing of reality (a.k.a. "amateur" or "homemade") porn, especially online, noting how the internet and related technologies have radically transformed practices of producing and consuming porn and how this reality genre trades on staged authenticity—its realness or naturalness is precisely what sets it apart from commercial porn. FFF shares this aesthetic, which it ties explicitly to its political mission: "Erotic activists showing you real idealism," the FFF website states, adding that "FFF is not really porn . . . not more than a private video of two lovers is porn." But, in fact, the organization knowingly deploys the imagery of reality porn (including its not-porn-ness) in order to communicate its political message of sexual freedom and ecopolitics.

FFF also aims to democratize public sex by naturalizing it, encouraging visitors to the group's site to participate as well as consuming its images, and "working to show that sex is not something you should fear": "It is possible if you take a walk in the forest one day that you will come across a couple having sex in nature. It is important that you are prepared then, we are trying to prepare people for this and of course at the same time create awareness about nature and FFF" (FFF 2007). FFF urges visitors to "live like animals, just being a part of nature, celebrating life" (FFF 2007) while also drawing on Gaian ideas about the Earth as a "sensitive system" and about nature-based spirituality: "We see this as a spiritual project, and often feel guided" (FFF 2007). Rainforest destruction and industrial forestry are emblematic of humanity's abuse of nature for FFF, and the group works with ecoprojects in the rainforests of Brazil and Costa Rica (having had their cash rejected by mainstream environmental organizations such as the World Wide Fund for Nature). While the Norwegian festival performance and subsequent court case has brought notoriety and media attention to FFF, the group downplays its provocative intent, arguing instead that it wants public sex and nudity to be seen as natural, not shocking. Yet in mobilizing the naturalness of sex and of "naturefucking" politically or counterculturally, FFF draws on a strong lineage of nature-based sex radicalism (or sex-based nature radicalism), with the nature of sex staged as a critique of both sex-negative and nature-destroying human cultures. Reconnecting to sex here renaturalizes humanity, too, by reminding us of our own embodied naturalness.

"To Conceive of those Magnificent Beasts as 'Queers'—Oh God!"

Work on "queer animals," such as Bruce Bagemilhl's (1999) *Biological Exuberance* and Joan Roughgarden's (2004) *Evolution's Rainbow* (which concerns human animals, too), posits nonhuman (a.k.a. more-than-human)[2] animal sex acts as evidence of the naturalness of homosexuality (as well as other nonreproductive sexual and gender practices, including transvestism and transgender). Nonhuman animal homosexuality is thus naturalized through the figure of the "queer animal" (Terry 2000), while homophobia is denaturalized as a culturally specific human response since animals do not exhibit hostility toward same-sex acts in their presence (Hird 2004).[3]

As with Simon LeVay's (1993) work on the "gay brain" and Gilbert Herdt's (1997) work on "same sex in different cultures," which use neuroscience and anthropology respectively in order to find the truth of human sexuality, research on queer animals stages a troubling re-essentialization or renaturalization of same-sex sex acts, often mobilized as part of the political project of staking rights claims for sexual minorities on the grounds that, because this is a natural phenomenon, denying rights is discriminatory. There is no denying the potency of this appeal, given the currency of the idea of the natural across a range of academic and popular domains. Thus it is perhaps unsurprising that a contemporary liberal political project appeals to nature—via science—as the proof of the unnaturalness of discrimination and the naturalness of polymorphous sexual practice, undermining the procreative and genetic logic that has previously underpinned biological models of sex. Bagemihl (1999) calls for a "new paradigm" in theorizing the nature of sex, which he calls "biological exuberance"—a notion of excess and extravagance, drawing on (1) post-Darwinianism, (2) Gaian and (3) chaos theory, along with (4) Bataille and (5) what he refers to as aboriginal or indigenous cosmologies, or the "vast storehouse of knowledge about the natural world" (215) that modern science has disavowed and that only something more akin to "postmodern science" can begin to reincorporate into this new paradigm.

Modern science, as Myra Hird (2004) argues, has busily ignored, denied, or explained away homosexuality in nonhuman animals, since the logic of much evolutionary theory emphasizes the primacy of sexual reproduction for species survival and development. This logic thereby denaturalizes all other forms of sexual activity, unless that can be explained or contained within the overall imperative of sexual reproduction (however tenuously). As critics such as Hird, Jennifer Terry (2000), Roughgarden (2004), and Bagemihl (1999) all suggest, this denial has served to legitimate reproductive opposite-sex acts as the only truly natural form of sex. This move is, of course, ideological, and articulates what Terry calls the traffic between nature and culture. This traffic is complexly two-way, with ideas projected back and forth, from human to nonhuman and back again. The search for the scientific truth of sex inevitably turns to nature as its proving ground, yet it brings to nature a powerfully normative set of ideas about the truth to be found there. As Hird explains:

> Research on nonhuman animals immediately raises a number of issues. Nonhuman animals are closely linked with "nature"; thus what animals do is considered to be "natural." In western cultures, "natural" is often attached to morality—"nature" becomes "natural" becomes "good." So when animals behave in ways that apparently reinforce normative conceptions, the moral economy runs smoothly. Problems occur when nonhuman animals do not behave in ways that are obviously interpretable within the normative framework. (2004, 117)

If nature behaves unnaturally, in short, then what lies ahead is, as Barcan (2004, 171) puts it, "nature trouble." Of course, turning to nature to uncover the nature of sex also trades on a remarkably resilient cultural narrative that sees humans as animals—a narrative that toes a tricky line, too, in terms of how much naturalness human nature can legitimately exhibit. The equation of nature with good that Hird outlines above tells only half the story: the brutish, cruel, instinctive side of nature "red in tooth and claw" is also something to be denied or explained away. The domestication of nonhuman animals and the "culturalization" of humans both attempt to contain "bad nature," while a strong discourse of "good nature" is used to critique humanity's seemingly anti-natural acts, as FFF elaborates. Clearly, the classification of good nature and bad nature is contingent—Bagemihl's recourse to indigenous cosmologies represents his attempt to shift context away from modern Western worldviews.

The project of reclaiming queer animals is, as already noted, driven by a political imperative to naturalize the rights of sexual minorities; it is also driven by a scientific imperative to get to the real truth of the nature of sex. Crossover texts such as *Evolution's Rainbow* and *Biological Exuberance* target scientists and educators as well as activists—Roughgarden imagines in the introduction to her book the range of potential readers, from scoutmasters to therapists, doctoral students to the "woman scientist wondering how to contribute to feminist theory" (2004, 5). Perhaps inevitably then, they trade on the dominant sense-making frame of their imagined audience, which combines the truth of science (underpinned by the proper legitimating apparatus of scholarly citation, etc.) with the populist nature wonder of what we might call the "naturalist media"— embodied in countless spectacular wildlife documentaries, programs that themselves are often called upon to narrativize and dramatize nonhuman animal reproduction through populist anthropomorphism (relatedly, see Halberstam 2008 and Terry 2000 on a *Nightline* discussion of the bonobo).[4] As Terry (2000, 160) also notes, texts (and shows) like these reflect the "obviously widespread cultural wish" to understand the "true nature" of sexuality—a wish that inevitably reaches to the explanatory potency of science.

The call upon science to explain the nature of sex sits at odds, of course, with the powerful anti-essentialism of queer theory and politics (see Alaimo, this volume). Wary of the uses of scientific discourses of sexuality, and equally wary of the problematic fixity of identity categories, queer theory and politics have proven resistant to claims to biological or natural explanation of sexuality. Yet there have been moments when a strategic essentialism has been mobilized in defense of minority rights claims, for example in rebuffing the logic of the UK government's notorious Section 28. This clause, within a broader Act of Parliament passed in 1988, forbade state organizations such as schools, libraries, and art galleries from "promoting" homosexuality as a "pretended family relationship" (see Smith 1994). Underpinning the clause was a moral panic about the contagiousness of homosexuality—the idea that people could be "turned gay" by exposure to gay-positive materials. Activists were quick to point out that no one could be turned gay if homosexuality was innate, using the "born gay" argument to contest the logic of Section 28. Moreover, queer's anti-essentialism has often been at odds with the agenda of activists, who did not want to be told that their fight against oppression was founded on a fiction, even if it was a "*necessary* fiction" (Weeks 1995). What this tension has meant, among other things, is a reopening of a gap between politics and theory in the context of queer, fracturing what could have been a more productive interplay of ideas and practices.

Appeals to nature have also to be understood as powerfully appealing and affirming, especially when science is used to "reveal" nature's truth. Simon LeVay's "gay brain" research was greeted positively by those who welcomed a final, tangible explanation for homosexuality (Bell 2006b). A similar anti-queer anti-essentialism is noted by Michael Cobb (2006) in the U.S. movement of "former homosexuals," who cite the pervasive "born-gay" message as a trap that they have finally managed to escape. The naturalness of sexuality can be deconstructed from very different angles, with very different motivations.[5] Nevertheless, in popular science formats, the new science of sexuality, in all its exuberant rainbows, challenges the natural history equation of procreative heterosexuality, sex selection, and nature, opening up a space to rethink the nature of sex and the sex of nature.

"A Gathering of Happy People Enjoying Life!"

My third lens is the contemporary naturist movement, and in particular how it attempts to contain its own ambivalent orientation toward sex. In this case, sex and the naturalness of the naked body are arguably decoupled, and sex becomes culture rather than nature. The naturist movement attempts to distance itself from sex-positive cultures, deploying a range of performative and discursive regulatory frames through its own internal organization and policing: prohibitions against single people, rules about bodily adornment, and so on (Bell and Holliday 2000). The naked body is thus coded as natural, and while sexual arousal is often also accommodated as a natural occurrence, the desire for sex acts is commuted from nature to culture in a move that cordons public nudity off from sexualization. In this formulation, it is human culture that codes nudity as sexual, and human nature is a model of naked restraint instead. The naturist movement is often ambivalent about homosexuality, which is similarly bracketed off as culture, while the procreative nuclear matrimonial family is the embodiment of naked naturalness.[6]

Yet the nature of naturism brings with it Barcan's nature trouble, and the histories of naturism speak of the various negotiations of this trouble. Barcan explains: "Nudists enjoy a form of naked embodiment that they idealize as authentic and natural and yet which is widely conceived of by others as perverse. Nudism is inherently paradoxical—the natural, authentic practice that needs to argue constantly for its own normalcy. Wholesome perversion, uncommon naturalness, nudism is a practice both banal and extraordinary" (2004, 167). The paradoxical nature of naturism lies in its claim to banal naturalism: It should be ordinary, natural, normal, but it is recast as deviant or perverse. Why? Because the "clothing compulsory" culture of humans has denaturalized and sexualized nakedness. As Rob Cover (2003) argues, the pervasive sexualization of the public sphere in Western societies has closed off spaces where nakedness can be seen as nonsexual. He attributes this to the sexualizing gaze, which frames the to-be-looked-at-ness of the naked body as always sexual—the display of nakedness cannot not be sexual, in short.[7]

Barcan is interested in interrogating the nature trouble at the heart of naturism, for what she describes as the movement's "'problem' with the erotic" (2001, 312) has shaped the ways in which naturists articulate the relationships between the naked body and nature. As she concludes, "both the nakedness and the nature at the heart of naturism are culturally unstable" (2004, 171): "Nudism has always had a troubled relation with the erotic. The popular equation of nudity with sex must inevitably cross paths at some point with nudism's core claim about the naturalness of nakedness, obliging nudist thought to grapple with the problem of conceptualizing the 'natural' place of sex in the human world" (172).

Barcan tracks four discourses used by naturists that, like those around queer animals, variously deny, ignore, or explain away sex in naturism. The first draws on puritanism to decouple nudity from sex, bracketing sex off to the private sphere; the second is based on asceticism, and sees nudity as sexually calming; the third borrows from sexology to see nudism as beneficial for proper development. The fourth discourse, according to

Barcan, radicalizes nakedness, drawing on 1960s countercultural ideas—though she concludes that this is a very rare discourse in contemporary naturism (though we can trace an obvious link here to FFF). More commonly, sexual pleasure is deprioritized, and other bodily pleasures of nakedness are emphasized instead, especially the "feel" of the natural elements on the unclothed body, and the "freedom" to move unencumbered by vestments. In this move, the connection between nakedness and the erotic is denaturalized—sex, like clothes, becomes part of the culture cast off, while the emphasis on family-oriented, nonsexual, nude recreation packages contemporary naturism as a leisure practice, a holiday from clothing and culture (Bell and Holliday 2000). Those poor "textiles" unable to see past the naked body as an object of arousal (or humor) are deprived of access to this utopian space of nature.

Of course, one of the key compromises of the contemporary naturist movement is to permit that utopian space to be bounded, demarcated, and privatized. While there are calls for a radical public naturism somewhat akin to FFF's ethos (but without the fucking), most contemporary organized Western naturism takes place in designated zones, in clubs and camps and on beaches, governed by rules and regulations. The nature of naturism requires much organization, and there is intense labor behind the production of a natural, leisurely, "relaxed lifestyle" (Barcan 2004, 171, e.g., her discussion of the labor of producing the "natural body"). A large part of this labor concerns boundary work, preventing the return of the repressed in the guise of the erotic. Hence, as already noted, there are proscriptions on bodily styling and decoration, and ambivalence toward singles and gay men (whose motives for naturism are more readily codable as sexual, given the unnaturalness of singledom and the hypersexualization of homosexuals). In naturism, then, the nature of sex is naturally restrained, civilized by the very fact of its nakedness.

Natural Sex, Public Nature

The three examples of the complex articulations of the sex of nature and the nature of sex discussed here all rest on the nature/culture divide, itself a powerful structuring binary in Western thought. In each case, certain things are parceled up as properly part of nature, others as part of culture. Sex is often a problematic case. Is sex nature or culture? While it might appear that discussions of queer animals want to argue that sex is natural, Hird (2004) cautions against this view that only humans have culture. This idea has long been used to police the human/nonhuman boundary. Now that such boundaries have been argued to have been thoroughly breached, it makes no sense to deny the idea of (nonhuman) animal cultures. In relation to sexual practices, Hird notes, for example, "animals clearly learn sexual behaviors within their social groups and pass sexual behaviors down from generation to generation" (105). So there is nature trouble in attempts to define nonhuman animal sex as natural. Yet the power of appeals to nature is resilient.

Haraway (2003) offers a way out of this cul-de-sac when she argues the need to bond the two terms across the divide, to always talk of naturecultures. This is certainly a useful shorthand that keeps visible the interconnections. It reminds us that the very idea of nature itself is not natural; *nature is cultural.* But the term does not simply want to erase nature and call everything culture. This would be to miss the point of entwined naturecultures: This is not an incorporation, but a grafting. In each of the three examples I have focused on here, this grafting works (or doesn't work) in particular ways. FFF wants to realign human with nature, to claim sex as a natural act but at one and the same time as a political act. And not just that: an *eco*political act. Here, natural sex is deployed as a critique of the devaluing of both sex and nature. The contemporary naturist movement, in my analysis, wants to naturalize only nuclear-family, reproductive sex. As Ralph Rugoff once wrote, "naturists don't fuck, they breed" (1995, 181). Other sexual acts belong to the sphere of culture, which is a degradation of nature (and naturism). On this last point, FFF and the naturist movement are in seeming agreement—culture is bad for nature. Meanwhile, the discussion of queer animals has been popularly positioned as a way to claim the naturalness of queer, to exemplify the "rainbow" of sexual practices manifest in nature. But, as noted, this powerful assertion rests on the denial of culture beyond the human. "Naturecultures" here reminds us that nature has cultures: *culture is natural.* Clearly, queer ecologists and ecological scientists should be talking the same language after all.

I want to end by returning to a point made earlier, one that recurs throughout this collection. FFF's eco-porn arguably does more than use nature as a backdrop. The importance of the setting connects to the group's "spiritual" view of nature. In discussions of nature as a space for queer desires to find liberation, nature itself is often evoked, giving its blessing: in the "queer pastoral," as noted in the introduction, nature becomes the natural setting for sexual desires outlawed by human civilization (Fone 1983). As seen in *Brokeback Mountain,* it's only when back among their fellow humans that Ennis and Jack are shamed. Remember, too, that writers such as Bagemihl (1999) and Hird (2004) note reports of the non-existence of homophobia in nonhuman animals. Bagemihl writes that the "animal public" is either nonchalant or else likely to join in with any sexual activity witnessed. While Queen Victoria might have, according to popular stories, expressed disgust at sex that "scares the horses," it seems she had neither consulted the relevant science periodicals nor watched enough of the *Discovery Channel,* as the horses don't seem to be scared by unnatural acts in nature, whether homosexual or bestial (as the film *Zoo* explores, Devor 2007). This point raises some last questions. In what ways can we see nature as making up (part of) the public in public sex? What would it mean for our understandings of public sex to think about nature-as-public? What does it mean to talk of the publicness of nature? And if we can speak of more-than-human publics, what does that mean for the politics of nature and the politics of sex?[8]

NOTES

1. "Welcome, Nature Lover!" is taken from the FFF website (Fuck For Forests 2007). All other FFF quotes are taken from same site.

2. Some writers prefer the phrase "more-than-human" to describe animals and plants, rather than the too-human-centric "nonhuman."

3. The title of this section is from Valerius Geist, *Mountain Sheep and Man in the Northern Wilds* (1975), quoted in Bagemihl 1999, 107.

4. Wildlife documentaries are often mocked as "animal porn," a notion captured perfectly in the lines of the Bloodhound Gang song: "You and me baby we ain't nothing but mammals, so let's do it like they do on *The Discovery Channel.*"

5. At times, the "gays in the military" debates also traded on the contagious nature of homosexuality as grounds for its prohibition in the forces.

6. The title of this section is spoken by Bert, nudist, respondent in Barcan's study, discussing whether he saw naturism as a "movement"; see Barcan (2004, 174).

7. Barcan (2001) contests this view in her work on how female nudists resist the sexualizing gaze.

8. Although there isn't room to discuss it here, this issue raises interesting questions for bestiality and transspecies sex, too.

REFERENCES

Bagemihl, Bruce. 1999. *Biological Exuberance: Animal Homosexuality and Natural Diversity.* New York: St. Martin's Press.

Barcan, Ruth. 2001. "'The Moral Bath of Bodily Unconsciousness'": Female Nudism, Bodily Exposure and the Gaze. *Continuum: Journal of Media and Cultural Studies* 13.3: 303–17.

———. 2004. *Nudity: A Cultural Anatomy.* Oxford, UK: Berg.

Bell, David. 2006a. Bodies, Technologies, Spaces: On "Dogging." *Sexualities* 9.4: 387–407.

———. 2006b. *Science, Technology and Culture.* Maidenhead, UK: Open University Press.

Bell, David, and Ruth Holliday. 2000. Naked as Nature Intended. *Body and Society* 6.3–4: 127–40.

Cobb, Michael. 2006. God Hates Cowboys (Kind of). *GLQ* 13.1: 102–105.

Cover, Rob. 2003. The Naked Subject: Nudity, Context and Sexualization in Contemporary Culture. *Body and Society* 9.3: 53–72.

Devor, Robinson, dir. 2007. Motion picture. *Zoo.* THINKfilm.

Dicum, Gregory. 2005. Eco-Porn: Great Sex for a Good Cause. *SFGate*, April 13. http://www.sfgate.com/cgi-bin/article.cgi?f=/g/a/2005/04/13/gree.DTL.

Fone, Byrne. 1983. This Other Eden: Arcadia and the Homosexual Imagination. *Journal of Homosexuality* 8.1: 13–34.

Fuck For Forests. 2007. About Fuck For Forests. http://www.fuckforforest.com/AboutFFF.html.

Giffney, Noreen, and Myra Hird, eds. 2008. *Queering the Non/Human.* Aldershot, UK: Ashgate.

Halberstam, Judith. 2008. Animating Revolt/Revolting Animation: Penguin Love, Doll Sex, and the Spectacle of the Queer Non-human. In *Queering the Non/Human,* ed. Noreen Giffney and Myra Hird, 265–82. Aldershot, UK: Ashgate.

Haraway, Donna. 2003. *The Companion Species Manifesto.* Chicago: Prickly Paradigm.

Herdt, Gilbert. 1997. *Same Sex, Different Cultures.* Boulder, Colo.: Westview Press.

Herring, Scott. 2006. *Brokeback Mountain* Dossier. *GLQ* 31.1: 93–109.

Hird, Myra. 2004. *Sex, Gender and Science.* Basingstoke, UK: Palgrave.

LeVay, Simon. 1993. *The Sexual Brain.* Cambridge, Mass.: MIT Press.

Roughgarden, Joan. 2004. *Evolution's Rainbow: Diversity, Gender, and Sexuality in Nature and People.* Berkeley and Los Angeles: University of California Press.

Rugoff, Ralph. 1995. *Circus Americanus.* London: Verso.

Shuttleton, David. 2000. The Queer Politics of Gay Pastoral. In *De-Centring Sexualities: Politics and Representations beyond the Metropolis,* ed. Richard Phillips, Diane Watt, and David Shuttleton, 125–46. London: Routledge

Smith, Anne. 1994. *New Right Discourse on Race and Sexuality: Britain 1968–1990.* Cambridge: Cambridge University Press.

Terry, Jennifer. 2000. "Unnatural Acts" in Nature: The Scientific Fascination with Queer Animals. *GLQ* 6.2: 151–93.

Weeks, Jeffrey. 1991. *Against Nature: Essays on History, Sexuality, and Identity.* London: Rivers Oram Press.

———. 1995. *Invented Moralities: Sexual Values in an Age of Uncertainty.* Cambridge, UK: Polity Press.

PART

2

Green, Pink, and Public:
Queering Environmental Politics

CHAPTER 5

Non-white Reproduction and Same-Sex Eroticism: Queer Acts against Nature

ANDIL GOSINE

In Euroamerican-dominant cultural contexts, two kinds of sex have been (are) said to be toxic to nature: reproductive sex between non-white people, and sex between men. From their preservationist-conservationist origins right through to the twenty-first-century canonization of Al Gore as global eco-crusader, leading North American environmental movements have invested in the production and circulation of discourses on "overpopulation" that pit blame for global ecological disaster on the re-producing proclivities of the world's poor; due to the easy collaboration of capitalism with patriarchy and racism, that has meant the economically dispossessed non-white peoples of the world, particularly child-bearing (or potentially child-bearing) women from Asia, Africa, and South and Central America, as well as First Nations and non-white women in North America. All were collectively held responsible for "overpopulating" the earth and placing too much pressure on its natural resources. Paul Ehrlich succinctly laid out the rationale for this position in his influential 1968 text, *The Population Bomb*: "too many people" with "too little food" leads to "a dying planet."[1] In more direct terms, Ehrlich and the rest were making (still make) the claim that heterosexual (reproductive) sex between poor men and women burdened natural environments and threatened the survival of earth itself. More recently, various scholars have called attention to ways in which male, homosexual sex has also been articulated in public policy discourses and legal frameworks as harmful to healthy environments. Public cruising and sexual activity by men in parks and beaches, in both rural and urban landscapes across the world, have historically been construed as illicit and dangerous acts that degrade the sites they cross (Castells and Murphy 1982; Chauncey 1995; D'Emilio and Freedman 1988; Ingram 1997; Schultz 1998).[2]

In this essay, I want to begin to think through the representation of both kinds of sex as ecological threats, and invite a more engaged consideration of them. Although overpopulation propaganda and its material offshoots (family planning programs, coercive sterilization practices, etc.) and the criminalization and policing of sexual acts between men have been and are generally treated as distinct phenomena, their genealogies are intimately interwoven through the projects of colonialism, development, and nation building. Read against the heterosexist, racialized formations of nature engendered through these projects (the creation of national parks, etc.), heterosexual, potentially reproductive sex between non-white people and homosexual sex, I argue, threaten colonial-imperialist and nationalist ambitions. Both are "queer acts" in that they challenge the stated norms of collaborating colonial narratives of race, sex, and gender, through which modern formations of nature have been constituted. Both fail to meet and are threatening to the white nation-building projects engendered through the process of colonization, and uncritically buttressed in historical and contemporary discourses of the environment and ecology.

I consider three shared features of discourses on the ecological dangers of overpopulation and homosexuality that demonstrate how they similarly function and are similarly invested in the production and maintenance of white heteronormativity: their commitment to projects of white nation-building; their use of linked arguments about public safety and morality to make claims about the dangers that non-white heterosexual and homosexual sex pose to nature; and their denial of the erotic, through their insistent nonrecognition of sexual desire and of sexual acts as pleasurable. Toward this end, I examine a range of texts in which these discourses take shape: newspaper and other media reports, textbooks and other scholarly publications, government documents, including those scripted by police agencies, and materials produced by environmental organizations.

My characterization of both kinds of sex acts as "queer" is a recognition of their imbrications, and is intended as a kind of provocation to the theorization and practice of queer ecology. Through this work, I am trying to think through how the production of racialized sexual anxieties links the colonial encounter to projects of industrialization-development and nation-building, as expressed, for example, in contemporary population control and HIV/AIDS prevention programs, as well as in the policing of homosexuality in parks and beaches. I argue that these projects strive for and work to sustain white heteropatriarchy, and any acts seen to upset this agenda are constituted as not just unnatural, but *toxic* to nature. This claim is not far removed from those made by postcolonial scholars and psychoanalysts who recognize sex as a primary site through which the terms of empire are negotiated and stipulated. Neither is it a claim that has been unexplored in queer ecological or environmental justice literature; my position relies very much on the work of other contributors to this volume who have described various ways in which nature is called upon to take up the task of the racialized, gendered, and sexual marking of certain bodies as toxic. In this paper, I shift attention from the bodies that are rendered toxic to the act of sex that makes them so. A focus on sex rather than on bodies resists any stabilization of race, gender, or sexuality, and turns attention to the acts that give bodies significance. Sex is where anxieties about the self motivate the production of race, gender, and sexual identity, and sex is the place that may present, I think, interesting possibilities for configuring an ecological politics that is keenly considerate of the multiple forms of oppression that produce and organize nature.

The Sex of Others

The sex of "Others" has long preoccupied the imaginations of social and economic stewards of Euroamerican culture. Prior to European colonization of the Global South, fantasies and anxieties about its "monstrous races" and lascivious "Wild Men" and "Wild Women" circulated in oral and written texts. Several European authors testified to the potent sexuality of Africans in sixteenth- and seventeenth-century texts: Leo Africanus, a Spanish Moroccan Moor, announced in 1526 that "there is no Nation under heaven more prone to Venery" than the Negroes of West Africa; in 1566, French political theorist Jean Bodin similarly concluded that "in Ethiopia . . . the race of men is very keen and lustful"; in 1624, Francis Bacon's *New Atlantis* referenced "an holy hermit" who "desired to see the Spirit of Fornication; and there appeared to him a little foul ugly Aethiop"; and in 1665, the English author of *The Golden Coast* reported that Negroes were "very lustful and impudent, especially when they come to hide their nakedness" (all quoted in Jordan 2000, 44–45). Many commentators surmised that Negroes had sprung from bestial relationships with apes. Bodin remarked, "[P]romiscuous coition of men and animals took place, wherefore the regions of Africa produce for us so many monsters" (43–44).

These fantasies "became intertwined with imagined encounters and imagined accounts of 'the East' or Africans, and exerted a powerful formative influence on figures such as Columbus," and informed the organization of colonial society around the tropes of race and gender (Rattansi 1994, 44). For example, in her study of the construction of colonial categories and national identities around the concept of *métissage* (interracial unions) in nineteenth-century French Indonesia, Ann Laura Stoler demonstrates how "the management of sexuality, parenting, and morality were at the heart of the colonial project" (1995, 226). Cohabitation, prostitution, and legally recognized mixed marriages, she says, "slotted women, men and their progeny differently on the social and moral landscape of colonial society," and "were buttressed by pedagogic, medical and legal evaluations that shaped the boundaries of European membership and the interior frontiers of the state" (226). Through the course of colonization, anxieties about non-white peoples' sexualities would also inform the constitution of natural space across the world. The creation of "wildlife preserves" and national parks across the colonized world was predicated on the removal of their human, reproductive presence: the areas' indigenous populations. Aboriginal peoples in Africa, North America, and Asia were viewed as both a part of and a threat to pristine nature, a contradictory argument that rested in no small part on fears about the potential reproduction and "abundance" of them.

Reproduction-Overpopulation

Of the various ways in which anxieties about the sex of Others have continued to shape the contemporary world, the production of discourses on overpopulation has been an especially powerful legacy. English cleric Thomas Malthus is credited with innovating the idea that the sheer growth of human population (and not what humans do) is socially and environmentally destructive. In his 1798 *Essay On Population,* Malthus (1958 [1798]) argued that since agricultural production increases arithmetically and population soars geometrically, poverty and disease acted to check excess numbers of people who were outstripping available resources. Malthus's thesis would be resuscitated and revised to serve many different interests in subsequent decades: racial theorists,[3] birth control advocates,[4] American military agents of imperialism and national security,[5] ethnonationalists, international development policy makers and project managers,[6] and environmentalists. The idea that population growth in non-white communities poses an ecological threat has throughout the twentieth century enjoyed considerable popular appeal, particularly in the Global North. Two 1968 publications were especially influential in advancing this philosophy. The journal *Science* published Garrett Hardin's polemical essay "The Tragedy of the Commons," in which he declared: "Freedom to breed is intolerable" (1968, 1246). The essay strongly criticized arguments for the redistribution of wealth and launched into a stirring defense of eugenics, privatized ownership of natural resources, and coercive practices of sterilization against the poor. At about the same time, the Sierra Club published Paul Ehrlich's (1968) *The Population Bomb,* a project it had commissioned. Many environmentalists hailed the "scientific" rewriting of Malthus's population law by Ehrlich,[7] and some, such as Earth First! founder Dave Foreman, went one step further to suggest that human death and suffering were both a natural consequence of and solution to the environmental problem of human overpopulation.[8]

Most credible scholarship has rejected outright Malthusian claims.[9] The overpopulation myth is simply bad science, unsubstantiated by lived experience and driven by particular ideological interests that serve to deflect attention from the fact that most environmental problems—global warming, pollution, deforestation, and so on—are the direct consequence of industrialization, overconsumption, and capitalist territorialization, and *not* simply the overabundance of people. Yet the idea continues to wield significant influence on analyses and responses of environmental problems. For preservationist-conservationist environmental movements in North America, the myth of overpopulation was an appealing distraction from the effects of capitalism and industrialization that became especially apparent in the 1960s, effectively turning attention away from the consumption activities of white, middle-upper-class Americans who often made up the movements' membership (Darnovsky 1992). That function of the discourse continues to resonate today. In his now celebrated 2006 documentary *An Inconvenient Truth,* Al Gore remains committed to the Malthusian rhetoric he had adapted from the Ehrlichs, and peppers his presentation of analysis on climate change with references to and assumptions about "the disaster" of population growth. In the student handbook that Gore produced in conjunction with the film, a section entitled "Collision Course" begins with the warning: "We are witnessing an unprecedented and massive collision between our civilization and the Earth. We are trashing the planet. How has this happened? One major reason is that there are so many of us on Earth" (2007, 136).

In typical Malthusian fashion, Gore includes a two-page spread showing population growth from 160,000 BC to 2050 AD, when over nine billion humans are anticipated to be living on the planet (138–39). This chapter also includes visual references to just two places that demonstrate the global "problem" of overpopulation: Tokyo and Brazil. About the former, Gore notes, "The population of the Tokyo metropolitan area, the largest in the world, has grown to more than 35 million." A picture of a tree logger at the Tapajos National Forest in Brazil is accompanied by the explanation that "because of this rapid rise in population, there's greater demand worldwide for food, shelter, water, energy, which in turn puts a strain on all our natural resources" (142). The logger's photograph is followed by and juxtaposed against a post–clear cutting image from Folks, Washington. Notably, no images of loggers are included in the image of the American Folks forest, but humans are introduced again in the third set of images, of a weapon-wielding, young, black man set against a burning forest in the backdrop, in the Rodonia, Brazil (144–45). The chapter's closing images reiterate the link between blackness and environmental destructiveness, as the reader's attention is called to the differences between the lush, green Dominican Republic and the Republic of Haiti, where "98% of their forests," Gore notes, "have been cut down" (146–47). Haiti's population growth rate, however, is a modest 1.6 percent (UNdata country profile -Haiti: http://data.un.org/CountryProfile.aspx?crName=Haiti).

One important point that is overlooked in discussions of Malthusianism is that in overpopulation discourse, the main culprit is sex. Although not much is about sex or sexuality in Malthusian work, identification of overpopulation as the cause of poverty and environmental degradation necessarily implicates the people said to be engaged in dangerously over-producing themselves: non-white men and women living in the Global South engaged in heterosexual sex. Sex itself, then, is the act of destruction.

Same-Sex Eroticism

In Malthusian environmental discourses, heterosexual, potentially reproductive sex between non-white people is a central cause of earth's demise. Nonreproductive homosexual sex has also been represented in dominant renderings of ecology and environmentalism as incompatible with and threatening to nature. In its early incarnations, streams of North American environmentalism were conceived as a response to industrial urbanization. As homosexuality was associated with the degeneracy of the city, "the creation of remote recreational wild spaces and the demarcation of 'healthy' green spaces inside cities was understood partly as a therapeutic antidote to the social ravages of effeminate homosexuality" (Mortimer-Sandilands 2005, 10). Indeed, the subsequent use of these spaces by queer men looking for sex was morally condemned and criminalized in the United States and Canada (Castells and Murphy 1982; Chauncey 1995; D'Emilio and Freedman 1988; Ingram 1997; Schultz 1998). Thus, male cruising in parks, beaches, and other nature spaces has been heavily regulated and attacked. Recent examples of police actions against public male homosexual activity in these areas have occurred across the United States, including: arrests of sixteen men in Bull Creek Park, in Austin, Texas, in November 2005 (Robuck 2005); police surveillance and arrests of men found cruising in a park near Dayton, Ohio, in October 2005 (Markham-Smith 2005, 14); arrests of dozens of men at a boat ramp on Lake Quinsigamond in Massachusetts between 1996 and 2006 (Thompson 2006, A1); arrests of men cruising for sex at parks in Merced, California (De La Cruz 2006, 1); the May 29, 2007, arrest of six men for indecent exposure at the Black Dog Preserve in the Minnesota National Wildlife Refuge, near Minneapolis, the latest of several dozen arrests in various parks across the state (Lemagie 2007); and the June 2007 arrests of six men at the Kokomo Reservoir Park in Indiana (Olsen 2007). In all of these cases, the arrests were made after planned "sting" operations in which police went undercover as men soliciting sexual activity. Anxieties about public sex are also not limited to just the United States. Newspaper searches of European, Australian, and Canadian publications also produce similar reports of arrests of men alleged to be engaged in looking for public sex (Baker 2006; Fraser 2007; Shand 2006). Most media coverage (discussed in more detail below) consistently adopts the same demeanor: public, homosexual sex is bad for the environment.

Making White Nations

The denunciation of homosexuality shares much in common with the attacks on the fertility and potentially reproductive sexualities of non-white men and women. First, nature stands in for nation in both narratives, an easy epistemological substitution, as nations have the same requirements as "healthy environments": reproductive species and resistance to the incursions of foreign bodies. As Sarah Ahmed suggests, "a good or healthy neighbourhood [or nation] does not leak outside itself, and hence does not let outsiders (or foreign agents/viruses) in" (2000, 25). There is, she adds, "no body as such that is given in the world: bodies materialize in a complex set of temporal and spatial relations to other bodies, including bodies that are recognized as familiar and friendly, and those that are considered strange" (40).

In white nationalist projects, including European colonization, homosexuals and non-white reproductive heterosexuals are "strange"; they make no contribution to the building and expansion of—and in fact threaten—white nations. Their significance derives instead from their manifestations of oppositional subjects, as the Others through whom the white subject can make sense of himself (for the "normal" human subject is always a biological male), and upon whom anxieties about identity may be focused. The articulation of nature within a white, nationalist framework, furthermore, produces homosexuals and non-whites as not just strange, but toxic. Working with Ahmed's theorization of nationalism, Berila points out that "who and what counts as toxic is . . . deeply contested ground" (2005, 130). "Since the bodies of particular others, usually people of color, queers, women, or people from other nations, are repeatedly targeted as threats to the nation," she adds, "the reading of which bodies are marked as toxic seems particularly important in any discussion of the landscapes of nation and national identity" (130).

Nationalism is always predicated on racialized heterosexuality, as the survival of nations demands the reproduction of bodies. It is for this reason that women have been regarded in nationalist discourses as objects of both reverence and slippage; they are biological reproducers of the nation, but any sexual transgressions on their part (lesbianism, interracial sex) mean that they also threaten its survival (Anthias, Yuval-Davis, and Cain 1992). The most expansive project of white nationalism, the colonization of North America, has been deeply informed by and achieved through the generation of responses to anxieties about homosexuality and the sexual liberties of non-white heterosexuals. Historian Ned Katz notes that "the widespread homosexuality of the North American Indians was given as an excuse by the invading whites for their extermination" and "the Christianization of Native Americans and the colonial appropriation of the continent by white, Western 'civilization' included the attempt by the conquerors to eliminate various traditional forms of Indian homosexuality—as part of their attempt to destroy that Native culture that might fuel resistance—a form of cultural genocide involving both Americans and Gay people" (quoted in Gaard 1998, 33).

White homosexual subjects betrayed the nation's reproductive imperative. The threat of non-white homosexual subjects to the nation was differently rationalized. They were problematic by virtue of their apparent potential to attract and "homo-sexualize" whites. Stoler notes that during the colonial period, "desires for opulence and sex, wealth and excess were repeatedly attributed to creole Dutch and lower-class Europeans, to those with culturally hybrid affiliations and/or of mixed-blood origin." Natives and these "fictive" Europeans, Stoler adds, were "persons ruled by their sexual desires" (1995, 183). The "homosexual native" and the "native woman" represented temptation, and threatened to unravel the European's self-discipline, unleashing his darkest fantasies.

These anxieties laid the groundwork for the theories of racialization that would emerge in the nineteenth century, such as those posited by Count Gobineau in his "Essay on the Equality of Races." Gobineau's core argument was that it was the white races who are inclined to be sexually attracted toward the other races, which is why they mix with them, while yellow and brown races were deemed to have a stronger repulsion to inter-racial sex, which is why, he says, they tended to remain relatively unmixed (quoted in Young 1995, 107). Indeed, nineteenth-century theories of race did not just consist of essentializing differentiations between self and other but also were, as Young points out, broadly about "a fascination with people having sex—interminable, adulterating, aleatory, illicit, inter-racial sex" (181). Such racial theory, Young argues, "projected a phantasmagoria of the desiring machine [of colonialism] as a people factory." There were great fears about

> uncontrollable, frenetic fornication producing the countless motley varieties of interbreeding, with the miscegenated offspring themselves then generating an ever increasing melange, "mongrelity," of self-propagating endlessly diversifying hybrid progeny: half-blood, half-caste, half-breed, cross-breed, amalgamate, intermix, miscegenate, alvino, cabre, cafuso, castizo, cholo, chino, cob, creole, dustee, fustee, griffe, mamaluco. (181)

Subsequent to the fall of European empires, these anxieties took new shape as anti-immigration discourses ("Yellow Fever," "Asian Invasion," etc.) and, as already noted, overpopulation propaganda. More recently, postindustrial concerns about environmental degradation have provided another prism through which xenophobia and racism could be articulated as environmental prudence. But make no mistake about it: Calls by groups such as the Sierra Club (U.S.)—some of them made as recently as 2006—to curb immigration and regulate the sexual reproduction of people in the Global South are merely a restatement of white nationalist ideals as a commitment to nature. This analysis is supported by research demonstrating North American environmentalists' commitment to white nationalist constructions of nature. As Noël Sturgeon points out,

> mainstream environmentalists, in their emphasis on wilderness, species extinction, and in general seeing the environment as excluding human beings, often fall into service to this dominant Western logic of seeing the natural as pure, unchanging, untainted by social influence and without history. This kind of mainstream environmentalism avoids environmental justice issues, which deal primarily with problems of human and community health using a broader, less reified definition of the environment and identifying power relations as central to the cause of environmental problems. (2004, 263)

Nature needs protection, this logic forwards, from the toxic presence of non-white bodies.

Coverage of arrests of men engaged in or looking for sex in natural spaces similarly reveals nature's parallel constitution (with nation) as a pure space that must be protected from the incursions of toxic homosexuals. One commonly employed strategy toward this effect has been to equate sex with pollution, and to focus on the litter and damage to the environment produced by homosexual acts. A news report filed by Sarah Lemagie for the *Star Tribune* on the Minnesota arrests provides one illustration of this approach. Lemagie begins the article by associating gay sex with garbage. "The trash-strewn pulloffs along the Minnesota River hardly look like Lovers' Lane," she notes, "but to Burnsville police who have been tracking lewd behavior between men there, that's basically what they've become." Writing about a popular cruising spot at Maple Grove, she quotes an officer who makes note of the damage men seeking sex inflict on the environment and litter they leave behind. "Men loitered in cars or at picnic benches and retreated in pairs to the bushes," where officers found mattresses and "condoms by the hundreds," she reports him as saying. In Canada, an article about male cruising in Stanley Park that appeared in the *Vancouver Sun* in 2001 reported, "Venture down one of the well-worn side paths into the trees and you can't miss it. The soggy ground is carpeted with used condoms, their wrappers, and tissues, the tell-tale remnants of what is widely known in the male gay community as park sex" (Zacharias 2001, A1). A June 2007 story appearing in the *National Post* repeated this association of homosexual sex with pollution of natural space, and condemned police for not taking punitive action. "Visitors to one part of famous Stanley Park may stumble upon men engaged in fellatio and intercourse," columnist Brian Hutchinson noted, "yet cruising areas, littered with used condoms and cigarette butts, seem sacrosanct" (Hutchison 2007, A1). Similarly, a report filed by Peter Baker for the *Essex Chronicle* focuses on the outrage expressed by Brian Olley in encountering homosexual acts taking place in Hylands Park. According to the article, park user Brian Olley "exercises his dog in Hylands by walking from his nearby home twice a day" (2006, 11). Although he had often seen "vehicles with male occupants park outside the main gate [to the Hylands]" on most evenings, he was "shocked to come across two men having sex on a path he used to walk his dog by the park's edge" (11). Olley, Barker reports, has noticed "there is unsavoury litter around the entrance area" frequented by men looking for sex. The Hylands estate manager is also quoted as saying, "The condoms and tissues presumably get deposited on the highway and in lay-bys" (11). This littering of parks is akin to "dirtying the nation," particularly in light of the historical constitution of parks as part of white nation-building.

Public Safety and Morality as Ecology

Employing a similar approach, ecology has also serviced the production of social and moral codes that are oppressive to queers and non-white people. Both homosexual sex and non-white heterosexual eroticism have been viewed, beginning (at least) in the colonial period and into the contemporary, as transgressions of morality and threats to public safety. Stoler points out that in the late nineteenth and early twentieth century Dutch Indies, "the equation of common-class origins and unchecked licentiousness was pretty much the same" (1995, 179). For settlers, concubinage with native women was weighed against and equated to homosexual sexual practices, whether between colonial men or with native men. "The dangers of a homosexual European rank and file were implicitly weighed against the medical hazards of rampant heterosexual prostitution," Stoler says; "both were condemned as morally pernicious and a threat to racial survival" (181). Indeed, sex with native prostitutes was excused on the grounds that a common European soldier had to satisfy his "natural sexual appetites," and that if prevented from exercising these natural sexual urges, he would resort to unnatural vices, that is, masturbation or homosexual sex (179–80). Stoler also points out that while "strident moral disparagements" were explicitly cast against racial mixing, the moral dangers of homosexuality often went unstated (181).

Malthus's warnings about the threat of overpopulation were also deeply informed by racialized moral panics related to sexuality. Most texts about Malthus, including ones critical of his thesis, reference only the British context that framed his original musings on overpopulation. Most attention to the clergyman's work in this literature is focused on the defense of capitalist interests in the context of class struggles in England. But as research by J. C. Caldwell (1998) makes clear, Malthus was also strongly influenced by his work as a colonial administrator in India. Malthus spent nearly his whole adult life working for the East India Company, and it was his aversion to the sexual habits of Indians that fuelled his rhetoric on overpopulation. "Malthus became increasingly interested in the lack of prudence about marriage in the uncivilized nations," Caldwell notes, "and in the conditions that nevertheless stopped them from being in a perpetual state of famine" (681). Anxieties about sex were intertwined, as they had been for the European explorers before him, with those of racial difference.

More recently, moral dangers about both homosexuality and non-white reproductive heterosexuality have been stated through the production of ecological discourses. In Malthusian renderings of environmentalism, the planet's demise is linked to the immoral ravishes of the polluting underclass. Sandilands notes that population discourse "relies on the bifurcation of the world into two: 'good' ecological citizens, who have listened to and understood the call for limits and do not require (further) regulatory intervention, and unruly bodies, who have not, might not and/or do not" (1999, 86). Nature has similarly been used as a means of production and site of moral regulation against homosexual sex, such as in the representation of public sex as polluting. Sandilands explains, "Bulldozing the trees or pulling up the undergrowth in a downtown park can be as much a threat to the public expression of gay male culture as it is to urban nature, and polluting a beach that acts as a center for outdoor lesbian activity can destroy both biotic and social communities" (2001, 175). Sandilands concludes that mainstream environmentalism, such as that involved in the creation of urban parks, "includes a strong historical tradition of marginalizing sexual expression; in order to approach moral purity, sexuality was excluded" (Ingram, quoted in Sandilands 2001, 176).

A 2005 U.S. Department of Justice guidebook entitled *Illicit Sexual Activity in Public Places,* produced by the Office of Community Oriented Policing Services, makes clear the equation of immoral with environmental transgressions insofar as homosexuality is concerned. Issued as part of a series that aims to "summarize knowledge about how police can reduce the harm caused by specific crime and disorder problems" (v) and written specifically for police officers, the guidebook starts off with identification of six main reasons "why the police should care about public sex." This list conjoins and conflates concerns about morality and social respectability ("Public sexual activity can offend inadvertent witnesses" and "can deter the legitimate use of public spaces"), health ("Public sexual activity may be related to the spread of sexually transmitted diseases, including HIV/AIDS" and is "associated with heavy drinking"), public security ("Public sexual activity can attract a hostile audience, creating a risk of violent crime such as assault and/or robbery, as well as non-violent crime such as blackmail"), and ecological degradation ("Discarded used condoms, lubricant containers, and other paraphernalia are unattractive and potentially hazardous"[2]).[10] None of these claims tend to hold up under more careful scrutiny (Chauncey 1995, Ingram 1997, Schultz 1998), and the positions advanced in many of them often defy logic: is it public sex—not homophobia, for example—that "attracts" a hostile audience to be violent? Public sex—not how it is performed (i.e., without condoms or other precautions)—is what causes AIDS. But the overarching message is clear: public sex, understood in the report as mostly homosexual sex between men, is socially dangerous and incompatible with the maintenance of healthy environments.

Speaking about the arrests of sixteen men in Black Dog Park, Minnesota, in May 2007, Police Sergeant Jeff Witte said, "We're not here to judge people on their behavior. We just don't want it out in public in our city parks" (Olsen 2007). Witte's claim that the policing of park sex is *not* about judging people doesn't hold up against closer examination of the language used to incite opposition to and punitive responses to public sex. One of the most popular strategies engaged by police and other opponents of sexual activity in natural spaces has been to present themselves as protectors of children. Very often, police explain their efforts to survey parks and make arrests in terms similar to those of Australian Senior Constable Mark Spencer. "I was receiving complaints every day from mums and dads taking their kids there and it got to the point no one wanted to be there," he said to one reporter covering Spencer's 2007 arrests of men at Burpengary Park (Fraser 2007). Like Witte's statement about how "our" city parks are used, Spencer's comment not only reiterates the notion that homosexuals do not belong to and instead pollute the nation ("no one wanted to be there"), he invokes a moral discourse that also emphasizes how exposure to images of gay sex might impugn the innocence of children. Concerns about ridding parks of gay sex toward transformation of them into places that have "a more inviting family atmosphere" are expressed by numerous other arbiters of planning (e.g., Osterwalder 2006, B01; Stepzinski 2007, B-1), and at least one anti-gay sex sting operation created by police is entirely premised on a moral responsibility to children. In 2002, the Fresno California police force set up operation "Protecting Our Children" in which officers pretended to be cruising for sex. According to court records, "an undercover deputy would enter the park restrooms, make eye contact with people and suggest they engage in sex acts. Those who agreed were either arrested on the spot or apprehended later" (Collins 2007, B4). Only male officers were engaged in the operation. A CBS news report on public sex in Fort Worth, Texas, similarly noted, "the close proximity of families and children to sex at Trinity and the garbage left behind is of paramount concern." Repeating the characterization of homosexual sex as a polluting act and using language that animalizes homosexual sex, the report added that "the darkest parts of the nest are feathered with used condoms, condom wrappers, used tissues and toilet paper and discarded clothes" ("FW Park Known" 2007). These excerpts demonstrate that surveillance and punishment of public sex between men is much less concerned with the material circumstances of the situations considered than with the maintenance of heteronormativity: men seeking sex in parks more likely seek them out because they provide visual cover and safety, not necessarily because of some exhibitionist drive. As even acknowledged in a 1993 editorial in the *Edmonton Journal* that condemned "sexual activity in public parks" (Victoria Park and Government House), "no one would want to stumble upon people engaged in public sex, but that is unlikely because the activity usually occurs in the middle of the night when picnickers and joggers are asleep in their beds" (Overactive Police Work? 1993, A8). As well, police entrapment of men in public washrooms hardly corresponds with evidence that clearly shows that children are far more likely to be sexually abused by people familiar to them in private spaces than they are by strangers in a washroom.

The efficacy of moral arguments is evidenced not just in the discursive practices of critics of public sex, but also in those of more sympathetic actors. Discussing the problem of sexual activity in Minnesota, Shakopee police captain Craig Robson repeats a common warning about dangers it poses to children. "When you're engaging in sexual activity in a public park where you have playgrounds and kids within close proximity of that area," he says, "that's not OK" (Lemagie 2007). Lorraine Teel, the executive director of the Minnesota AIDS Project, was harshly critical of the arrests made of the men charged for engaging in lewd acts. In an interview with Lemagie, she condemned the severity of the response by police, and points out: "We would prefer to use these situations as ways to educate." Cracking down on public sex, Teel notes, "takes men who are engaging in risky behavior and need help and drives them further underground" (Lemagie 2007). Yet, she too is convinced by the notion that sex between men poses a threat to "normal" uses of nature. "At the same time," she noted, "clearly, we recognize that there are public issues. If those venues are in the plain and full view of picnic areas or the Target parking lot or something, yeah, that's a problem" (Lemagie 2007).

One of the great ironies about the framing of public sex as dangerous to nature is that attempts to police and curtail homosexual acts in natural spaces have themselves been destructive. A common tactic employed by police and planners has been to clear areas thought to be amenable to concealing sexual activity. In Maple Grove, Minnesota, for example, the local police agency cut down bushes at a popular rest area and eventually built a ten-foot fence (Lemagie 2007). In Geelong, Australia, police concerned about public sex in Belmont Common's northern fringe advocated cutting down bushes. "To prevent [gay sex], . . . mow the joint down," Geelong inspector Wayne Carson told one reporter (Shand 2006, 1–4). Similar actions have taken place in Toronto, through the clearing of Cherry Beach, including as recently as in 2007. Reactions to the anxieties about the impact of homosexual sex on nature, in other words, have actually turned out to have a much more devastating impact. Indeed, some regulators of park space have taken a less polemical and ultimately more meaningful approach. Responding to condom litter in Stanley Park, the Vancouver Park Board Commission installed extra garbage receptacles in the area and, board member Duncan Wilson says, "has urged the gay community to clean up after itself" (Zacharias 2001).

Denying the Erotic

A necessary component of this characterization of homosexuality and non-white reproductive sexuality as dangerous and damaging to ecology is the denial of the pleasures they bring. Sexual pleasure is denied through two entwined strategies: the characterization of sex as an act of death and the denial of individual agency by non-white and homosexual subjects in forming sexual desire. Sex between Third World men and women brings death to the planet through the pressures of overpopulation, while homosexual sex brings death and disease. Sandilands suggests that in population-environment discourse, "the only possible relationship between humans and non-human nature is antagonistic, as nature exists only as a 'resource' for human use; more people inevitably means more degradation" (1999, 86). Second, "nature's primary appearance in human life is as a limit to human *excess,* including, potentially, an excess of human freedom (especially in the context of a crisis)" (1999, 86, emphasis in original). Not only is death the inevitable consequence of both forms of queer sex, but sex itself is seen as failure of its initiators to civilize; sex is not a conscious decision to seek out erotic pleasure, but rather the consequence of unfettered desire. This logic holds in the rationalization of both homosexual sex and non-white heterosexual sex.

The story of overpopulation is premised in large part on the idea that non-white people lack agency in forming and executing sexual desires. In metropolitan popular culture, sex is most often associated with individual types, desires, choices, and decisions. Movies, television series, pop songs, publications about sex between men and women tend to reduce the variety of political and social influences on desire to "personal feelings" and individual tastes. Not so in neo-Malthusian discourse. In stark contrast to the love songs and romantic comedies of Hollywood (and Bollywood) that emphasize ideas about sexual chemistry and courting rituals, both advocates and critics of population control reduce the complexity of sexual behavior to sociopolitical conditions *only.* References to sexual desire and pleasure are nowhere to be found in the development literature concerned with either overpopulation or its discursive successor, HIV/AIDS. At best, sexual health education strategies acknowledge the "need" for sex, but often, sex is associated with the coming of death, via AIDS or other sexually transmitted diseases. Even critics of Malthusianism have been complicit with this position. Murray Bookchin suggests, for example, that the sexual behavior of Third World peoples "is *profoundly conditioned* by their social status, as people who belong to a particular gender, hierarchy, class group, ethnic tradition, community or historical era, or adhere to any of a variety of ideologies" (1994, 32, emphasis in original). Although his primary purpose in making these comments is to refute the equation of humans with fruitflies, Bookchin places so much emphasis on the "conditioning" of human experience (and sexuality) that he implicitly adheres to this denial of love/desire; it is, after all, "social status, gender, hierarchy, class group, ethnic tradition," and so on, *not* individual desire, that conditions sexual relations. In "Reproductive and Sexual Rights" (1994), feminists Sonia Correa and Rosalind Petchesky propose four ethical principles to guide a reproductive rights agenda: bodily integrity, personhood, equality, and diversity. But the only overt reference to sexual pleasure in the entire document is in reference to disease and death:

The global crisis of HIV and AIDS complicates but does not diminish the right of all people to responsible sexual pleasure in a supportive social and cultural environment. For women and men of diverse sexual orientations to be able to express their sexuality without fear or risk of exclusion, illness, or death requires sex education and male and female resocialization on a hitherto unprecedented scale. (114)

Most other contributors suggest that sex among people living in the Third World is a global, political economic event—and for good reason. Fighting off the quick and harmful coercive sterilization techniques used to control Southern women's sexuality on one hand and masculinist pro-natalism and religious fundamentalism on the other, feminists have had to assert that reproductive *choices* are not just about using birth control. But left unchallenged in this framing is the categorization of Third World peoples as lacking agency.

The key idea, cutting across both neo-Malthusian and anti-Malthusian discourses, is that "the poor" have no agency. When the World Bank, the UNFPA, Ehrlich, and others call for the implementation of population controls, they imply that reproduction in the Third World can be systematically controlled through delivery of "the right information" and services. When feminists, (liberal) development planners, and others call for more accessibility to health and education, they make the same implication. Educating more girls, building more schools and clinics, and making birth control more accessible may be, in themselves, worthy goals, but their pursuit in the context of reproductive control is problematic in that they write out love, pleasure, and sexual desire.

Homosexual sex has been similarly characterized in both the Global North and Global South, from at least the colonial period to the contemporary moment. Citing Grosz's interpretation of Freud, Sandilands suggests that pleasure and death are "phylogenetically linked": "The pleasurable sexual activities of individuals are closely linked to the reproduction of the species, and the reproduction of the species is contingently dependent on the life, reproduction, and death of individuals. Sex, in this narrative, is a *compensation* for death" (2001, 181, emphasis in original). Sex is, in this framework, an *act* of death. Supporting Greta Gaard's contention that anti-eroticism and hegemonic heterosexuality not only are part of dominant Western ideas of nature, but also are interstructured with environmental degradation, Sandilands argues that "Western culture's profound erotophobia"—an erotophobia that is clearly linked to the regulation of sex—ensures the production of environmentalisms that cling to an understanding of nature that pathologizes sexual diversity.[11] Indeed, it is the figure that is mapped across both subject positions—the non-white homosexual man (more recently tagged as MSM, men who have sex with men)—that has become identified as the planet's greatest threat, his sexual indiscretions and his betrayal of the heterosexual family unit deemed responsible for the scourge of HIV/AIDS (Gosine 2007, 2009).

(Working) Toward Queer Ecologies

This description of the ways in which the relationship of non-white reproductive sex and homosexual sex to nature are similarly construed is as much a call to recognize those imbrications as it is a provocation to the making of "queer ecologies." Through my characterization of "non-white reproduction" as queer sex, I am trying to raise three sets of related concerns:

First, a concern about the political geography of queer ecology: Is the production of "queer ecology" a decidedly Euroamerican project? Work theorizing sexuality and nature has tended to assume (at the same time that it critiques) an understanding of environmentalism and nature as Western teleological narratives. This essay, for example, has been concerned with the representation of non-white reproductive and homo-sex in Euroamerican environmental discourses; non-white heterosexual reproduction is queer sex in the sense that it deviates from the social conventions advocated in North American environmental discourses. What are the implications of setting this historical-geographic limit to queer ecology? If the Euroamerican context always remains the primary reference point, how will its questions and analysis meaningfully contribute to the production of nature elsewhere, or to the contemporary articulation of environmentalism as a global project? Is the privileging of Euroamerican stories of environmentalism—even for the purpose of critical examination—complicit with the agendas of empire, and American imperialism in particular?

Second, a concern about race-racism: If queer ecology is to maintain a primary gaze on the production of nature in Euroamerican contexts— which, despite my reservations is, I think, a legitimate and viable option— what becomes of race-racism? Many scholars engaged in the production of the field of queer ecology (e.g., Ingram, Sandilands, and the contributors to Rachel Stein's *New Perspectives in Environmental Justice*) have certainly invited, even sometimes privileged, an analysis of race. In her important essay, "Toward a Queer Ecofeminism," Greta Gaard outlines some of the linkages between colonization and homophobia. She describes how homosexual relationships between North American Indians were viewed by colonial scientists as being responsible for their extermination, and engages a discussion of Cynthia Enloe's work on masculinity to demonstrate some links among the production of masculinity, sexual identity, and nationalism. Gaard also points out that "not only did transgender practices and sodomy disturb the colonizers; even heterosexual practices devoid of the restrictions imposed by Christianity were objectionable" (2004, 35). However, some of the claims of queer ecology about the construction of heterosexuality as natural become troublesome without a contaminant analysis of race-racism. For example, in the same essay, Gaard argues, as many others have done, how the natural is associated with the "procreative"; this may be true in the context of white nationalism, but the procreative proclivities of non-white people has certainly not been regarded as natural (rather, as I have outlined above, as dangerously perverse) in Western environmentalism. Given the recognized interwoven investments of sexuality with race in the production of nature and the nation, must we not always be alert to the simultaneous foregrounding of both? I would add to this list gender and class, which I have not discussed here, but which I also believe must always be primary considerations in our analysis. Also implicit in this analysis has been a separation of the queer subject from the racialized-as-non-white subject; that is, subjects are seen to occupy either position, not both, in effect disappearing the non-white queer and, I would also suggest, the diasporic subject. As I have already stated, it is the non-white queer subject that in this contemporary moment is cast as a deadly and dangerous deviant, through tropes of HIV/AIDS; I would suggest that a special focus on the constitution of the non-white queer subject might even provide for a more insightful project of queer ecology.

Third, a concern about the political resistance: Related to this point, my characterization of non-white reproduction and homosexual sex as queer acts against nature is not just a call for more determined engagement in an analysis of sexuality with race, gender, and class, but also for political projects that recognize and challenge the shared investments of projects of heterosexism, racism, and capitalism in the production of white nationalism (including white nationalism practiced by non-whites fully committed to the reproduction of Euroamerican model of capitalist nation-states). What I am trying to suggest is that the refusal of race-racism is not separate from the refusal of heteropatriarchy, as both are productions of capitalism-nationalism. Thus, rather than think about a "coalition" of "different" interests (e.g., Gaard's and others' calls for feminists, queers, and non-white people to forge alliances), might a queer ecological political project present a different kind of framework of resistance? Might queer ecology be better served, for example, by the kind of model of political resistance that has been articulated by black lesbian feminists such as Audre Lorde, M. Jacqui Alexander, and Dionne Brand, where its work is not merely to attend to the "sexuality" part of oppression, but to recognize and work with its full, complex rendering?

NOTES

Much thanks and appreciation to Ana Rico-Balanos and Marc Sinclair for their committed research assistance, and to Cate Mortimer-Sandilands.

1. The titles of the first three chapters of *The Population Bomb* were "Too Many People," "Too Little Food," and "A Dying Planet."

2. Public sex between women and public heterosexual sex have also been similarly positioned, but for various reasons have attracted considerably less critical attention. Not much research has been done on sex between women in public places—in part, no doubt, because of the organized relegation of women to the private sphere and their exclusion from the public sphere. Public heterosexual sex ("dogging," etc.) has gained some attention, but certainly less than male homosexual sex, and is generally less energetically scandalized.

3. In 1878, George Arthur Gaskell pronounced: "There is certainly a great danger in decreased fertility of some races, namely that the pressure for other races on them might extinguish them. The lessened fertility commences in the races which are stronger socially; I trust they will endure. The nations guided by reason could not long submit to having their standard of comfort or their means lessened by the influx of an inferior race" (quoted in Greer 1984, 255).

4. For example, in her 1919 *Birth Control Review,* leading feminist birth control advocate Margaret Sanger championed the popular position that continues today to motivate population control planning: "More children from the fit and less from the unfit—that is the chief issue of birth control" (quoted in Hartmann 1995, 99). In Sanger's book *Pivot of Civilization,* she similarly warned leaders that illiterate "degenerate" masses might destroy "our way of life" (99), and pursued partnerships with eugenicists.

5. U.S. military interests in "population matters" reached new heights in the 1940s. "It is probable that in the last five years," Pendell observed in 1951, "more copies have been published of discussions related to population than in all the previous centuries" (quoted in Escobar 1995, 34). By July 1959, a government committee chaired by military general William H. Draper recommended to President Eisenhower that the United States fund population research as part of its Mutual Security Program, and that aid be given to "those developing countries who establish programs to check population growth" (quoted in Hartmann 1995, 105).

6. Reinventing Third World states as "underdeveloped" and "poor" societies, development also explained poverty and strife in these societies as the direct result

of population growth (Hartmann 1995; Sen and Grown 1987). Indeed, development policies were generally based on the economic principles of John Maynard Keynes, a self-professed Malthusian. A member of two birth control organizations, the Malthusian League and Marie Stopes's Society for Constructive Birth Control and Racial Progress, Keynes believed that the working classes bred too much; he saw deaths from famine, war, and pestilence as the most effective means of raising living standards in overpopulated Third World countries (Toye 2002). With population control identified as a basic condition of these countries' social stability, reproductive sex among poor and non-white people, then, always jeopardizes their own security as well as the North's.

7. Included in the environmental organizations that promoted this doctrine were: the Audubon Society, the National Wildlife Federation, Population Action International, and the Sierra Club subgroup Campaign on Population and Environment (COPE). At the 1992 United Nations Conference on Environment and Development (UNCED), population lobbyists and environmentalists joined together to issue a "Priority Statement on Population" which stated: "Because of its pervasive and detrimental impact on global ecological systems, population growth threatens to overwhelm any possible gains made in improving living conditions" (quoted in Hartmann 1995, 145).

8. In a 1986 interview with Bill Devall, Foreman said that "the worst thing we could do in Ethiopia is to give aid—the best thing would be to just let nature seek its own balance, to let people there just starve" (in Bookchin, Foreman and Chase 1991, 108). In 1981, he also argued, "letting the USA be an overflow valve for problems in Latin America is not solving a thing. It's just putting more pressures on the resources we have in the USA" (108). Foreman says:

> For me, the problem is not just to figure out how to level off human population at a level that can be biologically sustained at equitable levels of consumption. . . . Other beings, both animal and plant, and even so-called "inanimate" objects such as rivers, mountains, and wilderness habitats are inherently valuable and live for their own sake, not just for the convenience of the human species. If we are serious then, about creating an ecological society, we will need to find humane ways to arrive at a global population level that is compatible with the flourishing of bears, tigers, elephants, rainforests and other wilderness areas, as well as human beings.
>
> This will undoubtedly require us to lower our current population levels which, even if we succeed at overcoming poverty and maldistribution, would probably continue to devastate the native diversity of the biosphere which has been evolving for three and a half billion years. I subscribe to the deep ecology principle that "the flourishing of human life and cultures is compatible with a substantial decrease of the human population and that the flourishing of non-human life requires such a decrease." (ibid. 53)

9. See Bookchin (1994, 30–48); Correa (1995); Hartmann (1995); Mies and Shiva (1993); Sen (1994); Sen and Grown (1987); and Yearley (1996, 51–55).

10. This statement is interesting for a number of reasons, including the fact that it is listed just after the concern about HIV/AIDS, at once using the disease to create anxiety and to dismiss the means to prevent its spread.

11. As Sandilands explains:

> Gaard's argument is that Western culture, with its post-Enlightenment emphasis on reason, devalues eroticism in the same conceptually dualized construction as that which subordinates women to men, body to mind,

non-white to white, queer to heterosexual and nature to culture. To Gaard, there is an ideologically reinforcing relationship among the normalization of heterosexuality, the devaluation of the erotic, and the understanding of the supremacy of human culture over nonhuman nature; the containment of nature supports the suppression of sexual diversity, and the regulation of sexuality is an active part of the oppression of nature. (2001, 177)

REFERENCES

Ahmed, Sara. 2000. *Strange Encounters: Embodied Others in Post-coloniality.* Liverpool, U.K.: Routledge.

Anthias, Floya, Nira Yuval-Davis, and Harriet Cain. 1992. *Racialized Boundaries: Race, Nation, Gender, Colour and the Anti-racist Struggle.* New York: Routledge.

Baker, P. 2006. Help Crack Park Sex Ring. *Essex Chronicle Series* (January): 11.

Berila, Beth. 2005. Toxic Bodies? ACT UP's Disruption of the Heteronormative Landscape of the Nation. In *New Perspectives on Environmental Justice: Gender, Sexuality and Activism,* ed. Rachel Stein, 234–56. New Brunswick, N.J.: Rutgers University Press.

Bookchin, Murray, Dave Foreman, and Steve Chase. 1991. *Defending the Earth: A Dialogue Between Murray Bookchin and Dave Foreman.* Montreal, Quebec: South End Press

Bookchin, Murray. 1994. *Which Way for the Ecology Movement?* San Francisco, Calif.: AK Press.

Bookchin, Murray, and Dave Foreman. 1991. *Defending the Earth: A Dialogue between Murray Bookchin and Dave Foreman.* Boston, Mass.: South End Press.

Caldwell, John C. 1998. Malthus and the Less Developed World: The Pivotal Role of India. *Population and Development Review* 24.4: 675–96.

Castells, Manuel, and K. Murphy. 1982. Cultural Identity and Urban Structure: The Spatial Organization of San Francisco's Gay Community. In *Urban Policy Under Capitalism,* ed. Norman I. Fainstein and Susan S. Fainstein, 237–59. Beverly Hills, Calif.: Sage.

Chauncey, George. 1995. *Gay New York: Gender, Urban Culture, and the Making of the Gay Male World 1890–1940.* Abingdon, U.K.: Carfax.

Collins, Chris. 2007. Roeding Park Sex Sting Ruling Faces Challenge; Judicial Panel Weighs Upholding Decision on Homosexual Bias. *Fresno Bee,* June 2, B4.

Connelly, Matthew. 2006. Population Control in India: Prologue to the Emergency Period. *Population and Development Review* 32.4: 629–67.

Correa, Sonia. 1995. *Population and Reproductive Rights: Feminist Perspectives from the South.* Atlantic Highlands, N.J.: Zed Books.

Correa, Sonia, and Rosalind Petchesky. 1994. Reproductive and Sexual Rights: A Feminist Perspective. In *Population Policies Reconsidered,* ed. Gita Sen et al., 107–108. Boston, Mass.: Harvard Center for Population and Development Studies.

Darnovsky, Marcy. 1992. Stories Less Told: Histories of US Environmentalism. *Socialist Review* 92.4: 11–54.

De La Cruz, Mike. 2006. Two Arrested in Park Sex Sting; Operation Will Continue at All Merced Parks. *Merced Sun-Star,* April.

D'Emilio, John, and Estelle B. Freedman. 1988. *Intimate Matters: A History of Sexuality in America.* New York: Harper and Row.

Ehrlich, Paul R. 1983 (1968). *The Population Bomb.* New York: Ballantine Books.

Escobar, Arturo. 1995. *Encountering Development: The Making and Unmaking of the Third World.* Princeton, N.J.: Princeton University Press.

Foreman, Dave. 1986. A Spanner in the Woods. Interviewed by Bill Devall, *Simply Living:* 2.12.

Fraser, Kelmeny. 2007. Struggle to Reclaim Park for Families. *Caboolture Shire Herald,* January.

FW Park Known to Some Men as a Place for Sex. 2007. *CBS 11/TXA 21—Dallas.* http://cbs11tv.com/topstories/local_story_165225727.html.

Gaard, Greta. 1998. *Ecological Politics: Ecofeminists and the Greens.* Philadelphia, Pa.: Temple University Press.

———. 2004 (1997). Toward a Queer Ecofeminism. In *New Perspectives on Environmental Justice: Gender, Sexuality and Activism,* ed. Rachel Stein, 21–44. New Brunswick, N.J.: Rutgers University Press.

Gore, Al. 2007. *An Inconvenient Truth.* Emmaus, Pa.: Rodale Press.

Gosine, Andil. 2007. "Race," Culture, Power, Sex, Desire and Love: Writing in "Men Who Have Sex with Men." *IDS Bulletin* 37.5: 27–33.

———. 2009. Monster, Womb, MSM: The Work of Sex in International Development. *Development* 52.1, 25-33.

Greer, Germaine. 1984. *Sex and Destiny: The Politics of Human Fertility.* New York: Harper and Row.

Guggenheim, Davis, dir. 2006. Motion picture. *An Inconvenient Truth.* Lawrence Bender Productions.

Hardin, Garrett. 1968. The Tragedy of the Commons. *Science* 162: 1243–48.

Hartmann, Betsy. 1995. *Reproductive Rights and Wrongs: The Global Politics of Population Control.* Boston, Mass.: South End Press.

Hutchinson, Brian. 2007. Against the Law; Vancouver; Brian Hutchinson; [National Edition]. *National Post,* June 9, A1.

Ingram, Gordon Brent. 1997. Marginality and the Landsacpes of (Erotic) Alienation. In *Queers In Space: Communities|Public Places|Sites of Resistance,* eds. Ann Marie Bouthillette, Yolanda Retter, and Gordon Brent Ingram, 27–54. Seattle, Wash.: Bay Press.

Jordan, Winthrop D. 2000. First Impressions. In *Theories of Race and Racism,* ed. Les Back and John Solomos, 33–50. New York: Routledge.

Linden, Eugene. 1996. The Exploding Cities of the Developing World. *Foreign Affairs* 75.1: 52–62.

Lemagie, Sarah. 2007. Policing the Shadows. *Star Tribune,* June 13. http://www.startribune.com/332/v-print/story/1239363.html.

Malthus, Thomas R. 1958 (1798). *An Essay on Population.* London: Dent.

Markham-Smith, Ian. 2005. Priest Park-Sex Charge. *Mirror,* October 25.

Mies, Maria, and Vandana Shiva. 1993. *Ecofeminism.* London: Zed Books.

Mortimer-Sandilands, Catriona. 2005. Unnatural Passions? Notes toward a Queer Ecology. *Invisible Culture: An Electronic Journal for Visual Culture* 9. http://www.rochester.edu/in_visible_culture/Issue_9/title9.html.

Olsen, Julianna. 2007. Police Raid Park to Stop Sex Crimes. *Kare 11 News,* June 20. http://www.kare11.com/news/news_article.aspx?storyid=255817&GID=Tp1wk31ZWxrePi5IYNdlpTPvU60teZn3yY+OSO1RBss%3D.

Osterwalder, Joan. 2006. Park's Return to Former Glory. *Press Enterprise,* sec. B.

Overactive Police Work? [Editorial—Op-Ed]. (1993). *Edmonton Journal:* A8.

Rattansi, Ali. 1994. "Western" Racisms, Ethnicities and Identities in a "Postmodern" Frame. In *Racism, Modernity and Identity on the Western Front*, ed. Ali Rattansi and Sallie Westwood, 15–86. Cambridge, U.K.: Polity.

Robuck, Bob. 2005. Police Sting Nets 16 Arrests for Lewd Acts. *News 8 Austin*, November 30. http://www.news8austin.com/content/top_stories/default.asp?ArID=150946.

Sandilands, Catriona. 1999. Sex at the Limits. In *Discourses of the Environment*, ed. Eric Darier, 79–94. Oxford, U.K.: Blackwell.

———. 2001. Desiring Nature, Queering Ethics: Adventures in Erotogenic Environments. *Environmental Ethics* 23.2: 169–88.

Schultz, Mark Talbott. 1998. Policing Public Space: Community Response to Park Cruising and Sexual Activity. MA thesis, Department of Landscape Architecture. Seattle, Wash.: University of Washington.

Sen, Amartya. 1994. Population: Delusion and Reality. *New York Book Review* 41.15, September.

Sen, Gita, and Caren Grown. 1987. *Development, Crises and Alternative Visions: Third World Women's Perspectives*. New York: Monthly Review Press.

Shand, Jenny. 2006. Police Want Park Sex Lair Cleaned Up. *Geelong Advertiser*, May.

Six Arrested in Park Sex Sting. 2007. *Indy Channel*. http://www.theindychannel.com/news/13540972/detail.html.

Stepzinski, Teresa. 2007. 2 Nabbed in Park Sex Sting. *Florida Times-Union*, May 7, sec B.

Stoler, Ann Laura. 1995. *Race and the Education of Desire: Foucault's History of Sexuality and the Colonial Order of Things*. Durham, N.C.: Duke University Press.

Sturgeon, Noël. 2004. "The Power is Yours, Planeteers!" Race, Gender and Sexuality in Children's Environmental Popular Culture. In *New Perspectives On Environmental Justice: Gender, Sexuality and Activism*, ed. Rachel Stein, 262–76. New Brunswick, N.J.: Rutgers University Press.

Thompson, Elaine. 2006. Gay Sex-Site at Lake Busy Despite Arrests. *Worcester Telegram and Gazette*, June, sec A.

Toye, John. 2002. Keynes on Population. *Economic Journal* 112.480: F391–94.

U.S. Department of Justice, Office of Community Oriented Policing Services. 2005. *Illicit Sexual Activity in Public Places*, by Kelley Dedel Johnson. Washington, D.C. http://www.vcpa.org/Resources/ Illicit%20Sex%20in%20Public%20Places.pdf.

Weinberg, Bill. 1991. *War on the Land: Ecology and Politics in Central America*. London: Zed Books.

Yearley, Steven. 1996. *Sociology, Environmentalism, Globalization: Reinventing the Globe*. London: Sage.

Young, Robert J. C. 1995. *Colonial Desires: Hybridity in Theory, Culture and Race*. London: Routledge.

Zacharias, Yvonne. 2001. Inside Stanley Park's Gay Sex Scene: Why Some "Trail Hoppers" Choose Anonymity over the Club Scene. *Vancouver Sun*, November, sec. A1.

CHAPTER 6

From Jook Joints to Sisterspace: The Role of Nature in Lesbian Alternative Environments in the United States

NANCY C. UNGER

Despite the depth and breadth of Catriona Sandilands's ground-breaking "Lesbian Separatist Communities and the Experience of Nature," with its emphasis on communities in southern Oregon, Sandilands does not consider her article, published in 2002, to be "the last one on the topic." Instead she hopes "fervently that other researchers will enter into the ongoing conversation [about queer landscapes]" (136). This essay is an answer to her invitation to draw further "insight from queer cultures to form alternative, even transformative, cultures of nature" (135). It examines the role of place in the history of American lesbians, particularly the role of nonhuman nature in the alternative environments lesbians created and nurtured in their efforts to transcend the sexism, homophobia, violence, materialism, and environmental abuse afflicting mainstream society. Certainly such an investigation supports the challenge, detailed in Katie Hogan's essay in this collection, to the notion of queers as "unnatural" and "against nature." Lesbians' ways of incorporating nonhuman nature into their temporary and permanent communities demonstrate how members of an oppressed minority created safe havens and spaces to be themselves. In addition to offering mainstream society insight into the impact of place on identity, in some instances lesbian communities also provide some important working examples of alternate ways of living on and with the land.

Early Lesbian Environments

Place has played an important role in the creation of lesbian identity and community. Although modern urban environments, with their softball fields and lesbian bars and bookstores, are conventionally perceived as most conducive to lesbian life, pockets of safe spaces for women who loved women existed earlier, even in the more conservative rural south. Angela Davis's *Blues Legacies and Black Feminism* details the explorations of sexuality granted to African Americans following their emancipation from slavery. Prohibited from frequenting white establishments by virtue of their race and economic status, rural African Americans danced, drank, and socialized to blues music in ramshackle jook joints, also called barrelhouses, frequently located in wooded, remote areas away from disapproving eyes and ears. These informal nightclubs "where blues were produced and performed were also places of great sexual freedom" (1998, 133). Davis examines in particular female African American blues performers who were "irrepressible and sexually fearless women," many of whom were openly lesbian and whose songs celebrated sexual love between women (137).

Most lesbians, however, associated sexual freedom with urban rather than rural life. To Mabel Hampton, a young African American lesbian who moved from Winston-Salem, North Carolina, to New York's Harlem in 1920, the idea that non-urban, outdoor settings might prove to be a valuable partner in creating and fostering a positive lesbian identity would have been a total anathema. For Hampton, there could be no more nurturing and empowering environment for lesbians than the open atmosphere of Harlem, a small section of racially segregated Manhattan. "I never went in with straight people," she recalled decades later in the film documentary *Before Stonewall*. "I do more bother [have more contact] with straight people now than I ever did in my life." She summed up her memories of the clubs and nightlife available to openly lesbian women with a wistful, "[you had] a beautiful time up there—oh, girl, you had some time up there" (Rosenberg, Scagliotti, and Schiller 1984).

In Hampton's heyday, it was indeed cities, with their potent combination of proximity and privacy, that promised the greatest liberation for most homosexuals. The very notion of homosexuality as a lifestyle grew out of the urban centers of newly industrialized nations. Many cities included a more "bohemian" area in which people who were considered to be outside mainstream society found a home. In these centers lesbians found each other. They enjoyed the chance to experience nightlife in clubs featuring lesbian entertainers, some of whom got their start in the jook joints of the rural south.

Private parties were far more common than nights on the town, however, because they were cheaper and provided both safety and privacy. During non-work hours "'I didn't have to go to bars,' Hampton recalled, 'because I would go to the women's houses'" (quoted in Nestle 2001, 346). During periods when she was not working at the Lafayette Theater, Hampton and her friends "used to go to parties every other night. . . . The girls all had the parties" (quoted in Garber 2009). As Hampton recalled, lesbians "lived together and worked together. When someone got sick the friend [lover] would come and help them—bring food, bring money and help them out . . . I never felt lonely" (quoted in Nestle 2001, 346).

Urban lesbians created informal communities, providing places to connect with each other as well as generate emotional and financial support and solidarity. Throughout the first half of the twentieth century, these urban (as opposed to rural) environments represented freedom and opportunity for lesbians (see Chauncey 1994, Atkins 2003). As Hampton noted, "[I]n a small town you wouldn't have a chance to get around and meet [gay] people. Now in New York, you met them all over the place, from the theater to the hospital to anything," concluding, "Yes, New York is a good place to be a lesbian" (quoted in Nestle 2001, 346). Urban environments, with their occasional lesbian bar and clusters of same-sex living spaces, including the YWCA and other women-only boarding and rooming houses, also offered the greatest potential for the creation of lesbian community.

An Early Alternative Environment: Cherry Grove

Urban life offered only fleeting and furtive opportunities for white middle- to upper-class lesbians to find each other (primarily in the form of visits to bars discreetly catering to lesbians) and to carry out relationships. Some of these women began to seek out environments more conducive to living as they desired. Esther Newton's "The 'Fun Gay Ladies': Lesbians in Cherry Grove, 1936–1960" details the role that physical environment played in creating a unique lesbian community (1995). Cherry Grove is on Fire Island, a long, narrow sandspit about thirty miles long between the Atlantic Ocean and the southern coast of Long Island. It was, even in the 1930s, a relatively easy commute via boat from the New York metropolitan area and served as the perfect antidote to the huge, dirty, crowded, overwhelming—and in most sections overwhelmingly homophobic—city.

Few cars were allowed on the island, and it was "so wooded, and so beautiful, [with] a canopy of trees wherever you'd walk" (Newton 1997, 145). One-time resident Natalia Murray recalled coming to Cherry Grove in 1936: "[In] this place, so close to New York, you can breathe the fresh air; when we found it it seemed so secret, [so] wonderful." Its lack of electricity and running water dictated a simpler lifestyle. Island life allowed people to "breathe freer" (quoted in Newton 1997, 147). In addition to its refreshing physical characteristics, Cherry Grove was already home (at least in the summer and on weekends) to the same kind of arts-and-theater crowd that had helped to cement Harlem's bohemian reputation. The energetic white women who flocked to Cherry Grove "enjoyed independent incomes, professional occupations, or both. . . . [M]ost were connected to or identified with the theater world," making them, in the words of Murray, "Interesting, talented people . . . who had so much fun!" (quoted in Newton 1997, 147–48).

Being near the beach contributes to a more relaxed dress code. For women, time at Cherry Grove meant discarding the constraints of mainstream society, sometimes literally: "We could throw off our girdles, dresses, heels," elements of the uniform virtually required of middle-class women. Lesbians gloried in being able to "wear slacks and to be with and talk to others like [themselves]," providing "a simply extraordinary feeling of freedom and elation," unlike the rest of the world where "there was nothing" (Newton 1997, 149). Cherry Grove offered unprecedented freedom. Women could walk alone, even at night, without fear of violence, harassment, or arrest: "The Grove offered lesbians a breather from the strains of continual concealment, and from straight men's unwanted sexual attentions, in a glorious, natural setting" (Newton 1997, 150).

The results of all this freedom were more personal than political. Unlike the lesbians who sought alternative environments in the 1970s and 1980s, the "fun gay ladies" of Cherry Grove were not consciously political or inspired to activism. "Closeted Grovers had desperate reasons to go . . . where they could be what they felt was their authentic selves . . . to be openly gay—expressive, honest, and sexual" (Newton 1997, 150). Despite their appreciation of the natural beauty around them, they were not especially concerned with environmental protection. The negative environmental impact of the lack of indoor plumbing, for example, was never mentioned. Their goal was not to improve, let alone remake, the greater society, but simply to enjoy a respite from its incessant expectations that all women be heterosexual and conform to the demands of patriarchy. Nevertheless, compared to the elaborate housing developments that were to come, their environmental impact was relatively small. They didn't come to transform Cherry Grove physically, to "civilize" the land, to tame or develop it. They sought privacy and were content to live in relatively simple dwellings that fit their budgets and blended with the natural setting rather than dominating it.

The early residents of Cherry Grove frequently spoke of it as another world, including Peter Worth, who gloried in being, for once, in the majority: "This was my world and the other world was not real" (quoted in Newton 1997, 149). Although the white middle- to upper-class lesbians at Cherry Grove were able to shrug off the homophobia of that other world, its racism and classism remained: they did not reach out to their working-class sisters nor to lesbians of color. As one resident recalled, "In those days, the Grove was like a very private gay country club" (Newton 1997, 156).

Beginning in the 1950s, the tenor of Cherry Grove changed. Early in the decade a younger generation, still middle-class but more committed to butch and femme identities, took up residence. After electricity and running water were installed in 1961, construction of new homes doubled, then tripled. "The old-timers looked on aghast as the 'unspoiled' natural setting of their 'gay country club' was 'raped,'" as Natalia Murray put it (quoted in Newton 1997, 156). The passage of the National Seashore Act in 1964 froze the limits of Cherry Grove, prohibiting further sprawl, but by then its transformation into what resident and film historian Vito Russo called "a Coney Island of [male] sex" was already complete (quoted in Newton 1995, 186).

An overwhelming percentage of the buyers of the newly constructed homes were gay men, who, by virtue of their sex, had more purchasing power than most women. The lesbian "country club" became a gay man's "sexual social club" (Newton 1995, 185). As Cherry Grove became a playground almost exclusively for gay men during the 1960s, virtually all of the original "gay ladies" of Cherry Grove moved on, many becoming part of the "Bermuda shorts triangle," so named to indicate the imaginary line between their apartments in Manhattan and their summer cottages in the Hamptons or near Westport, Connecticut. Significant numbers of lesbians of all classes began returning to the Grove only in the 1980s as a result of their greater purchasing power (Newton 1997, 157).

Despite the near total absence of communal activism, the history of Cherry Grove between 1930 and 1960 offers a glimpse into a pioneering experience, highlighting the way living a simple, more sustainable lifestyle in a natural setting can contribute to an exhilarating rejection of society's condemnation of lesbianism. Cherry Grove was valued as an apolitical alternative environment offering its lesbian residents a sense of belonging in the more natural world, and respite from that other world: the artificial urban jungle of patriarchy, misogyny, and homophobia. It became the work of a later generation of lesbians to tackle the myriad problems of that other world head on, and to create alternative environments not as respites, but as viable models of just how that other world might be recreated socially, politically, and environmentally.

Laying the Groundwork for a New Kind of Alternative Environment: *Silent Spring* and *The Feminine Mystique*

In 1954, best-selling naturalist and pioneer ecofeminist Rachel Carson publicly proclaimed women's "greater intuitive understanding" of the value of nature as she denounced a society "blinded by the dollar sign" that was allowing rampant "selfish materialism to destroy these things" (Lear 1997, 259–60). Just when the old lesbian environment of Cherry Grove grew obsolete, Carson's *Silent Spring* (1962) used arguments featuring the traditional female emphasis on beauty, spirituality, and future generations to dramatically question the governmental fathers' wisdom concerning industrial waste and the vast reliance upon pesticides, especially DDT. Women in particular perceived Carson's work as an invitation to environmental activism.

The "female" values stressed by Carson were very much in evidence in *Silent Spring*. Chastening "man" for his "arrogant" talk of the "conquest of nature," Carson warned that the power to achieve that boast had not been tempered by wisdom. *Silent Spring*'s attack on the government's misplaced and ineffectual paternalism appeared just one year before Betty Friedan's assault on patriarchy, *The Feminine Mystique*. Many of the women originally "awakened" by Friedan's work to take themselves seriously were white and middle class, and took their first steps into finding a larger place in the world by responding to Carson's call, written in terms they could understand about a cause with which they could identify. Friedan's urging that women throw off patriarchy reinforced Carson's message that they no longer assume "that someone was looking after things—that the spraying must be all right or it wouldn't be done" (Lear 1997, 423). In response women questioned authority and embraced environmental activism. As environmental historian Adam Rome notes, "Carson cultivated a network of women supporters, and women eagerly championed her work" (2003, 536–37).

Rachel Carson herself chose not to identify as a feminist or as a lesbian, but her work contributed to the significant role that lesbians play in imagining environmental alternatives (see Unger 2004, 54–55). At the same time that *Silent Spring* was transforming environmental thought, the feminist movement was taking hold, dedicated to a rejection of prevailing gender spheres in favor of the political, economic, and social equality of the sexes. Although Friedan would betray lesbians by attacking them as the "Lavender Menace" in 1969 and purging them from the National Organization for Women, they remained at the forefront of the burgeoning women's rights movement. As they promoted the rights of all women, lesbians openly claimed the right to their own sexuality.

The Birth of Ecofeminism

As the environmental movement became increasingly mainstream, many women believed that their traditional role as housekeeper, mother, nurturer, and caregiver made them uniquely qualified to contribute. In particular, the feminist and environmental movements of the 1960s contributed significantly to the environmental justice and ecofeminist movements of subsequent decades and to the role of lesbians within them.

The basic concept of ecofeminism is grounded in the movements launched to no small degree by the writings of Carson and Friedan, but its definition depends on which ecofeminist, scholar, or critic is asked (see MacKinnon and McIntyre 1995, Sturgeon 1997, Warren 1997). At its core, ecofeminism unites environmentalism and feminism, and holds that there is a relationship between the oppression of women and the degradation of nature. Some argue that, because of that relationship, women are the best qualified to understand and therefore to right environmental wrongs. In most parts of the world, women are the ones who are "closest to the earth," the ones who gather the food and prepare it, who haul the water and search for the fuel with which to heat it. Everywhere they are the ones who bear the children, or in highly toxic areas, suffer the miscarriages and stillbirths or raise damaged children. According to one Brazilian ecofeminist, "Men have separated themselves from the ecosystem." It therefore falls to women to fight for environmental justice and to save the earth (Merchant 1992, 205). Within the United States, a variety of mutually exclusive forms of ecofeminism rival for dominance. One branch emphasizes the power of goddess mythology. Practitioners of Goddess spirituality seek to reclaim ancient traditions in which, they assert, a Mother Goddess (rather than a Holy Father) was revered as the great giver of life. Some argue that despite the efforts of the patriarchal Judeo-Christian tradition to eradicate this belief, all women, especially mothers, are the natural guardians of "Mother Earth."

Their horrified feminist rivals counter that these kinds of claims perpetuate old gendered stereotypes and are a violation of the egalitarianism of true feminism. Nature should not be anthropomorphized into a mother to be protected but instead be respected as a nonhuman, nongendered partner in the web of life. They argue that women and nature are mutually associated and devalued in Western culture and that it is strictly because of this tradition of oppression that women are uniquely qualified to understand and empathize with the earth's plight, and to better conserve and more fairly distribute its resources. These ecofeminists see the anthropocentrism that is so damaging to the earth as just one strand in a web of unjust "isms," including ageism, sexism, and racism, that must be destroyed in order to achieve a truly just world. In the words of 1980s activist Donna Warnock, "The eco-system, the production system, the political/economic apparatus and the moral and psychological health of a people are all interconnected. Exploitation in any of these areas affects the whole package." "Our only hope for survival," concludes Warnock, "lies in taking charge: building self-reliance, developing alternative political, economic, service and social structures, in which people can care for themselves . . . to promote nurturance of the earth and its peoples, rather than exploitation" (Warnock, circa 1985). Lesbians created some of the earliest and most comprehensive efforts to forge the kinds of earth-saving alternative communities Warnock proposed.

Back to the Land

During the 1960s a trickle of people, mostly white and middle class, including many lesbians, some of whom identified as ecofeminists, began moving to rural communities across the nation. They were determined, in becoming part of the burgeoning "back to the land" movement, to be the "hope for survival" by transcending the sexism, homophobia, violence, materialism, and environmental abuse afflicting mainstream society (Agnew 2004). The proliferation of ecological problems and the ongoing war in Vietnam significantly contributed to a radical lesbian-feminist vision of an American nation in such deep trouble that only drastic measures could reverse its course. Some women, convinced that the root causes of America's problems were male greed, egocentrism, and violence, believed that only a culture based on superior female values and women's love for each other could save the nation. Others embraced separatism for different reasons: some lesbians insisted that "women-only" spaces were the only way to ensure that lesbians' needs came first. Living in the country was considered superior to living in cities created and dominated by men because in urban centers both lesbian sexuality and efforts to transform society were constantly oppressed and diverted. The separation from cities and suburbia offered by country life was considered crucial in the creation of models that would allow women to reclaim their sexual and environmental rights (Agnew 2004; Splitrock 1985). Moreover, these women, although often derided as unnatural by the straight community and therefore suited only to urban life, confidently took a holistic approach to society's problems by making nature central (see Cheney 1985).

In southern Oregon in 1972, the trickle of members of the back to the land movement became "a wave of women immigrants" (Corinne 1998). The lesbians who settled in rural Oregon between Eugene and California's northern border were a far cry from the "gay ladies" of Cherry Grove. They sought not a temporary retreat into a kind of fantasy world but rather the creation of a new and viable alternative. Ideology rather than economics was the primary factor in their efforts to eschew sophisticated development and expansion in favor of simple dwellings. They strove to adapt to the natural environment rather than to transform it. In their early rhetoric, notes Sandilands, "rural separatists viewed the land as a place that could restore physical and spiritual health to a group of people sickened, literally, by (heteropatriarchal capitalist) corruption and pollution and thus as a sort of paradise on earth to which women could be admitted if they recognized their oppression at the hands, and in the lands, of men" (2002, 138).

Women erected (or adapted from existing shacks and cabins) small housing units that were easy to build and manage. These tiny residences (frequently less than ten by twelve feet—smaller than Thoreau's cabin at Walden) represented safety, economy, and autonomy. These structures did not dedicate space to entertaining or child rearing due to the conscious rejection of traditional women's roles. The emphasis tended to be collective rather than communal. One resident recalls that "so much of the back to the land movement was about coming out, and coming into our power and identities as Lesbians. We intuitively knew we had to get out of the patriarchal cities, and redefine ourselves and our lives. We actually tried to build a new culture . . . not [just] back to the land but back to ourselves" (Corinne 1998).

This new culture included "a desire to live lightly on Mother Earth and in sympathy with nature" (Corinne 1998). Instead of celebrating unbridled production, it valued salvaged, recycled, and handcrafted materials over those industrially produced and store-bought. These women eschewed sophisticated technology, heavy machinery, and animal products in favor of solar power, hand tools, and vegetarian organic foods in their desire to protect the environment as part of a larger effort to combat the evils of patriarchy and heterosexism. As one informational pamphlet from the Oregon Women's Land Trust put it, "We want to be stewards of the land, treating her not as a commodity but as a full partner and guide in this exploration of who we are" (quoted in Sandilands 2002, 139).

Sandilands details the struggles as well as the triumphs of the various communities' efforts to remake the world: "After 27 years of Oregon women's lands, not a single lesbian I spoke to in the course of my research subscribed to the view of the women's lands as a utopia on earth" (2002, 140). Despite the communities' desire to create an inclusive and diverse lesbian society, few women of color came to Oregon, and the mountainous terrain proved a barrier to women with disabilities and to the elderly. Relatively poor soil and chronic water shortages contributed to the "ongoing dynamic between a separatist utopian ideology and an everyday practice of subsistence culture located in a particular place" (Sandilands 2002, 140). Residents were frequently divided over what constituted acceptable spiritual practices (see Kleiner 2003). And yet none of the lesbians in residence termed their efforts a failure. They spoke of the empowerment they found in doing things for themselves and their recognition that nature is not an abstraction to be idealized, nor an "other" to be feared, tamed, subdued, or exploited, but rather "a friend, a sister, a lover (not to mention a workplace, a home, a refuge, and on some days a nuisance)" (Sandilands 2002, 146). These lesbians proved that there were ways of living, however imperfect, that did not hinge on profit or patriarchy and that instead allowed lesbians to live openly, freely, and consciously as partners with nature.

The Pagoda: "An Island of Lesbian Paradise"

Just as the lesbians of Cherry Grove thrived due to their physical distance from mainstream society, the lesbian communities of the Pacific Northwest enjoyed the privacy rendered by isolation. Few lesbians were willing or able to live in such complete separation from the mainstream world. Even those who sought to create alternative communities were not necessarily drawn to rural life; others wished to pursue professions not valued or practicable in rural collective settings. In contrast to the back-to-the-land lesbians of southern Oregon, a group of lesbians in Florida took an entirely different approach to creating a lesbian environment. In 1977 Morgana MacVicar, a ritual performer and matriarchal belly dancer, combined resources with three other lesbians, all in their early thirties and "very much impacted by the 60s revolution in America" (Greene 2009). On the Coastal Highway at Vilano Beach, they purchased four cottages that had originally been units in the Pagoda motel. This marked a new beginning for the Pagoda as a womynspace in St. Augustine.[1]

The reborn Pagoda was less an effort to remake the world than an attempt to carve a uniquely lesbian residential and retreat space within the existing one. During its first four years the Pagoda served as a vacation destination for lesbians, then became increasingly residential. For both spiritual and financial reasons, the building at the community's center was granted tax-exempt status as a religious institution in 1979, strengthening the residents' communal identity and allowing the complex to exist legally as a women-only space. It took several years for the Pagoda to take shape as a community and ten years to complete its acquisition of properties. Because lesbianism was not an accepted lifestyle in St. Augustine and the Pagoda was not in a secluded location, the community did not publicly proclaim a lesbian identity. Residents necessarily kept a "very low profile" in the outside community (The Womyn of the Pagoda). Unlike the lesbians in southern Oregon who, weather permitting, enjoyed music, nudity, and sexual activity out of doors, Pagoda residents were prohibited from appearing nude on the grounds or on the beach and were urged to keep the volume of all voices and activities low, especially after dark.

Beneath the Pagoda's veneer of repression and orthodoxy was a vibrant experiment in lesbian community. "We maintain a very special energy here," noted Pagoda resident Elethia in 1982; "when I drive into the Pagoda, I feel like I've entered another space and time" (Morgana and Elethia 1985, 113). Emily Greene bought a cottage at the Pagoda in 1978. Looking back on her life there, her "memory was not of being overwhelmed by rules" because she saw them as necessary to the lesbian paradise being created (Greene 2009). She found the Pagoda to be "life transforming" for herself and for others: "There was a real desire for egalitarianism, [and an] openness to diversity." The "rich, deep bonds we formed as we worked, played, and struggled to keep the Pagoda going" helped her to realize that she "wanted to always live in community, especially with Lesbians" (Greene 2009).

This unique lesbian space was "amazing" according to founder MacVicar, "when you think of the fact that we own very little land—two fifty foot strips surrounded by development, [with] a busy street out front" (Morgana and Elethia 1985, 113). Pagoda residents bought the swimming pool they had originally shared with a third strip of cottages, and enjoyed a community space featuring Persephone's garden and firepit. In addition, the community had a cultural center "open to ALL womyn," housing a small theater and a store featuring natural foods and products handcrafted by women (The Womyn of the Pagoda). In the center building, called the Pagoda, the Temple of Love, residents were encouraged to participate in various activities and events celebrating women's culture and spirituality.

Recalled early resident Emily Greene, "[I]t really did have the feel of an island of Lesbian paradise." Significantly, the Pagoda was a one-minute walk from the beach, offering immediate access to all the natural beauty and sense of timelessness, wonder, and freedom that the ocean evokes. The ocean had "invaded the soul" of Greene at an early age, and she recalls that "the beautiful setting of the Pagoda by the Sea was a big draw for so many women: as we traveled through this uncharted territory [of creating an egalitarian lesbian community], the ocean was such a comfort." Greene recounts walking on the beach "when life was almost overwhelming," then returning to "my little cottage with renewed strength to carry on" (2009). "Rituals and bonfires by the beach were common and sustained community identity" (Rabin and Slater 2005, 175). The Pagoda's "sweet little" beach cottages "needed a lot of fixing up," but were, in the community's early years, relatively affordable (Greene 2009). Measuring six hundred square feet, they boasted "rustic-tacky charm," had heat and air-conditioning, and in addition to a stove and refrigerator were fully furnished. Lesbians at the Pagoda chose housing that offered convenience without extravagance, consciously living a relatively simple, environmentally friendly lifestyle. The dune grass that separated the structures from the beach, for example, remained undeveloped and without paved paths.

In this intimate environment, lesbians of the Pagoda were free to practice (or to reject) wide-ranging spiritualities, including goddess worship. Some residents who practiced Wicca participated in a variety of rituals, including Moon Circles, which honor the various stages of the moon's appearance and draw from its power. Their beliefs, emphasizing the influence on humans caused by cycles in nonhuman nature, fostered environmental awareness. Practitioners sought to protect the earth they viewed as a Holy Mother.

In this nonviolent, women-only "lesbian paradise" in a beautiful natural setting, members of the Pagoda sought to create genuine community (Kershaw 2009). Residents gathered together one evening each week to discuss any interpersonal issues. Differences or issues affecting the entire community received top priority. Support and feedback were also available to residents struggling with a particular need or problem (The Womyn of the Pagoda). In short, the Pagoda was not just a pretty place for lesbians to live while basically carrying on as if in the outside world. "It was a truly transformative experience," according to Emily Greene. "We were all given the golden opportunity to delve deeply into our hearts and search our souls for what truly had meaning . . . learning to live co-operatively, helping to promote the cultural and spiritual expression of women" (Greene 2009).

The Pagoda's inhabitants were not as pointedly environmentally aware and active as their separatist sisters in Oregon, but certainly they were more conscious of the need for the conservation and preservation of resources than were the early residents of Cherry Grove. The way of life at the Pagoda represented an effort to live simply and more in conscious harmony with nature. Residents sought to celebrate and protect the area's wild beauty and to create a supportive sisterhood of like-minded lesbians who could pursue their chosen spiritual practices and offer each other support and guidance.

Six long-term community members made plans to expand the Pagoda in order to make room for the "Crone's Nest," a new kind of environment dedicated to the needs of aging lesbians (Greene 2009). It was not to be. The Pagoda's physical environment, primarily its proximity to the beach that had been key to its success, contributed to its decline in the 1990s as a haven for lesbians living with an emphasis on simple, low-impact ways of living with nature. The dune grass providing the community easy access to the beach was replaced by condominiums, and a new bridge built directly in front of the property further diminished the peace and beauty that had played a large role in the community's founding. Life at the Pagoda became more expensive and "things started to become difficult," according to a former resident. "Newer women [did not] want to continue struggling to work [out] our issues through our feelings meetings and consensus" (Greene 2009). Beach erosion and the high price of local land contributed to the decision by three of the founding members to leave.

Although heterosexuals bought some of the Pagoda properties, in the first decade of the twenty-first century the remaining lesbian residents retain aspects of lesbian community, albeit in reduced form (Rabin and Slater 2005).

Temporary Alternative Environments: The Power of Women's Festivals

Most lesbians rejected the call to separatism and sought instead to find their rightful place in mainstream society. But this, too, often included a strong environmental element. Many closeted lesbians, emboldened by the women's rights movements that erupted in the 1960s, no longer felt compelled to live a lie and left their heterosexual marriages. Other women allowed themselves to honestly examine their sexuality for the first time. Free from the assumption that they must be heterosexual, they discovered, and celebrated, their same-sex desires. Many experienced this epiphany in a unique environment conducive to the empowerment of women: the women's music festival.

Women started performing in church basements and bookstores in the early 1960s, but soon were gathering larger audiences in bigger venues. The impact of hearing lesbian-themed music with an audience of other women is impossible to exaggerate. In the 1999 film documentary *After Stonewall*, Torie Osborn highlights the large number of women then in their mid-40s and 50s who remember vividly their first women's music concert. Osborn certainly had not forgotten hers:

> I can remember piling six . . . women . . . into my little baby blue Volkswagen and driving down from Burlington, Vermont, where there was no gay subculture, to see my first [women's music pioneer] Cris Williamson concert. One [of the six women] quit her job as a nurse so that she could form Coven Carpentry, so she could do lesbian carpentry. One left her husband—we're talkin' this concert literally changed people's lives. The empowerment had an ongoing impact. It was an extraordinary force. (quoted in Scagliotti, Baus, and Hunt 1999)

Women's concerts grew into festivals, described by feminist scholar Bonnie J. Morris as "a vibrant subculture" welcoming "the female outsider in search of an alternative community." Women's festivals rejected "the material objectification of women in violent U.S. media" and celebrated "the female sphere as a source of empowerment apart from men's gatherings" (quoted in Scagliotti, Baus, and Hunt 1999; see also Ciasullo 2001). "The only place we really feel safe," reflected one festival attendee in 1983, "is on the land, not in the city run by men. A lot of times we don't realize it until we leave and then we get slapped in the face by the contrast" (Wiseheart et al. 1985, 97). Women camped out and had the opportunity to buy and sell arts and crafts, carry out a variety of spiritual rituals and practices, go naked, and make social and sexual contacts. Perhaps the best known of the variety of annual music events that began during the 1970s and 1980s and includes Pennsylvania's Campfest is the Michigan Womyn's Music Festival.

Since its debut in 1976, the Michigan festival has been held every August, welcoming women of all nationalities, ages, races, sexualities, and physical abilities. In 1982 it moved to a private rural setting of more than 650 acres, where it consistently attracts thousands of women each year, and has been "celebrated for decades as a must-see destination for activists in lesbian cultural production" (Morris 2005, 623). Diversity is strongly valued. In addition to the Womyn of Color Tent, features include networking spaces for teens, over-40s, Jewish womyn, the Deaf, and womyn from other countries; dances, musical performances, a film festival, a crafts bazaar, and a wide array of workshops. Tickets are priced on a sliding scale to encourage attendance by women of all economic abilities. The festival's emphasis is on community: "Each womon [staying the entire week] does two shifts in a community area during her stay (one for the week-enders), adding her own splash of color to the fabric of the Festival. Every womon's personal involvement forms the foundation of the Festival spirit, built on the energy, ethic, good fun and challenge of living and working together" (General Festival Information 2007).

Part of that working together to create a truly alternative environment is dedicated to respecting the earth and leaving the lightest possible footprint. Central to the Michigan experience are the "forest, meadow, and sky [that] stretch out in all directions" (General Festival Information 2007). Participants are required to be "land stewards" and honor nature as a partner rather than a backdrop. This involves living simply for the duration of the festival, thereby consuming fewer resources and creating as little waste as possible. This creation of an "ecology consciousness," reflected one participant in 1983, offers a "real hands-on experience in 'what are we doing here? How are we living here?'" and a lesson in "how fragile the ecology is . . . thru more than a textbook." She spoke for many attendees when she emphasized her "vested interest in more and more women feeling connected to the land" (Wiseheart et al. 1985, 97).

For many participants an environmental consciousness is further fostered by woman-centered spiritual practices emphasizing women's "oneness" with the earth, with the moon, and with natural cycles. From its earliest beginnings, "[p]art of Michigan's radical mission," according to Morris, "was its safe space for woman-identified and woman-centered spiritual practice. Events and Goddess rituals . . . allowed women who had been hurt by their exclusion from (male-only) religious office or women recovering from male-dominated fundamentalism to find themselves in feminine images of the divine" (2005, 622).

Whether or not attendees participate in nature-centered spiritual rituals, all are required to clean up after themselves and respect their surroundings. The land is valued for its own sake, not merely for the special qualities it brings to the various events. Rather than create a permanent infrastructure on the land to facilitate the elaborate set-up procedures necessary to put on such a large event, after each Michigan festival much effort is expended to return the land as completely as possible to its natural state. All nonorganic materials are removed. The electrical boxes that power the festival are buried so that no visible trace of human activity remains. Nonhuman rather than human nature takes precedence and is sustained. "We reduce it all back to that meadow and ferns," notes organizer Sandy Ramsey. "If there is a very high impact deterioration happening somewhere . . . maybe we would do some mulching, seeding, landscaping. . . . We're very aware that we have to watch these things and do what needs to be done to make sure that we can continue to reuse them" (quoted in Lo 2005).

Morris calls the Michigan festival "a wonderland of cultural anthropology" offering "a record spanning two generations or more of musicians, dancers, technicians, craftswomen, comedic emcees, workshop speakers, healthcare workers, kitchen chefs-for-8,000, and land stewards [that] represents the opportunity to examine the absolute best in cooperative community and what might be called an ongoing city of women (akin to 'Brigadoon,' appearing magically at yearly intervals)" (Morris 2005, 627). A Michigan regular celebrates important differences rather than the similarities between Michigan and Brigadoon: "Unlike Brigadoon, where everything is clean, the weather is perfect, and everyone is rich, white, heterosexual, able bodied, politically homogenous (i.e., unaware), Michigan brings together a largely lesbian sample of *everyone*" (Morris 2005, 627; Wiseheart et al. 1985, 100). Despite the fleeting nature of the festivals themselves, the sense of community and lesbian sisterhood and environmental awareness they instilled was permanent. "We go," asserts

Morris, "because festivals offer the possibility of what our lives *could* be like year-round if we lived each day in a matriarchy actively striving to eliminate racism and homophobia . . . [while] living tribally" (1999, xiii). One 1990 attendee said simply, "The planet should be like this" (Morris 1999, 328).

Although attendance is down to about half of the 8,000–9,000 reached during peak years, and Morris laments the passing of some of the early leaders and guiding lights of the festival, more than thirty years after Michigan's debut, it lives on. Even late into the first decade of the twenty-first century, the festival continues to invite women "into the familiar comfort of a time and space where we celebrate all things female." "The magic of Michigan" is described as "a city built up from the ground up by feminist values," where "healthy food, clean air, green woods, art and music will recharge batteries you didn't know were fading." "Make it to Michigan one time," organizers promise, "and it will call to you each and every August" (General Festival Information, 2007).

Exclusively Lesbian Workshops and Meetings as Alternative Environments

Although lesbians flocked to Michigan, the festival is open to all women-born-women (that is, those who were born and raised as girls and who identify as women, excluding transsexual and transgender women—one of several policies generating heated debate within the queer community) (Lo 2005; Morris 1990). Many lesbians sought exclusively lesbian gatherings in which to meet, network, find strength, and create community. Lesbian meetings and political workshops, like Sisterspace, held annually in the Pocono Mountains beginning in 1975, and the ones organized in Gainesville, Florida, in 1984 and 1985 by LEAP (Lesbians for Empowerment, Action, and Politics), were frequently held at remote, outdoor sites that ensured privacy and encouraged "a passionate love for the natural world." LEAP organizers wanted lesbians to learn more about their connection to the earth. Seeking to heal both the environment and themselves they worked to create a community that "will give us energy and power in our work of transforming the effects of the white man's patriarchy on this achingly beautiful planet" (Next Southern Leap 1985, cover).

Two hundred and fifty lesbians gathered on October 19–21, 1984, at "a beautiful wooded private campground on the Suwannee River near Gainsville, Florida" where LEAP created its first "self-sufficient community by sharing . . . dreams, feelings, knowledge, skills, hopes, fears, art, spirituality, food, chores, tears, support and love." The result, according to the organizers of the following year's event "has been enlightening, empowering, and is something we will carry through the rest of our lives" (Next Southern Leap 1985, cover). Key to LEAP's success in "shar[ing] our actions . . . shar[ing] our ways of living lesbian lives" was its emphasis on partnership with the land, which was "beautiful with shaded oak groves, huge pines, open sunlit clearings, patches of deer moss, [and] sprinklings of zillions of kinds of Florida plant life." "We are here among the long leaf pines to find out more about ourselves and each other [and] more about our connection to the earth," LEAP reminded attendees, and urged them to "Please enjoy the beauty of this land" but take care not to disrupt its delicate ecosystems. Further evidence of LEAP's emphasis on nature as partner is apparent in much of its literature: "We are . . . sharing this space with coral snakes, prickly pear cactus, and scorpions. . . ." "We are here," urged LEAP, "to help each other explore and discover the wisest, healthiest way to use the power that springs from our individual truths— for changing the world." A community vegetarian kitchen was partially dependant upon attendees' donations and "organized around the grand lesbian traditions of anarchy and chaos" (1985, cover–1). Because of the privacy the woods provided, nudity was "highly encouraged on the interior of the land," also contributing to the sense of being in a unique and accepting space (1985, 2).

LEAP's literature emphasized the power inherent in this alternative environment: "Coming into an all-lesbian space provides us with a particular kind of safety that is basically unknown in the world where most of us live. All of a sudden we are able to be ourselves in a truer way. The protective walls we keep up as we move through the patriarchal culture often come tumbling down—and sometimes real fast and dramatically. . . . Letting these feelings out is an important step toward our personal freedom and happiness and it also provides us with more energy for doing our political work" (1985, 6). Like the more inclusive women's festivals, LEAP was intended not as a temporary respite, but as a catalyst for creating permanent change, including awareness of the earth and its resources as a partner requiring respect, careful use, and protection. Attendees were warned that as they moved "back into patriarchal culture," they would likely find themselves "bombarded by the sickening truth of what . . . patriarchy is." LEAP organizers urged that attendees use the strength they gained through the LEAP experience: "[T]ake a clearer look at our lives and figure out ways we can change things to better express our power; organize groups for political action and consciousness-raising; constantly validate ourselves and each other and the true incredible power of our presence in this world" (1985, 6).

Lesbian festival regular Retts Scauzillo

attended because it was crucial to my survival as a lesbian feminist. I needed to be with like-minded dykes, living and working together, to create our culture and practice our lesbianism. I went there hungry for love and sex and it was a place I could be all of me. I could take my shirt off, wear ripped or revealing clothes, flirt, be sexy, laugh, and talk lesbian feminist politics. We would agree on some things and disagree on others, but by the end of the night we were holding each other and dancing under the stars. I could be outrageous and radical, truly what they call high on life.

Such liberation could take place only if one felt truly free. For Scauzillo and thousands of lesbians like her, the lesbian festival offered "the safest place on the planet. It made the outside world tolerable. . . . I grew up at these festivals and learned lessons that are with me today. Plus it was FUN!" (2007).

Many of the women's and/or lesbian festivals that flourished in the 1970s and 1980s disappeared in the 1990s due to poor attendance, in large part due to the success of feminism and the gay and lesbian liberation movements. "The woman-identification of earlier festivals simply does not call out as spectacularly to young women who have grown up with more rights, with Title IX, with greater possibilities of becoming rabbis, lawyers, or politicians," notes Bonnie Morris (2005, 625). Festival regular Scauzillo acknowledged in 2007 that she had become part of the older generation and recognized that "it is the right [sic] of passage for the young queer women to rebel against us." She doubted that the 2007 festivals' intergenerational emphasis, such as Sisterspace's ODYQ (Old Dyke, Young Queer) forum, would succeed in bringing in substantial numbers of young lesbians: "I try to think as a young queer woman now, would I need or want to go to women's music festivals?" Scauzillo understood the draw of lesbian-only cruises, vacations, and Dinah Shore parties, and yet complained that "the F-word [feminism] is missing" from most of these retreats that are more in the pleasure-seeking tradition of Cherry Grove than Michigan-style consciousness raising. In her view, as "queer" replaces "dyke," "women are invisible in the new 'gender/studies' world." She recalled her recent positive experience at the Sisterspace festival, whose objectives focused exclusively on making women both visible and empowered. Features included education regarding issues of concern to the lesbian community

and the fostering of a positive self-image for lesbians. Scauzillo emphasized a trait conspicuously absent from the retreat activities enjoyed by
younger lesbians: the communal aspect of traditional women-only festivals
such as Sisterspace and Campfest. She singled out for praise "the unpaid
workers, most of them lesbians who created these festivals and keep them
going" and the sense of community that kind of participation produces.
Also missing from most resort experiences (which frequently promote
consumption rather than conservation) is the kind of environmental consciousness overtly cultivated and honored by back to the land lesbians, the
residents of the Pagoda, and festivals such as Michigan and LEAP. Despite
her doubts, Scauzillo hoped that "festivals will start popping up and young
dykes will start [re]claiming these institutions as their own" (2007).

Back to the Land Redux: Alapine Village

Scauzillo's desire for a revival of lesbian institutions is shared by former members of the Pagoda. After leaving Florida in 1997, three Pagoda
co-founders relocated to northeastern Alabama, where, over time, they
acquired nearly 400 acres of rural land. They established a legal corporation and began developing about 80 acres into a lesbian community
they named Alapine Village. On this land they carried out some of their
original goals in far more isolation from the outside world than was ever
possible at the Pagoda (Kershaw 2009). Former Pagoda member Emily
Greene came to Alapine because she wanted "to be in nature" and to have
lesbian neighbors. She was happy "to be back in community with people
who want to live simply so that others may simply live." Her dreams were
"to help us age the way we want without leaving our community, to be
good care takers of this beautiful land and save some of it for our fellow
creatures, [and] to have as low an impact as I possibly can on my environment" (Greene 2009).

Environmental protection and sustainability were paramount at
Alapine. In 2009 Greene sought to negotiate the swap of some Alapine
land for an adjoining 60-acre forest that was home to "the trees, deer,
coyote, squirrels, rabbits, and birds," in order to permanently protect that
"pristine forest" from development (2009). Like most Alapine residents,
she practiced many environmentally friendly ways of living: she collected rain as her water source, and used a tankless hot water heater and
a wood-burning stove. Vegetables grown in Alapine's community garden
were another indication of the group's dedication to sustainability—and

to eating as nutritiously as possible, good health being at a premium to the many members without medical insurance.

Alapine residents valued the many additional benefits of their deep connections with the earth. Barbara Stoll shared many of Greene's dreams, and she too found in Alapine the opportunity to turn those dreams into reality. Stoll "just knew from an early age" that she was "meant to live in the woods." Finding "the consumerism and materialism of suburbia" to be "more than I could bear," she referred to Alapine as "my paradise." For Stoll, who had read "everything I could get my hands on regarding homesteading, alternative energy, sustainability, etc.," it was the place where she could "get back to the basics of life, the rawness of carving out a life that wasn't consumed by things and manmade ideologies." Life at Alapine allowed her to find answers to life's most important questions: "How little could I live on, how much could I produce myself, how might I take life down to its simplest elements so that nature could flow through me without hindrance?" (Stoll 2009).

Like the lesbians in rural southern Oregon, Stoll designed her small, one-room cabin "for the highest efficiency," allowing her to "live lightly on the land" because "the most important aspect of living on the land for me was having as small a footprint as I possibly could." Although she described herself as a hermit, Stoll rejoiced in her ability to live in a like-minded community and "visited other intentional communities in other states to learn about this much needed and wonderful way of life." Living at a "much calmer, more serene pace . . . surrounded by other like minded women," according to Stoll, allowed for "stretching of the mind and new ideas to be considered and possibly implemented." She refused, however, to romanticize her "very simple and frugal life," noting the psychological as well as the physical struggles at Alapine, where "the land brings emotion to the surface . . . [and] the woods do not let you hide from yourself," and where communal living in "a group of strong women with strong opinions" can be "very challenging" (2009). For all its difficulties, life at Alapine had profound meaning for Stoll: "I live an authentic life [because] I touch nature and the sacredness of life everyday." She vowed to "heal the planet and its non-human inhabitants with my every action," and hoped that even after she was "long dead," other women would "carry the torch and continue what we are trying to accomplish here, to preserve the beauty of life through nature and gentle, light-footed actions" (2009).

The community worried about who those women bearing torches into the future might be. While at the Michigan festival in 2005, Alapine resident Emily Greene "became really aware and concerned about the lack of younger womyn attracted to living in community on the land" (Greene 2009). By 2009, her worry became more acute. Although home to only twenty residents, Alapine was nevertheless one of the largest of the remaining "about 100 below-the-radar lesbian communities in North America." "We are really going to have to think about how we carry this on," noted Greene, or "in twenty to twenty-five years, we [lesbians in alternative communities] could be extinct" (Kershaw 2009). At age sixty-two, Greene recognized that younger lesbians were not eager to withdraw from heterosexual society because "the younger generation has not had to go through what we went through." Many Alapine residents were "deeply scarred" by the discrimination and persecution they suffered at the hands of an openly homophobic society. They felt in the 1960s and 1970s "a real sense of the need to strongly identify as a woman and have women's space ... the need to be apart" in order to draw on their own strength and empowerment. They recognize that "young feminists today recoil at the idea of identity politics" (Kershaw 2009).

Although the members of Alapine Village lived quietly and avoided publicity, in 2009 they were willing to be the subject of a feature story in the *New York Times* as one way of reaching out to younger lesbians in their efforts to remain a viable and vibrant community. The web version of the story included a multimedia presentation featuring Alapine residents and their natural setting.[2] To help achieve its shared goal of "expanding into an intergenerational community, especially welcoming younger women," Alapine created a website (Alapine Community Association 2009). In addition to celebration of the many social features of community living, much was made in the inviting Web pages of the land's rolling hills, hardwood and pine forests, flowing mountain river, and hiking paths, as well as the ready availability of outdoor activities (bicycling, canoeing, kayaking, camping, and gardening). The Web site also featured the community's use of wood heat, solar energy, propane, composting toilets, and recycling, its self-sufficiency, and its work toward making "homes, gardens and community buildings sustainable, with the ability to survive off grid" (Alapine Community Association 2009).

Nature remained an important component in this lesbian alternative environment and, its residents hoped, one of the keys to attracting like-minded lesbians and assuring its future. The response generated by the *New York Times* was overwhelming. It "warmed the heart" of Greene, and convinced her that "we are not a 'dying breed,' and that our form of community is very vibrant and alive." With "plenty of land [and] hard-working women," this former nursing-home care provider has renewed confidence that the women of Alapine can "create a new environment for Lesbians as we age" (Greene 2009).

Conclusion

Place matters. In times of oppression and intolerance, there were few spaces that allowed for lesbian sisterhood. Lesbians used existing built environments, such as the nightclubs of Harlem and beach cottages of Cherry Grove, to carve out rare opportunities for lesbian community. Following the rise of environmental and feminist consciousness, spaces were made into more than just enclaves of same-sex desire. Some lesbians made ambitious efforts to create settings in which they could also put into practice their ecofeminist philosophies. These efforts, whether temporary, like Michigan, or permanent, like Alapine Village, offered participants not just safety and freedom, but the opportunity to carry out experiments in both egalitarianism and environmental sustainability.

Such lesbian alternative environments are by no means obsolete, but no longer do they provide the only safe space in which lesbians can enjoy the freedom to be themselves, find solidarity, and build community. Esther Rothblum and Penny Sablove's edited 2005 collection *Lesbian Communities: Festivals, RVs, and the Internet,* for example, includes an essay on virtual lesbian communities that do not even exist in physical space. Environmental consciousness and protection are, however, increasingly promoted in both gay and lesbian cyberspace and real-life communities. In 2008, *Out Front Blog* documented that as "consumer engagement in all things 'green' has taken off in the past year, engagement and recognition of gay and lesbian audiences with environmental issues has also increased. . . . For many gays and lesbians in 2008, green is the new pink" (Finzel 2008). According to Emily Greene in 2009, "lesbians as a group are more conscious of how they are impacting their environment now more than ever before." Growing lesbian attention to environmental issues does not change the fact that many of their efforts to remake the world by creating environmental alternatives have fallen casualty to the rise of multiple new spaces and opportunities for lesbian sisterhood.

Through their efforts to transcend sexism, homophobia, and violence, lesbian communities sometimes intentionally and sometimes inadvertently made important contributions to environmental history and environmental justice movements. Some groups' recognition of nature as partner and de-emphasis on materialism make them particularly valuable models of efforts to create sustainable ways of living. Further research on lesbian alternative communities, past and present, will not only shed light on important aspects of lesbian history, but also provide thought-provoking examples of new ways of thinking, living, and valuing both human and non-human nature.

NOTES
Minor portions of this essay originally appeared in Unger (2004). A Mary Lily Grant funded research at the Sallie Bingham Center for Women's History and Culture at Duke University. Emily Greene, Barbara Stoll, and Morgana MacVicar contributed generously to this essay. Don Whitebread, Mary Whisner, and Susan Goodier provided editing expertise.
1. In the documents of many of these efforts to create lesbian alternative communities, "woman" is spelled variously as "womyn," "womon," and "wimmin." Those original spellings are maintained in this essay.
2. Article at www.nytimes.com/2009/02/01/fashion/01womyn.html?_r=2&scp= 2&scp=sarah%20kershaw&st=cse. Multi-media presentation at
www.nytimes.com/interactive/2009/02/01/style/20090201-women-feature/ index.html.

REFERENCES
Agnew, Eleanor. 2004. *Back from the Land*. Chicago: Ivan R. Dee.
Alapine Community Association, Inc. 2009. http://www.alapine.com.
Atkins, Gary. 2003. *Gay Seattle*. Seattle, Wash.: University of Washington Press.
Carson, Rachel. 1962. *Silent Spring*. Boston, Mass.:Houghton Mifflin.
Chauncey, George. 1994. *Gay New York*. New York: Basic Books.
Cheney, Joyce, ed. 1985. *Lesbian Land*. Minneapolis, Minn.: Word Weavers.
Ciasullo, Ann. 2001. Making Her (In)Visible: Cultural Representations of Lesbianism and the Lesbian Body in the 1990s. *Feminist Studies* 27.3: 577–608.
Corinne, Tee. 1998. Little Houses on Women's Lands. http://www-lib.usc.edu/~retter/ teehouses.html.
Davis, Angela Y. 1998. *Blues Legacies and Black Feminism*. New York: Pantheon Books.
Finzel, Ben. 2008. Earth Gay. *Out Front Blog: The Full Spectrum of Gay and Lesbian Communications*. http://www.fhoutfront.com/2008/04/earth-gay.html.
Garber, Eric. 2009. A Spectacle in Color: The Lesbian and Gay Subculture of Jazz Age Harlem. http://xroads.virginia.edu/~UG97/blues/garber.html.
General Festival Information. 2007, 2008. *Michigan Womyn's Music Festival*. http:// www.michfest.com/festival/index.htm.
Greene, Emily. 2009. Personal correspondence with author.
Kershaw, Sarah. 2009. My Sister's Keeper. *New York Times,* February 1, ST1.

Kleiner, Catherine. 2003. Nature's Lovers: The Erotics of Lesbian Land Communites in Oregon, 1974–1984. In *Seeing Nature through Gender,* ed. Virginia. Scharff, 242–63. Lawrence: University Press of Kansas.

Lear, Linda. 1997. *Rachel Carson: Witness for Nature.* New York: Henry Holt.

Lo, Malinda. 2005. Behind the Scenes at the Michigan Womyn's Festival. http://www.afterellen.com/archive/ellen/Music/2005/4/michigan3.html.

MacKinnon, Mary Heather, and Moni McIntyre, eds. 1995. *Readings in Ecology and Feminist Theology.* Kansas City, Kans.: Sheed and Ward.

Merchant, Carolyn. 1992. *Radical Ecology.* New York: Routledge.

Morgana and Elthia. 1985. The Pagoda. In *Lesbian Land,* ed. Joyce Cheney, 111–15. Minneapolis, Minn.: Word Weavers.

Morris, Bonnie J. 1999. *Eden Built by Eves: The Culture of Women's Music Festivals.* New York: Alyson.

———. 2005. Valuing Woman-Only Spaces. *Feminist Studies* 31.3: 618–30.

Nestle, Joan. 2001 (1993). Black Entertainer Mabel Hampton Recalls Lesbian Life in the 1920s and 1930s. In *Major Problems in the History of Sexuality,* ed. K. L. Peiss, 345–46. New York: Houghton Mifflin.

Next Southern Leap. 1985. Box 8. File 15. Atlanta Feminist Lesbian Alliance. Rare Book, Manuscript, and Special Collections Library. Duke University.

Newton, Esther. 1995. *Cherry Grove, Fire Island: Sixty Years in America's First Gay and Lesbian Town.* Boston, Mass.: Beacon Press.

———. 1997. The "Fun Gay Ladies": Lesbian in Cherry Grove, 1936–1960. In *Creating a Place for Ourselves: Lesbian, Gay, and BiSexual Community Histories,* ed. B. Beemyn, 145–64. New York: Routledge.

Rabin, Joan S., and Barbara Slater. 2005. Lesbian Communities across the United States: Pockets of Resistance and Resilience. *Journal of Lesbian Studies* 9.1–2: 169–82.

Rome, Adam. 2003. "Give Earth a Chance": The Environmental Movement and the Sixties. *Journal of American History* 90.2: 525–54.

Rosenberg, Robert, John Scagliotti, and Greta Schiller, prod. 1984. Motion picture. *Before Stonewall.* First Run Features.

Rothblum, Esther, and Penny Sablove, eds. 2005. *Lesbian Communities: Festivals, RVs, and the Internet.* New York: Harrington Park Press.

Sandilands, Catriona. 2002. Lesbian Separatist Communities and the Experience of Nature. *Organization and Environment* 15.2: 131–61.

Scagliotti, John, Janet Baus, and Dan Hunt, prod. 1999. Motion picture. *After Stonewall.* First Run Features.

Scauzillo, Retts. 2007. Women-Only Festivals: Is There a Future? *About: Lesbian Life.* http://lesbianlife.about.com/od/musicreviews/a/WomenOnlyFest.htm.

Splitrock, Myra Lilliane. 1985. Traveling in Dykeland. In *Lesbian Land,* ed. Joyce Cheney, 167–68. Minneapolis, Minn.: Word Weavers.

Stoll, Barbara. 2009. Personal correspondence with author.

Sturgeon, Noël. 1997. *Ecofeminist Natures.* New York: Routledge.

Unger, Nancy C. 2004. Women, Sexuality, and Environmental Justice in American History. In *New Perspectives on Environmental Justice: Gender, Sexuality, and Activism,* ed. Rachel Stein, 45–60. New Brunswick, N.J.: Rutgers University Press.

Warnock, Donna. Circa 1985. Pamphlet. What Growthmania Does to Women and the Environment. Syracuse: Feminist Resources on Energy and Ecology. Box 14. File 6. Atlanta Feminist Lesbian Alliance. Rare Book, Manuscript, and Special Collections Library, Duke University.

Warren, Karen J., ed. 1997. *Ecofeminism: Women, Culture, Nature.* Bloomington: Indiana University Press.

Wiseheart, Susan, et al. 1985. Michigan. In *Lesbian Land,* ed. Joyce Cheney, 96–98. Minneapolis, Minn.: Word Weavers.

The Womyn of the Pagoda. (n.d.) The Pagoda. Box 10. File 26. Atlanta Feminist Lesbian Alliance. Rare Book, Manuscript, and Special Collections Library, Duke University.

CHAPTER 7

Polluted Politics? Confronting Toxic Discourse, Sex Panic, and Eco-Normativity

GIOVANNA DI CHIRO

The body as home, but only if it is understood that bodies can be stolen, fed lies and poison, torn away from us. They rise up around me—bodies stolen by hunger, war, breast cancer, AIDS, rape; the daily grind of factory, sweatshop, cannery, sawmill; the lynching rope; the freezing streets; the nursing home and prison. . . . Disabled people cast as supercrips and tragedies; lesbian/gay/bisexual/trans people told over and over again that we are twisted and unnatural; poor people made responsible for their own poverty. Stereotypes and lies lodge in our bodies as surely as bullets. They live and fester there, stealing the body.

—Eli Clare

As genderqueer author Eli Clare notes, there are myriad terrible ways that bodies are stolen, violated, and poisoned. Enumerating the diverse messages of "body hatred" that he has lived with throughout his life owing to the "irrevocable difference" of his queerness and disability—perverse, unnatural, defective, tragic—Clare explains how these expressions of abnormality "sunk beneath his skin" and would tear him from his body (2001, 362). Bodies can be torn and stolen away in multiple ways (rape, murder, poverty, disease, trauma, numbness), and Clare keys into the various and intersecting techniques through which injustice can mark a body:

I think of the kid tracked into "special education" because of his speech impediment, which is actually a common sign of sexual abuse. I think of the autoimmune diseases, the cancers, the various kinds of chemical sensitivities that flag what it means to live in a world full of toxins. I think of the folks who live with work-related disabilities because of exploitative, dangerous work conditions. I think of the people who live downwind of nuclear fallout, the people who die for lack of access to health care, the rape survivors who struggle with post-traumatic stress disorder. (2001, 362–63)

"But just as the body can be stolen, it can also be reclaimed" (363). According to Clare, this means "refiguring the world" into one composed of bodies unique and precious to the earth and all who live on it. The body can be reclaimed and refigured as *home*—that desired place of connectedness, family, and well-being—with full realization that the body/home is sometimes the site of exposure to just the opposite: abuse, hunger, polluted water and air. Clare's analysis of difference and connection as being located in the body/home and his social-environmental politics based on reclaiming and learning from those stolen bodies that have been deemed out of place, against nature, broken and deformed, produces what Catriona Mortimer-Sandilands has termed a *queer ecology* that is "both about seeing beauty in the wounds of the world and taking responsibility to care for the world as it is" (Mortimer-Sandilands 2005, 24).

In environmental studies, the term "ecology"—whose root comes from the Greek *oikos,* meaning an inhabited house or household—describes the web of relationships and interconnections among organisms and their "homes" (their communities and biophysical environments) (Ward and Dubos 1972). Thinking of the body as home/ecology, especially in consideration of those bodies, communities, and environments that have been reviled, neglected, and polluted, provides an apt metaphor and material grounding for constructing an *embodied* ecological politics that articulates the concepts of diversity, interdependence, social justice, and ecological integrity. In recent years, the environmental justice movement has elucidated the ways that poor communities and communities of color have shouldered an unequal burden of the negative externalities of modern, industrial society—their lands, homes, communities, and bodies have been exploited, dumped on, and contaminated with toxic emissions resulting in disproportionate rates of environmental illnesses, reproductive harms, and degraded homelands. In contrast to mainstream environmentalism, which has historically viewed social and ecological issues as separate concerns, environmental justice activists construct a more inclusive vision of human-nature interactions generating an ecopolitics that brings environmentalism *home,* so to speak, and defines the environment as our *communities:* the places where "we live, work, play, and learn."[1] Along with the more commonly understood view of nature as the living biosphere, activists also embrace inhabited/built places—cities, villages, reservations, agricultural fields, workplaces, and poor and low-income neighborhoods located next to hazardous industrial facilities—as *environments* worthy of recognition and protection (Di Chiro 1996). Moreover, the environmental justice challenge to the dominant (primarily white, middle-class, and male) environmental movement espouses human *diversity* as a shared value and locates its historical lineage in struggles for civil rights and social and economic justice (Bryant and Mohai 1992; Bullard 1994). Can such an ecopolitics committed to inclusivity and diversity—which offers an essential corrective to the environmental movement—also embrace as worthy of recognition and protection the unseen bodies, homes, and environments about which Clare writes?

In this chapter I discuss how the dominant anti-toxics discourse deployed in mainstream environmentalism adopts the potent rhetoric that toxic chemical pollution is responsible for the undermining or perversion of the "natural": natural biologies/ecologies, natural bodies, natural reproductive processes. This contemporary environmental anxiety appeals to cultural fears of exposure to chemical and endocrine-disrupting toxins as troubling and destabilizing the normal/natural gendered body of humans and other animal species, leading to what some have called the "chemical castration" or the "feminization of nature" (Cadbury 1998; Hayes 2002). Particular anxiety has been focused on the perils to humanity of our "swimming in a sea of estrogen" (Raloff 1994b, 56; Sumpter and Jobling 1995, 173), a consequence, according to many environmental scientists, of the rising levels of estrogenic, synthetic chemical compounds emitted into our water, air, and food. This concern about the excesses of estrogenic pollution (what some refer to as "ova-pollution") is commonly articulated in popular scientific media as explaining the pan-species *instability* of maleness and as putting at risk the future existence of *natural* masculinity. Invoking an oft-used environmentalist metaphor, this anti-toxics discourse warns that the rising incidences of male-to-female gender shifts and intersex conditions observed in the "lower" species of animals, such as frogs, fish, and salamanders, represents the newest "canaries in the coalmine" portending an uncertain fate for human maleness and for the future of *normal* sexual reproduction (Roberts 2003). Moreover, this anti-toxics discourse argues that many estrogenic chemical toxins disrupt or prevent normal *prenatal* physiological development and disturb natural reproductive processes, leading to rising cases of infertility and producing disabled, defective, and even monstrous bodies. What are presented by many environmentalists as critical scientific facts (and quite rightly worthy of alarm) can, however, work to create a "sex panic," resuscitating familiar heterosexist, queerphobic, and eugenics arguments classifying some bodies as being not normal: mistakes, perversions, or burdens. This version of anti-toxics environmentalism, while professing laudable and progressive goals, mobilizes the knowledge/power politics of normalcy and normativity and reinforces what queer and disability theorists have analyzed as a *compulsory* social-environmental order based on a dominant regime of what and who are constructed as normal and natural (Davis 1995; Garland-Thomson 1997; McRuer 2006). Clare's critical melding of queer theory, disability theory, and environmental justice politics illuminates the cultural and ideological work performed by the hegemonic concept of the normal in mainstream environmentalism. Scratch a liberal environmentalist and you might find polluted politics enforcing "eco(hetero)normativity" lurking underneath; disability becomes an environmental problem and lgbtq people become disabled—the unintended consequences of a contaminated and impure environment, unjustly impaired by chemical trespass.

The very *real* issue of the myriad grave consequences (in terms of both mortality and morbidity) of the widespread contamination and worldwide bioaccumulation in bodily tissues of hazardous chemicals known as POPs (persistent organic pollutants)[2] becomes distorted by the alarmist focus on one piece of their toxic story. That selective telling of the story which zeroes in on toxic chemicals' role in disturbing hormonal systems, damaging the reproductive organs, and creating sexual instability and impairment has functioned strategically to appeal to the society's basest fears of an ominous disruption in the normal gender order and ultimately the challenge to heteronormativity. If the resuscitation of old and the generation of *new* eco-normative forms of heterosexism were not enough, the media fixation on gonadal deformities and sexual/gender abnormalities as the most treacherous concern ends up perilously de-emphasizing and, in fact, *naturalizing* and *normalizing* the many other serious health problems associated with POPs, which are on the rise: breast, ovarian, prostate, and testicular cancers, neurological and neurobehavioral problems, immune system breakdown, heart disease, diabetes, and obesity.[3]

In the spirit of unearthing counter discourses to these "polluted politics" and queer(y)ing the liberal stance on environmentalism, I examine several examples of research practices, environmental criticism, and social activism that incorporate an anti-toxics emphasis and profess allegiance to ecofeminist and/or environmental justice politics. One of the key principles of ecofeminist and environmental justice perspectives is a commitment to what might be called a normative politics of inclusiveness, diversity, and social justice. Again, how inclusive and diverse are these progressive social movements? What are the toxic residues of unrecognized or unacknowledged polluted politics that continue to reassert the normalized body and the naturalized environment and therefore impede the potential for forging coalition politics that move us toward a more *just,* green, and sustainable future? Can we imagine environmental-feminist coalitions that can forge a critical normative environmental politics (we *all* should live in a clean environment; we *all* should have the right to healthy bodies) that resist appeals to normativity?

New Gender Troubles

Kermit to Kermette? It's Not Easy Being Green
—Dr. Frank J. Dinan

In the spring of 2008, a *New York Times* article reported on a study by a Yale University biologist on the alarming numbers of "hermaphrodite" frogs (male frogs with ovaries growing in their testes) observed in upscale suburban neighborhoods in the northeastern United States. The article opened with the following attention-getting sentence: "Just as frogs' mating season arrives, a study by a Yale professor raises a troubling issue. How many frogs will be clear on their role in the annual spring-time ritual?" (Barringer 2008, D2).

Although wildlife, evolutionary, and developmental biologists have since the early 1990s observed changes in the physiological development of several species of birds, reptiles, mammals, and fish, and a global decline in the populations of over 30 percent of the known species of amphibians (Alford and Richards 1999), the representation and circulation of this information has in recent years taken on a new sense of urgency. Headlines in scientific and news media have raised the alarm that evidence of the links between species fitness and ecological decay generated from animal studies is surely telling us that "something is sinister underway in the environment" and that humans may ultimately be affected (Amphibian Decline 2006). While the news of rising incidences of fish tumors, clam and mussel lesions, Beluga whale breast and ovarian cancers, and disappearing amphibians have attracted a following in environmentalist circles, the documentation of gender-bending, homosexual, and emasculated frogs, fish, birds, and alligators has caught the attention of the mainstream media and the blogosphere. Kermit the Frog a Transsexual? Intersex Fish? Lesbian Gulls? Hermaphrodite Frogs? "Teeny Weenies" (Dunne 1998)?[4] "Silent Sperm" (Wright 1996)?[5] "Sexual Confusion in the Wild" (Cone 1994)?[6]

In the late 1970s and 1980s, following the EPA's banning of the carcinogenic and persistent organochlorines DDT and PCB, studies were conducted on these chemical toxicants and several other classes of halogenated aromatic pollutants, including the infamous and highly toxic 2,3,7,8-tetrachlorodibenzo-p-dioxin (TCDD, dioxin) to determine their ongoing and long-term health effects, specifically in relation to breast, uterine, and other cancers (Colborn and Clement 1992; Colborn, Vom Saal, and Soto 1993; Steingraber 1997). In the early 1990s, a bumper crop of publications in toxicology and public health journals heightened concerns about the potential adverse human health effects associated with background environmental exposures to so-called endocrine disruptors, chemicals that disrupt endocrine signaling pathways.[7] The harmful effects of TCDD-Dioxin and related compounds on wildlife and laboratory animals had earlier been established, and researchers set upon new studies hypothesizing that other endocrine-active compounds such as estrogenic chemicals that bind directly to the estrogen receptor (including the organochlorines PCB, DDE, PVC, TCE, and synthetic xenoestrogens in birth control pills) may pose environmental and human health problems. The work of Theo Colborn and her coworkers was some of the first to sound the alarm, presenting evidence of the pervasiveness of environmental contaminant-induced wildlife problems, especially those associated with reproduction and development, and suggested that these animal studies need to be seen as sentinels warning us about an impending human health crisis threatening the "human prospect" (Colborn, Dumanoski, and Myers 1996, 258). According to Colborn and her co-authors, the most disquieting consequences of endocrine-disrupting chemicals may not be their effects on some "individual destinies or the most sensitive amongst us, but a widespread erosion of human potential" (232), which we are already witnessing in the current "breakdown of the family" and "dysfunctional behavior in human society" (186, 238). Warning the problem goes "beyond cancer" (198), they predict that endocrine-disrupting chemicals threaten to transform the normal order of things: "We are confident that ongoing research will confirm that the hormonal experience of the developing embryo at crucial stages of its development has an impact on adult behavior in humans, affecting the choice of mates, parenting, social behavior, and other significant dimensions of humanity" (238).

The framing of the so-called endocrine disruptor thesis emerged from a "new synthesis" of scientific and biomedical information introduced in 1991 at the Wingspread Conference held in Racine, Wisconsin.[8] This meeting brought together a multidisciplinary group of researchers to assess what they considered to be the growing evidence that exposure to synthetic chemicals was interfering with the hormonal signals in wildlife and humans, altering their normal sexual development. The group of ecologists, anthropologists, endocrinologists, toxicologists, wildlife biologists, immunologists, lawyers, and psychiatrists drafted a consensus statement that was intended to integrate and evaluate the findings from the scholarly literature, to establish a research agenda to address remaining uncertainties, and to propose policy recommendations to protect the public health (Wingspread Statement 1991). The endocrine disruptor thesis would now claim the status of a scientific-environmental theory that "places the idea of *abnormal* or *disruptor* at the center of the theoretical framework. This is not a theory about normal processes, but a theory about the abnormal" (Krimsky 2002, 139, emphases in original). More specifically, it is a theory not of genetic, biological, or moral abnormality/deviance, but of the abnormal as the unintended and potentially deadly consequences of perturbing "natural" developmental and reproductive processes.[9]

Despite the Wingspread Statement's apocalyptic words warning of widespread developmental and reproductive *disruption* being caused by environmental contamination, and the broadcasting in 1993 of the BBC documentary (Cadbury 1993; aired on the Discovery Channel) titled *The Estrogen Effect: Assault on the Male,* the information about chemicals interfering with the hormonal system of humans and animals did not attract a lot of media attention (Myers, Krimsky and Zoeller 2001, 557). The publication of *Our Stolen Future* (Colborn, Dumanoski, and Myers 1996), the first mass-marketed book on the subject, would transform the media environment generating extensive news coverage. With the provocative subtitle "Are we Threatening our Fertility, Intelligence, and Survival?" *Our Stolen Future* garnered passionate media reviews describing it as a "chilling," frightening," "catastrophic" cautionary tale, and catapulted the theory of endocrine disruption into the public eye. While the book chronicles a *host* of harmful effects to humans and wildlife, including carcinogenicity and neurotoxicity—both associated with exposure to several known "hormonally active agents" such as DDT and PCB—"the images

that most appealed to the media involved reproduction and sexuality"
(Myers, Krimsky, and Zoeller 2001, 557).

Toxic Assault on the Male or:
The Emergence of the Incredible Shrinking Man

Speaking in 1995 to a group of U.S. congressional representatives
(predominantly men) at the House Subcommittee on Health and the Environment, University of Florida biologist Louis Guillette reported on the
startling statistic issued by Danish endocrinologist Neils Skakkebaek that
global human sperm counts had declined by 50 percent. In his concluding statements to the traumatized group of congressmen, Guillette stated:
"Every man sitting in this room today is half the man his grandfather was.
Are our children going to be half the men we are?" (Twombly 1995, 4).
Guillette testified that his research on the decline in alligator populations
in Florida's Lake Apopka represented animal studies that were consistent
with this evidence of an emergent "syndrome" signaled by "decreased
male reproductive capacity" on a worldwide scale (Raloff 1994b; Sharpe
and Skakkebaek 1993, 1393). Alligator populations were rapidly declining
in several Florida lakes located adjacent to a Superfund site that had in
the 1980s been contaminated with hormonally active pesticides, including dicophol and toxaphene. Apparently more shocking than the actual
decrease in numbers of these Apopka alligators was the fact that their
reproductive failure was probably due to the "tiny members" of the males,
which had been observed over several years to be shrinking to one-third
to one-half the normal size (Colborn, Dumanoski, and Myers 1996, 151).
Guillette and his colleagues also noted that female alligators displayed
"abnormalities in their ovaries and follicles," and males were discovered
to have testicular problems, but the "teeny weenies" were of most interest
to the "parade of journalists" willing to slog through the swampy wetlands
to photograph alligator penises (151).

According to the researchers, shrunken penises were partly responsible for the 80–95 percent egg-hatching failure rate in Apopka alligators, resulting in population decline, but so was the out-of-balance hormone ratio
of both males and females—female alligators appearing as "superfemales"
with twice the estrogen typical of a female and almost no testosterone in
the males (Guillette, Gross, Masson, Matter, Percival and Woodward,
1994). Earlier animal studies in birds examining the correlation between
exposure to estrogenic compounds such as DDT and its metabolite DDE
and the precipitous decline in the 1960s and 1970s of the populations of

western gulls in the Channel Islands and herring gulls in Lake Ontario also demonstrated "skewed sex ratios biased toward females" resulting in the so-called gay gulls or lesbian gulls because female gulls were observed sharing clutches with other females (Colborn, Dumanoski, and Myers 1996; Fry, Toone, Speich, and Peard 1987, 30). Similarly, the female birds presented with "grossly feminized reproductive tracts" and males' gonads had "tissues that were both ovarian and testicular, an intersex or hybrid gonad" (Fry et al. 1987, 31). Avian toxicologists hypothesized that the intersex conditions found in males most likely accounted for their lack of sexual interest in females and therefore explained the "homosexual behavior" in the cohabiting females.

Many other wildlife sentinel species have been studied and have provided evidence of the potential impacts on the health and reproduction of human populations of exposure to the many identified hormonally active/endocrine-disrupting chemicals that contaminate the water, air, soil, and food supply (Fox 2001). In the late 1990s, the National Academy of Sciences (NAS) established committees on (1) Animals as Monitors of Environmental Hazards and (2) Hormonally Active Agents in the Environment and concluded:

> Reported reproductive disorders in wildlife have included morphological abnormalities, eggshell thinning, population declines, impaired viability of offspring, altered hormone concentrations, and changes in sociosexual behavior. . . . Many wildlife studies show associations between reproductive and developmental defects and exposure to environmental contaminants, some of which are HAAs (hormonally active agents). (NAS 1999, 21)

Since the publication of *Our Stolen Future* in 1996, many wildlife biologists, endocrinologists, and toxicologists have argued in support of the use of "wildlife health data in a larger epidemiologic weight-of-evidence context upon which to base decisions and policies regarding the effects of chemical exposures on human populations" (Fox 2001, 859). But the human evidence in support of the endocrine disruptor thesis has been much more controversial, even though many scientists have postulated a link between these hormonally active agents and a number of "human abnormalities," including problems in "male reproductive capacity," breast, testicular, and prostate cancer, and neurological and neurobehavioral effects (Krimsky 2000). As with wildlife studies, the popular media dissemination of the research examining human effects of toxic exposure adopts the "assault-on-the-unstable-male-as-the-most-terrifying-thing-of-all" premise. Despite the evidence demonstrating links between exposure to endocrine-disrupting toxicants and breast, ovarian, prostate, and testicular cancers, immune system function, metabolic diseases, mutagenic effects, and neurological problems, what has made it to the headlines and what has been highly debated in the scientific and popular literature has been the seemingly unrelenting offensive on the stability and reliability of the human male reproductive capacity and sexual orientation. A few examples:

- The evidence of a worldwide decrease in sperm counts and sperm motility and quality, and the subsequent proliferation of supporting research (Tummon and Mortimer, 1992).
- The effects of *in utero* exposure to high doses of estrogen or the potent synthetic estrogenic drug diethylstilbestrol (DES) on the fertility of male offspring. (Wilcox , Baird, Weinberg, Hornsby, and Herbst 1994; Raloff 1994a).
- A decline in the "normal" birth sex ratio of 1.06–1.0 male to female (Davis, Gottlieb, and Stampnitzky 1998).
- An international increase in cases of hypospadias and cryptorchidism in male infants (Paulozzi 1999).[10]

The expressions of alarm in both the scientific community and the popular media of falling sperm counts, male infertility, deformed genitals, and disappearing baby boys were countered with equally forceful denials criticizing the claims that environmental contamination by endocrine-disrupting POPs, including pesticides, plastics, and solvents, were placing male reproduction and sexuality at risk. Some scientists challenged the validity of extrapolating the endocrine disruptor thesis from wildlife to humans (Safe 2000), and other commentators blamed lowering sperm counts and infertility on "lifestyle" choices, such as drinking, smoking, obesity, and wearing too-tight underpants (Larkin 1998). Writing in the *National Review,* conservative analyst John Berlau dismissed the endocrine alarmists as being manipulated by the proliferation of man-hating feminists: "Whereas man-made chemicals used to be characterized as the Grim Reaper, they're now a stand-in for Lorena Bobbitt" (1995, 45). Evidence of "toxic trespass" challenged societal assumptions about male virility and invulnerability to harm and raised the alarm of a masculinity at risk. The reactions would fall into two camps: the endocrine disruptor thesis deniers, who vehemently rejected the suggestion that *real* men could be negatively affected (generally the "conservative" position) and the thesis proponents (tending toward "progressive" environmentalists), who were troubled by the chilling proposition that endocrine disruptors were perverting humanity's natural sexual dimorphism, blurring the natural divide between men and women and producing abnormal bodies—feminized males, intersexed individuals, and hermaphrodites. Either way, denial or panic, the virulent debates about toxic assaults by estrogenic chemicals on male reproductive capacity were not simply about an impending human health problem, but about a newly troubled masculinity threatening to "throw into question not just gender but all of the social order" (Daniels 2006, 69).

Fallout from the Endocrine Disruptor Thesis: The Persistence of and Challenge to Eco-Normativity

As mentioned above, the endocrine disruptor thesis (renamed as HAAs) was taken up by the panel of experts assembled by the NAS in the late 1990s to critically review the scientific literature on the subject of hormone-related toxicants in the environment and their impacts on wildlife and human populations. The final report published in 1999 would reflect the seventeen-member panel's deep disagreements and concluded that the data were inconclusive, especially in respect to humans. Confirming the results of research documenting worldwide increases in rates of hypospadias, cryptorchidism, testicular cancer, and changing sex ratios, the NAS report concluded that the causes of these conditions is unclear and that they could not definitively be "linked to exposures to environmental HAAs at this time" (NAS 1999, 135).

On an international scale, most environmental scientists, endocrinologists, and toxicologists are in agreement that the weight of the scientific evidence implicates the global spread of POPs in population decline and extinctions of many species of wildlife and in the rising rates of many serious human health problems (Schapiro 2009; Steingraber 1997, 2007; Whitty 2007). Despite the U.S. government's claim that the evidence is "inconclusive" and that more research is needed, other countries have taken action to protect the public health and the environment by banning the most dangerous and commonly used chemicals (e.g., the European Union's ratification in 2004 of the United Nations Stockholm Convention on POPs).

Given this overall consensus on the problem of toxic contamination, how are concerned scientists, environmentalists, and other "progressive" analysts engaging with the endocrine disruptor thesis in the 2000s? I am interested in the contradictory ways that even progressive environmental science and policy circles can mobilize socially sanctioned heterosexism and queer-fear in order to generate public interest and a sense of urgency to act on this serious environmental problem. Do the knowledge politics surrounding the endocrine disruptor thesis function to set off a sex panic relying on the assumption that the public would react more strongly to news of impending gender perversions and would consider this prospect even more frightful, unnatural, and unacceptable, than other more ordinary concerns such as environmentally induced cancers, asthma, and heart disease, normalized diseases that are killing people in alarmingly high numbers?

Cynthia Daniels (2006) argues that some conservatives blame feminism (rather than endocrine disruptors) for the feminization of men and the erosion of natural masculinity (as evidenced in lowered sperm counts and developmental disorders, but also in the increased numbers of women in the workplace and women students outnumbering men at universities). Yet, in what ways can even feminist environmentalisms unwittingly call upon these same assumptions of eco(hetero)normativity in their critical analyses of the unnatural disruptions that underlie social and environmental injustices? And, how might we develop a more proactive (rather than polluted) politics that argues for the integrity, security, and health of bodies, homes, families, and communities without reproducing the eugenics discourse of the "normal/natural"?

Feminism, Multiculturalism, and the Unearthing of Environmental Normality

To reiterate my fundamental argument, I fall squarely in the ranks of the proponents of an anti-toxics environmental justice–ecofeminist politics and am outraged at the indifference and foot-dragging that has been the modus operandi of government regulators and the corporate lobbyists who are in bed with them. There is good reason for alarm concerning the continued use and accumulation of toxic chemicals that are wreaking havoc on the health and reproductive possibilities of the living world. Our cumulative exposures to endocrine disruptors, carcinogens, neurotoxins, asthmagens, and mutagens in our normal, everyday lives from our daily contact with plastic water bottles, shampoos, and kitchen cleaners to insect repellants, food preservatives, and factory farmed meats, among others, are most certainly putting at risk the health of our own bodies and our earth. There is good reason for alarm, but where should the critical attention lie? The hyperfocus on the world turning into hermaphrodites participates in a sexual titillation strategy summoning the familiar "crimes against nature" credo and inviting culturally sanctioned homophobia while at the same time sidelining and naturalizing "normal" environmental diseases such as cancer. This is not a good strategy either for coalition building or for developing a comprehensive politics of pollution prevention and environmental health justice. In the following examples, I examine—in critical solidarity with—several progressive feminist, environmentalist, and reproductive justice scholars' and activists' anti-toxics strategies, analyzing both the mobilization of and resistance to environmental normativity. In each example, my goal is not to argue with a particular author's rank order of socially critical priorities (race or gender or class or sexuality), but to examine through an inclusive environmental justice lens how appeals to the natural and normal in anti-toxics discourse stressing toxic chemicals' threats to natural sexuality, gender balance, and the balance of nature (1) tend to de-emphasize (and normalize) the many other health and reproductive effects of toxic chemical exposure (e.g., increased rates of cancer and other diseases) increasing morbidity and mortality rates, and (2) may unintentionally reinforce the oppressive ideology of heteronormativity and limit coalition politics across a diversity of social and environmental issues.

.   .   .

In his dynamic and popular slide presentation, "From Silent Spring to Silent Night," endocrinologist and amphibian biologist Tyrone Hayes (2007) frankly admits that he is a man with a message and has chosen to "cross the line" to become a scientist-advocate, urging his audiences to take action against the widely used herbicide and known endocrine disruptor atrazine. In the late 1990s, the Swiss-owned biotech giant Novartis (now Syngenta) approached Hayes, asking him to conduct scientific studies on the dose-response effects of its big money-maker, atrazine (at the time the most commonly used herbicide, which has only recently been eclipsed by glyphosate, commercially known as Roundup and manufactured by the Monsanto Corporation). The company-sponsored research was intended to provide proof of the chemical's safety as it was up for review and reapproval by the EPA. Syngenta was confident that atrazine, long thought to be nontoxic at concentrations below 3.0 parts per billion (ppb), would pass with flying colors, but Hayes's thorough investigation showed otherwise.

Starting in 1998, Hayes grew frog larvae in water samples collected from ponds and streams from agricultural regions in Wisconsin, Minnesota, and Indiana, some of which had been treated with atrazine and others that had reported little or no use. He grew the larvae in water samples containing a wide range of atrazine concentrations and then observed the developmental stages of the growing tadpoles and mature frogs. Within months of starting the research Hayes was surprised to find that doses of atrazine as low as 1.0 ppb were inhibiting the growth of the larynxes of male frogs (making them sound like female frogs and therefore unattractive and unable to mate), and at levels as low as 0.1 ppb (thirty times lower than the level the EPA allows for drinking water) Hayes observed intersex frogs with both ovaries and testes. Exposed frogs exhibited levels of the male sex hormone testosterone ten times lower than the control group of untreated animals. Hayes ultimately demonstrated that atrazine exposure stimulates the rate of production of aromatase, an enzyme that converts testosterone to estradiol, a potent form of estrogen, thereby "feminizing" male frogs or creating "hermaphroditic, demasculinized frogs" in up to 90 percent of exposed animals (Hayes 2002; Hayes, Haston, Tsui, Hoang, Haeffele, and Vonk 2002).

When in 1999 Hayes delivered his research findings to Syngenta, the company was less than impressed. Thus began a widely publicized, Hollywood-worthy story (complete with mysteriously disappearing data, federal officers dispatched to protect him if he testified at EPA hearings, and environmental lawyers advising him to stay in a different hotel each night) of a heroic battle between corporate malfeasance and a young scientist in the pursuit of truth whose integrity was not for sale.[11] Clearly, Hayes is working in hostile territory as he works to publicize his frightening tale of an approaching time when croak-free "silent nights" may become more common as amphibian populations throughout the world are decimated from exposure to widely available and EPA-approved endocrine-disrupting agricultural chemicals. Yet, by upfront appealing almost exclusively to the looming threats to eco-normativity, his equally powerful information on other lethal wildlife and human health problems become tangential.

By his own account, Hayes is "several standard deviations from the norm" (Royte 2003, 156). As one of only a handful of African Americans in the rarified field of endocrinology, Hayes talks about his childhood roots in South Carolina exploring the reeds and mudflats of the Congaree Swamp, and his father's urging him to study hard and pursue his passion for biology. Hayes earned a scholarship to Harvard University, completed his Ph.D., and accepted an academic job at UC Berkeley. In his early thirties he became the youngest full professor in the university's history.

Hayes's laboratory in UC Berkeley's Department of Integrative Biology has attracted scores of undergraduate and graduate students of color and has remained the most diverse in the sciences. He prides himself on having large lecture classes in biology that are nearly 20 percent African American at a university where fewer than one percent of the scientists are black. Arguing that "diversity makes science better," Hayes has been committed to promoting ethnic diversity in his department because "people from different backgrounds have different perspectives and take different approaches to the same problem" (Parks 2005, 3). A practitioner of rigorous scientific research, Hayes also believes that science must be more accessible to the general public and that scientists cannot separate themselves (their histories, families, and ethics) from the knowledge they are generating, especially if it could help people who may be disproportionately exposed to chemicals such as atrazine. Articulating an environmental justice perspective, Hayes states:

> As scientists we're arguing in front of the EPA, but the farmworkers and the public don't ever know about it. Ethnic minorities and people of low income are more likely to hold the "unskilled" laborer positions in agriculture and pesticide production that would put them at higher risk of exposure. They are also least likely to have access to the emerging science demonstrating the dangers of that exposure. So this environmental and public health issue is also a racial/social justice issue because minority and working class people are the primary targets of pesticide exposure. (quoted in Thomas 2006, 19)

Hayes's recognition of his own incongruousness in the predominantly white, high-status world of bioscience and his willingness to deviate from the political norms of science clearly situate him as an outsider within. Even though his own research and his critical review of others' research on the wildlife and human health effects of exposure to low levels of atrazine reveal a long list of potential health problems over and above its feminizing and gender-bending effects—including the stunting of frog growth, leading to smaller mouths that are not large enough to catch and consume its usual prey and thus leading to starvation, or frogs' much higher susceptibility to parasitic infections resulting in massive frog die-offs—his truly electrifying presentations highlight for his audiences that what really is *not normal* are the facts of "chemical castration" and "demasculinization."[12]

Likewise, the observations of human responses to atrazine exposure through drinking contaminated water have demonstrated a higher rate of breast cancer in women and prostate cancer in men. Workers at Syngenta's atrazine plant in St. Gabriel, Louisiana, were reported to suffer cancer rates more than three and a half times greater than the Louisiana state-wide average (Thomas 2006, 20). Despite the availability of data on these dire consequences of toxic chemical exposure, Hayes (and others) lead with the "imperiled normal" and generally achieve the desired response.[13] At the start of his lecture, "From Silent Spring to Silent Night" (2007), Hayes establishes *both* his outsider status (minority racial and working-class background, the integration of personal, political, and participatory policies in his scientific practice) *and* his normality (pictures of his parents and his wife and children). This stage-setting assertion of heteronormativity effectively sets up the norm against which the deformed frog bodies are contrasted and works to create the impression that atrazine's greatest danger is the threat to gender norms, the family, and the stability of the society. What gets lost in this chilling story of sexually and physiologically deformed frog bodies, I argue, is his important main point—that his research provides clear evidence of what is causing the massive decline in amphibian populations and, more important, that lacking swift regulatory action and responsibility from government and industry, this lethal situation could also be humanity's fate. Challenging certain norms but reasserting others, Hayes's decision to foreground atrazine's demasculinization of male frogs and the creation of abnormal hermaphrodites as his take-home message while de-emphasizing the other harmful health effects may play into culturally acceptable queer-fears, and may limit its coalitional possibilities and broader objectives of social justice. Such broad-based and sustained political coalitions are what will be required to demand effective government and industry action to prevent environmental contamination.

. . .

In her meticulously researched article, "Gender Transformed: Endocrine Disruptors in the Environment," environmental historian Nancy Langston focuses on the history and toxicology of endocrine disruptors providing important historical details on the physiological and environmental consequences of living in a "sea of estrogens," which she fears may be "changing the nature of gender" (2003, 133, 130). Langston sets out to examine and substantiate the biological/material realities at the root of *gender,* which she describes as being under siege by the many industrial and commercial endocrine-disrupting chemicals that have polluted our bodies and environment since the 1930s. Critiquing what she considers to be the postmodernist-feminist turn away from the facts of biology, Langston argues that "sexual differentiation is not just a cultural construction" (148) and insists upon the overwhelming truth of the hormonal determinism of gender:

> Postmodernists like to imagine that gender is culturally constructed, and clearly cultural forces do shape the expression of gender differences in our society. But gender is also profoundly biological. Hormones control the biological construction of gender, and now hormone mimics may control the biological deconstruction of gender as well. To complicate matters, cultural constructions influence the biological constructions of gender because behavior, social interactions, and expectations can all change the ways our bodies produce sex hormones. On a more direct level as well, culture alters the biological control of gender differences because many of the chemicals our culture produces have powerful effects on hormonal functions. (133–34)

Chronicling in careful detail the list of examples from both animal and human studies of how "hormones create gender" and how hormonally active agents are "seriously confusing [our] genitalia" (136), Langston hammers home the point that the normal gender regime (both bodies and behaviors) is being damaged, a dire situation that portends an uncertain future. As a biologist, environmentalist, and feminist, Langston persuasively critiques the Western philosophical nature/culture divide and argues that one of our "fondest illusions" is that we can separate ourselves from the natural world:

> What we do know is that we're all in this together: the atrazine that gets sprayed on my neighbor's cornfields ends up in the river water, then in the fish, then in the herons and the raccoons that eat the fish—and it also ends up in my breasts, my belly, and my blood. What's out there in wildlife and wild places is also in our bodies . . . endocrine disruptors connect environmental histories of the body with environmental histories of wild places and wild animals. (153)

Langston's arguments urging feminists to rethink materiality are most effective and invite greater possibilities for a politics of articulation with other discourses of interrelationship and justice when she demonstrates clearly the damage to health and the environment that occurs when humans do not integrate the "intimate" and the ecological and imagine instead our bodies as separate from, unaffected by, and unconnected to our environments. On the other hand, her writing forecloses on potential articulations when she appeals to corporeal and environmental normality: "Our most intimate reproductive environments, the places that make us most female or most male, the places we are most vulnerable and most natural, may have been hijacked by the residues of our industrial world. This is a disturbing thought" (154). The move to locate the danger of an unbridled and unjust industrial society in the callous hijacking of our sexual dimorphism ends up obscuring our vulnerability to the wide range and diversity of hormonally sensitive diseases and physiologic changes, including, for example, pancreatic cancer and early onset of puberty. This too is a disturbing thought.

Invoking the "naturalness" of binary gender, Langston raises the specter of a crisis of heteronormativity, thereby eclipsing a comprehensive analysis of toxins in the environment that would more fully interconnect ecosystem cycles and "intimate" bodily/physiological systems, what I have called an *embodied* ecology.

. . .

The publication in 1997 of Sandra Steingraber's *Living Downstream: An Ecologist Looks at Cancer and the Environment* established her as an important voice in the anti-toxics environmental movement. Focusing on the environmental links to cancer—as compared to *Our Stolen Future*, published a year earlier, which described itself as moving "*beyond* cancer" to focus on the presumably more serious problems of hormonal disruption and dysfunctional sexual reproduction—*Living Downstream* became the industry standard for environmental writing that blended the personal and the political and made accessible to a broad audience the scientific information and controversies relating to the increasing rates of cancer worldwide. Steingraber's later book *Having Faith: An Ecologist's Journey to Motherhood* (2001) again combines personal and scientific inquiry to examine her own pregnancy with her daughter Faith—an unexpected event, she explains, as she had been presumed infertile after her diagnosis and treatment for bladder cancer at the age of nineteen. With its focus on the effects of exposure to environmental toxins at every stage of maternal and fetal development during the nine months of pregnancy, *Having Faith* takes up more directly than her earlier work the endocrine disruptor thesis and examines the potential effects of the global distribution of POPs on human reproductive capacity. One reviewer succinctly summed up the overall message of the book: "[Steingraber's] findings strongly suggest that having a healthy child today is even more of a miracle and is increasingly threatened" (Miller 2002, 2).

Steingraber's subsequent work looked at historical trends in the onset of puberty in girls and represents her most in-depth foray into the field of endocrine disruption and its impacts on sexuality and sexual "disorders."[14] In a monograph on the subject, "The Falling Age of Puberty in U.S. Girls: What We Know, What We Need to Know" (2007), Steingraber overviews what is known about the trend of earlier pubertal age by reviewing the literature in the fields of epidemiology, endocrinology, toxicology, and evolutionary biology, as well as in sociology, child development, nutrition, veterinary medicine, media studies, and anthropology. Her broadly interdisciplinary investigation reveals information about pubertal trends that is widely accepted and also information that is uncertain and inconclusive. The preponderance of the evidence shows that breast development (thelarche) and menstruation (menarche) are both occurring earlier in the lives of U.S. girls, with the age of thelarche falling more rapidly. In addition, the average age of menarche among U.S. girls steadily declined throughout the first half of the twentieth century, and the rates differed markedly among racial and ethnic groups. The average menarchal and thelarchal ages of African American and Latina girls are lower than those of white girls. Theories about the triggering mechanisms driving these trends show less consensus in the literature, but what is known is that low birth weight, premature birth, obesity, and environmental exposures to endocrine-disrupting chemicals can set off the neuroendocrine apparatus controlling pubertal onset.[15]

Throughout the voluminous study, Steingraber's analysis consistently speaks to the multitude of factors—biological, environmental, and social—that have contributed to this change in the sexual development of U.S. girls, and, although her focus is on the age of puberty, she insists on connecting this problem to a wide array of health and social risks for girls and women. In the preface, she opens by connecting the issue of "early puberty" to women's health: "Early puberty—in particular, early menarche—is a known risk factor for breast cancer" (2007, 2). She continues:

In the puberty story, so many variables are interwoven and interdependent that, as I began to trace the threads of causality to their beginning points, I sometimes felt as though I were caught in a Mobius strip. For example, obesity raises the risk for early puberty in girls, but weight gain itself is a consequence of early pubertal development. And risks for both obesity and early puberty are raised by being born to small or too soon—risks for which are modulated by maternal exposure to certain environmental chemicals during pregnancy. (4)

The monograph then lays out the evidence demonstrating the complexity of the interactions among the diverse social and physiological health risks that are associated with early puberty, including reduction of complex brain function and the brain's ability to recover from injury, slower bone growth, breast cancer, obesity, diabetes, polycystic ovary syndrome, depression, teenage pregnancy, low performance in school, and cardiovascular diseases (32–37).

As a scientist-advocate (much like Hayes and Langston), Steingraber offers suggestions for proactive and preventative "actions that can be taken on the basis of what is already known" (16), which include: strategies to phase out or ban the endocrine-disrupting chemicals to which girls are exposed (including phthalates and bisphenol A) and endorsement of action-based monitoring policies such as the California Environmental Contamination Biomonitoring Program, which in 2006 became the first statewide monitoring system to test for the presence of toxic chemicals in the bodies of the population at large and in targeted studies of communities of concern; strategies to tackle childhood obesity, including offering healthy food in schools and opportunities for sports and physical activity; investments in urban agriculture and farm-to-school programs; availability of non-organochlorine cleaning and pest control products for use in homes and schools; strategies to lower preterm and low-weight births by providing affordable prenatal care; elimination of air pollution and mercury contamination from coal-fired power plants; and community-based strategies promoted by the environmental justice movement to "lower the combined burden of psychosocial, socioeconomic, and environmental stressors, which disproportionately affect poor and minority communities" (17).

Adopting a "weight of the evidence" methodology (Krimsky 2000, 232), Steingraber's work represents an anti-toxics approach that demonstrates the interconnection of environmental and health problems with gender, class, and racial injustices. Rather than resorting to the discourse of environmental normality to drive home her point, she stresses the centrality of health and well-being and offers a host of alternative strategies that she argues will ensure a healthy and sustainable environment for all. Insisting on the articulation of all of these diverse factors, Steingraber concludes:

> Because it arises from a combination of many different stressors in several different aspects of the environment—psychosocial, nutritional, behavioral, chemical—early puberty in girls is not a trend that will be reversed by single actions by single-purpose agencies. It is a multi-causal threat to the well-being of girls and women that ultimately requires a comprehensive, integrated, unified response. . . . The environmental justice community, with its long experience with cumulative risks and impact, has many insights to offer here. Any meaningful attempt to mitigate the problem of early sexual maturation in girls must draw on the collective wisdom of its leadership. (2007, 97–98)

. . .

In "Changing Sex," a chapter in the book *Courage for the Earth,* the anthology of writings published in 2007 in celebration of the centennial of the birth of Rachel Carson, Janisse Ray, the award-winning author of *Ecology of a Cracker Childhood,* a social and ecological memoir of growing up in a rural, poor, white, Southern community, writes:

> In the past two decades, study after study has shown what Rachel Carson predicted. Chemicals are disturbing normal hormone-controlled development, affecting gender, sex, and reproduction. . . . In Florida's Fenholloway River, mosquitofish females developed a male sex organ called a gonopodium and attempted to mate with female fish. The scientific term for dual sex anatomy is *intersex,* which means an abnormal presence of traits of both sexes in one specimen . . . smallmouth bass in the South Branch of the Potomac River [were almost all] intersex in that they contained immature eggs in their testes. (2007, 112–13)

Ray declares that she is not a chemist and "loves macro, not micro" so would much rather be writing about "ancient mountains" and "caribou running like a low dark cloud across the Arctic plain in advance of the oil drillers" (115) than about "life-threatening" invisible chemicals. In the literary nonfiction style reminiscent of Carson and Steingraber, Ray blends the personal voice with her no-nonsense, straight-talking explanations of the science of endocrine-disrupting chemicals to narrate the story of her awakening to this particularly disturbing information pointing to the phenomenon of changing sex. One of the early experiences alerting her to the dangers of endocrine disruptors is recounted in the story of meeting Tracy and C. B., a young couple living on a farm in Vermont who had decided to eat locally, buy organic, and eliminate all plastics, phthalates, and bisphenol A from their lives. As Ray writes, "Tracy was a woman in her late twenties, with strawberry blond hair . . . and wore long skirts" (117). Describing C. B., on the other hand, was a little trickier: "C. B. is Tracy's husband, but we were at first confused because he looked like a woman, with a feminine figure and delicate features. He wore jeans and a plain T-shirt, his dark hair cropped short" (117).

Ray then relates her awakening to the existence of transgender people by describing her childhood friend Anna, who had recently confessed that she had "always felt like a boy and was going to change her sex" and would soon become Andrew (124). But, as Ray explains,

> This is not a story about being transgender. That subject is too personal, too political, too nuanced. On occasion I had met transgender people. But at Tracy and C. B.'s home, for the second time in a month, I was sitting with a transgender person. Suddenly I was calling a friend who looked like a she a he. He, him, his. I was watching my young friend Anna/Andrew using the men's bathroom, and listening to him tell me about not being able to check either gender box on job applications. (124)

Getting the courage to ask the "politically incorrect question" to Tracy and C. B. as to whether they thought C. B.'s transgender identity might be connected to endocrine disruption, Ray was surprised when they both nodded yes and immediately mentioned Christine Johnson, a transgender author and administrator of the Web site trans-health.com who has published articles on the issue of the link between endocrine disruptors and the increased numbers of trans people (Johnson 2004). Quoting Tracy, Ray expresses her own politically correct position on this issue of changing sex: "I don't think that being intersex or being trans is a problem, any more than being just male or just female is a birth defect. But when we start having babies who are developing in one direction and switch them chemically to develop differently, it shows that chemicals are powerful and are affecting us at levels many of us are exposed to on a daily basis" (125).

While Ray—who has raised awareness of classist and racist assumptions in the environmental movement through her environmental memoir on growing up poor, white, and Southern—acknowledges her potentially "politically incorrect" stance and her ignorance of "gender variance," it seems these social/bodily "ambiguities" are easier attributed to a poisoned environment than to normal human sexual difference. The other health impacts of hormonally active chemicals are mentioned briefly in her chapter, but they pale next to the specter of environmental contamination causing sexual abnormality.

As an homage to Rachel Carson's legacy, Ray's essay appropriately points to the risks to reproductive health in humans and other animals that are associated with exposure to endocrine-disrupting chemicals. In her widely read book, *Silent Spring*, Carson cites the link between the carcinogenicity of the chlorinated hydrocarbons such as DDT to the human reproductive system and their known toxicity to the liver, one of the organs associated with the maintenance of healthy hormone levels in the body (Carson 1962, 207). In other words, Carson explains, exposure to DDT (which would later be classified as an endocrine-disrupting chemical) compromises the liver's capacity to maintain hormone balance, which could potentially lead to cancers of the reproductive organs in men and women and could increase the risk of reproductive problems, including infertility. Although the connections Carson made among DDT, cancer, and reproductive disorders (including possible genetic damage) compelled then secretary of agriculture Ezra Taft Benson to wonder "why a spinster with no children was so concerned about genetics" and the problems of human reproduction (Lear 1997, 429), her writing never worked to instigate a selective sex panic. Granted, Ray is writing in a different historical moment, but her expressions of terror at the prospect of changing sex without a serious engagement with either trans people themselves or with the literature theorizing how "power in contemporary society habitually passes itself off as embodied in the *normal*" (Dyer 1997, 45) participate in the reinforcement of compulsory eco(hetero)normativity and may limit the possibilities for diverse environmental coalitions.

.   .   .

The community-based organization Asian Communities for Reproductive Justice (ACRJ), based in Oakland, California, develops what its leaders call an "intersectional" analysis of reproductive justice that articulates the many social, economic, cultural, and environmental factors affecting the lives of poor and low-income Asian and Pacific Islander (API) communities in the East Bay region. As the organization's executive director, Eveline Shen, explains:

> Our goals are to address reproductive freedom within a social justice context, because we realize that you can't disentangle the issues that intersect with reproductive freedom that are most important to the communities we work with, which include immigrant rights, workers rights, queer rights, environmental justice, educational justice, ending violence against women, and the empowerment of youth. ... Reproductive justice is really about fundamental changes in individual, community, and institutional power structures. (2005)

Popular education approaches are at the center of ACRJ's organizing strategy, which is committed to leadership development and focuses on action-based research and educational and political campaigns identified as important to the local community. One such campaign, the fight against IES (Integrated Environmental Systems), a waste management company that owned and operated two solid-waste incinerators located in East Oakland, brought the ACRJ in alliance with a San Francisco Bay Area-wide environmental justice coalition helping to expand the grassroots base of the local environmental justice movement and introducing critical gender and reproductive justice components to the coalition's environmental justice frame (Shen 2005). Other campaigns have helped to broaden the reproductive justice movement by building alliances with a wide range of social justice and mainstream women's organizations.[16]

The ACRJ's youth program, SAFIRE (Sisters in Action for Issues of Reproductive Empowerment) joins together reproductive and environmental justice issues in their initiative known as POLISH (Participatory Research, Organizing, and Leadership Initiative for Safety and Health). The project focuses on women's and girl's exposure to chemical toxins in beauty products both personally as consumers and on the job as beauty/nail salon workers (80 percent of whom are Vietnamese immigrant women). Partnering with Asian Health Services, UC Berkeley's School of Public Health, and the NIH, the POLISH project examines the cosmetic industry's continued use of reproductive and developmental toxins such as dibutyl phthalates in its products and joins with statewide and nationwide efforts to mandate stronger FDA regulation of personal care products. Committed to a coalition politics that does not pit environmental protection against economic security, the POLISH project deploys a community-based participatory action research approach that connects the environmental health, safety, and livelihood concerns of both consumers and workers (Shah and Paredes 2005). The intersectional politics practiced by the SAFIRE activists link reproductive justice and environmental justice issues and have created a movement of young API women who now identify themselves as "environmentalists," and who are becoming community leaders in the San Francisco Bay Area.

With the commitment to respond to the needs and concerns of all members of the community, ACRJ organizers recognized that the focus on reproductive justice was not resonating with the large queer and trans community with whom many of the organization's leaders identified and worked. Striving to broaden further their concept of reproductive justice, organizers have deepened their analysis to further challenge the heteronormative construction of the body and sexual binary models of reproduction and have focused on how bodies are defined and affected by social, economic, *and* environmental injustices. ACRJ communications director Diana Yin Ming explains: "Discussions of the body as the site of analysis are very metaphorical and political and often focus on symbols and representations, but the body is also very literal and material, and what's happening in our workplaces, homes, communities, and environments have a very specific impact on all our bodies" (Ming 2007).

Speaking directly to the necessity of forging a coalition politics to counter the full range of assaults on reproductive justice—including environmental contamination—Eveline Shen calls for "an integrated analysis, holistic vision, and comprehensive strategies that push against the structural and societal conditions that control our communities by regulating our bodies, sexuality and reproduction. This is the time to come together across issue areas, across separate change efforts, and across identities to achieve this vision" (2006, 14). Shen argues that "toxic pollution creating reproductive disorders affects us all" and that "focusing on the abnormality of intersex frogs rather than on how oppressive political and economic systems such as globalization are creating injustices that affect our self determination and the self determination of *all* beings, including the frogs!" is a divisive strategy. She asserts that effective coalitions between reproductive and environmental justice issues enable "all people to have the economic, social, and political power and resources to make healthy decisions about our bodies, sexuality and reproduction for ourselves, our families and our communities" (Shen 2007).

Conclusion: Queering Environmentalism, Refiguring the World

Environmental theory and politics in the United States have historically mobilized ideas of the normal, or what Rosemarie Garland-Thomson
refers to as "the normate," that is, "the social figure through which people
can represent themselves as definitive human beings" (1997, 8), to determine which bodies and environments/landscapes *embody* the distinctly
American values of productive work, rugged individualism, masculinity,
independence, potency, and moral virtue, upon which environmental
advocacy movements should be based (e.g., Haraway 1989; Cronon 1991).
Critical histories of U.S. environmentalism have revealed the capitalist,
patriarchal, colonialist, heteronormative, eugenicist, and ableist histories
underlying its "progressive" exterior (e.g., Boag 2003; Darnovsky 1992;
Evans 2002; Gaard 2004; Jaquette 2005; Sutter 2001). In this chapter, I
have examined the residues of what I have called eco-normativity (or,
eco[hetero]normativity) that appear in the alarmist discourse of the anti-
toxics arm of the environmental movement, residues that, I argue, appeal
to pre-existing cultural norms of gender balance, normal sexual reproduction, and the balance of nature. The deployment of the anti-normal
or anti-natural in anti-toxic discourse is questionable political-ecological
strategy and can work to reinforce the dominant social and economic
order (the forces actually behind environmental destruction and toxic
contamination of all our bodies and environments) by naturalizing the
multiple injustices that shore it up. In short, this unexamined toxic discourse produces *polluted politics* even while claiming to stand for diversity
and justice.

I have also examined feminist and environmental justice *challenges* to
normal environmentalism, which, I argue, are *queering* ecological thinking and creating new possibilities for genuine coalition politics with the
aim of disrupting the social power of eco-normativity. The question remains: Can the environmental coalitions we develop succeed in calling
for stronger environmental protections, the right to a healthy body, and
the need for sustainable communities in such a way that resists appeals to
normalcy and normativity? And, furthermore, can our coalitions be capacious enough to embrace and care for *all* community members (human
and nonhuman) even in their "irrevocable difference" (Clare 2001, 361)?

In closing, I return to Clare's creative politics of articulation, in which
he links queer and disability theorists' critiques of the compulsions of heterosexuality and able-bodiedness together with the environmental justice
movement's redefining of nature and environment as "community" and

"home." While those bodies, communities, and environments that stray from the "normate" may be hated, impoverished, and poisoned, Clare maintains that seeing and knowing from *non*-normate positions may offer outsider views for imagining new, just, and sustainable ways of living on the earth—our home. "And as for the lies and false images, we need to name them, transform them, create something entirely new in their place, something that comes close and finally true to the bone, entering our bodies as liberation, joy fury, hope, a will to refigure the world. The body as home" (12).

NOTES

1. See Di Chiro (2003), LaDuke (1997), and Stein (2004), for more discussion about this conceptual and political intervention.

2. The United Nations Environment Programme (UNEP) established a program on POPs in the late 1990s, which set in motion the organizing of the UN Stockholm Convention on Persistent Organic Pollutants, held in 2001 to address the global circulation of these dangerous compounds and to protect human health and the environment. Parties to the Stockholm Convention agree to eliminate or reduce the twelve identified POPs of greatest concern: aldrin, chlordane, DDT, dieldrin, dioxins, endrin, furans, heptachlor, hexachlorobenzene, mirex, polychlorinated biphenyls (PCBs), toxaphene.

3. For overviews and recent research findings, see the Science and Environmental Health Network (SEHN), http://www.sehn.org/ and the Collaborative on Health and the Environment (CHE), http://www.healthandenvironment.org/.

4. A reference to the size of the penises of alligators found in Lake Apopka, Florida, a body of water abutting a federal Superfund site.

5. A reference to the lowered sperm counts observed in wildlife and humans from around the world.

6. Published after the BBC documentary *The Estrogen Effect: Assault on the Male* was aired in September 1994.

7. For example, see Birnbaum 1995; Colborn, Vom Saal, and Soto 1993; El Bayoumy 1993; Hunter and Kelsey 1993; and Sharpe and Skakkebaek 1993.

8. The crux of the endocrine disruption thesis was that some exogenous compounds (both natural and synthetic) can interact with hormonal systems by either (1) blocking or mimicking receptor binding, (2) altering the rates of hormonal synthesis or metabolism, or (3) affecting receptor availability. The list of known endocrine-disrupting chemicals that were of central concern to the conferees includes: DDT and its degradation products, DEHP (di)2-ethylhexyl)phthalate), dicofol, HCB (hexachlorobenzene), kelthane, kepone, lindane and other hexachlorocyclohexane congeners, methoxy-chlor, octachlorostyrene, synthetic pyrethroids,triazine herbicides, EBDC fungicides, certain PCB congeners, 2,3,7,8-TCDD and other dioxins, 2,3,7,8-TCDF and other furans, cadmium, lead, mercury, tributyltin and other organo-tin compounds, alkyl phenols (nonbiodegradable detergents and anti-oxidants present in modified polystyrene and PVCs), styrene dimers and trimers, soy products, and

laboratory animal and pet food products (Wingspread Conference Statement, July 1991).

9. The use of the language of "disruption" was opposed by some scientists from the National Research Council, who argued instead for the term HAAs (hormonally active agents) because, they argued, there exist several chemicals, such as plant-based estrogens, that are hormonally active but are not known to cause harmful effects. The term HAAs preserved "the distinction between chemicals that interact with hormone receptors or other hormone-mediated pathways and chemicals that cause adverse physiological effects on an organism" (Krimsky 2001, 22).

10. Hypospadias refer to a developmental condition in which the urethra opens on the underside of the penis or on the perineum instead of at the tip of the glans penis. Cryptorchidism is a condition in which one or both of the testicles fail to descend during fetal development from the abdomen cavity to the scrotum. Both of these conditions have been associated with infertility, testicular cancer, and other health problems.

11. See Pierce (2004) and Thomas (2006).

12. Hayes's Powerpoint presentation includes several slides displaying cross-sections of the atrazine-induced "feminized testes" of exposed Northern Leopard frogs. For most nonbiologists, a scientific slide of a cross-section of a frog testis sprouting ovaries appears as a brown, grainy background with clumps of lighter-colored masses scattered throughout. To help elucidate the slide for the audience and to draw attention to this gonadal abnormality, large arrows point to bundles of cells labeled "ovaries" or "testes," and the words "NOT NORMAL" are stamped across the image in upper-case, bright-red letters. To view the slide, see http://www.youtube.com/watch?v=z4lijvIjpRw at 10:27.

13. In earlier conversations with Hayes, he told me that during his presentations on the dangers of atrazine his audiences regularly express the two responses of either denial or panic that I discussed earlier. Specifically, he explained, burly, white male farmers from Wisconsin tended to represent the *deniers* ("That's about frogs, not us men!"), and male farmers in Angola reacted with *alarm* ("Smaller penises? Gender-bending? No way!"), resulting in the Angolan government banning atrazine. Author's personal communication, University of Massachusetts, Amherst, May 2, 2005.

14. Puberty in girls is signaled when the brain instructs the ovaries to begin secreting estradiol, which results in breast development (thelarche) and the onset of menstruation (menarche). Another brain signal stimulates the secretion of androgens from the adrenal gland, which results in pubic hair growth (pubarche).

15. Another recently published study on endocrine disruptors' dangers to women and girls also presents a complex analysis of the health risks associated with exposure, rather than the exclusive focus on these toxins destabilizing maleness and gender balance (Collaborative on Health and the Environment 2009).

16. For example, ACRJ partnered with a wide coalition of organizations, including the ACLU, Planned Parenthood, the League of Women Voters, immigrants' rights organizations, and educational reform groups, to defeat Propositions 73 and 85, ballot initiatives put on the California special elections in November 2005 and again in the general elections in 2006, to amend the state's constitution to prohibit a physician from performing an abortion on an unemancipated minor until forty-eight hours after the doctor notifies in writing the minor's parent or guardian, except in the case of a medical emergency or with a parental waiver. For more information on the defeat of these propositions, see http://www.smartvoter.org/2005/11/08/ca/state/prop/73/, and http://reproductivejustice.org/download/Prop85/ACRJDefeating85.pdf.

REFERENCES

Alford, R. A., and S. J. Richards. 1999. Global Amphibian Declines: A Problem in Applied Ecology. *Annual Reviews in Ecology and Systematics* 30: 133–65.

Amphibian Decline Is Rapidly Worsening. 2006. *Associated Press.* http://www.msnbc. msn.com/id/6249901/.

Auger, J., Jean Marie Kunstmann, Françoise Czyglik, and Pierre Jouannet. 1995. Decline in Semen Quality among Fertile Men in Paris during the Past 20 Years. *New England Journal of Medicine* 332 (1995): 281–85.

Barringer, Felicity. 2008. Hermaphrodite Frogs Found in Suburban Ponds. *New York Times,* April 8, D2.

Berkson, L. D. 2000. *Hormone Deception.* Chicago: Contemporary.

Berlau, John. 1995. Case of the Falling Sperm Counts. *National Review,* June 26, 45–48.

Birnbaum, L. S. 1995. Developmental Effects of Dioxin. *Environmental Health Perspectives* 103: 89–94.

Boag, Peter. 2003. Thinking Like Mount Rushmore: Sexuality and Gender in the Republican Landscape. In *Seeing Nature through Gender,* ed. Virginia Scharff, 40–59. Lawrence: University Press of Kansas.

Bryant, Bunyan, and Paul Mohai. 1992. *Race and Incidence of Environmental Hazards.* Boulder, Colo.: Westview Press.

Bullard, Robert.1994. *Unequal Protection: Environmental Justice and Communities of Color.* San Francisco: Sierra Club Books.

Cadbury, Deborah, writer and prod. 1993. Documentary. The Estrogen Effect: Assault on the Male. *Horizon.* London: British Broadcasting Corporation.

———. 1998. *The Feminization of Nature: Our Future at Risk.* London: Penguin Books.

Carson, Rachel. 1962. *Silent Spring.* Boston, Mass.: Houghton Mifflin.

Clare, Eli. 1999. *Exile and Pride: Disability, Queerness, and Liberation.* Cambridge, Mass.: South End Press.

———. 2001. Stolen Bodies, Reclaimed Bodies: Disability and Queerness. *Public Culture* 13.3: 359–65.

Colborn, Theo, and C. Clement, eds. 1992. *Chemically Induced Alterations in Sexual Development: The Wildlife/Human Connection.* Princeton, N.J.: Princeton Scientific Publishing.

Colborn, Theo, D. Dumanoski, and J. P. Myers. 1996. *Our Stolen Future: Are We Threatening Our Fertility, Intelligence, and Survival? A Scientific Detective Story.* New York: Penguin Books.

Colborn, Theo, F. S. Vom Saal, and A. M. Soto. 1993. Developmental Effects of Endocrine-Disrupting Chemicals in Wildlife and Humans. *Environmental Health Perspectives* 101: 378–84.

Collaborative on Health and the Environment. 2009. Girl Disrupted: Hormone Disruptors and Women's Reproductive Health. http://www.healthandenvironment. org/articles/doc/5492.

Cone, Marla. 1994. Sexual Confusion in the Wild. *Los Angeles Times* October 2, A1.

Cronon, William. 1991. *Nature's Metropolis.* New York: W. W. Norton.

Daniels, Cynthia. 2006. *Exposing Men: The Science and Politics of Male Reproduction.* Oxford, U.K.: Oxford University Press.

Darnovsky, Marcy. 1992. Stories Less Told: Histories of U.S. Environmentalism. *Socialist Review* 22.4: 11–54.

Davis, Leonard. 1995. *Enforcing Normalcy: Disability, Deafness and the Body.* London: Verso.

Davis, D. L., M. B. Gottlieb, and J. R. Stampnitzky. 1998. Reduced Ratio of Male to Female Births in Several Industrial Countries: A Sentinel Health Indicator. *JAMA* 279: 1018–23.

Di Chiro, Giovanna. 1996. Nature as Community: The Convergence of Environment and Social Justice. In *Uncommon Ground: Rethinking the Human Place in Nature,* ed. William Cronon, 298–320. New York: W. W. Norton.

———. 2003. Beyond Ecoliberal "Common Futures": Environmental Justice, Toxic Touring, and a Transcommunal Politics of Place. In *Race, Nature and the Politics of Difference,* ed. Donald Moore, Jake Kosek, and Anand Pandian, 204–32. Durham, N.C.: Duke University Press.

Dunne, Kyla. 1998. Teeny Weenies: Alligators in Florida's Lake Apopka have Smaller Penises. PBS interview, June 2.

Dyer, Richard. 1997. *White: Essays on Race and Culture.* New York: Routledge.

El-Bayoumy, K. 1993. Environmental Carcinogens That May Be Involved in Human Breast Cancer Etiology. *Chemical Research in Toxicology* 5: 585–90.

Evans, Mei Mei. 2002. "Nature" and Environmental Justice. In *The Environmental Justice Reader: Politics, Poetics, and Pedagogy,* ed. Joni Adamson, Mei Mei Evans, and Rachel Stein, 181–93. Tucson: University of Arizona Press.

Fox, Glenn. 2001. Wildlife as Sentinels of Human Health Effects in the Great Lakes-St. Lawrence Basin. *Environmental Health Perspectives* 109.6: 853–61.

Fry, D. M., C. K. Toone, S. M. Speich and R. J. Peard. 1987. Sex Ratio Skew and Breeding Patterns of Gulls: Demographic and Toxicological Considerations. *Studies in Avian Biology* 10: 26–43.

Gaard, Greta. 2004 (1997). Toward a Queer Ecofeminism. In *New Perspectives on Environmental Justice: Gender, Sexuality, and Activism,* ed. Rachel Stein, 21–44. New Brunswick, N.J.: Rutgers University Press.

Garland-Thomson, Rosemarie. 1997. *Extraordinary Bodies: Figuring Physical Disability in American Culture and Literature.* New York: Columbia University Press.

Guillette, Louis J., Timothy S. Gross, Greg R. Masson, John M. Matter, H. Franklin Percival, and Allan R. Woodward. 1994. Developmental Abnormalities of the Gonad and Abnormal Sex Hormone Concentrations in Juvenile Alligators from Contaminated and Control Lakes in Florida. *Environmental Health Perspectives* 102: 680–88.

Haraway, Donna. 1989. *Primate Visions: Gender, Race, and Nature in the World of Modern Science.* New York: Routledge.

Hayes, Tyrone. 2002. Hermaphroditic, Demasculinized Frogs Following Exposure to the Herbicide, Atrazine, at Ecologically Relevant Doses. *Proceedings of the National Academy of Sciences* 99.8: 5476–80.

———. 2007. *From Silent Spring to Silent Night.* Video of lecture, sponsored by the Friends of the Mississippi River, the Humphrey Institute for Public Affairs, St. Paul, Minnesota, March 23. http://www.youtube.com/watch?v=z41ijvIjpRw.

Hayes, Tyrone B., Kelly Haston, Mable Tsui, Anhthu Hoang, Cathryn Haeffele, and Aaron Vonk. 2002. Herbicides: Feminization of Male Frogs in the Wild. *Nature* 419: 895–96.

Hunter, D. J., and K. T. Kelsey. 1993. Pesticide Residues and Breast Cancer: The Harvest of a Silent Spring. *Journal of the National Cancer Institute* 85: 598–99.

Jaquette, Sarah. 2005. "Maimed Away from the Earth": Fitting Disabled Bodies Back into the Wilderness. *Ecotone* (Spring): 8–11.

Johnson, Christine. 2004. Transsexualism: An Unacknowledged Endpoint of Developmental Endocrine Disruption? M.A. thesis, Evergreen State College, Olympia.

Krimsky, Sheldon. 2000. *Hormonal Chaos: The Scientific and Social Origins of the Environmental Endocrine Hypothesis*. Baltimore, Md.: Johns Hopkins University Press.

——. 2001. Hormone Disruptors: A Clue to Understanding the Environmental Causes of Disease. *Environment* 43.5: 22.

——. 2002. An Epistemological Inquiry into the Endocrine Disruptor Hypothesis. *Annals of the New York Academy of Sciences* 948: 130–42.

LaDuke, Winona. 1997. Voices from White Earth: Gaa-waabaabiganikaag. In *People, Land, and Community*, ed. H. Hannum, 22–37. New Haven, Conn.: Yale University Press.

Langston, Nancy. 2003. Gender Transformed: Endocrine Disruptors in the Environment. In *Seeing Nature through Gender*, ed. Virginia Scharff, 129–66. Lawrence: University Press of Kansas.

Larkin, Marilynn. 1998. Male Reproductive Health: A Hotbed of Research. *Lancet* 352: 552.

Lear, Linda. 1997. *Rachel Carson: Witness for Nature*. New York: Henry Holt.

McRuer, Robert. 2006. *Crip Theory: Cultural Signs of Queerness and Disability*. New York: New York University Press.

Miller, Elise. 2002. Book Review: *Having Faith: An Ecologist's Journey To Motherhood* by Sandra Steingraber. *YES Magazine* (Summer): 9.

Ming, Diana Yin. 2007. Interview with the author, Oakland, March 31.

Mortimer-Sandilands, Catriona. 2005. Unnatural Passions? Notes towards a Queer Ecology. *Invisible Culture* 9. http://www.rochester.edu/in_visible_culture/Issue_9/ sandilands.html.

Myers, John Peterson, Sheldon Krimsky, and R. Thomas Zoeller. 2001. Endocrine Disruptors: A Controversy in Science and Policy. *NeuroToxicology* 22: 557–58.

National Academy of Sciences. 1999. *Hormonally Active Agents in the Environment*. Washington, D.C.: National Academy Press.

Parks, Clinton. 2005. Balance and Love. *Science* (October 7). http://sciencecareers .sciencemag.org/career_development/previous_issues/articles/2005_10_07/ bal ance_and_love/(parent)/12097.

Paulozzi, L. J. 1999. International Trends in Rates of Hypospadias and Cryptorchidism. *Environmental Health Perspectives* 107: 297–302.

Pierce, Alison. 2004. Bioscience Warfare. *SF Weekly*, June 2, 1.

Raloff, Janet. 1994a. That Feminine Touch: Are Men Suffering from Prenatal or Childhood Exposures to "Hormonal Toxicants"? *Science News* 145.4: 56–58.

——. 1994b. The Gender Benders: Are Environmental "Hormones" Emasculating Wildlife? *Science News* 145.2: 24–27.

Ray, Janisse. 1999. *Ecology of a Cracker Childhood*. Minneapolis, Minn.: Milkweed.

——. 2007. Changing Sex. In *Courage for the Earth: Writers, Scientists and Activists Celebrate the Life and Writing of Rachel Carson*, ed. Peter Matthiessen, 109–28. New York: Houghton Mifflin.

Roberts, Celia. 2003. Drowning in a Sea of Estrogens: Sex Hormones, Sexual Reproduction and Sex. *Sexualities* 6.2: 195–213.

Royte, Elizabeth. 2003. Transsexual Frogs. *Discover Magazine* 24.2: 155–63.

Safe, Stephen. 2000. Endocrine Disruptors and Human Health: Is There a Problem? An Update. *Environmental Health Perspectives* 108 (June): 1.

Schapiro, Mark. 2009. *Exposed: The Toxic Chemistry of Everyday Products and What's at Stake for American Power*. White River Junction, Vt.: Chelsea Green.

Shah, Aparna, and Dana Ginn Paredes. 2005. Interview with the author. Oakland, October 31.

Sharpe, R. A., and N. F. Skakkebaek. 1993. Are Oestrogens Involved in Falling Sperm Counts and Disorders of the Male Reproductive Tract? *Lancet* 341: 1392–95.

Shen, Eveline. 2005. Interview with the author, Oakland, October 28.

———. 2006. Reproductive Justice: Toward a Comprehensive Movement. *Mother Jones,* January/February. http://www.motherjones.com/commentary/col umns/2006/01/reproductive_justice.html.

———. 2007. Interview with the author, Oakland, July 25.

Stein, Rachel, ed. 2004. *New Perspectives on Environmental Justice: Gender, Sexuality, and Activism.* New Brunswick, N.J.: Rutgers University Press.

Steingraber, Sandra. 1997. *Living Downstream: An Ecologist Looks at Cancer and the Environment.* New York: Vintage.

———. 2001. *Having Faith: An Ecologist's Journey to Motherhood.* Cambridge, Mass.: Perseus.

———. 2007. The Falling Age of Puberty in U.S. Girls: What We Know, What We Need to Know. San Francisco: A Report for the Breast Cancer Fund. www.breastcan cerfund.org/puberty/.

Sumpter, John P., and Susan Jobling. 1995. Vitellogenesis as a Biomarker for Estrogenic Contamination of the Aquatic Environment. *Environmental Health Perspectives* 103, supp. 7: 173–77.

Sutter, Paul. 2001. Terra Incognita: The Neglected History of Interwar Environmental Thought and Politics. *Reviews in American History* 29 (June): 289–98.

Thomas, Pat. 2006. Sex, Lies, and Herbicides. *Ecologist* (February): 14–21.

Tummon, S., and D. Mortimer. 1992. Decreasing Quality of Semen. *British Medical Journal* 305: 1228–29.

Twombly, Renee. 1995. Assault on the Male. *Environmental Health Perspectives* 103.9: 802.

Ward, Barbara, and René Dubos. 1972. *Only One Earth: The Care and Maintenance of a Small Planet.* New York: W. W. Norton.

Whitty, Julia. 2007. Gone. *Mother Jones,* May/June. http://www.motherjones.com/ news/feature/2007/05/gone.html.

Wilcox, Allen J., Donna B. Baird, Clarice R. Weinberg, Paige P. Hornsby, and Arthur L. Herbst. 1995. Fertility in Men Exposed Prenatally to Diethylstilbestrol. *New England Journal of Medicine* 332: 1411–16.

Wingspread Conference Statement. 1991. Statement from the work session on chemically induced alternations in sexual development: the wildlife/human connection. Wingspread Conference Center, Racine, Wisconsin, July 26–28. Reprinted in *Chemically Induced Alterations in Sexual Development: The Wildlife/Human Connection,* ed. Theo Colborn and C. Clement, 1–8. Princeton, N.J.: Princeton Scientific Publishing (1992).

Wright, Lawrence. 1996. Silent Sperm. *New Yorker,* January 15, 42–48, 50–53.

CHAPTER 8

Undoing Nature: Coalition Building as Queer Environmentalism

KATIE HOGAN

> Ecocritique is similar to queer theory. In the name of all that we
> value in the idea of "nature," it thoroughly examines how nature
> is set up as a transcendental, unified, independent category. . . .
> Far from remaining natural, ecocriticism must admit that it is
> contingent and queer.
>
> —Timothy Morton

> Queer . . . is a coalition-building word.
>
> —Eli Clare

Queer Ecocritique

The denunciation of queers as "unnatural" and as "crimes against nature" has a long history that continues to endanger queer lives and complicate queer environmental desires. Elected officials, popular athletes, and
powerful religious authorities routinely evoke crimes against nature ideology, affecting most queer people's lives on a daily basis.[1] A literal example
took place in the United States in March 2004 when Rhea county officials
in Tennessee voted to amend the state's criminal code so that "the county
[could] charge homosexuals with crimes against nature" (Monkey Trial
2004). Commissioner J.C. Fugate explained, "we need to keep them out of
here" (Monkey Trial 2004). Another stunning instance of "against nature"
emerged on February 16, 2007, in a statement by retired NBA athlete Tim
Hardaway: "You know, I hate gay people, so I let it be known. I don't like
gay people and I don't like to be around gay people. I am homophobic. I
don't like it. It shouldn't be in the world or in the United States" (Hardaway

2007). A recent religious ceremony became the occasion for against-nature sentiment in December 2008 in Pope Benedict XVI's Christmas "greeting" to senior Vatican staff. In this talk, the pope spoke of nature as man and woman and referred to an "ecology of the human being" (Donadio 2008). The pope explained that to ignore this human ecology—by engaging in destructive unnatural behaviors—would be on par with destroying the world's vulnerable rainforests. Such discourse reinforces the entrenched idea of queers as unnatural; it affects how queers think about—and relate to—natural spaces, the environment, and environmental language and issues, and it complicates queer experiences of ease in nature. But it also inspires a queer ecocritique.

In response to repeated condemnations, queer activists, theorists, artists, writers, and filmmakers—with impressive critical force, ingenuity, and creativity—have directed intense theoretical and activist attention to the undoing of the natural and unnatural. This body of work challenges not only heteronormativity, but uncritical nature-based arguments and ideologies. A fully conscious queer ecocritique, as Timothy Morton suggests above, is precisely what contemporary ecocriticism needs. In fact, Morton calls for a "partnership between queer theory and ecological criticism," a collaboration that he says "is long overdue" (Morton 2007, 186). Similarly, although focusing on affinities between ecocriticism and postmodernism, scholar Peter Quigley echoes Morton's ideas in "Nature as Dangerous Space" (1999). In this article, Quigley urges ecocriticism to critically rethink nature: "If nature could be seen as a force that disrupts, overwhelms, undermines, explodes or otherwise 'makes strange' our ideological consensus, our anthropocentrism, then it is possible to see it as an agent of criticism" (198). Treating nature as criticism means revealing the hidden ideologies, assumptions, and politics of the term.

Queer ecocritique shares in these scholars' determined skepticism about discourses of nature and environmentalism, not because queers are innately urban and "hate" nature or environmentalism, or because nature and environmentalism are "naturally" oppressive to queers, but because queer theories are designed to challenge the assumption that nature and the natural are neutral, independent categories exempt from critical challenge. Queer ecocritique takes the alleged "against nature-ness" of queers as the focus of its work. Whether formally recognized or not, a queer ecocritique is a powerful contribution to ecocriticism and environmental justice theory and activism; it keeps the focus on how the seemingly innocent realm of nature and ecological protection is potentially rife with ideology and violence. Queer ecocriticism relentlessly uncovers nature as, to quote again from Quigley, "a weapon of oppression," thus offering a critical practice from which to build theoretical partnerships and multi-issue political actions (1999, 202). Quigley sees this oppressive aspect right alongside an activist potential too when he writes that nature is also "a place to gather strength against the forces of domination" (201–202). In other words, nature is an opportunity to build theoretical overlaps and an opportunity for activist coalitions among seemingly disparate groups and communities.

In *Eight Bullets: One Woman's Story of Surviving Anti-Gay Violence* by Claudia Brenner and Hannah Ashley (1995), Brenner evokes Quigley's vision of nature as both weapon of oppression and place "to gather strength." A queer memoir about a hate crime that resulted in the murder of Brenner's life partner during the couple's hike on the Appalachian Trail in eastern Pennsylvania, *Eight Bullets* unwittingly demonstrates a queer ecocritique by recording the consequences of heteronormative ideas of nature and environment—that queer groups and individuals do not deserve to be in nature because they are "unnatural"—and by responding with images of queer cultures in nature to resist "the forces of domination." Using nature as a chance to fight domination is specifically voiced in the following statement of the design of the murdered queer woman's memorial service: "Evelyn and Rebecca's closest friends had planned this memorial service, deliberately choosing a beautiful, outdoor place both to honor Rebecca's love of nature and to reclaim the outdoors after her murder. The clearing seemed to grow to the perfect size for the huge circle of over 150 people who had come to celebrate her life" (Brenner and Ashley 1995, 104–105). Queer ecocritique not only shows us how to undermine and challenge the "against nature" ideology eloquently charted in *Eight Bullets;* it also highlights how queer texts create interesting and resistant political cultures using nature as an organizing focus.

Coalitions of the Unfit

The numerous historical examples of oppressive ideas of unnatural and unfit that we associate with hate crimes and murders make queer interventions into nature and environmentalism relevant, if not urgent. Betsy Hartman (2006) and Nancy Ordover (2003) have explored the implications of eugenics discourses for socially vulnerable groups, including immigrants, queers, women, people of color, the ill and disabled, and working-class and poor people. Hartman's essay "Everyday Eugenics" urges progressive scholars to consider the subtle ways that environmentalism and nature are potentially saturated with ideas of the unfit and un-natural: "American environmentalism has had a long and strong relationship with eugenics. Many of the early conservationists were eugenicists who believed in maintaining the purity of both nature and the gene pool as well as the manifest destiny of the white Anglo-Saxon race to steward (and colonize) the environment" (2006).

Hartman insists that "the problematic assumptions, languages and images that make American environmentalism particularly susceptible to eugenic influences" ought to be a main focus of contemporary progressive critical inquiry. Queer theory aids enormously in this critical project. Pure nature and pristine wilderness, two seemingly neutral organizing concepts of dominant American environmentalism, have been linked to various kinds of racial, sexual, and gender oppression throughout American history, with specific instances of social purity and racial hygiene campaigns involved in eugenics-like ideologies.

Like Hartman's work, Nancy Ordover's (2003) *American Eugenics: Race, Queer Anatomy, and the Science of Nationalism* traces the influence of eugenic philosophies and practices in such areas as medicine, immigration/nationalism, education, law, public policy, and, most relevant to my argument, environmentalism. She points out that in some historical eras, such as the early part of the twentieth century, U.S. state-funded sterilization programs were openly implemented and praised. Eugenics projects garnered legislative funding in the form of government- and university-sponsored sterilization programs, such as the program promoted by Harvard university professor Robert DeCourcey Ward. Ward, a leader in the U.S. eugenics movement, called for strict immigration laws to prevent what he called "crimes against the future" (Ward 1912), referring specifically to the unfit children of inferior immigrants. Many states in the United States, from Vermont to Oregon, had official sterilization and castration programs. For example, Peter Boag's (2003) *Same-Sex Affairs: Constructing and Controlling Homosexuality in the Pacific Northwest* analyzes early-twentieth-century eugenics programs targeting gay men of various racial, ethnic, immigrant, and class backgrounds. But even when eugenics programs are abolished and outlawed, as they are today, eugenics ideology lingers, as Hartman suggests, and often under the guise of protecting nature.

Ordover singles out the rash of anti-gay ballot measures of the early 1990s—I will be focusing on one of these campaigns in this chapter—as contemporary examples of eugenics-like discourses of the late twentieth century. Ordover also points to scientific and medical research into the alleged "gay gene" as a medical instance of a contemporary eugenics-like project. And although Ordover does not devalue mainstream environmental movements, she nevertheless demonstrates how these movements can be cannibalized by eugenics ideas, evident in the current "greening of hate" phenomenon that has emerged in the last decade. For instance, some members of local chapters of the mainstream environmental group the Sierra Club have created alliances with anti-immigrant campaigners to oust immigrants from the United States on the grounds that they are environmental threats; the rhetoric of "protecting nature," repeatedly evoked, resonates with a eugenics ideology (Ordover 2003, 50; also Hartman 2006). In other words, eugenics and environmentalism, while not one and the same, have been historically linked as projects that operate in tandem, rather than in opposition, and often in terms of ideas of the unfit and unnatural.

Perhaps one of the most disturbing examples of nature as a platform for eugenics purposes is analyzed in Bruggemeier, Cioc, and Zeller's volume, *How Green Were the Nazis: Nature, Environment, and Nation in the Third Reich* (2005). Using the lens of environmental history to shed light on Nazis' manipulations of environmental preservation programs as a cover for racial genocide, the essays in this collection address annexation of lands in Eastern Europe in an effort to "Germanize" the landscape. To implement these programs German officials relocated and/or exterminated those communities deemed inferior, unfit, and insufficiently Aryan to live on German land. Although the collection does not directly analyze connections between American eugenics and Nazi environmentalism, several essays do link America's eugenics-like programs, including the United States' seemingly innocent program of building national parks, as an aspect of purity and nationalism campaigns that later inspired Nazi environmental policies. For instance, the Nazis took inspiration from the United States' extermination and relocation of Native peoples from lands in order to create national parks and control natural resources. Of course, the Nazis took things further; they cleansed the unfit throughout Eastern Europe in order to purify the German landscape, but they made the link between land, nation, and unfit/unnatural by studying U.S. policies.

These theoretical and historical perspectives on environmentalism serve as dramatic instances of how, in the name of nature, racial eugenics ideologies are reformulated as caring for the environment. Nature and environmentalism are categories that are uniquely susceptible to this kind of exploitation because these categories are often assumed to be benign, neutral, or innocent. Yet the disturbing links between eugenics and environmentalism in modern history suggest how "everyday eugenics" masquerades as ecological preservation.

Queer critical interventions into such uses of nature and environment expose the dark purposes to which nature and environmentalism can be put. Disrupting, challenging, and undermining normative ideas of what counts as naturally fit and unfit is the primary emphasis. Such critical work is as important to humans and all nature as is the work of identifying environmental racism and stopping toxic dumping in poor rural and urban areas. Furthermore, while typical instances of environmental degradation include a focus on chemical toxicities and vulnerable ecosystems, the destruction of queer bodies, communities, and cultures through toxic discourses of unnatural and unfit are also outrageous instances of environmental destruction as urgent as disappearing species and global warming. This powerful reframing of what "counts" as environmental damage—and seeing environmental discourse as a potential location of harm and damage—opens up affinities between ecocriticism and queer theory, but also between the more directly activist approaches of environmental justice theory and activism and queer intellectual activity and thought. Since both queer and environmental justice perspectives assume that nature and environment are not neutral ahistorical categories, and each critical practice looks at how the very language of nature and environmentalism can often mask harm to humans and nature, this shared theoretical and historical experience could serve as a basis for coalition. If divided and disparate groups agreed to consider how nature is often a "weapon of oppression" used against them, and, equally important, if these same groups saw how nature is also an opportunity for creative resistance, an unusually strong coalition could be formed (Quigley 1999, 202). Like environmental justice, queer critical consciousness continually exposes the violence and ideology of these taken-for-granted terms. In this way, queer theory's preoccupation with the uses of nature operates as a form of environmentalism that is useful to all communities deemed unfit.

The Nature of Coalitions

Communities deemed unfit and unnatural draw on that experience as the basis for resistance and coalition in Heather MacDonald's 1995 documentary film *Ballot Measure 9* and in Joseph Hansen's 1984 detective novel *Nightwork*. As if heeding Greta Gaard's call for coalition building as set forth in her classic essay, "Toward a Queer Ecofeminism," *Ballot Measure 9* and *Nightwork* deconstruct and resist ideas of pristine nature and notions of the fit and unfit and instead show how such ideas are wielded against various groups (Gaard 2004). MacDonald's and Hansen's narratives urge us to work collaboratively to challenge nature as a weapon of oppression, thus offering a realistic and hopeful vision of coalition.

MacDonald's *Ballot Measure 9* highlights Oregon's well-documented history of driving the uncivilized from land, nature, space, and environment, and illustrates how discriminatory legislation there has targeted African Americans, Asian Americans, and Catholics in turn. The careful inclusion of this focus is highly significant; it is one of the most distinguishing features of this documentary as it illustrates correspondences between racial and gender-queer violence.[2] The Oregon Citizens' Alliance sought to amend the state constitution to discriminate against lesbian, gay, and transgender people, and the proposed amendment specifically characterized queers as "abnormal, wrong, and unnatural." MacDonald carefully juxtaposes the amendment's language with previous legislation throughout Oregon's history that targets certain groups or activities as wrong and unnatural.

Joseph Hansen's detective novel *Nightwork* uses a popular genre to offer an original response to the crimes-against-nature paradigm as it affects both queers and working-class communities and people of color. In this text, a wealthy white gay detective and his middle-class African American lover expose toxic dumping as an aspect of toxic heterosexuality. The main characters are acutely aware of how ideologies of race, sexuality, and economic privilege are linked to environmental degradation, and Hansen portrays the queer interracial relationship as a symbol of healing coalition.

Uncovering the ecoqueer sensibility of the film and novel offers critics, readers, viewers, and activists alternative perspectives on seemingly ordinary texts devoid of ecological significance. An ecoqueer perspective brings into bold relief how resistance to "against nature" can take many forms, and that resistance itself can expand knowledge and practices of environmentalism. Rather than reinforcing the traditional view of nature and environment as an escape from the social world, ecoqueer critique positions nature and environment as rooted in the social world. For queers, as for many racial, ethnic, gender, and religious minorities, nature is not a hiding place from ideology but often its location, and using nature as a resource or tool for ecocritique is a way to broaden what "counts" as environmentalism.

Understanding how environmentalism can function as an aspect of eugenics ideology is a disturbing project, as the volume *How Green Were the Nazis* (Bruggemeier, et al. 2005) makes clear, but it is also an extremely productive point of view through which to interpret queer texts such as Heather MacDonald's (1995) *Ballot Measure 9*. The time period covered in the film is the eight months leading up to the 1992 presidential elections when a Christian-right group with national funding and resources, the Oregon Citizens' Alliance (OCA), presented Ballot Measure 9 to the voters. If the measure passed, queer citizens could have been denied housing, employment, and other civil rights without legal recourse. Measure 9 also included language stating that homosexuality was "wrong, abnormal, and unnatural" and that all public educational institutions, including colleges and universities, would be in violation of the law if they "promoted" homosexuality.[3] By making this high-stakes conflict her focus, MacDonald's film explores in vivid detail the against-nature paradigm of Measure 9 while also showing how this same ideology became the basis for effective coalition politics. Alternating between the voices and activities of the Oregon Citizens' Alliance and their efforts to Christianize and heterosexualize the state, and the views and activism of the "No on 9" organizers—overwhelmingly comprising queers, people of color, progressives, and religious moderates—MacDonald's film unexpectedly captures the deeply entrenched eugenics-like aspect of the against-nature ideology as an inspiration for coalition politics.[4]

However, perceiving this queer ecocritique of the film is, to my knowledge, a unique take on the documentary film. For instance, while many viewers and critics experience *Ballot Measure 9* as a progressive, riveting documentary, it has been categorized as simplistic, earnest, and assimilationist, and its focus on coalition politics has been singled out as particularly naive. The film's presentation of queers in what is considered highly sanitized terms is troubling, and the images of vulnerable lgbt Oregonians in kitchens, living rooms, or workplaces are problematically juxtaposed with images of the OCA as foul-mouthed brutes and fascist clods.

Ronald Gregg (1997), a "No on 9" queer activist who organized against the OCA's ballot measure while he was a graduate student at the University of Oregon, notes the narrative's simplistic villain/victim structure and suggests that the film does not effectively challenge homophobia and heteronormativity. Despite its sincere commitment to recording how queer Oregonians were victimized by severe discrimination and how they fought back, Gregg points out that the film does not address the underlying issues of queerness and heteronormativity and that it downplays the diversity of queer sexualities/cultures. Gregg is correct that many Oregonians voted "no" on Measure 9 because of the measure's extreme language, not because they genuinely thought queer cultures, particularly in the area of sexual relationships, were equal to heterosexual cultures and relationships. Many who voted against Measure 9 did not want to see themselves as bigots, yet many still believed that queers were inferior human beings. Stated differently, while Oregonians did not think queers should be exterminated, driven out of the state, or denied housing and jobs, nevertheless queer sexual cultures, relationships, and families were not seen as equal to heterosexual relationships and families. In fact, some newspaper editorials suggested that, had Measure 9 been written using less incendiary, hateful language, it probably would have passed, even in urban centers.

In short, Gregg categorizes *Ballot Measure 9* as a well-meaning documentary forged in the heat of a frightening assault on queer rights, but he ultimately dismisses the film as capitulating to mainstream heterosexual ideology; I think Gregg is underestimating the film's emphasis on coalition building and its creative resistance to ideas of the unnatural and the lingering manifestations of everyday eugenics of the Measure 9 ballot initiative. While it is true that MacDonald does not show a range of sexual practices and cultures, neither does her film capture the infighting, misunderstandings, and different forms of prejudice that created enormous stress in building a cross-racial, -ethnic, -religious, -class, and -sexual coalition, MacDonald does document that coalitions organized around contesting the against-nature paradigm can work.

For instance, she shows that when a Catholic priest publicly denounced Measure 9, his church was vandalized and the sanctuary walls covered with spray-painted terms such as "Kill gays and Catholics," "Jews & Spics & Gays," and "OCA Yes on 9." Included in this section of the film is footage of various parishioners, many of whom are Catholic senior citizens who remember being persecuted by the KKK in the 1920s, reading the graffiti. Memories of this kind of abuse, hatred, and attack among Oregonian religious, racial, and sexual minorities strengthened, rather than diluted, the No on 9 coalition. These groups, at one time or another, were seen as against nature, as unfit to live in Oregon. From the perspective of queer approaches to environmentalism, this seemingly mainstream political documentary inadvertently deconstructs the politics of the fit and unfit that bolstered the OCA's key ideas and strategies. When the film is viewed as contesting the alleged against-nature-ness of the unfit, I think it is slightly more difficult to dismiss it as simply pandering to mainstream America. MacDonald effectively illuminates the against-nature pattern that has permeated Oregon's history and that played out in this latest eugenics-like campaign.

The documentary opens with Lon Mabon, the organizer of Measure 9 in Oregon, driving his car with the luminous Oregon landscape in view as he spouts homophobic hatred. Dramatic music merges with Mabon's statements, suggesting, says Gregg, how Mabon and his ilk are villains who actively disrupt the gentle beauty of Oregonian nature. But from a queer environmental justice perspective, this same opening segment illustrates the idea of nature as a resource for heterosexualizing and Christianizing Oregon: Mabon, the Oregon landscape behind him, shares his view that homosexuality is a defect of nature, and nature is on Mabon's side. Here, the nature is neither a backdrop nor a neutral or benign category; it is the stage or vehicle upon which Mabon's against-nature-ness of queers is framed in his Measure 9 legislation.

Organizing the film around numerous groups and communities with a shared history of being the target of such eugenics discourse, MacDonald clears ground for coalition among queers, women, people of color—that is, any group or community deemed unfit, unnatural, or against nature. While the unfit paradigm is not used against groups and communities in identical ways, the marginalized groups respond and resist the OCA's ballot measure because of their shared experience. They understand how terms such as "nature" and "the natural" have been used to drive out and/ or control the bodies, lives, and cultures of diverse Oregonians.

What this means is that one of the consequences of belonging to a group or community targeted as unfit is experiencing restricted access to nature and natural resources. Queer access to American nature, as Mei Mei Evans argues, is complicated by the fact that American nature has been historically embroiled in ideas of racial purity and nationalism. Consequently, American nature is often constructed as "the province of [heterosexual] white men" (Evans 2002, 188). As Evans explains, "One way of understanding the culturally dominant conception of what constitutes 'nature' in the United States is to ask ourselves who gets to go there" (Evans 2002, 191–92). Frank Peterman, an African American environmentalist, talks about this idea in terms of his family's reaction to his plans for an extended stay in national parks in the western United States (Kelly 2006). Peterman's family members were so concerned for Peterman and his spouse's safety that they bought the couple loaded guns. Peterman understood his family's reaction as historical memory of the Ku

Klux Klan. Although Klan activity did occur in cities, the Klan carried out many of its acts of terror, murder, and torture in the wilderness: "African Americans still think of some of the dirty deeds that were done by the Klan out in the woods," said Peterman (Kelly 2006).

Gender, race, sexuality, religion, physical ability, and class figure prominently in who is assumed to belong in nature and who is not, who has safe access to nature and who does not. For queer citizens in particular, the language of ecological protection has been especially problematic since for centuries gay men, lesbians, and transgender individuals have been characterized as "pollution" threatening the moral fabric of society through a willful creation of dirty, diseased, and immoral environments. A 1960s Senate subcommittee report on homosexuals in the U.S. military concluded that "one homosexual can pollute an entire office" (Carter 2004, 14). The findings of the report were quickly applied to civilian work settings, with fears that homosexuals could potentially infect and pollute the entire country. Thus, openly claiming a queer place-based identity, as Evans puts it, challenges Western Christian ideology and social customs that have defined queers as "freaks of nature" and "defects of nature." Again, such ideas about unfit people resonate with the language and ideology of the OCA's Measure 9. For instance, one OCA supporter and harasser is heard saying on an answering machine message, "Save America, kill a fag!" Queers perceived both as "out of place" and as "opposed" to nature and environment are cornerstone ideas of the OCA's ballot Measure 9 initiative.

MacDonald's film frames homophobia as structurally linked to racial and ethnic racism in Oregon, a suggestion that strikes some critics, such as Gregg, as dubious. In her research on Oregon's Ballot Measure 9 campaign, Arlene Stein found disturbing overlaps between racism and the homophobic violence that erupted in the public school during the OCA campaign. "[A] group of [school] boys constructed plywood figures hanging from nooses with 'kill fags' written on them and wore them on chains around their necks" (2001, 199). According to Stein's findings, no teacher or other school authority challenged the boys or asked them to remove the chains while on school property. Furthermore, Nancy Ordover's research on American eugenics supports MacDonald's view of Measure 9; the enormous increase in violence that erupted during the campaign echoes historically documented racist eugenics-like ideas of the fit and unfit, the natural and the unnatural. While racism and homophobia have their own historical and material specificities, both are inextricably linked to the everyday racial eugenics that has saturated Oregon (and U.S.) history.

Presenting these connections in terms of the OCA campaign indicates how destructive uses of nature can link queers to other historically marginalized groups. OCA supporters cultivated an environment of hate targeted at queers and their allies; hate crimes increased in quantity and severity; people's private homes and workplaces were vandalized; some queers were killed; allies and No on 9 supporters were harassed, and their lives, family, animals, and property were threatened and/or harmed. Queer citizens, in the words of OCA members, are not only "against" the Christian Bible: queerness is a plague akin to rats and pollution, and therefore should "be discouraged and avoided." By carefully documenting this environmental disaster of hate, MacDonald resists Oregon's legacy of affirming itself through the exclusion of racial, cultural, and sexual others while eradicating those it perceived as different, a practice that successfully drove queer citizens out of the state. In a 1992 *New York Times* article, "Behind the Hate in Oregon," Michelangelo Signorile reported that lesbians and gay men reacted to the violence and hate by selling their homes and leaving the state, a response the OCA clearly encouraged in its campaign.

MacDonald also captures Measure 9's curtailment of the physical and social freedom of citizens. The OCA's Ballot Measure 9, reminiscent of Oregon's "sundown laws," which "prohibited blacks from circulating freely at night" (Stein 2001, 144–45), causes activists living and working in Grant's Pass, a rural area located in southern Oregon and populated with lesbian "back to the land" communities founded in the 1970s, to fear for their safety. MacDonald depicts women discussing their fears of being shot at by young men in pickup trucks or having their homes trashed by supporters of the OCA. As Sky, a local activist explains, "we live real isolated here." While many of the concepts informing Sky's back-to-the-land endeavors are essentialist and rooted in white, middle-class privilege, marginalized communities such as hers, argues Catriona Sandilands, "craft new cultures of nature against dominant social and ecological relations of late capitalism" (2004, 109). They also contribute to the idea, as Gill Valentine puts it, that "lesbians and gay men can disrupt the taken-for-granted production of everyday space as heterosexual space" (2000, 100).

MacDonald exposes the assumption that Oregon is heterosexual land by highlighting the testimony of Scott Seibert, a gay activist, ex-marine, and police officer, and one of MacDonald's main subjects in the film. Seibert explains that he was born in Oregon, that he considers Oregon his state, and that it is a beautiful place. His identity as a gay man is inextricably linked with his identity as an Oregonian; Seibert's Oregon car license plate reads "GAYMAN." But after months of threats, his home is vandalized and he wonders where he will live and how far he will run since the OCA plans to organize anti-gay ordinances throughout the country. By focusing on the way queer Oregonians were being driven from their homes and state, and by showing how they were being violated and murdered, MacDonald's film reverberates with standard ideas of environmental justice perspectives, which stress the right of all individuals to safe environments.

The grassroots environmental justice movement's overall goal "to fight against the destruction and taking of our lands and communities," coupled with Principle Six, which states that environmental justice "affirms the fundamental right to political, economic, cultural and environmental self-determination of all peoples," has profound meaning for queer social justice activism and theory (Seventeen Principles of Environmental Justice, quoted in Kirk and Okazawa-Rey 2001, 499). It also supports a more complex interpretation of *Ballot Measure 9*. Applying these environmental justice concepts to queer communities and cultures makes clear that the physical, emotional, social, economic, political, and psychological violence and injustice directed toward queers, particularly when they openly claim their right to a "place," is an environmental justice issue that MacDonald's film intuitively understands. Seeking to drive queers out of Oregon was a central focus of the Ballot Measure 9 campaign, and MacDonald's film skillfully captures the efforts of the OCA, who wanted Oregon to be a Christian heterosexual space.

Rural Queers and Queer Theory

In addition to showing what happens when lesbians and gay men claim a place-based identity rooted in a queer environmental justice framework, MacDonald's film also quietly challenges the dominance of urban definitions of queerness, activism, and community. Rural queers threaten the still pervasive assumption held by many Americans that rural space is heterosexual and urban space is homosexual and "unnatural." Such beliefs fuel the violation of queer bodies and justify the forced removal of "unfit" queers from supposedly "natural" heterosexual spaces; they also facilitate the equally problematic myth of urban space as naturally queer and more accepting. As Eli Clare repeatedly argues in *Exile and Pride: Disability, Queerness, and Liberation,* many queer theorists and activists who challenge the ideologies of nature and the unnatural nevertheless espouse a simplistic view of rural cultures: "the people and institutions defining queer identity and culture are urban" (1999, 37). This sentiment is echoed in William J. Spurlin's essay, "Remapping Same-Sex Desire: Queer Writing and Culture in the American Heartland": "very often queer studies focuses its attention on queer public space in large metropolitan centres as if queer activism is absent or non-existent in non-urban locations" (2000, 184). Judith Halberstam includes an extended analysis of the structure of urban queer predisposition in the Brandon Teena murder that occurred in rural Nebraska in 1993 (2005a). And Beverly A. Brown's *In Timber Country: Working People's Stories of Environmental Conflict and Urban Flight* is another essential text that breaks down class bias in queer theory (1995).

The work of Alan Berube (1990) and John D'Emilio (1993) has shed light on the social construction of queer identity and culture as urban. Berube argues that World War II functioned as the watershed event that helped create the modern, urban lesbian and gay identity and movement. Thousands of men and women from small cities, towns, and farms traveled to port cities to enter the sex-segregated armed services; when the war ended, these same individuals remained in port cities such as Los Angeles, San Francisco, and New York. Joining the service allowed millions of lesbians and gay men to meet, socialize, and create romantic relationships, and when the war ended, they did not want to return to the environments of small towns and rural areas.

D'Emilio also interprets World War II as a pivotal event in the creation of a modern lesbian and gay urban identity, but he points to the emergence of industrialism and consumer capitalism as setting the stage for the creation of urban gay identity. Capitalism shifted the country from an agricultural, home-based, family-run production economy to a capitalist manufacturing and consumer economy. The new economy loosened the grip that the heterosexual, nuclear family traditionally had on its members, freeing them to create a personal identity based on erotic and emotional attraction.

Ironically, the social construction of queers as linked to capitalist urban space has meant, in the minds of many Christian fundamentalists, that lesbians and gays do not belong in small towns and rural areas. In her book, Arlene Stein includes the words of a Christian preacher who denounces cities as moral cesspools populated with "gays, Asians, New Agers, and other undesirables" (2001, 231). For fundamentalist Christians, the notion of cities as unnatural and decadent is one of the reasons they are equated with queers; but even non-fundamentalists may equate cities with gay and lesbian people. Given the popular assumption that to be gay is to be urban, it is not surprising that rural queers live in exile, leaving rural spaces behind. But such departures highlight what happens when queer citizens openly claim their right to a place-based identity in geographic spaces deemed heterosexual, not that queers do not, and should not, inhabit rural space.

While, as Berube and D'Emilio suggest, many lesbians and gay men leave small towns and rural areas for urban centers, many do not. According to the 2000 U.S. census results, "partnered lesbians and gay men reside in 99.3 percent of all the counties in America" (Martinac 2001). In Michael Nava's (1999) novel, *The Burning Plain,* he gives voice to the desire to stay in one's hometown despite the stigma of being gay. Through the melancholic voice of his main character, Henry Rios, Nava explores the longing many lesbians and gays have for their hometowns and rural areas. Rios grew up in an immigrant Chicano section of a small town in California's Central Valley. Now, as an "out" lawyer living in Los Angeles—a city described as the "burning plain" in the novel's title—Rios often "wondered how it felt to belong to a place. My homosexuality had exiled me from my own hometown, where the local prejudices would have kept me in the closet had I remained. . . . [But] what would it be like to die in the same place where you were born, to grow old with people you knew as children, to be compared to your grandfather or grandmother by people who had actually known them" (Nava 1999, 118)? What authors like Nava, Clare, Spurlin, Halberstam, and Brown are suggesting is that the specific experiences, histories, and theories of rural and small-town queers need to be more carefully integrated into our concepts and understanding of queer intellectual activity, creativity, and organizing. In order to carefully illuminate the subtle presence of everyday eugenics that often flows from protectionist discourses of nature and environment, it is vital to analyze the ideologies and cultural myths informing representations of rural and urban nature and environments. Such work broadens our understanding of who and what deserves environmental freedom, so that queer bodies, sexualities, and cultures are seen as worthy of ecological and cultural protection on par with urban national parks and wilderness areas. The razor-sharp ability of queer intellectual practices to detect "everyday eugenics" in the urban/rural split inspires interesting coalitions that potentially benefit all people and nature.

Challenging the idea that queers are naturally inferior and highlighting the power and possibility of alliance renders *Ballot Measure 9* an important queer environmental justice text. MacDonald's focus on rural and urban queers who create alliances with racial, ethnic, and religious communities and groups dovetails with Judith Halberstam's call for a shift away from identity toward coalition building as a focus for organizing: "While identity obviously continues to be the best basis for political organizing, we have seen within various social movements of the last decade that identity politics must give way to some form of coalition if a political movement is to be successful" (2005b, 555). The destructive uses to which notions of fit and unfit, natural and unnatural, have been put throughout Oregon's history are thoughtfully exposed, documented, and resisted in *Ballot Measure 9*, enacting a powerful framework for queer environmental protection based in coalition.

Nightwork

Queer critical interventions into the eugenics-like potential of nature discourses exists side by side with desire for cultures of nature that queers create and practice. Such a complex ecological sensibility permeates Joseph Hansen's 1984 detective novel *Nightwork: A Dave Brandstetter Mystery*. By the narrative's end, Hansen's main character, queer white insurance investigator Dave Brandstetter, has uncovered illegal midnight toxic dumping—the "night work" of the book's title—and begins to speak like a bona fide environmentalist: "The air is poisoned, ponds, rivers, lakes, whole oceans. The water under the land. The land itself. Farms, the animals on the farms. People. Whole towns have to be abandoned. Somebody has to stop it" (1984, 155–56). Although Dave is officially an insurance investigator who is also independently wealthy, he detects the impact of environmental social injustices as they affect humans and non-human physical nature. Hansen's text articulates a subtle queer critique of the often coded discourses of the fit and unfit, and his narrative uncovers toxic heterosexuality and capitalism as environmental threats. Similar to *Ballot Measure 9*, Hansen's narrative includes activism and coalition work as a central theme. But unlike *Ballot Measure 9*, *Nightwork* explicitly draws on the language, issues, and themes of mainstream environmentalism, espoused by an out queer man.

Akin to grassroots environmental justice theory and activism, Hansen's narrative connects seemingly unrelated issues: exposure to workplace toxins, gang violence, police neglect, high unemployment among black teenagers, an inferior public educational system, shoddy housing, and illegal dumping of toxic waste in wilderness areas are all linked to destructive ideological conceptions of nature. It is significant that Hansen presents these troubles as interlocking; the text refuses to compartmentalize the various social issues, echoing a key strategy of environmental justice theory. In this way, Hansen's text interweaves queer perspectives with standard environmental justice concerns. It is Dave Brandstetter's marginalized sexuality—his "queerness"—that renders him "naturally" inferior and that facilitates his skepticism about how nature is misused; it is also his "queerness" that produces his understanding of the interconnections between racial, gender, and economic injustice and environmental issues. For example, Hansen's narrative includes the eccentric character DeWitt Gifford, who wears women's hats and makeup, about which Dave is neither unnerved nor disapproving. And after DeWitt is murdered by one of Gifford Gardens's gangs, Dave places a 1920s woman's hat on De-Witt as his body lies on a stretcher. "'You're kidding,'" says a member of the coroner's office, referring to Dave's action. Dave replies, as he looks at DeWitt's dead body, "'He wasn't'" (162). In other instances, Hansen uses humor to stand gender on its head: "Men with cameras on their shoulders. Pretty girls of both sexes with microphones" (112). A combination of queerness in terms of environmental issues renders *Nightwork* a unique example of queer ecocritique and queer environmental justice.

The narrative opens with a significant description of the altering of nature in the construction of what eventually becomes the working-class neighborhood of Los Angeles called, ironically, Gifford Gardens: "Before the construction of these acres of shacky stucco houses in 1946, the creek bed was shallow, cluttered with boulders from the far-off mountains, shaded by live oaks, and clumpy with brush. He remembered it that way from the 1930s" (1). What makes this passage about a changing landscape different from the traditional lament over the loss of nature is Hansen's understanding that the alteration of the land is a violation not only of nature, but the people who will live there. Nature, people of color, and the working class will be sacrificed for this "development"—their lives, health, and families are fodder for capitalist accumulation. In order to turn a profit, the developers had to build Gifford Gardens quickly; the trees were cut down and the creek bed was covered over with concrete slabs so that housing could be hastily erected. When the rains came, all of the houses flooded "until the County at last gouged out the creek bed and lined it with concrete slabs. Much too late" (2). This historical information—that Gifford Gardens residents live in shabby, unsound housing slapped together because of greed—is thematically connected to Dave's investigation into present-day Gifford Gardens, where cracked sidewalks (or no sidewalks at all), roads with broken pavement, tacky homes with chain-link fences, visible gang activity, high unemployment, alcoholism, and shoddy services create a landscape of injustice.

Dave, his lover, Cecil Harris, an African American television news reporter, and a working-class African-American boy whose father has died from handling hazardous waste discover the behind-the-scenes actions of Tech-Rite managers. Working with organized crime, the managers hire outside truckers to perform so-called night work, the illegal midnight dumping of toxic waste in wilderness areas. In pursuing the mystery of the death, the narrative incorporates a critique of two seemingly contradictory conceptions of nature: as refuge for white male heterosexuality and as profitable dumping ground for unscrupulous capitalists.

The senior vice president of Tech-Rite, Lorin Shields, has built an expensive house in the woods for his young, beautiful wife, only to learn that she has developed cancer caused by exposure to one of Tech-Rite's illegal toxic dumps. The spouse's exposure to toxicity is clearly connected to Shields's contradictory conceptions of nature as the location for white, heterosexual intimacy while, at the same time, dumping ground for toxic waste. As Shields explains, "You don't understand how impossible all those government regulations make doing business" (169). Shields literally "shields" himself from his dark culpability; instead of acknowledging that he has poisoned his wife, nature, and working-class truckers, he murders the truckers who engage in the illegal night work that he alone is responsible for authorizing. Employing a queer environmental justice perspective, Hansen shows how Shields's toxic conceptions of nature are linked to white, heterosexual privilege. He destroys nature, women, and the working class by practicing corporate capitalism's plundering of resources and people for profit while, simultaneously, feeling entitled to nature as refuge from the stressful, high-pressured world of corporate capitalism he cultivates.

Hansen presents a unique interpretation by including Shields's characterization of his dead wife's relationship to nature as passive, luminous escape: "Do you know what she wanted from life? Everything gentle and beautiful. A house in the woods. Quiet. Solitude. Nature. Away from the world" (168). Nature as people-less landscape, as retreat from "the world," is precisely the politics of nature that Hansen's queer ecological perspective challenges. Historically, nature as enchanting escape has been an experience for some maintained at the expense of many socially marginalized groups and communities. Environmental justice theorists and activists Robert Regina Austin and Michael Schill identify this deeply entrenched dynamic as "favor [ing] nature over society and the individual's experience of the natural realm over the collective" (Austin and Schill 1994, 58).

To challenge this prevalent view of the wilderness, Hansen deliberately departs from the typical case of a toxic dump in a poor urban or rural community of color. Emphasizing wilderness as a site of one heterosexual man's conceptions of nature, Hansen zeroes in on this widely held conception of nature as retreat for the privileged and wealthy, but implies that such ideology has toxic consequences for humans and nature alike.

Gifford Gardens, located miles away from the rural midnight dumping, is nevertheless significantly affected by Lorin Shields's actions, but because Gifford Gardens, as Dave puts it, is a "mixed town," where African American, Latino American, and white working-class people are pitted against each other, there is initially little hope for coalition building as a response (Hansen 1984, 16). A few white and Asian families are able to save enough money to send their children to a private academy, but the majority of the children attend unsafe, low-quality public schools. Gang violence between Chicano and African American youth is so severe that people stay in their homes, and the police refuse to respond to the community's calls for help. Dave's lover, Cecil, characterizes Gifford Gardens as "a killing ground," and the community's black minister, Luther Prentice, says, "We are in the last days, it appears" (63, 31).

Despite the unrelenting economic injustice and racism challenging this community, white trucker Paul Myers and African American trucker Ossie Bishop are close friends; it is Ossie who tells Paul about the high-paying night work that will allow these men a financial plan for their children's futures. Unfortunately, it is also the night work that leads to both men's exploitation and death. Like many members of working-class communities and communities of color, Ossie and Paul are being asked to choose between making a living and environmental health. Through what happens to these two characters, Hansen incorporates into his narrative the realities of toxic exposure on the job and illegal toxic dumping in wilderness by presenting them as motives for murder.

Echoing the cross-racial friendship of Myers and Bishop, Dave forges relationships across sexuality, age, race, class, gender, and neighborhood, challenging the traditional view of the hard-boiled, isolated, heterosexual male detective who, in solving crimes, routinely makes disparaging remarks about gays, women, and people of color. In contrast, Hansen's detective collaborates with those positioned as marginal and never removes himself from social relationships or activism to solve a mystery. Additionally, Dave's response to nature and environment as neither outside of ideology nor completely determined by it drastically differs from

Lorin Shields's conception of nature as escape from ideology or a resource for profit.

Although Hansen's text was published in 1984, when the environmental justice movement was just beginning to form, the narrative foretold much of what has happened and is currently happening in environmental justice theory and activism today. In fact, Hansen's 1984 novel resonates with the youth group Sierra Youth Coalition of Canada, a contemporary environmental justice coalition that states on its organization's Web site that it is committed to examining "how all forms of oppression are interconnected and how they correspond to the degradation of the physical environment. . . . Furthermore, racism, sexism, classism, transphobia, ableism and heterosexism (among other things) are just as harmful to our human environment as is its physical degradation" (n.d.). Like the Sierra Youth Coalition, Hansen understood environmental violations as a nexus of structures, involving racism, labor, and sexuality as central environmental themes. The notion of nature as property and sanctuary for entitled men is powerfully resisted in this text, as is the overall theme that nature and environment are poisoned by ideological misuse.

As a queer man, Dave encounters all of the real-life challenges and difficulties facing environmental justice activists, including corrupt legal systems, corporate greed, and organized crime, and he intuitively knows that activism and alliance across cultural difference are the solutions. When Hansen's text is read alongside the famous environmental justice principles, an implicitly queer sensibility encoded in environmental justice emerges. Through his tender attention to communities and the natural world and its people, the author makes clear that exposing the ideological ways in which nature and the natural are used is one of the highest forms of activism.

Taken together, *Ballot Measure 9* and *Nightwork* show us what a queer ecocritique and queer environmental justice looks like. These interesting—yet overlooked—texts contribute queer critical perspectives on the languages, assumptions, and images of environmentalism and discourses of nature, envisioning an environmental justice for all. Cultivating and refining critical perspectives on nature-based and environmental paradigms and exposing the subtle eugenics-like ideology often accompanying them is a central feature of queer thought and activism. Like traditional environmental justice, the queer ecocritique of these texts not only protects vulnerable groups and communities from toxic ideologies but creates "cleaner" uses of the categories of nature and environment. Instead of nature and ecological protection as a way to mask an "everyday eugenics," a queer environmental justice framework exposes the potentially sinister misuses of nature in terms of race, sexuality, gender, and class. Uncovering the ways in which nature and the natural are used to label some groups and communities as unnatural and unfit is deeply disturbing work, but such contestation inspires organized social justice, ideas that both *Ballot Measure 9* and *Nightwork* illustrate.

What these texts also show is that queer skepticism is good for queers, nature, and environmentalism because it questions how all of these terms can be put to use in harmful ways. Responding to condemnation, exclusion, and mistreatment with enlivened theoretical and activist work is what queer critique and environmental justice theory make possible. For queer citizens, environmentalism is radical skepticism about the very categories upon which environmentalism depends, as well as appreciation for the earth and human communities. Challenging uncritical nature-based discourses and practices and encouraging queer access to nature and queer environmental cultures indicates an extraordinary commitment to environmental issues. Projects that seek to "green" queer theory might acknowledge the powerful ecological sensibility that is already there.

NOTES

A portion of the section *"Nightwork"* appeared previously in Hogan (2004).

1. The most current inclusive term for queer identities is lgbtqqi: lesbian, gay, bisexual, transgender, queer, questioning, and intersex.

2. Judith Halberstam's analysis of a documentary film on a famous rural hate crime, *The Brandon Teena Story*—which is about the murder of a young transgender person living in rural Nebraska—argues that the documentary misses the centrality of racial politics in queer violence in largely rural white areas (Halberstam 2005a). Halberstam's concern is that *The Brandon Teena Story* does not fully acknowledge the racial dimension of the murders of Brandon Teena, Lisa Lambert, and Phillip DeVine, even though one of the murderers was a member of a white hate group and one of the victims African American (2005a, 29). This is not the case with *Ballot Measure 9*. As one of the "No on 9" organizers in MacDonald's film points out, the OCA's attacks were based in racism.

3. For more specific information on the language of the measure, see Arlene Stein (2001) and Ronald Gregg (1997).

4. At the statewide level the measure was defeated, largely because it did not pass in urban areas. But it was heavily supported in rural areas, and the OCA put its focus there after losing at the state level. Since 1992, many towns and counties have passed some version of Measure 9.

REFERENCES

Austin, Regina, and Michael Schill. 1994. Black, Brown, Red, and Poisoned. In *Unequal Protection: Environmental Justice and Communities of Color,* ed. Robert Bullard, 53–74. San Francisco: Sierra Club Books.

Berube, Allan. 1990. Marching to a Different Drummer: Lesbian and Gay GIs in World War II. In *Hidden from History: Reclaiming the Gay and Lesbian Past,* ed. Martin Duberman, Martha Vicinus, and George Chauncey, 383–94. New York: Meridian.

Boag, Peter. 2003. *Same-Sex Affairs: Constructing and Controlling Homosexuality in the Pacific Northwest.* Berkeley and Los Angeles: University of California Press.

Brenner, Claudia, and Hannah Ashley. 1995. *Eight Bullets: One Woman's Story of Surviving Anti-Gay Violence.* Ithaca, N.Y.: Firebrand Books.

Brown, Beverly A. 1995. In *Timber Country: Working People's Stories of Environmental Conflict and Urban Flight.* Philadelphia, Pa.: Temple University Press.

Bruggemeier, Franz-Josef, Mark Cioc, and Thomas Zeller, eds. 2005. *How Green Were the Nazis: Nature, Environment, and Nation in the Third Reich.* Athens: Ohio University Press.

Carter, David. 2004. *Stonewall: The Riots That Sparked the Gay Revolution.* New York: St. Martin's Press.

Clare, Eli. 1999. *Exile and Pride: Disability, Queerness, and Liberation.* Cambridge, Mass.: South End Press.

D'Emilio, John. 1993. Capitalism and Gay Identity. In *The Lesbian and Gay Studies Reader,* ed. H. Abelove, M. Aina Barale, and D. M. Halperin, 467–77. New York: Routledge.

Donadio, Rachel. 2008. The Vatican: In Speech, Pope Calls Homosexual Behavior a Violation. *New York Times.* http://www.nytimes.com/2008/12/23/world/europe/23briefs-INSPEECHPOPE_BRF.html.

Evans, Mei Mei. 2002. "Nature" and Environmental Justice. In *The Environmental Justice Reader: Politics, Poetics, and Pedagogy,* ed. Joni Adamson, Mei Mei Evans, and Rachel Stein, 181–93. Tucson: University of Arizona Press.

Gaard, Greta. 2004. Toward a Queer Ecofeminism. In *New Perspectives on Environmental Justice: Gender, Sexuality and Activism,* ed. Rachel Stein, 21–44. New Brunswick, N.J.: Rutgers University Press.

Gregg, Ronald. 1997. Queer Representation and Oregon's 1992 Anti-Gay Ballot Measure: Measuring the Politics of Mainstreaming. In *Between the Sheets, in the Streets: Queer, Lesbian, and Gay Documentary,* ed. C. Holmlund and C. Fuchs, 15–29. Minneapolis: University of Minnesota Press.

Halberstam, Judith. 2005a. *In a Queer Time and Place: Transgender Bodies, Subcultural Lives.* New York: New York University Press.

———. 2005b. Transgender Butch: Butch/FTM Border Wars and the Masculine Continuum. In *Feminist Theory: A Reader,* ed. W. Kolmar and F. Bartkowski, 550–60. Boston, Mass.: McGraw Hill.

Hansen, Joseph. 1984. *Nightwork: A Dave Brandstetter Mystery.* New York: Henry Holt.

Hardaway, Tim. 2007. Retired NBA Star Hardaway Says He Hates "Gay People." *ESPN.* http://sports.espn.go.com/nba/news/story?id=2766213.

Hartman, Betsy. 2006. Everyday Eugenics. *Z Net.* http://www.zmag.org/znet/viewArticle/3126.

Hogan, Katie. 2004. Detecting Toxic Environments: Gay Mystery as Environmental Justice. In *New Perspectives on Environmental Justice: Gender, Sexuality, and*

Activism, ed. Rachel Stein, 249–61. New Brunswick, N.J.: Rutgers University Press.

Kelly, Erin. 2006. Parks, Conservation Groups Aim to Attract Minorities. *USA Today,* March 19. http://www.usatoday.com/news/nation/2006-03-19-environment-minorities_x.htm.

Kirk, Gwyn, and Margo Okazawa-Rey. 2001. *Women's Lives: Multicultural Perspectives.* 2nd ed. Boston, Mass.: McGraw Hill.

MacDonald, Heather, dir. 1995. Motion picture. *Ballot Measure 9.* Toots Crackin Productions.

Martinac, Paula. 2001. Will Ellen's New Show Debunk Stereotypes? *Planet Out.* http://www.planetout.com/news/feature.html?sernum=315.

"Monkey Trial" County Trying to Outlaw Homosexuality. 2004. *USA Today,* March 17. http://www.usatoday.com/news/nation/2004-03-17-rhea-county_x.htm.

Morton, Timothy. 2007. *Ecology without Nature: Rethinking Environmental Aesthetics.* Cambridge, Mass.: Harvard University Press.

Nava, Michael. 1999. *The Burning Plain.* New York: Bantam.

Ordover, Nancy. 2003. *American Eugenics: Race, Queer Anatomy, and the Science of Nationalism.* Minneapolis: University of Minnesota Press.

Quigley, Peter. 1999. Nature as Dangerous Space. In *Discourses of the Environment,* ed. Eric Darier, 181–202. Oxford, U.K.: Blackwell.

Sandilands, Catriona. 2004. Sexual Politics and Environmental Justice: Lesbian Separatists in Rural Oregon. In *New Perspectives on Environmental Justice: Gender, Sexuality and Activism,* ed. R. Stein, 109–26. New Brunswick, N.J.: Rutgers University Press.

Sierra Youth Coalition. n.d. http://www.syc-cjs.org/sustainable/tikiindex.php?page=anti+oppression.

Signorile, Michelangelo. 1992. Behind the Hate in Oregon. *The Gist,* Sept. 21, 2008. http://www.signorile.com/2008/09/this-op-ed-piece-ran-in-new-york-times.html.

Spurlin, William. 2000. Remapping Same-Sex Desire: Queer Writing and Culture in the American Heartland. In *De-centering Sexualities: Politics and Representations Beyond the Metropolis,* ed. Richard Phillips, Diane Watt, and David Shuttleton, 182–98. London: Routledge.

Stein, Arlene. 2001. *The Stranger Next Door: The Story of a Small Community's Battle over Sex, Faith, and Civil Rights.* Boston, Mass.: Beacon.

Valentine, Gill. 2000. "Sticks and Stones May Break My Bones": A Personal Geography of Harassment. In *From Nowhere to Everywhere: Lesbian Geographies,* ed. Gill Valentine, 81–112. London: Harrington Park Press.

Ward, Robert DeCourcey. 1912. "Our Immigration Laws from the Viewpoint of Eugenics." *American Breeders Magazine* 111 (1): 21–22.

CHAPTER 9

Fragments, Edges, and Matrices: Retheorizing the Formation of a So-called Gay Ghetto through Queering Landscape Ecology

GORDON BRENT INGRAM

Can interdisciplinary sciences such as landscape ecology, fields of inquiry that fully engage natural and social sciences, be adapted for better understanding the dynamics of networks of sexual minorities, and more broadly the patterns across space and time of participants of various kinds of sex that do not specifically lead to reproduction? If most scientific inquiry in recent centuries in the West has had a "heteronormative" (Warner 1991) bias, of what could queered forms of landscape ecology studies consist? In this chapter, I revisit some early discussions on neighborhoods of visible sexual minorities sometimes labeled "ghettos," along with literature from past decades on the formation of landscape ecology, in order to shed light on these questions. This chapter re-examines the environmental context of the formation of one so-called gay ghetto, Vancouver's West End, and explores more nuanced, spatial, and materialist means of describing social processes involving sexual minorities across metropolitan areas. Through revisiting primarily materialist frameworks, such as landscape ecology's notions of fragments, edges and matrices, I hope to build a theoretical bridge to better blend biophysical and empirical descriptors in investigations of social networks and physical sites of sexual minorities with critical forms of cultural theory.

The afterlife of the queer theory of the 1990s is shifting to fuller recognition of and engagement with material conditions (Shapiro 2004) that can be termed "queer ecologies." Broadening the theories and practices that underlie how marginalized groups come to perceive, assess, and claim sites, neighborhoods, and social resources has become a project in contemporary sexual cultures and politics (Ingram 1997a). But what do we need to know about our communities and associated physical environments to better defend and expand newfound gains? This chapter explores some opportunities provided by and limits to adapting the field of landscape ecology for providing and organizing information on neighborhoods that in turn can be used in local activism. My focus is on gay male community formation processes that took place in Vancouver's West End until the onslaught of AIDS in the 1980s, when the neighborhood's white gay male demographic began to peak. The West End has been a strategic and mythic locale in Canada's homosexual male, gay, lesbian, and queer cultures and politics but was particularly important to the formation of notions of gay rights in the 1960s and 1970s. The historical moments that saw the urban changes that created a self-defined gay ghetto (even as long-term resident lesbians were moving away) comprise the focus of this chapter.

Until recently, most of the earth's ecosystems have been transformed by human cultures that have coupled heterosexuality with reproduction, socialization, and survival. While exceptions have existed, notions and spaces of sex for pleasure outside of heterosexual reproductive units often remained decidedly marginalized. Well into the twentieth century, studies of biological exuberance (Bagemihl 1999), of pleasure in general, were often considered "unscientific," especially any explorations of the implications of certain human cultures and pursuits of erotic pleasure on ecosystems. Over the last forty years, the combined movements for women's reproductive freedom, gay liberation, lesbian feminism, transgender activism, and queer theory have transformed the formerly heteronormative notions of the biosphere. In the more affluent parts of the world, urban life is being restructured by pursuits for satisfaction, diversifying practices of biological reproduction and modes of families and socialization. The implications of these queer human ecologies on an urbanizing world already degraded by globalization, consumerism, contamination, destruction of habitat, loss of species, and climate change have barely been explored.

In these uncertain times, any utopian anticipation of a planetary *lustgarten* would be premature and naive. Instead, we are in an era where *any* space (and associated ecosystems and landscapes) capable of supporting consensual intimacy is increasingly vulnerable to violence or privatization or both, and thus becomes a site for contestation. So while there may be a queering of ecological investigations, through at least a tolerance of notions of biological exuberance that include sexual intimacy between two or more members of the same gender and/or sex, the totality of the habitat (indeed the biosphere) of human sexual expression remains conflicted and "uncomfortable" within the broader contexts of the now lurching globalization of capital and environmental deterioration.

In this chapter of *Queer Ecologies*, therefore, I explore an expanded paradigm for understanding the biophysical and cultural environments of networks of public and private sites. In so doing, I hope to contribute to erotic expression, there and elsewhere, that is defined by erotic desire rather than procreation, and that is "queer" at least in the sense of the dismantling of the poisonous blend of racism and heteronormativity that was consolidated in the late Victorian period. In particular, I want to queer the vocabulary of landscape ecology in order to better describe and understand the shifting relationships between those physical spaces, increasingly influenced by urban design, ecosystem management, and aspects of sites marked in some ways by the rich combination of homoerotic social networks, forms of private and perhaps public erotic expression, and resistances to homophobia.

The central argument of this chapter is that landscape ecology holds some theoretical and methodological tools that can be adapted to understanding material aspects of processes of queer urbanization, but that in order to achieve that understanding it will be necessary to rethink ways to combine the natural and social sciences with a kind of eroticized cultural studies. In particular, it will be necessary to build theoretical bridges linking research methods on cognitive maps to better the defining of erotic subcultures, on one side, and to inventorying uses of particular sites and landscapes by specific groups along with notions of agency, on the other side. Landscape ecology as a field of inquiry consists of interdisciplinary approaches for studying the interplay of biophysical ecosystems and human communities—including culture. Some European schools of landscape ecology have focused on cultural transformations of ecosystems and physical space. Some associated research methods, which map shifting culture landscapes at various scales over time, can be applied for more nuanced understandings of sexual subcultures (which of course have a material basis), and also for the queering of neighborhoods and even for identifying contemporary policy and design agendas. But queering landscape ecology, as contesting the cultural biases in any science, will not be easy.

A second argument emerges from applying landscape ecology to understanding community formation for sexual minorities in Vancouver's

West End: in describing material aspects of queer social relationships, there is a basis for identifying important dynamics between the physical environment and economic relations, on one hand, and culture and popular political ideas, on the other. Some of these relationships can be dialectical, yet they are only partially mediated by political economy. In other words, environmental contexts and city forms have impacts on sexual cultures, while sensibilities and ideas directly influence urban policy, design processes, neighborhood landscapes, and metropolitan ecosystems. These dynamics between and among physical contexts, political economy, and culture—including erotic cultures—are not symmetrical across space or time. Ideas, including ones that are key ingredients for sexual cultures, lead to the transformation of urban spaces just as biophysical environments can foster certain experiences and ideologies. A kind of queered landscape ecology, as a mode of investigation, could be a pillar of a renewed and more empirically based body of activist theory and associated research methods, especially useful for better understanding persistent social inequities that extend to sexual expression.

Beyond Ghettoes: Revisiting Shifting Relationships across Networks and Communities of Sexual Minorities

We have fled here from every part of the nation, and like refugees elsewhere, we came not because it was so great here, but because it was so bad there. By the tens of thousands, we fled small towns where to be ourselves would be to endanger our jobs and any hope of decent life. . . . And we have formed a ghetto out of self-protection. It is a ghetto rather than a free territory because it is still theirs. (Wittman [1969] 1972, 330)[1]

In relatively new Canadian cities such as Vancouver, open space contains a mixture of landscape elements of both the city and the frontier. Central Vancouver is exceptional in that a large area of forest and beaches, Stanley Park, dominates its central peninsula and has provided an alternative space to the adjacent areas of intensive urbanization (figure 9.1). Over the last century, this frontier, softened to a cusp of forested parkland and residential streetscapes, has functioned as a refuge for a range of marginalized social groups. Here, divergent processes of community formation, repression, resistance to patriarchy and homophobia, and institutionalization of human rights protections, to mention only a few social processes, have been played out, "naturalized," and normalized.

Vancouver's West End was mythologized in the pantheon of places in Canada as one in which newly politicized gay men could be fully "out" in the 1970s and 1980s. But the West End did not often function as a real ghetto (or refuge) for gay men, and was never so for lesbians. In terms of the initial usages of the term *ghetto* or *geto* (Foa 2000, 139), the West End was quite different from the much larger gay ghettoes that emerged in the years before and decades after the rise of the Gay Liberation movement in larger North American cities such as San Francisco, Toronto, and New York. As a regional center of gay and lesbian activism, the West End had far more modest demographic forces. But there was repression and resistance similar to that in other North American cities such as Toronto. The one set of processes that gave the West End some semblance of a ghetto was the remarkable network of public spaces, often in or near relatively secluded forested parklands, that allowed a range of sexual networks and politicized subcultures to express themselves erotically and to coalesce into the beginnings of self-defined networks and communities. My underlying argument in this chapter is that over and above political economic forces, these neighborhood spaces were successfully claimed and eventually queered because of material conditions associated with the urban landscape ecology. The West End has supported an exceptional amount of open space, which, because of the vegetation and relatively high population, has for well over a century been particularly difficult to police. This notion of the West End's public space as an anchor or organizer of a location of resistance contrasts markedly with experiences of other gay enclaves in North America in the mid twentieth century.

By the mid to late 1970s, the use of the term "gay ghetto" in Vancouver had become self-fulfilling. Gay men were attracted to the West End as one of the easiest places in Canada to be open about their sexuality. Four decades ago, Don Hann left Newfoundland and moved to the West End, as part of a network of gay male activists from his island. In a recent conversation, he stated that the West End "was a ghetto in the 1970s" where there was "more dick" and where the neighborhood was "relatively safe" (Hann 2009). In the same period of gay male ghettoization, lesbians, who had been a significant demographic group in the wooden boarding houses that were prevalent from before World War II until they were demolished in the 1960s and 1970s, were pushed out and moved east. By the mid 1970s, a demographic shift had been established, with gay men becoming a significant population and voting block in central Vancouver, though never anywhere near a majority. Thus, the use of "the gay ghetto" was part of a process of myth making and empowerment (for gay men) under the

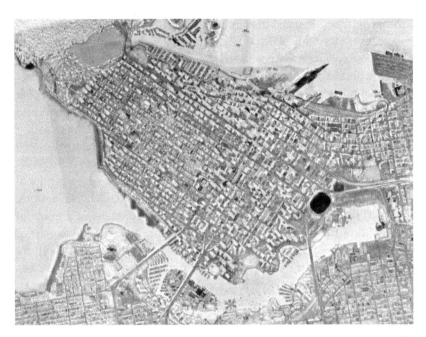

FIGURE 9.1. Aerial view, West End, Vancouver, BC, showing Stanley Park (upper left).

rubric of identity politics, but also was part of claiming particular spaces, territories, and resources (Ingram 1997a).

While the West End barely had ghetto-like traits in terms of general forms of marginalization, stigmatization, cordoning, and related forms persecution, the term obfuscated more nuanced and localized processes of community formation and transformation of public space that hold more resonance to queer movements and initiatives of today. However, it was clear that the ghetto metaphor held exceptional currency in building one of the first of the more diverse and gay- and lesbian-"friendly" neighborhoods in Canada, one that for a time had some of the largest concentrations of active and self-identified homosexual males in North America. At the same time, the use of the term "ghetto" in the 1970s and 1980s paralleled and often obscured a male gendering of the area. To put it simply, the West End "worked" for nearly three decades as a ghetto as defined by early gay rights and gay liberation but was almost an anathema for lesbian feminism. Revisiting the idea of the ghetto allows us to re-examine queer demographics and use of public space as forms of physical as well as cultural relationships (only partially defined through successive social movements). But how can we revisit the social processes that established the West End as a site of national and international importance for discourses in justice for sexual minorities along with the persisting disparities that women experienced in public space in the neighborhood? What historical, empirical, and cultural research methods can help us reconceive of this so-called ghetto across time and space?

Some methods used in environmental research and related history can be adapted to highlight a shift in intellectual production from positing queer *theory* to describing queer *ecologies*. Queer theory was part of an agenda to build solidarity between and among genders, sexualities, and cultures. Queer ecology, by contrast, could function as a mode of investigation that better recognizes more nuanced differences as part of broader initiatives for environmental justice. Today's emphasis on culture in studies of sexual minorities is in large part a response to the deficiencies in earlier forms of materialist social science that obscured or underacknowledged the diversity of subjectivities. Many of the activist social sciences of the early- and mid-twentieth century were grounded in forms of historical materialism and respective "scientific" approaches that provided only partial bases, if any at all, for the articulation of both erotic expression and marginality. The shift from the primacy of Marxist theory to struggles for social justice contributed directly to today's preoccupation with "sexual stories" for better understanding sexual cultures.[2] But "stories" are only stories and are only part of the picture of the landscape. The form of engagement in political economy and environmental contexts that is provided by a queered landscape ecology will posit the existence of landscape ecologies that subvert the heteronormative with a myriad of relationships barely fathomed in the bygone notions of gay ghettos that formed a half century ago.

One attempt to adapt some of the lineages of Hegelian historical materialism to more critical cultural analyses was Stanley Aronowitz's 1981 *The Crisis of Historical Materialism:*

> Beyond the demand for equal rights . . . each of [these] struggles challenges the social, economic, or ideological reproduction of society, either because it makes problematic capital accumulation processes or erodes the legitimacy of those institutions that embody normative structures necessary for social and cultural domination. At the core of these challenges are again questions of nature and human nature. (106)

Nearly three decades later, both nature and culture have been contorted in very new ways under globalization and now the international financial crisis. Now we see advanced capitalism in disarray while homophobia is often being de-institutionalized. The Hegelian historical materialism that was defined in the nineteenth century was not able to provide a sufficient means for addressing issues of inequities for marginalized sexual cultures and the extent of the democracy of urban space at the scale of neighborhoods and metropolitan areas. The subsequent avoidance of material or environmental indicators was only partially reversed by Fredric Jameson's interest in cognitive maps (Jameson 1984).

In exploring the theoretical and descriptive potentials of landscape ecology for describing mélanges of sites, landscapes, individual acts, collective events, and processes of institutional formation, a broader framework is necessary that links material indicators to culture in the context of analyses of local and global political economy. I term this paradigm for a broader understanding of both the culture and the physical aspects of our communities "New Materialism"; with human ecology and landscape ecology, it is grounded in biophysical and spatial contexts having central positions. In turn, this new form of engagement in political economy and environmental contexts posits the existence of queer ecologies with a myriad of relationships barely fathomed in the bygone notions of gay ghettos that formed a half century ago.

Landscape Ecology as a Queer Spatial Vocabulary

Freedom of action in public spaces is defined and redefined in each shift of power and custom.
—Kevin Lynch

Landscape ecology is the science of investigating inherently interconnected biophysical and cultural processes across space and time. Landscape ecology methods provide one of a number of more materialist or, more correctly, "ecological" methods that can help us understand the dynamics that link and play out across networks of homoerotic subjectivities.[3] Landscape ecology holds particular promise as an expanded spatial framework that links the biophysical to human erotic subjectivities over time, as Zev Naveh argued that

as a holistic order seeking science of nature and man [*sic*] in their totality, landscape ecology can serve as bridge between bio-ecology and human ecology. But for this purpose it has not only to transcend natural sciences but also go beyond paradigms of prevailing, mostly mechanistic, positivistic and reductionistic conceptions of scientific knowledge in general. (1990, 54–55)

By the 1980s, landscape ecology began to codify a spatial vocabulary with some relevance for understanding subcultures and sexualities across neighborhoods (Naveh and Lieberman 1984, 3–25; Schreiber 1990, 21–33). But well over three decades into landscape ecology as a field of inquiry of human and environmental dynamics, I know of no study that squarely considers gender and sexuality. Why such an enigmatic gap in a field that considers human beings within the context of nature and nature within the context of often human-induced environmental change? There are numerous reasons, the most important of which has been the preoccupation with using landscape ecology to understand community-wide, macro-level ecological deterioration even though the core of this science is spatial and temporal inquiry at a range of scales, including the finer site levels. Sexual interaction, even when partially disembodied through digital artifice, is site-based. Aside from aversions to site-specificity, landscape ecology in the last several decades has been more preoccupied with the biophysical impacts of macro-level cultural change such as between indigenous and other tribal cultures under assault and various kinds of settlement demographics, economic globalization, and neoliberalism. The two discourses of sex-as-site-specificity that *could* be linked to landscape ecology studies have been around epidemiology, especially as related to strategies to obstruct the spread of HIV, and violence against women and sexual minorities.

In exploring how to construct a queer environmental history and time-series map of Vancouver's West End, I turn to Forman and Godron (1986), the most widely influential text of the field, in order to begin to adapt and to queer four of landscape ecology's most basic concepts and descriptors.

1. A *patch* (83–95) represents a contiguous area with some common landscape characteristics, and a *fragment* is a portion of a formerly larger spatial unit that has broken down through marked disturbance such as logging or climate change–related storms or more subtle forms of environmental change such as gradual shifts in annual temperatures. Much of the conceptualization of the concept of patches has been derived from the anthropogenic fragmentation of forest, but a patch could be a grassland being invaded by woodland or a bare understory trampled through certain kinds of public sex.

2. An *edge* or *ecotone* (108–109, 60–61) comprises the exterior territory of a patch or corridor that touches on another kind of fragment of a landscape. Edge in landscape ecology comprises the zone where two landscape patterns or habitats overlap. Edge comprises the transition zone between one set of biophysical and cultural elements, relationships, and processes and another. There are high-contrast *ecotones,* such as beaches and the zones between ancient forest and grassland or woodland and pavement. And there are lower-contrast edges, such as between relatively recent woodland and ancient coniferous forest, between beaches and adjacent terrestrial vegetation that is influenced by salty air, and between edges and centers of playing fields with their highly social dimensions.

3. *Connectivity* (127) represents various flows of nutrients, disturbances, organisms, and even language, concepts, and cultural practices, that shift across the landscape at various scales. A stream represents a high level of connectivity through the flows of water and nutrients. A busy, well-lit street represents relatively high levels of connectivity for automobile-driving people but something of an obstacle for pedestrians. And a relatively safe and well-used pathway has higher degrees of connectivity, in terms of supporting social contact, for groups vulnerable to harassment and violence.

4. A *matrix* (155–77) is the most connective set of elements, habitat, and social practices (or lack of practices) that span and touch on territories and aspects of particular landscapes and neighborhoods. In highly urbanized areas, the matrix of the landscape has typically shifted to streets and asphalt. But for some "well-treed" neighborhoods, such as much of the West End, the matrix is still open, public space and streets with relatively high levels of native and planted vegetation. Over the twentieth century, most higher-density North American neighborhoods lost this green matrix, making the West End particularly attractive to men and women who enjoyed social contact out-of-doors.

Even Fuzzy Ideas Can Be Part of Landscape Ecology Processes

The landscape phenomenon outlined above might appear, in terms of the twentieth-century vocabularies of both the natural sciences and cultural studies, to be relatively inert and without links to thought, culture, or even desire. But landscape ecology has been the first science to confirm that all ecosystems and places have cultural dimensions. Therefore, there must be a place, a possibility perhaps, for a vernacular, for describing the implications of ideas, modes of communication, alliances, and sex— across space and time at various scales. While there is insufficient space in this chapter to describe a nuanced framework for assessing sex and culture in landscape ecologies, it is necessary, in order to understand the transformations in the West End, to appreciate the power of ideas and their implications for the partially shared, cognitive maps that allow individuals and groups to use and transform public space. The point of inquiry in this chapter, of the West End as a so-called gay ghetto that really was not a ghetto but was sufficiently ghetto-like to be a major subject for de-ghettoization within the sexual politics of Canada, is valuable for appreciating how even fuzzy ideas can become part of powerful processes within the landscape.

The West End has supported an exceptional amount of open space and, because of the vegetation and relatively high human population, has been particularly difficult to police. This notion of the West End's public open space, as an anchor or organizer of a location of resistance, contrasts markedly with experiences of other gay enclaves in North America in the mid twentieth century. The West End represented a rich set of spaces in which to hide and find intimacy rather than, for example, a locale for the corralling and controlling of Jews. But the notion of a ghetto and various forms of both complacency with and resistance to social constraints that have similarities with ghettoization came to shape the sexual subcultures and their associated environments in the West End for three decades.

The notion of the gay ghetto was a central concept for gay liberation and gay rights activism that traveled by word of mouth, newsletters, and a small number of books. The gay ghetto concept had far less currency in lesbian feminism. Carl Wittman's 1969 essay on San Francisco, "A Gay Manifesto" ([1969]) 1972, is the best example of the adapting of the modern notions of the ghetto, recast since the 1944 Warsaw Uprising, for homosexual males. Even though Wittman did not spend much time in Vancouver, he had a knowledge of and interest in the West End (Wittman 1974), and his essay was the most widely read piece of theory of gay community activism in the years directly after the Stonewall Riots. But how Wittman's ideas were then stretched to be applicable to activism in a relatively high density but comfortable community, with spectacular open space, low levels of crime, and moderate levels of income, remains enigmatic. One explanation is that the ghetto metaphor was the nearest term in an impoverished vocabulary to explain the persistent homophobia and hostility that many gay men still experienced—both inside and outside of the West End. So the idea of identifying a fuzzy, only partially relevant idea as an additional descriptor for the processes in a (cultural) landscape fills a major theoretical gap. An underlying function of the following chronology of the West End is in sketching the environmental linkages between desire and ideas, ideas and culture, culture and landscapes, and the feedback loops of biophysical change that transform culture. In other words, at the core of exploring the utility of landscape ecology for (eroticized) cultural studies and similarly the potential uses of cultural studies in landscape ecology processes is identification of a rather queer set of relationships between desire, ideas, and the natural world.

In Wittman's North American gay ghetto, so-called refugees were forced into relatively pleasant neighborhoods (such as the West End):

> We have fled here from every part of the nation, and like refugees elsewhere, we came not because it was so great here, but because it was so bad there. By the tens of thousands, we fled small towns where to be ourselves would be to endanger our jobs and any hope of decent life.... And we have formed a ghetto out of self-protection. It is a ghetto rather than a free territory because it is still theirs.... So we came to the ghetto—and as other ghettos it has negative and positive aspects. Refugee camps are better than what preceded them or people never would have come. (Wittman 1972, 330, 339)

By the mid to late 1970s, the use of "the Gay Ghetto" in the West End was widespread and had become, in part, self-fulfilling. But instead of a minority being forced by a hostile state into a ghetto, gay men were attracted to the West End as one of the easiest places in Canada to be open about their sexuality. Rather than a fact or a particularly clear concept, the use of "the Gay Ghetto" in the West End was part of a vocabulary and set of practices for resistance and reconstructed entitlement. Here the idea, metaphor, practices, strategies, and biophysical impacts associated with Wittman's notion of the ghetto blurred into a process of myth making and empowerment (for gay men) under the rubric of identity politics as part of claiming of particular spaces, neighborhoods, and socially apportioned resources (Ingram 1997a). By contrast, landscape ecology provides an alternative narrative to explain the choice and impacts of de-ghettoization practices for an urbanized peninsula that was barely ever a ghetto and of a more a privileged enclave for white male "boomers." And while some of the common terms of landscape ecology that are discussed here might appear deceptively biophysical and without a relationship to culture, words such as "fragment," "edge," "flow," and "matrix" can take on cultural resonances that have yet to be fully explored. In the second half of this chapter, I sketch the environmental, social, and cultural changes, across this metropolitan area, that, for a few decades, gave the fuzzy set of ideas about the ghetto particular currency for restructuring the social and erotic dimensions of the West End—in which a more nuanced set of processes that can be expressed in terms of the vocabulary of landscape ecology were also interacting and transforming urban space, sexual practices, social relationships, and culture.

A Modern History and Landscape Ecology of Homosexual Social Spaces in the West End

The history of the place
    (like) a whip across the face
        —Stan Persky[4]

The villages that came to comprise central Vancouver were incorporated as a city in 1886, just a few months after the Victorian codification of Britain's anti-sodomy laws. "The Terminal City"[5] was a highly divided, working-class city with northwestern Europeans in largely white enclaves on the two peninsulas (which included the West End) on the west side of the city and the more multicultural Eastside supporting an often transient working-class culture (McDonald 1996, 57) that, until well into the twentieth century, was overwhelmingly male. Soon after Vancouver's incorporation, recurring race riots established an initial racial line running north to south, with northwestern Europeans on the west side of Carroll Street. Construction of the West End began adjacent to recently protected Stanley Park. Relatively far from Chinatown, the West End was to be the middle-class enclave on what many envisioned as a white peninsula. However, Stanley Park still had one Native village, whose residents had no intention of moving. The efforts to depopulate Stanley Park would provide opportunities for the formation of a culture of public sex that could not be practically controlled by the often underfunded city police. And as Vancouver further industrialized in subsequent decades, the West End also became an attractive area in which to relax because it had the least polluted air and beaches in the city.

The aboriginal landscape ecology of the West End was marked by the high-contrast ends of land and sea, with fragments of more mature and denser forest set in a matrix of beach and culturally modified vegetation. The hand and horse logging that took place in the mid-nineteenth century

widened and transformed that aboriginal matrix. The modern homosexual male genesis in the West End in the early decades of the twentieth
century was along a frontier, a high-contrast ecotone, of forest and houses
that secondarily exploited the edges between the denser vegetation, which
was often used for sex, and the more open areas in which there were trails
that were used for cruising and other socializing. But the West End was
not entirely immune to the growing movement to police homosexuality.
"The definition of a sex crime in the late Victoria and Edwardian era in
Canada knew no boundaries" (Chapman 1986, 277). It was during the
construction of the fine houses that were to dominate the first seventy
years of the West End that the notion of a male homosexual identity as a
specter and even a threat to imperial society was imported from London
after public opinion was solidified by news of the Oscar Wilde trials. This
early notion of homosexual orientation in British Columbia was associated with the middle and upper classes well into the twentieth century
(Waugh 1996, 290), with violence and perversion associated culturally
with the male working class. So as a middle-class, seaside enclave, the
West End was a relatively easy landscape for visual contact between homosexual males and for camouflage of minority orientations and public
sexual acts.

Well into the second quarter of the twentieth century, most of the arrests for consensual homosexuality between adults were of working-class
males, often men of color, and took place in the downtown area near lines
of racial segregation such as Carroll Street. Adele Perry (1997) argued
that "mixed-race relationships remained a constant if contested aspect
of British Columbian society throughout the nineteenth century" (515),
and anxieties blended with the rising phobia against intimacies between
consensual adult males. Many of the early-twentieth-century arrests for
consensual homosexuality as "gross indecency" involved South Asian
men who were targeted and entrapped by the city police in the historic
downtown of Vancouver, which was within blocks of Chinatown (Ingram
2003). In contrast, the West End, as a nearly totally white enclave well
into the twentieth century, saw few arrests for consensual homosexuality between adults that led to trial. The Edwardian fusing of phobias of
sexual deviance and miscegenation left the West End out of the limelight
of homophobic repression.

For white, middle-class homosexual males at the turn of the twentieth
century, the West End appears to have been an exceptional refuge. The
only other Canadian urban area west of Winnipeg where homosexual
males could have had an opportunity to meet in such numbers (and to

engage in regular public sex all year round), was the still larger city across the Strait, Victoria. But with fewer single and transient males, and with open space consisting of open meadows providing far less visual cover to avoid detection, prospects for homosexuality in the City of Victoria were modest.

Since the first decades after the Parks Board's inception in September 1888, discussion about controlling cruising and public sex has not been far from the minds of the politicians and managers of Stanley Park and Vancouver's entire network of parks in general. Well into the 1970s, police on trails, often on horseback, have harassed individuals whom they suspected of engaging in public sex. But while increasingly diminished and fragmented, patches of dense forest have remained refuges for men to engage in intimate acts while avoiding detection. But the only partially successful protection of the park's forests was not as a refuge for public sex. As early as the late nineteenth century, a stalemate became evident over management of Stanley Park between advocates of facilities such as sports fields and building infrastructure and those who did not want to levy municipal tax dollars. This stalemate effectively contributed to relatively large areas of mostly vacant forest (only decades before it was still being modified by resident aboriginal communities and through selective logging). And the facilities that were funded created a range of soft edges among forest, field, and building that further confounded the policing of social behavior. Rather than broach the topic of the growing indications of homosexuality in the park, early discussions on the management of Stanley Park and adjacent beach area focused on the extent to which the park was to be left "in a state of nature." This commitment to supposed naturalness was a useful cover for park commissioners who were busy leasing out concessions on the cusp of the park and the residential areas of the West End (McDonald 1984, 138–39).

As the remaining Native residents were pushed out, a process that took decades, Stanley Park was effectively depopulated. With so few people entering the more remote parts of the park, the odds of public sex being observed continued to diminish well into the twentieth century. In this social vacuum, an early culture of public sex emerged around Stanley Park on a scale that was sometimes conceived, by mid-twentieth-century homosexual males in Canada, in almost mythic proportions. In the decades before and after World War I, the first wave of city of Vancouver police crackdowns against homosexuality, it became much easier for men residing in the Eastside, where the arrests were nearly all occurring, to travel to Stanley Park. New streetcar lines to Stanley Park were opened at a time when the still-segregated West End increasingly saw its use by laborers from Asia and Southern Europe. The streetcar line along Robson Street repopulated the West End with men on furtive quests for sex with each other.

The West End and Stanley Park were increasingly reduced to dense patches of public space connected by a matrix of muddy walkways and trails. A pedestrian culture was re-inscribed at a time when much of the rest of the city was being reconstructed for the automobile. As facilities and business establishment were constructed on the cusp of Stanley Park and the residential areas, the edge, as a kind of frontier, was softened and its contrast lessened. But Stanley Park remained a location, well into the twentieth century, that did not serve well the needs and interests of women and children, and thus the space continued to be one for mostly single males.

Initially a white and largely segregated, middle-class neighborhood, the West End became a major center for women's suffrage, which was obtained for white women in 1916. The West End's effective residential segregation was an important factor as Asian and aboriginal women continued to be denied voting rights until after World War I. The first half of the twentieth century saw the largest wave of immigration, in terms of the city's overall demographics, in Vancouver's history. The Women's Building at Thurlow and Robson, on the eastern, downtown side of the West End, was established in 1913 (*Vancouver Sun* 1913, 1) and operated until around the outbreak of World War II. Political and cultural organizing fostered crucial spaces to discuss women's reproductive and sexual rights, often in times of marginalization and isolation of "spinsters" and women of color. And the West End had most of the rooming houses in the city where unmarried adult women could find their own housing.

Stanley Park also played an important role in the formation of some proto-lesbian social space. In the decade before World War I, there was a hysteria against women going into Stanley Park alone. Until after World War I, the city's leaders refused to allocate public funds for toilets and washrooms in the park, in a thinly veiled effort to keep women out. But one group of women did take outdoor space for themselves in the West End: the region's pioneering women athletes, who struggled hard in the early days of enfranchisement to have access to the higher-quality sports fields that were in or near the edge of Stanley Park (McKee 1976, 14–15).[6] These female-tolerant enclaves made up less than one percent of the total area of the park. The more confined spaces of women functioning in self-identified groups thrived on the soft edge between Stanley Park and the adjacent beach, residential, and business areas. While some women began to walk alone in Stanley Park, no records have been so far found of a culture of female public sex or related arrests at the time.

The new urban subculture of men and women enjoying nature in the West End flourished with little public acknowledgment for over half a century—with a male subculture focused on anonymous sex and a female sports subculture built around social solidarity and furtive romances. Arrests, imprisonment, and state harassment intensified against homosexual men and women from World War II through to the mid 1960s, with the War Measures Act effectively legalizing the dismissal of homosexuals from their jobs without cause until 1950. Only after that was lesbianism formally criminalized.[7] In this climate of intensifying repression, Stanley Park became increasingly used for male public sex, while the old houses of the West End were converted to rooming houses for single women and men. By the end of World War II, unmarried women in particular had few housing options in Vancouver outside the West End. Parallel cultures of single men and women, defined by drinking establishments, fostered an additional set of homoerotic networks for the West End. On the other side of the West End, two nascent entertainment enclaves emerged. Males began to frequent a rundown part of downtown along Robson and Seymour Streets, while lesbian corners emerged in some of the city's toughest and filthiest bars along Main Street. In Vancouver's boom-and-bust economy that was quite depressed after World War II, these new indoor spaces were funded through heavy alcohol consumption. Members of sexual minorities were effectively welcome in these otherwise marginally profitable businesses when they spent a great deal. An exception to these sites of abjection was the upper-class male subculture that coalesced in the plush basement of the Hotel Vancouver, and in the lounges of other fine hotels nearby—all a pleasant walk from Stanley Park.

Much of the male homoerotic public space of the West End was expanded during the Cold War where a landscape narrative was formed, as part of a nascent subculture of public sex between males, with the bars as sites for socializing and verbal contact at the downtown end of the West End, and the depth of Stanley Park, on the other side of the neighborhood, often a site of anonymous sex and little talk. Whereas homophobic repression under McCarthyism began to subside in the United States by the late 1950s, the Canadian government's security interests in homosexuality often led to arrests, questioning, and harassment; these practices were not curtailed until the mid 1960s (Kimmel and Robinson 1994, 345). Thus the proliferating sites of male cruising and sex in Stanley Park did not see coordinated repression until the late 1950s, and police presence was largely on blocks adjacent to and very near the boundaries of the green space. Hundreds and probably thousands of men who walked by Stanley Park, only some of whom actually engaged in homosexual behavior, were harassed, arrested, and subsequently hounded by security authorities. The landscape ecology of thick forest patches combined with a diversity of ecological and visual edges, which had drawn so many men, came to support an additional social niche of police predation for over three decades. And this tension contributed to re-inscription of this refuge also as a ghetto.

While the pressures of the Cold War primed the West End for the activism of the 1970s, it remains problematic to have labeled the West End a (pre–Stonewall Riots) ghetto (and only for males) except in terms of the sustained interest of the municipal and federal (RCMP) police, in which men suspected of engaging in public sex in the West End and Stanley Park were harassed and then listed as potential security risks, with many subsequently losing their jobs. There was, however, a small "ghetto" in Vancouver at the time in the sense of more similarities with the term's initial usage in the formation of the original Venetian *ghetto* in the late fifteenth century. Lesbianism in Canada was not formally criminalized in the early 1950s, and in this same period, butch women began to be forced out of West End boarding houses. Most women moved east, such as to the gritty, port-side section of Main Street. Those few blocks that tolerated self-described "bad girls" coalesced along Main Street, in bars so low-lying that their washroom plumbing often did not work. These few blocks functioned more like one of the original Jewish ghettos of Italy, as shaped through several papal edicts in the late-fifteenth and early-sixteenth centuries, in a number of ways. The grittier blocks of Main Street, between False Creek and Vancouver Harbour, constituted one of the few areas where openly butch women could find housing—in rooms that often were crowded, lacking in basic sanitation, unhealthy, and dangerous. Secondly, butch lesbians could interact in this small area along Main Street at night without much police harassment, whereas "out" butch behavior in the day, or presence in other parts of the city, would risk arrest. This lesbian enclave of butch (and femme) lesbians was adjacent to an African Canadian enclave called Hogan's Alley (Fatona and Wyngaarden 1994),[8] which had private homes serving food and musicians playing jazz; these "Chicken Houses" (because they often served fried chicken) were run by women. Both of these enclaves were destroyed by the City of Vancouver in 1967 with funds from the Government of Canada, ostensibly for construction of the Georgia Viaduct expressway. The West End then became the faux ghetto oriented to gay white male Canadian discourses about sexual liberation, while lesbians were pushed into lower-rent neighborhoods such as Commercial Drive, in which a lesbian subculture coalesced in the last 1970s and which became a major space for female and male queer activism in the early 1990s.

Throughout the 1960s and 1970s, as the women's spaces near Stanley Park were constrained and curtailed through underfunding and were being bulldozed along Main Street, some of the public sites in the West End of strategic importance to males saw the beginnings of some of the self-identified "queering" (a word not used in this sense before the 1990s) processes that were to shape it for decades. The first homophile organization in Canada, the Association for Social Knowledge, was formed in Vancouver in April 1964 (Kinsman 1996, 230–35) after a year of continued police harassment in the city's gay male bars (most being on the downtown edge of the West End). The now decaying wooden houses of the West End were being torn down for towers envisioned to be for so-called swinging singles. But few single women had the means to qualify to live in the new high-rises, and many butch lesbians, already suffering economically for being "out," were forced out of the dwindling number of rooming houses and then out of the neighborhood altogether. The economic dynamic that pushed often poor lesbians to the eastern part of the city was well underway before the rise of any popular understanding of lesbian feminism and gay liberation. In contrast, gay males, especially those who were financially successful, and often closeted, were aggressively welcomed into the West End by the landlords of the new towers. The year 1967 was a defining time for the emerging gay rights movements. That year, Justice Minister Pierre Trudeau, who a year later became leader of the federal Liberal Party and Canada's prime minister, announced plans to decriminalize homosexuality (Bill C-150) with the celebrated statement that the state had no place in the bedrooms of Canada. A number of levels of the state from the municipal police to the Government of Canada, however, remained very interested in intimacies in the parks and on the streets.

The Coalescence of a Matrix of Resistance to Homophobia

At first, gay institutions and cruising places spring up in urban districts known to accept variant behavior. A concentration of such places in specific sections of the city . . . results. This concentration attracts large numbers of homosexual men, causing a centralization of gay culture traits. Tolerance, coupled with institutional concentration, makes the areas desirable residential districts for gay men. (Levine 1979, 375)

As homosexuality between two consenting adults in one of their bedrooms was formally decriminalized in 1969, the battle lines were drawn for the activism of the 1970s that focused on visibility in public space: confronting police entrapment and harassment along with fighting for human rights protections.[9] The battleground was more often than not the public outdoor space of the West End. In this shift, sexually active gay men literally came out of the shadows of the patches of remaining denser forest to engage more openly in the matrix of highly visible public space. In contrast, lesbians tended to move out of the West End and took their institutions with them to indoor sites that were far less conflicted. In other words, men chose to fight in the West End, while women, with markedly fewer economic resources, were forced to take flight, with many moving east into less desirable housing.

So the West End as a ghetto was actually more of a juncture in two different and gendered migrations across Vancouver. To use the vocabulary of landscape ecology, in the West End males found greater connectivity and lesbians encountered harsher edges. The matrix of the West End, the open space, became more combative, and there were sufficient gay male numbers for a sense of security or at least solidarity; in contrast, lesbians, who were also likely to experience greater violence by the simple fact of being women, were overwhelmed, as well as more attracted to reconstructing the family-oriented Commercial Drive neighborhood a few miles to the east (Bouthillette 1997, Ingram 1998).

By the time of decriminalization, the most important of the male outdoor cruising sites in the West End had been established, most notably the "Fruit Loop" parking lot, the English Bay men's washroom, and Lee's Trail in Stanley Park. As late as 1977, openly gay men were harassed and assaulted by city police, sometimes to the point of requiring hospitalization (Hann and Joyce 1977). In that year, an anti-entrapment committee appealed for caution, noting in its newsletter: "Imagine the satisfaction of a young police officer in plain clothes LEANING INVITINGLY against a tree on English Bay at midnight. Waiting to lure the safe quarry, savouring the thrilling culmination of another arrest on this record and the moral satisfaction of catching a 'pervert'" (SEARCH 1977).

One of the earliest episodes of gay male activism focused on the neighborhood space of the West End was in a public meeting on April

6, 1977. Organized to discuss "the problems of Davie Street" (Volkart 1977), this meeting was initiated by City Hall to quietly discuss ways to move homosexuals out of public space (and out of the neighborhood). What was to have been a small meeting organized by the police became a raucous confrontation with four hundred people. A reporter from the *Vancouver Sun* stated, "Most visible—and vocal—were the homosexuals, who charged that police had called the meeting to manipulate public sentiment in support of an intensified campaign against gay people" (Volkart 1977). The same meeting saw some of Vancouver's first public resistance to the police by prostitutes.

As in most North American cities, the 1970s saw the first articulation and constructed visibility of specific lesbian and gay networks. In Vancouver, the more overtly gay West End Slo-Pitch Association (WESA) was first organized in 1978 (Hirtle 1998). The first recorded public Jewish involvement in decriminalized gay Vancouver was around the High Holidays in 1973. In subsequent years, Chinese, Italian, and Asian gay networks emerged, with many of their events taking place in the West End, though often out of the public eye. The bar-financed Dogwood Monarchist Society became the prototype for the charities that were to become prominent in the first two decades of the AIDS pandemic. In the 1970s, the leather and S/M scenes became visible and expanded rapidly. A prototype for partying-oriented organizations came with the formation of the gay motorcycle club the Border Riders in 1971. Openly gay and lesbian clubs emerged in the aftermath of the June 30, 1973, police raids of the Hampton Court Pub on Seymour Street. Discrimination in the licensing of gay clubs began to ease in the mid 1970s. By 1973, Vancouver had seven gay and lesbian clubs that served alcohol and five bathhouses, nearly all of which were in the West End or nearby in the downtown. Throughout the 1970s, demonstrations and public events organized by lesbians and gay men in Vancouver were virtually always held in the West End. Local observances of the 1969 Stonewall Riots began in 1971 and after intermittent events throughout the 1970s were reorganized as "Gay Pride,"[10] with an annual celebration in the first week in August. In comparison to larger cities such as San Francisco and Toronto, events in the West End were subdued and small and remained so for two decades. Celebrations nearly always took place in shore parkland in the West End.

By the late 1970s, another set of social forces in the West End collided with those that concentrated gay men and pushed lesbians to around Commercial Drive. Davie Street in the West End became the "high end" area for female (heterosexual) street prostitution in Vancouver; by the end of the decade it was joined by a low-end area for male-to-female (MTF) transvestite and early transsexual prostitution. The West End's gay male identity was formed through a social contest that came to pit gay bars against female street prostitution. Streetwalker space and gay bar space,[11] like tectonic plates, came to collide along Davie Street. Ironically, it was the sexual freedom exuded by "hookers" and "drag queens" that provided the bridge to move the early 1970s gay scene along Seymour and Richards Streets, with its historic links to Gastown and Robson Street, onto Davie Street. By the early 1980s, the gay-male-friendly space along Davie expanded and moved west (Anonymous 1982), as Seymour Street, an increasingly exhausted scene, moved south to intersect it. This intersection formed the core of the city's gay male commercial enclave in the 1980s and 1990s. Even as late as 1982, gay male spaces in the core of the city were as much along Robson, Seymour, and Richards Streets as along Davie Street. As gay male space shifted southwest, female, male, and transgender street-based prostitution was pushed east by city policies, and the police to fill the vacuum.

In the early 1980s, both the left and the right in the West End were allied in the fight against prostitution, including such events as the 1981–82 construction of street dividers to slow down the increasingly noisy automobile traffic associated with heterosexual males procuring female prostitutes (City Clerk 1981). The dividers made the streets far more pedestrian-friendly and conducive to chatting and cruising at the same time as they obstructed sex work that catered to car drivers. In the early 1980s, more centrist gay males formed an alliance with anti–street prostitution groups and engaged in such events as the 1984–85 "Shame the Johns" actions in the West End. But the shame campaigns made many women uncomfortable, leading to even more females moving out of the West End, effectively keeping rents lower for gay men and contributing to the appearance of a ghetto.

Increased gay male visibility and creation of visible homoerotic space occurred at a dizzying pace in the West End throughout the 1970s and early 1980s. As one *Vancouver Sun* reporter described life in the West End, "at one time, gays were a novelty, a visible aberration. Now, it's a mature, stable community" (Andrews 1983). But that sense of singularity, with its emphasis on white, middle-class gay men, was soon shattered by the pressures for broader coalitions to educate against the spread of AIDS, to care for the sick, and to confront the local conservative agenda with its formidable homophobic backlash. By the early 1980s, the bar economy of Davie and Richards Streets began to change, shifting from a focus on alcohol consumption and meeting for sex to a diversification of establishments providing a range of services. The emergence of western Canada's early gay and lesbian bookstore, Little Sister's, and this effective culture center's weathering of several violent attacks,[12] symbolized this hard-fought diversification from a bar culture catering to white gay men. But few of even these more diverse establishments provided much space for women, queer families with children, and groups of males other than young and middle-aged ones.

Most of the early conversations on more aggressively confronting racism and cultural chauvinism in communities of sexual minorities in the 1980s, in this exceptionally multicultural city, were initiated by lesbians (Silvera, Gupta, and Anonymous 1982) who often felt pointedly excluded from the West End. Throughout the late 1980s and 1990s, the queer politics of the West End was dominated by AIDS organizations along with some modest interventions by campaigns against homophobic violence and small queer projects. Efforts to gain more local human rights and initial marriage protections were remarkably successful. Immigrants, some of whom were asylum seekers, were attracted to the West End. And by the turn of the century, globalization had so penetrated Vancouver's land market that the lower-income gay men, now middle-aged or near retirement age, were increasingly forced out of the West End. As the economic gap between women and men lessened, single lesbians began to move back into the West End. Thus, a cycle of forces that created a ghetto for one sexual minority, and displaced others, was played out in half a century.

As the gay ghetto demographic peaked in the mid 1980s, roughly parallel to that of the post–World War II "baby boom," the public space matrix of the West End became more tolerant, thus making room for other social groups as homosexual men either died from sexually transmitted diseases or moved elsewhere for better housing. The deep forest patches, so crucial to the invisibility needed for community formation during repressive times, became less important; they also declined through the ecological deterioration associated with urban areas. And as the matrix of public open space became more tolerant, in part because of the male-oriented conflicts of the previous decades, new niches became available to more vulnerable networks, including some dominated by homoerotic women. The processes of decolonization broke down the monolithic notions of a (primarily white) gay male community into far more complex networks not marked as white or male. The forging of more tolerant and democratic experiences of the matrix of public space has had a rough parallel in landscape ecology to the removal of more severe predation pressures.

Conclusions: Toward a Landscape Ecology of Urban Activism

That is the ghetto trip. At one time there was no alternative, no
way out.
    Now there is. It's called liberation to those who can dig it.
        —The Body Politic

This chapter has been focused on "environmental factors," effectively ecological threats and opportunities across a dynamic cultural landscape, and how they mesh with erotic acts and ideas, along with other aspects of culture, to transform a neighborhood. As for understanding the participation of networks of sexual minorities, the once-salient notion of a gay ghetto was challenged and partially replaced by descriptors of more nuanced, human-environmental relationships and processes. The landscape ecology terms of "patch," "edge," "flow and connectivity," and "matrix" were recast as shifting spaces for human intimacies and sites of resistance to avoid police harassment. Queer activists and scholars of the last two decades have too often learned more about the rhetoric and metaphors of social change and less about the human-environmental aspects of what Madonna Ciccone alluded to her 1985 anthem as "the material world." In this chapter I have explored some uses for landscape ecology terms for revisiting spatial aspects of community formation interactions across one celebrated neighborhood, one in which modern Canadian notions of democratic society and public space were first imagined and tested. While my adaptations of landscape ecology concepts are still rudimentary, this spatial vocabulary can be mapped and chronicled far more precisely than the vocabulary and measures provided by gay liberation's ghetto and queer theory's sites and closets. My adaptations of terms such as "fragment," "edge," "flow and connectivity," and "matrix" to the contexts of subcultures of sexual minorities remain crude—as is contemporary theory on the relationship of sex to culture and place. Just as today's increasing discomfort with use of the term "ghetto" suggests a more nuanced vocabulary, in coming decades we might well discard some of these new labels to be reconceptualized, reworked, and reinserted into the increasingly fertile cusp of the fields of landscape ecology and cultural studies.

In contrast to all but a few other neighborhoods in Canada, the West End has supported a particularly rich public space matrix comprising vegetation, beach, open space, and pavement. This exceptional set of public spaces effectively allowed one group of sexual minorities, homosexual males, to interact in a wide range of poorly policed settings and to act sufficiently freely as to build social networks and institutions. Due to a range of human-induced changes unrelated to public sex, the deep forest patches have been degraded and diminished over the last century and a half. But while the visual protection that the forest initially provided has declined, paradoxically the need for protection from the police has become less acute. In contrast to the experience of adult males, women have had far less access to this matrix of relatively democratic space because they were more often denied access to housing in the neighborhood, because of economic injustice, and because of continued worries about violence from males in areas of denser cover. As economic disparities and threats of violence have diminished, however, lesbians have repopulated the West End, further transforming its matrix of rich and relatively democratic public space.

In further constructing an environmental history of the sexual minorities of Vancouver's West End, what additional information on environmental factors, culture, and subjective experience is necessary? Certainly both maps and ecological information of the past could help us maneuver through the present and envision a preferred future. But how can more material indicators be inserted and combined with cultural studies and sexual stories? And how can we engage a new generation of activists in further community building as older forms of social infrastructure, including aspects of the matrices of public space, are jeopardized through the recent succession of economic crises? In a time of growing concern over human health, the environment, and sustainability, one of the bodies of knowledge that holds the most promise for understanding the trajectory of the "queerscapes" (Ingram 1997b, 29) of the West End for the coming century is landscape ecology. And queer ecology as a fusion of the science of biological exuberance with some cultural studies and urban planning could provide a basis to reconstruct landscape ecology to help us better see, enjoy, and, when necessary, defend all that we love in the communities in which we live.

NOTES

1. The original form, title, and sequence of reproductions of "A Gay Manifesto" (1972) is unclear to me though I do recall, from a personal conversations with Carl

Wittman in 1974 after he'd eschewed the urban ghettos for rural life, that he described the essay's circulation in pamphlet form.

2. Perhaps the discussions that best codified this shift from ethnographic and cultural studies, as being the currency of studies of communities of sexual minorities, are contained in Plummer 1995.

3. Sexual acts can be reviewed in a number of ways. Behavior can be abstracted to a kind of higher primate ethology—across urban space. For studies of the use of public spaces, there are participant-observer methods for seeing patterns of human use (including for sex). And the field of environmental history has increasingly supported work that links social groups over time to aspects of their associated ecosystems.

4. When Stan Persky wrote this poem he was heavily engaged in gay and left politics in Vancouver.

5. The label "the Terminal City" was the alternative moniker for Vancouver, going back to the city's incorporation and the conflicts around the new city's multicultural demographics, where individuals with northwestern European heritages were often "in the minority" (Roy 1976, 44).

6. For a sense of the economic interests evident in the beginnings of the Parks Board, see Board of Parks and Recreation, Vancouver (1991).

7. See Fernie and Weissman (1992).

8. In 1994 and 1995, both Fatona and Wyngaarden provided additional information on Hogan's Alley and early lesbian bar space in conversations with me.

9. For one of the more candid discussions of entrapment in Canada in the 1960s, see Batten (1969, 32).

10. As with most cities, the actual title of the "Pride" events has shifted over the years to include bisexual, transgender, and various other minority sexual subcultures. And then there have been various women-only events such as the Dyke Marches. The original pride-type, or proto-pride, event in Vancouver was a Gay Rights demonstration, focused on Pacific Canadian issues, with commemoration of Stonewall only coming years later. And there were long periods when events were labeled as "Gay" and others as "Gay and Lesbian" and others as "Queer." And in some periods "Pride" was specifically used with other events focused on terms such as "Stonewall." So I use "Gay Pride" here to refer to a host of unevenly allied institutions involving mass demonstrations and partying, typically with an element of procession, that in Vancouver, over the last three and half decades, have been scheduled twice a year, in both late June and early August. And the nature of these exceptionally bifurcated, neighborhood-based events, in comparison to other North American cities, has been very much shaped by the uneven experience of and responses to "ghettoization" and "de-ghettoization" (Duggan and Hunter 1995, 168), illustrated in this sketch of the landscape ecology of the sexual politics of the West End.

11. A map in the December 1983 issue of *Angles* (19), Vancouver's major lesbian and gay newspaper in the 1980s and the first half of the 1990s, illustrated how small enclaves of gay-male-friendly (and sometimes lesbian-friendly) establishments were forming in Vancouver (and clearly had been coalescing for two decades). The Seymour and Richards Street "Theatre Row" area of gay establishments (that nearly all were in business because of alcohol sales) had begun to form a separate enclave rivaling that in Gastown and was almost merging with the more recent Davie Street spaces. Compared to information from the 1970s, the Robson Street gay businesses were on the decline. All of these early enclaves were within easy walking distance of most of the West End.

12. In the heart of the West End, Little Sister's Bookstore was bombed three

times: in December 1987, in February 1988, and in January 1992. There were injuries but no fatalities. Cleaning up after the attacks did cost the bookstore's owners a great deal of money and time—in the same period when they were mustering funds to make legal challenges to Canada Customs against the agency's policies against material depicting certain sexual practices.

REFERENCES

Andrews, Michael. 1983. Getting the Lowdown on the Gay Community. *Vancouver Sun*, November 19, D2.

Anonymous. 1982. Listings. *NW Fountain* (Seattle), March, 20–21.

Aronowitz, Stanley. 1981. *The Crisis of Historical Materialism: Class, Politics and Culture in Marxist Theory*. New York: Praeger.

Bagemihl, Bruce. 1999. *Biological Exuberance: Animal Homosexuality and Natural Diversity*. New York: St. Martin's Press.

Batten, Jack. 1969. The Homosexual Life in Canada (Will Trudeau's change in the law make any difference? An answer from the gay world). *Saturday Night* (Toronto) 84.9: 28–32.

Blumenthal, Walter. 1971. Editorial. We Name Thee . . . *Gay Tide* (Vancouver) 1.1: 2.

Board of Parks and Recreation, Vancouver (1991). Board Minutes. September 1988–December 1991. On file, CVPA MCR-47. 48-A-1.

The Body Politic. The Gay Ghetto [of Vancouver]. *The Body Politic* (Toronto), November–December, 17.

Bouthillette, Anne-Marie. 1997. Queer and Gendered Housing: A Tale of Two Neighborhoods in Vancouver. In *Queers in Space: Communities|Public Places|Sites of Resistance*, ed. Gordon Brent Ingram, Anne-Marie Bouthillette, and Yolanda Retter, 213–32. Seattle, Wash.: Bay Press.

Chapman, Terry L. 1986. Male Homosexuality: Legal Restraints and Social Attitudes in Western Canada, 1890–1920. In *Law and Justice in a New Land: Essays in Western Canadian Legal History*, ed. Louis Knafla, 277–92. Toronto, Ontario: Carswell.

City Clerk. 1981. Extract from City Council Minutes, November 3. Social Service and Health Matters, "West End Prostitution / Nuisance Problem." On file in the Archives of the City of Vancouver. Dossier 81-G-4, file 4.

Duggan, Lisa, and Nan D. Hunter. 1995. *Sex Wars: Sexual Dissent and Political Culture*. New York: Routledge.

Fatona, Andrea, and Cornelia Wyngaarden, dirs. 1994. Video. *Hogan's Alley*. Video In.

Fernie, Lynne, and Aerlyn Weissman, dirs. 1992. Motion picture. *Forbidden Love: The Unashamed Stories of Lesbian Lives*. National Film Board of Canada.

Foa, Anna. 2000. *The Jews of Europe after the Black Death*. Berkeley and Los Angeles: University of California Press.

Forman, Richard T. T., and Michel Godron. 1986. *Landscape Ecology*. New York: John Wiley.

Hann, Don, and Rob Joyce. 1977. City Police Record: Smash Hit. *Gay Tide (Vancouver)* 16: 4.

———. 2009. Personal communication with author, Melriches Café, Vancouver, BC, March 8.

Hirtle, Blair. 1998. 20 Years Throwing Balls. *Xtra West* (Vancouver) 129: 15.

Ingram, Gordon Brent. 1997a. "Open" Space as Strategic Queer Sites. In *Queers in Space: Communities\Public Places\Sites of Resistance,* ed. Gordon Brent Ingram, Anne-Marie Bouthillette, and Yolanda Retter, 95–125. Seattle, Wash.: Bay Press.

———. 1997b. Marginality and the Landscapes of Erotic Alien(n)ations. In *Queers in Space: Communities\Public Places\Sites of Resistance,* ed. Gordon Brent Ingram, Anne-Marie Bouthillette, and Yolanda Retter, 27–52. Seattle, Wash.: Bay Press.

———. 1998. It's a Time Warp: Commercial Drive Has Transformed from Women's Places to Lesbian Feminist Spaces to a Queer Neighborhood. *Xtra West* (Vancouver) 138 (November 26): 20–21.

———. 2000. (On the Beach): Practising Queerscape Architecture. In *Practice Practise Praxis: Serial Repetition, Organizational Behaviour and Strategic Action in Architecture,* ed. Scott Sorli, 108–23. Toronto, Ontario: YYZ Books.

———. 2003. Returning to the Scene of the Crime: Uses of Trial Narratives of Consensual Male Homosexuality for Urban Research, with Examples from Twentieth-Century British Columbia. *GLQ* 10.1: 77–110.

Jameson, Fredric. 1984. Post-modernism, or the Cultural Logic of Late Capitalism. *New Left Review* 146: 53–92.

Kimmel, David, and Daniel Robinson. 1994. The Queer Career of Homosexual Security Vetting in Cold-War Canada. *Canadian Historical Review* 75.3: 319–45.

Kinsman, Gary. 1996. *The Regulation of Desire.* 2nd ed. Montreal, Quebec: Black Rose.

Levine, Martin. 1979. Gay Ghetto. *Journal of Homosexuality* 4: 363–77.

Macdonald, Bruce. 1992. *Vancouver: A Visual History.* Vancouver, B.C.: Talonbooks.

McDonald, Robert A. J. 1984. "Holy Retreat" or "Practical Breathing Spot"? Class Perceptions of Vancouver's Stanley Park, 1910–1913. *Canadian Historical Review* 65.2: 128–53.

———. 1996. *Making Vancouver: Class, Status and Social Boundaries 1863–1913.* Vancouver: University of British Columbia Press.

McKee, William Carey. 1976. The History of the Vancouver Park System 1886–1929. M.A. thesis in History, University of Victoria.

Naveh, Zev. 1990. Landscape Ecology as a Bridge between Bio-ecology and Human Ecology. In *Cultural Aspects of Landscapes,* ed. Hana Svobodova, 45–58. Wageningen, Netherlands: PUDOC. (Orig. 1982. Landscape Ecology as an Emerging Branch of Human Ecosystem Science. *Advances in Ecological Research* 12: 189–237).

Naveh, Zev, and Arthur S. Lieberman. 1984. *Landscape Ecology: Theory and Application.* New York: Springer-Verlag.

Perry, Adele. 1997. "Fair Ones of a Purer Caste": White Women and Colonialism in Nineteenth-Century British Columbia. *Feminist Studies* 23.3: 501–24.

Persky, Stan. 1977. *Wrestling the Angel.* Vancouver, B.C.: Talonbooks.

Plummer, Ken. 1995. *Telling Sexual Stories: Power, Change and Social Worlds.* New York: Routledge.

Roy, Patricia E. 1976. The Preservation of Peace in Vancouver: The Aftermath of the Anti-Chinese Riots of 1887. *BC Studies* 31: 44–59.

Schreiber, Karl-Friedrich. 1990. The History of Landscape Ecology in Europe. In *Changing Landscapes: An Ecological Perspectives,* ed. Isaak S. Zonneveld and Richard T. T. Forman, 21–33. New York: Springer-Verlag.

SEARCH. 1977. Police at English Bay. *SEARCH Newsletter* (Vancouver), February, 1.

Shapiro, Stephen. 2004. Marx to the Rescue! Queer Theory and the Crisis of Prestige. *New Formations* 53: 77–90.

Silvera, Makeda, Nila Gupta, and Anonymous. 1982. Lesbians of Colour: Loving and Struggling—A Conversation between Three Lesbians of Colour. *Fireweed* 16: 66–72.

Vancouver Sun. 1913. Vancouver Women's Building. March 19 Special edition—Women's Extra, 20 pp.

Volkart, Carol. 1977. Prostitutes, Gays Clash with Residents: West End's Many Faces Exposed. *Vancouver Sun,* April 7, 25.

Warner, Michael. 1991. Introduction: Fear of a Queer Planet. *Social Text* 9.4: 3–17.

Waugh, Thomas. 1996. *Hard to Imagine: Gay Male Eroticism in Photography and Film from Their Beginnings to Stonewall.* New York: Columbia University Press.

Wittman, Carl. 1972 (1969). A Gay Manifesto. In *Out of the Closets: Voices of Gay Liberation,* ed. Karla Jay and Allen Young, 330–42. New York: Douglas Books.

———. 1974. Personal communication with author.

PART 3

Desiring Nature?
Queer Attachments

CHAPTER 10

"The Place, Promised, That Has Not Yet Been": The Nature of Dislocation and Desire in Adrienne Rich's *Your Native Land/Your Life* and Minnie Bruce Pratt's *Crime Against Nature*

RACHEL STEIN

> The hatred baffles me . . . /the way she pulled the statute book down like a novel/ . . . *crime against nature*. . . . /That year the punishment was: not less than five nor more/ than sixty years. For my methods, indecent and unnatural/ of gratifying a depraved and perverted sexual instinct./For even the slightest touching of lips or tongue or lips/to a woman's genitals.
> —Minnie Bruce Pratt

> I need to understand how a place on the map is also a place in history within which as a woman, a Jew, a lesbian, a feminist I am created and trying to create. Begin, though, not with a continent or country or a house, but with the geography closest in—the body. . . . Begin, we said, with the material, with matter, mma, madre, mutter, moeder, modder, etc., etc.
> —Adrienne Rich

Adrienne Rich and Minnie Bruce Pratt are contemporary U.S. lesbian feminist poets whose work overtly challenges many sorts of social inequalities and exclusions, including heterosexism, which rests upon the formulation of homosexuality as a crime against nature. Both poets expose how this discourse of unnatural sex dislocates lesbians from the social-natural order by framing homosexuals as societal pariahs and felons who are then excluded from social spaces and endangered within natural terrains. Rich and Pratt contest this "crime-against-nature" ideology by locating lesbian speakers within beloved landscapes, and through this strategic, nonessential identification of women with the natural world, they stake a claim for what Pratt describes as "the place, promised, that has not yet been—" (Pratt 1990, 18), a revolutionary environment of sexual freedom. Both writers call into question the ways that our ideas of the "natural" have permeated social formations and have been used by the hegemonic culture to naturalize and legalize social norms; while their poetry consciously redeploys the natural so as to reaffirm lesbian desires, it also emphasizes that appeals to nature have troubled histories and violent results that we must always address. Their poetic subversion of crime-against-nature ideology brings together struggles for environmental justice and sexual justice and offers us one approach toward a queer ecology.

Historically, United States religious and legal prohibitions against homosexuality have framed such desire as a crime against nature or unnatural perversion, as described in Pratt's lines above. From colonial times through the present, American laws regulating sexual behavior have drawn upon the Judeo-Christian belief that certain sexual practices are natural and others are unnatural, even crimes against nature. The Pauline epistle to the Romans sets forth this doctrine of "vile affections." Paul condemns those who pervert nature: "women did change the *natural use into that which is against nature;* and likewise also the man, leaving the *natural use* of the woman; (they) burned in their lust one toward another, men with men working that which is unseemly" (quoted in Bullough and Bullough 1977, 24, emphases mine). While leaving unspecified exactly which acts are "against nature," Paul's passage bases its regulation of sexuality upon distinctions between natural and unnatural use of human bodies. In his era, Christian thinkers compared human sexual actions to planting a field and only those activities that corresponded to "seeding," or procreation, were accepted as natural; other activities impeding or ignoring reproduction, whether performed with members of the same or the opposite sex were forbidden as against nature (Bullough and Bullough 1977, 28).

This vague category of crime against nature became the basis of English and American laws regulating sexuality that set severe punishments for such acts while seldom specifying exactly what these crimes entailed. In the United States, state laws known as the sodomy statutes or crime-against-nature codes criminalized different forms of nonreproductive sexual acts, including homosexuality, which became the primary target for prosecution and was punishable by execution.[1] Furthermore, because homosexuality was deemed so repellently unnatural, it was also believed unspeakable, for, supposedly, even to discuss it violated human nature. Thus the Pauline application of agricultural analogies to human sexual practices has undergirded centuries of social stigma, legal persecution, and cultural silencing of same-sex desire.[2] The U.S. sodomy statutes that criminalized homosexuality were finally overturned by the 2003 *Lawrence v. Texas* U.S. Supreme Court decision, but this decision still did not grant homosexuals the same legal rights as heterosexuals, and many communities still regard same-sex desire as immoral and unnatural.

While this use of agricultural analogies to denaturalize homosexuality has held sway in the social, legal, and ideological realms, it has also problematized the way that lesbians and gays have been situated in relation to natural environments. As Mei Mei Evans argues, in the United States, wilderness and rural areas have been deemed the exclusive province of straight white men, who adventure in nature in order to establish their manhood. Other marginalized groups, such as women, gays and lesbians, and people of color, are construed by the dominant culture as either too similar to wild nature or too unnatural to have rightful place in the more-than-human world, and so they are punished for venturing into wild spaces. Evans notes:

> We can see the way that representations of U.S. nature as a physical location are overdetermined as white, male, and heterosexual when we look at what happens to people who are *not* white, male, and/or straight when they attempt the same sort of transformative experiences in nature. . . . Nature or wilderness as *culturally constructed* locations have been foreclosed to women, people of color, and gays and lesbians. (2002, 181–93)

She explains that historically, such marginalized people have experienced discriminatory violence in natural settings—for example, blacks being lynched in southern trees and lesbians and gays being raped and murdered in wilderness locations: "Whereas straight white men look to nature to offer up something . . . against which they can prove themselves; people of color, and gays and lesbians go into nature in fear of encountering straight white men" (191). Crime-against-nature ideologies thus curtail lesbian and gay access to natural environments, which makes sexual justice also an environmental justice issue.

Because reference to the natural was used to police sexuality, turning natural environments into dangerous sites, a number of modern and postmodern theorists and activists promoting sexual freedoms such as contraception, abortion rights, and acceptance of homosexuality have been moved to reject the natural as a pertinent category.[3] However, Adrienne Rich and Minnie Bruce Pratt instead challenge proscriptions against homosexuality by directly confronting the premises and effects of crime-against-nature ideology: First, they detail how such ideologies dislocate lesbians from social and natural environments; then Rich and Pratt strategically resituate homoerotic desire within the natural landscape and use this identification of lesbianism with natural terrain and phenomenon as means of unsettling Pauline prohibitions and reaffirming same-sex desire.[4] In effect, their poetry "queers nature," in the manner called for by Catriona Sandilands, as she envisions ways of bringing environmentalism and queer politics into productive conversation:

> Rather than enumerate some series of points where lesbians, gay men, bisexuals and transgender [folk] can carve out some sort of unique "position" in relation to environmental issues, perhaps the point is to "queer" nature itself, to create "queer" environments. To queer nature is to question its normative use, to interrogate relations of knowledge and power by which certain "truths" about ourselves have been allowed to pass, unnoticed, without question. It is a process by which all relations to nature become de-naturalized, by which we question the ways in which we are located in nature, by which we question the uses to which "nature" has been put. . . . Queer environments are thus those in which the boundaries between "nature" and "culture" are shown to be arbitrary, dialectical, mutually constitutive. (1994, 22)

By emphasizing lesbian dis-location from social/natural spaces, and then also resituating lesbian desire within natural contexts, Rich's and Pratt's poetry queers nature in the way that Sandilands invokes, exposing how nature has often been called upon by the hegemonic society to determine the sexual norms, but then rearticulating nature and sexuality as more abundantly various than Pauline doctrine would allow.[5] Rich and Pratt articulate the damaging effects of this use of nature against homosexuals, including exclusion from both social and natural environments, and so, for these lesbian poets, reclaiming space in, and identification with, the natural world is one means of striving for sexual justice. In these volumes of poetry, Rich and Pratt articulate intersections between sexual and environmental justice: As I have argued elsewhere, when we frame sexual justice issues also as issues of environmental justice, we can make it evident that people of diverse sexualities have the human right to bodily sovereignty and to live safely as sexual bodies within social/physical environments (Stein 2004, introduction).

Adrienne Rich's *Your Native Land, Your Life* (1986b) and Minnie Bruce Pratt's *Crime against Nature* (1990) were written during the 1980s, a period of political retrenchment and renewed conservative antagonism to homosexuality. During the preceding decades of the 1960s and early 1970s, gay and lesbian liberation activists had achieved increased human rights, including the repeal of the sodomy codes by some states, the passage of numbers of city/county human rights ordinances that prohibited discrimination based on sexuality, and the American Psychiatric Association's removal of homosexuality from its list of mental illnesses. While this was substantial progress, twenty-five states still upheld crime-against-nature statutes that criminalized homosexuality, and most local anti-discrimination policies did not include sexuality as a protected category. Yet, by the late 1970s, in reaction to progress toward dismantling heteropatriarchy, the religious right mounted a backlash to reinstate religiously based legal proscriptions against gays and lesbians. Starting in 1977, this fundamentalist movement was given momentum through the Save Our Children campaign to repeal the anti-gay-discrimination ordinance of Dade County Florida, led by former beauty queen and orange juice spokeswoman Anita Bryant. (What better spokesperson for renaturalizing heteropatriarchy?) Bryant's rationale for her heterosexist campaign referenced the Pauline views of homosexuality as nonreproductive and therefore unnatural: "As a mother, I know that homosexuals cannot biologically reproduce children; therefore they must recruit our children" and "What these people really want . . . is the right to propose to our children that theirs is an acceptable alternate way of life" (Bryant 1977). Emphasizing the nonreproductivity of gay and lesbian sex—and ignoring the fact that gays and lesbians do in fact often have children through other means, as well as the fact that sexuality is not an inherited trait—Bryant implied that homosexuals were pedophiles who would prey upon the children of heterosexuals, and so her campaign for the denial of homosexual rights was built upon the notion of protecting children from the depredations of these unnatural sexual outlaws. She also conflated homosexuality with other forms of illegal sex, stating: "If gays are granted rights, next we'll have to give rights to prostitutes and to people who sleep with St. Bernards" (Bryant 1977). Bryant's campaign was successful in revoking the Dade County anti-discrimination ordinance, and this sparked a wave of other reactionary anti-gay campaigns across the United

States. Bryant's Save Our Children ideology also reinforced prohibitions against homosexual custody/adoption of children in many states, as she asserted that lesbians and gays are immoral and unnatural, and that they will therefore provide a negative environment for children that might influence them to accept this deviant sexuality and perhaps even become homosexual themselves. Even after the U.S. Supreme Court overturned the sodomy statutes with the 2003 *Lawrence v. Texas* decision, adoption laws in some states still reflected the Save Our Children anti-gay ideology (Mariner 2004).

Anita Bryant incited rampant right-wing heterosexism in the ensuing decades. Her campaign unleashed waves of anti-gay violence, persecution, and legal initiatives to limit gay rights. Gayle Rubin recounts an increase in police raids on gay bars and cruising areas across the country, and notes that by the early 1980s anti-gay violence was on the rise: "Queerbashing has become a significant recreational activity for young urban males. They come into gay neighborhoods armed with baseball bats and looking for trouble, knowing that the adults in their lives either secretly approve or will look away" (Rubin 1993, 6). Anti-gay platforms of religious right organizations such as the Moral Majority and Citizens for Decency gained mass appeal and contributed to conservative success in the elections of 1980, which would set the sexually repressive tone for that decade (8). In fact, the Web site of the Moral Majority—an organization with a "pro-life, pro-traditional family platform"—boasts that in 1980, "the Moral Majority backs the presidential candidacy of Ronald Reagan and helps sweep him into office in dramatic fashion. In addition, 12 liberal Democrat senators and several liberal House members are also defeated, launching a new wave of political activity within the evangelical community. The political landscape is spectacularly altered" (Moral Majority Timeline). Indeed, during the Reagan-Bush era, the religious right reasserted that heteropatriarchy was the only natural Christian-ordained sexual/family arrangement, once again framing homosexuality as a heinous crime against nature, both sinful and illegal. In fact, even as late as 2005, Pope John Paul II assailed gay marriage as challenging the "natural structure" of families and promoting an "unnatural vision of man" (quoted in Townsley 2005).

Adrienne Rich and Minnie Bruce Pratt resist the reactionary backlash of the 1980s in their volumes of poetry, reasserting the revolutionary belief in social and sexual justice, and situating lesbian desire out in the social/natural world. While their poetry exposes the violent dislocation of lesbians due to the heterosexist attitudes that re-emerged in that decade, they resist this doctrine by inscribing lesbian desire within natural settings and through natural phenomena. Their poetry stakes a claim to a rightful space in the landscape of the nation and reaffirms the potency, productivity, and possibilities of lesbianism through this strategic, positive affiliation with nature.

Published in 1986, Adrienne Rich's *Your Native Land, Your Life* is an expansive, political sequence of poems in which Rich foregrounds the oppression of those who deviate from social norms and so have been dislocated from secure relationship to their native land.[6] Rich explains: "I have been trying to speak from, and of, and to, my country. To speak a different claim from those staked by the patriots of the sword; to speak of the land itself, the cities, and of the imaginations that have dwelt here, at risk, unfree, assaulted, erased" (Rich 1986b, cover notes). Throughout *Your Native Land, Your Life,* Rich explores how our position within political/ natural environments, or "native lands," is determined according to our identities, or "lives," and vice versa. Rich first reveals the many ways in which marginalized persons have historically been "assaulted and erased" from their rightful place within political/natural environments and then she "speak(s) a different claim" to native land, for those who have been devalued and displaced.[7] Within this larger project, a number of her poems focus on the particular way that lesbians and gays, who are deemed unnatural, are violently dislocated from wild natural environments. After exposing this dynamic, Rich then claims a right to her native land by situating lesbian desire within natural landscapes, particularly gardens.

In the complex poem "Yom Kippur 1984" Rich challenges the privileged model of solitary ventures into pristine natural terrains practiced by canonical nature poets, such as Robinson Jeffers, to whom much of the poem is addressed. Writing as a Jew, as a lesbian, as a woman, as one deeply committed to social justice, and also as one committed to the natural world, Rich considers the problematic meaning of solitude in nature when it is defined by Jeffers in opposition to what he calls "the human-bodied . . . multitude" (Rich 1986b, 75). As I have discussed elsewhere (Stein 2000), Rich explains that, unfortunately, solitude is a luxury of those who fit the social norms, while those who are persecuted as deviants can be most vulnerable to attack when alone in remote places, away from the protection of others like themselves:

What would it mean not to feel lonely or afraid
far from your own or those you have called your own?
What is a woman in solitude: a queer woman or man?

In the empty street, on the empty beach, in the desert
what in this world as it is can solitude mean? (Rich 1986b, 75)

Ironically, while for the white, straight, male Jeffers, wilderness is a refuge
from fellow humans, for lesbians and gays wilderness is deadly terrain
where they are most exposed to heterosexist attacks encouraged by the
crime-against-nature ideologies that view queers as antagonistic to the
natural order and therefore permissible targets of hatred and violence.
Through these incidents of homophobic violence, queers are denied secure
access to wilderness.

"Yom Kippur 1984" goes on to detail murders of solitary Others in
remote terrains:

> . . . to love solitude—am I writing merely about
> privilege
> about drifting from the center, drawn to edges,
> a privilege we can't afford in the world that is,
> who are hated as being of our kind: faggot kicked into the icy
> river, woman dragged from her stalled car
> into the mist-struck mountains, used and hacked to death
> young scholar shot at the university gates on a summer evening
> walk, his prizes and studies nothing, nothing
> availing his Blackness
> Jew deluded that she's escaped the tribe, the laws of her exclusion,
> the men too holy to touch her hand; Jew who has
> turned her back
> on *midrash* and *mitzvah* (yet wears the *chai* on a thong between her
> breasts) hiking alone
> found with a swastika carved in her back at the foot of the cliffs
> (did she die as queer or as Jew?) (Rich 1986b, 77)

Rich describes the violence meted out to those who are "hated as being
of our kind" when they venture alone into wild environments. While the
lesbian hoped to escape the heteropatriarchal "laws of her exclusion" as
she hiked alone along the cliffs, crime-against-nature ideology dogged her
footsteps and endorsed her murder. When queers are viewed as unnatural,
entering nature becomes taboo and trespass is punishable by violent death;
and while Rich does not specify that the incidents she describes are based
on actual incidents, as is often true in her work, these hate crimes resonate
with the murders of lesbians hiking the Appalachian trail in Pennsylvania and Virginia, and the infamous murder of Matthew Shepard in rural

Wyoming.[8] Through these examples, Rich demonstrates how negative construction of homosexuality as unnatural violently dislocates homosexuals from the natural order and from natural environments.

This violence directed against lesbians and gays who seek solitude in nature prompts Rich's speaker to cry out for sexual justice, even to consider retaliatory violence to protect the right of all to solitary experiences of natural environments. By using the term "endangered species" to describe homosexual access to the natural world, Rich places this issue within the context of popular mainstream environmental campaigns to protect other animals from extinction, implying that lesbians and gays, too, merit environmental justice activism to assure their continuance within the larger natural order:

> Solitude, O taboo, endangered species
> on the mist-struck spur of the mountain, I want a gun to defend
> > you
> In the desert, on the deserted street, I want what I can't have:
> your elder sister, Justice. . . . (Rich 1986b, 77)

Rich ends the poem by asking how lesbians and gays might challenge this deadly heteropatriarchal formulation of wilderness as the exclusive purview of straight men such as Jeffers who go there to escape from the marginalized "multitudes" whom they despise:

> when we who refuse to be women and men as women and men are
> > chartered, tell our stories of solitude spent in
> > multitude
> in that world as it may be, newborn and haunted, what will
> > solitude mean? (Rich 1986b, 77–78)

Similar to Evans and Sandilands, Rich believes that by telling their own stories of deviance from and resistance to the naturalized norms, lesbians and gay men might dismantle the longstanding Pauline ideology that categorizes sexual acts and sexual identities as natural or unnatural, and might thereby produce a different social/natural world, "newborn and haunted" with possibility for sexual/environmental justice. Subverting the deadly use of nature to police sexuality, these stories would generate another world in which diverse sexualities were accepted; such persons might enjoy solitude in natural environments, without violent punishment from the dominant culture.

Your Native Land, Your Life concludes with a long series entitled "Contradictions: Tracking Poems" containing poems in which the speaker does tell her own stories of lesbian desire sited within the natural world. Overall, the "Contradictions" series emphasizes the painful paradoxes at the heart of American life, including poems on difficult subjects such as women in prison, sexual violence, progressive disease and surgery, radiation sickness resulting from nuclear tests, the effects of dioxin on soldiers. Interspersed within this sequence are several more apparently pastoral poems that situate lesbian love within the context of rural New England. In them, Rich queers nature by strategically equating the precious and precarious nature of lesbian love within a heteronormative society to the endangered plenitude of the New England landscape, in order to openly reassert women's same-sex desire against a history of suppression and violation.

Poem 3 presents a lesbian homoerotic interlude in the context of a winter's day, claiming the women's lovemaking as a pleasure of the season. While winter is often portrayed as the deadly, barren time within the natural cycle and while same-sex desire had historically been similarly portrayed as reproductively sterile, Rich instead emphasizes the lively pleasures of both season and sexual encounter:

> My mouth hovers across your breasts
> in the short grey winter afternoon
> in this bed   we are delicate
> and tough   so hot with joy we amaze ourselves
> tough   and delicate   we play rings
> around each other   our daytime candle burns
> with its peculiar light   and if the snow
> begins to fall outside   filling the branches
> and if the night falls   without announcement
> these are the pleasures of winter
> sudden, wild and delicate   your fingers
> exact   my tongue exact at the same moment
> stopping to laugh at a joke
> my love   hot on your scent   on the cusp of winter
> (Rich 1986b, 85)

In defiance of the homophobic 1980s, Rich boldly describes the homoerotic union of the female lovers against the backdrop of a wintry world. Rich interweaves descriptions of the women's acts of love with the signs of winter outside their home, and while the heat and light of the women's desire might be seen in contrast to the darkness and snow outside, the phrase "the pleasures of winter" encompasses not only snow-filled branches but also the two women, "wild and delicate," "tough and delicate," in the midst of love. The women's homoerotic union occurs on the "cusp of winter," serving as the crowning moment of the season, a poetic fusion that proclaims the naturalness of their desire by equating their partnering with the natural occurrences that surround them, and while winter is often referred to as a barren and unproductive season, Rich instead emphasizes the pleasures, rather than reproductivity, of the women and natural setting: the women are "hot with joy," they "play rings around each other" and they "laugh at a joke" while their fingers and tongues give each other the "exact" sexual pleasures that they desire. This joyous poem queers the nature of desire by replacing the negative Pauline focus upon sex as solely reproductive with a paean to the satisfying exuberance of lesbian sexual pleasures.

Two other poems use the fierce ephemerality of summer gardens to signify the courageous resistance of lesbians whose erotic commitment stands against a hostile, homophobic world. Joni Adamson notes that Native American cultures term gardens "the middle space," which humans and nature co-construct, because gardens offer a more reciprocal and interactive relationship between human and environment than does the fetishized wilderness adventure that has been the domain of straight white men (Adamson 2001). Gardens have also often been deemed a properly feminine form of women's interaction with nature in Euroamerican tradition. Even so, in Rich's poems, domestic natural environments are also subject to invasion: garden and women are still under external threat in Poem 21:

> The cat-tails blaze in the corner   sunflowers
> shed their pale fiery dust   on the dark stove-lid
> others stand guard   heads bowed   over the garden
> the fierce and flaring garden you have made
> out of your woes and expectations
> tilled into the earth   I circle close to your mind
> crash into it sometimes   as you crash into mine
> Given this strip of earth   given mere love
> should we not be happy?
> but happiness comes and goes as it comes and goes
> the safe-house is temporary   the garden
> lies open to vandals
> this whole valley is one more contradiction
> and more will be asked of us   we will ask more
> (Rich 1986b, 103)

The poem emphasizes both the difficulties of lesbian immersion in nature and also the productivity of this relationship. The lover has created this lush garden out of her "woes and expectations"—a phrase that signals both her painful dislocation from native land and also her determination to remake a positive relationship with natural environment—that she has "tilled into the earth." The garden is co-constructed by woman and nature together, offering an alternative model to straight male wilderness explorations. Through her labor, the lover has produced flowers that "stand guard" against external dangers, representing the "fierce and flaring" nature of the women's love; the speaker emphasizes the martial posture of the flowers: "cat-tails *blaze*," sunflowers shed *"fiery"* pollen, and others perform sentry duty with *"heads bowed,"* posing vigilantly against a hostile outside force (emphases added). The poem draws parallels between the fertile "strip of earth" and the couple's "mere love" (and we may perhaps read "mere" as a pun on the French "mère," or mother, signifying a love of women, of female corporeality) and both lovers and garden stand poised against intrusions such as vandals and other violators that loom ominously on the outskirts of the poem. Rich emphasizes the fertility but also the ephemerality of the home-space that the valley provides to relationship and garden: Both exist here in a sort of "safe-house," a temporary respite within a hostile world (such as the battered women's shelter mentioned in another poem of the "Contradictions" sequence), and knowledge of the corresponding endangerment of women and garden poses an enormous contradiction that Rich wants us to question. Rich queers nature by showing that for these lesbian lovers, the garden makes visible the dislocation of those persons construed as sexual pariahs, even while it simultaneously embodies the lush productivity of this union. Through their garden, these women have indeed staked a different claim to native land—but this claim remains precarious, subject to threat until the damaging practices of heterosexism end.

Similarly, in poem 28 Rich again subverts the Pauline use of agricultural metaphors to damn homosexuality as nonreproductive, drawing parallels between the lesbian lovers and the close of the summer season in their bountiful garden.

> This high summer we love will pour its light
> the fields grown rich and ragged in one strong moment
> then before we're ready will crash into autumn
> with a violence we can't accept
> a bounty we can't forgive

Night frost will strike when the noons are warm
the pumpkins wildly glowing   the green tomatoes
straining huge on the vines
queen anne and blackeyed susan will straggle rusty
as the milkweed stakes her claim
she who will stand at last   dark sticks barely rising
up through the snow   her testament of continuation
We'll dream of a longer summer
but this is the one we have:
I lay my sunburnt hand
on your table: this is the time we have (Rich 1986b, 110)

While proscriptions against homosexuality deemed such relationships barren, and therefore unnatural, Rich emphasizes the "rich" "bounty" that the lovers have produced within their garden and within the "high summer" of their love. Their crops are exceedingly prolific—the "pumpkins wildly glowing" and the "tomatoes straining huge"—and this image of fruitful harvest overturns the Pauline use of the agricultural analogy in order to condemn homoeroticism. Yet, the poignant end of summer, presaging the unforgivable ravages that autumn will bring, also hints at the social ravages that threaten the women's union from without. The dream of a longer summer is a dream of possibility, expansiveness, and growth cut short by the limits imposed by a homophobic society. Corresponding to the feminized flowers that "stand at last" in "testament of continuation," the speaker's closing gesture of laying her hand on her lover's table pledges the continuation of their love despite the struggles that may be yet to come. Using the garden to "stake(s) her claim" to the resourcefulness of lesbian love, Rich requires us to revalue the productive power of same-sex commitment, in direct challenge to the heteronormative condemnation that reigns beyond the boundaries of the lovers' garden plot. Rich asks us to see the way that the criminalization of homosexuality and attendant homophobia weigh upon the lovers, intruding even into the private natural space of their garden, and thus she queers nature by showing how the women's relations to each other and the surrounding world must stand against the religious/legal uses of nature to police sexuality. Gays and lesbians, living in the long shadow of crime-against-nature ideology, must stake another claim, reframing the intersection of native land and sexual identity.

Like Rich, Minnie Bruce Pratt is a contemporary lesbian poet and essayist who often interweaves attention to the natural landscape with a layered analysis of the personal, social, and political geography of the human communities sedimented upon the land, consciously interrogating the way that recourse to nature has been used to naturalize a hierarchical arrangement of social identities. Much as Rich wrote of marginalized U.S. groups reclaiming native land, Pratt describes her attention to landscape, history, and Otherness in her recent poetry: "It's a reinterpretation of the history of the South from the underneath point of view. . . . It's an attempt to retravel the landscape and see it from this Other point of view" (quoted in Hunt 1997, 99). In particular, in Pratt's autobiographically based collection of poems, *Crime Against Nature,* we revisit the landscape of the contemporary southern United States through the perspective of a lesbian mother who has lost custody of her two sons due to the North Carolina sodomy laws criminalizing homosexuality and rendering severe punishments for lesbian desire, as Pratt describes in the title poem, "Crime Against Nature" quoted as the epigraph for this essay. The speaker of these poems, like Pratt herself, must contend with the negative effects of Anita Bryant's Save Our Children campaign against homosexuals, particularly lesbian and gay parents. Threatened with the force of the sodomy statutes that mandate prison sentences of between five and sixty years for supposedly unnatural sexual acts such as cunnilingus, the speaker of Pratt's volume of poems relinquishes custody of her sons to her husband and reluctantly accepts limited visitation with the boys on her husband's terms, which precludes hosting them in her own home (Pratt 1990, 116). The sequence of poems in *Crime Against Nature* is testament to the material/maternal dislocation that Pratt's speaker has suffered, as she is torn over and over from her children by the laws that criminalize homoerotic desires as unnatural. Pratt makes very clear the painful irony and circular logic of the sodomy laws that deem lesbian desire unnatural since it is not inherently reproductive, yet mete out harsh punishments to lesbians who do reproduce by deeming them as unfit mothers and removing their children from their care. Ironically, because lesbian mothers *have* fulfilled the Pauline mandate to reproduce, they are punished by the laws and social norms for their contradictory status as lesbian/mothers by having to choose to live an either/or existence—either lesbian or mother, but not both/ and at once. Through her sequence of poems that expand out from the speaker's own situation to expose the losses suffered by silent legions of lesbian mothers, Pratt illuminates the terrible force of the sodomy laws, even while she undermines the logic of defining homosexuality as the crime against nature.

Throughout *Crime Against Nature* Pratt works to overturn the cultural assumption that lesbian desire is unnatural, to challenge the worldview inherent in the sodomy laws, and, in particular, to free herself and her sons from the heteronormative worldview that has separated them. As the sodomy laws limit the speaker's free movement through the social world—when she loses her marital home, and the right to visit her children in their home or hers—Pratt's speaker claims temporary home-spaces in the wilds of the natural world, where she is more free to be her own complex lesbian and maternal self, and to introduce her sons to natural phenomena that defy the limited logic of the patriarchal laws. Pratt queers nature by representing the larger natural world as a sort of momentary "safe-house" space for the speaker and her sons, similar to the garden in Rich's poems, and by describing the natural terrain and phenomena as wild and mysterious, beyond the boundaries of the unjust and unnatural sodomy laws still upheld by many states at the time of her writing.

Pratt shows us the terrible force of the laws that dislocate her from the foundations of her former life. Early in the volume, a poem entitled "No Place" emphasizes the way that her husband's recourse to the sodomy laws displaces the speaker from her former position as wife and mother, rendering her both physically and figuratively homeless. Bolstered by the laws, the husband forces the speaker to make a series of impossible choices between different aspects of herself, and between different parts of her life that she had not considered to be opposed or divisible:

One night before I left I sat halfway down,
halfway up the stairs, as he reeled at the bottom,
shouting, *Choose, choose.*   Man or woman, her or him,
me or the children.   There was no place to be
simultaneous or between. (Pratt 1990, 18)

Through these forced choices, the husband divides the speaker's life into a series of false oppositions—desire for men or women, commitment to self or motherhood—leaving the speaker "no place" for the complex realities that place her "simultaneous(ly) between" the binarisms mandated by the heteropatriarchal law of the fathers. While she is poised "halfway" up/down the stairs, her husband cannot accept this ambivalent placement, and so she loses him, home, and children as she chooses self, woman, and a new amorphous life—because there is "no place" in the social system for her to retain all aspects of her complex identity. Leigh Gilmore and Marcia Aldrich argue that Pratt makes visible "the homelessness of lesbianism" as she is outlawed from domestic space, and the remainder of the poem

describes the speaker's state of physical, social, and emotional dislocation as a lesbian mother whose car has become the place in which she
visits with her children, since she is forbidden to have them in her home
(Gilmore and Aldrich 1992):[9]

> How tired we got of traveling the night land;
> how we crossed river after river in the dark,
> The Reedy, the Oconee, the Cahaba, all unseen;
> how night and the rivers flowed into a huge void
> as if that was where we were going, no place at all. (Pratt 1990, 19)

Dislocated from the social spaces they once inhabited together, mother
and sons must instead navigate the surrounding natural world, which,
even though it is a "no place" and "a huge void," yet is still freer from
social strictures than other public space, the one site where the speaker
may enact all of the socially contradictory aspects of herself. While Rich's
"Yom Kippur, 1984" had described violent exclusions *from* wild areas,
Pratt instead describes exclusion from home space *to* wild areas. As an
outlaw from the sodomy statutes, Pratt dreams of finding a place in the
natural world where she can be freely and fully herself, the space of an
imagined future world beyond the forces of heteronormative laws and
power. Such a place is "unfamiliar," completely "changed" from her imperfect present social/natural geography:

> The month before I left I dreamed we three waded
> across a creek, muddy green, blood warm, quick cold.
> . . .
>   . . . There is milkweed, purple bronze
> wild hydrangea, and an unfamiliar huge openness.
> It is the place, promised, that has not yet been,
> the place where everything is changed, the place
> after the revolution, the revelation, the judgment.
>   . . .
>   . . . We are together, we have come across.
> We have no place to go. (Pratt 1990, 18–19)

Pratt calls upon this creek scene to represent a dream image of hopeful
"openness," a site of anticipated possibility and "promise" following a
social revolution that would move us beyond the false, punitive divisions
currently enforced by our homophobic laws. Throughout the sequence
of poems, Pratt queers nature in this way, presenting natural settings,
often rivers, as the physical and figurative place of possibility for out-

casts/outlaws from the social order. But the temporary sanctuary that she finds in these sites only heightens their contrast to the social spaces that remain intolerant of sexual difference and complex identities; and even while natural sites offer transitory respite, the speaker and her children still "have no place to go," because heteropatriarchy dislocates them from secure attachment to any physical environments.

Even so, the speaker of these poems finds in the natural world an antidote to heteronormative oppression, an alternative space in which to mother and where she may teach her sons the falsity of the patriarchal structures that have separated her from the boys. Repeatedly, Pratt emphasizes the way that an alternative vision of natural phenomena may decenter the rigid social order, and may recenter a more egalitarian mode that allows the speaker to be a lesbian mother to her sons even while she is exiled and absent. The natural world also becomes the site where her sons can exhibit their attachment to her, as Pratt describes in "The Place Lost and Gone, the Place Found." When the speaker arrives to visit her boys, they take her on a tour of their special places around the yard: "They have asked me into their tree and, satisfied,/we sit rather large in its airy room. Their house/slides away across the lawn to the edge. Now/we are in the middle . . ." (Pratt 1990, 37). In this image, the tree becomes a hospitable space, embracing lesbian mother and her sons, and decentering the house of the father, which slides away to the edge of their world. Floating in the tree-space, mother and sons can once again become a "we," a family unit, recentered firmly in the "middle" of their lives. As the boys continue to share with their mother the pond and creek, the plants, the light, the creatures and mysteries they have discovered, she comments: ". . . They show me everything,/saying, with no words, they have thought of me here,/and I am here with them in the in-between places" (Pratt 1990, 37–38). The boys view the details of the yard as wonders for them to share with their mother that are marked with her presence even in her absence, spaces that are queered, and therefore open to the in-between state of lesbian motherhood that she inhabits. Nature and lesbianism have become equated for her sons, and so, their love of the natural world subverts the assumption that homoeroticism is a crime against nature.

Similar to Rich, Pratt uses pastoral imagery to describe the sexual acts forbidden by the sodomy statutes, directly countering the letter and language of the law with her emphasis upon the naturalness of her homoeroticism. In the title poem, "Crime Against Nature," Pratt's speaker responds to the lawyer's glib reading of the sodomy statutes that deem cunnilingus one of the crimes against nature, by mentally comparing tongue and vulva to powerful, mysterious natural phenomena: "the tongue trail of saliva like an animal track quick/in the dew. . . . / . . . tongue like a snake (*bestial* is in the statute)/ winding through salty walls, the labyrinth, curlicue,/ the underground spring, rocks that sing . . ." (Pratt 1990, 116). In this poem and throughout the volume, Pratt uses the image of the snake as emblem for the way that lesbian desire transgresses the standard binarisms, such as male/female, active/passive, planting/receiving, inherent in the legal statutes, since a woman's tongue can play the snaking, phallic role of traversing the terrain of her lover's vulva, causing it to flow and sing with pleasure. While the speaker realizes that this animal/landscape imagery, too, would be deemed "bestial" by the creators of the laws, for her the images are full of beautiful, natural power, and so they renaturalize the desires that the laws condemn. Whereas Christian doctrine drew upon an agricultural analogy to define proper sexual activities, Pratt offers us instead the more slippery natural analogy of a snake winding through a landscape: both images are drawn from nature, and so therefore Pratt is able to queer nature, to demonstrate that while recourse to nature was used to police sexuality, a different framework of natural imagery might dismantle this entire ideology.

Similar to Rich, Pratt continuously frames her desire for her female lover within a register of natural imagery, in defiance of the legal code and homophobic social norms that punish such desires. In fact, in the poem "Dreaming a Few Minutes in a Different Element" homoerotic desire is portrayed as more natural, more "pure," more genuine, than the stale, diminished heterosexual desires that Pratt's speaker is relinquishing at this juncture in her life:

> . . . How to explain
> a kind of doubling back to myself, selfish or
> the difference between the stale fountain I stare at,
> and the creek, pure unknown, upwelling, sex, what
> I put my hands in, how it was to touch her,
> like me running down to be the first to meet
> enter, and be taken by the creek in the early morning. (Pratt 1990, 91)

The analogy between lesbian sex and a morning swim in the creek not only presents homoerotic desire as natural, unstoppable, and attractive as clear, fresh water welling up from the ground, it also recasts the creek itself as an earlier lesbian lover whom the speaker "enters" and is "taken by," thus queering nature by figuring this interaction between human and natural world as homosexual rather than the standard heterosexual relationship assumed within much nature writing.

All of the ways in which Pratt queers nature come together within the complex title poem, "Crime Against Nature," one section of which was discussed above. In section five of this poem, Pratt's speaker describes a river outing with her sons, using this event as the basis to speculate about homophobic fears of lesbian mothering and its supposedly dangerous, but actually liberatory, effects upon her sons. In this poem, nature is once again represented as that in-between space of free self-exploration, and as an example of the contradiction and complexity that defy the limited illogic of the sodomy laws:

Last time we were together we went down to the river,
the boys and I, wading.   In the rocks they saw a yellow-
striped snake, with a silver fish crossways in its mouth,
just another one of the beautiful terrors of nature,
how one thing can turn into another without warning

When I open my mouth, some people hear snakes slide
out, whispering, to poison my sons' lives.   Some fear
I'll turn them into queers, into women . . .

Some fear I've crossed over into capable power
and I'm taking my children with me.   My body a snaky
rope, with its twirl, loop, spin, falling escape,
falling, altered, woman to man and back again, animal
to human: And what are the implications for the political
system of boy children who watched me like a magic
trick, like I had a key to the locked-room mystery?
(Will they lose all respect for national boundaries,
their father, science, or private property?) (Pratt 1990, 119)

Once again, the river serves as site where lesbian mother and sons may be reunited, where they encounter natural phenomena that symbolically subvert the fixed social order that criminalizes homoeroticism: the striped snake mouthing the crossways fish is an image of sudden, unexpected change, of crossing and contradiction, of the physical transformation that pervades the natural order, and yet, ironically, it is just this sort of dynamic alteration and growth that the restrictive sexual laws and social norms strive to prevent—fearing them as dangerous processes because they entail change and risk.

Pratt's speaker understands that others view her as an agent of such metamorphosis, and that they fear her as they would the snake, as something ominous to the rigid existing order, a woman who refuses to stay within the boundaries of the heteropatriarchal laws, and instead transgresses the supposedly fixed binarisms of hierarchical social systems, such as man/woman, animal/human, showing them to be cultural creations rather than natural facts. While others of the ilk of Anita Bryant and her followers fear how this might adversely affect her sons, Pratt's speaker sees the liberating potential of her influence upon them. The boys' acceptance of the exigencies of the natural world and the complexities of lesbian mothering might undermine their allegiance to the political system that interweaves patriarchy, nationalism, capitalism, and science, and that depends upon principles such as rigid divisions, ownership, control, and objectivity—principles that the speaker and the snake defy. In this segment and throughout the entire volume, Pratt emphasizes the interconnectedness between our stance toward nature and the operations of our culture, exposing the way ideas of nature have been used to police sexuality and other aspects of social identity, and suggesting that more inclusive perceptions and mobile images of nature are crucial to freer, more egalitarian and unfixed and complex social formations.

Perhaps even Senator Jesse Helms negatively realized the force of Pratt's oppositional representations of lesbian dislocation and desire in *Crime Against Nature,* when in 1990 he asked the National Endowment of the Arts to rescind grants to Minnie Bruce Pratt and two other lesbian poets, on the grounds that their writings about lesbianism were inherently obscene. Pratt had dared to challenge the premises of the sodomy statutes and to oppositionally inscribe lesbian desires in the context of nature, and Helms reacted by once again censoring creative rendering of homosexual acts that he considered too blasphemous to put into words. Pratt comments on her response to Helms's attack upon *Crime Against Nature:*

> I lived through punishment for my rejection of male authority over my life and my children; lived on to reclaim my relationship with my sons, and to write poetry about those years of struggle and triumph; lived to see my work and that of others create some widening in the public space where we could live as lesbian and gay people. And then, ironically, or inevitably, I watched that space, and my art, threatened by censorship forces led by a senator from North Carolina, Jesse Helms. . . . My disbelief at Helms' attack came in part because I had written the very poems he pointed at exactly to answer and turn inside out such lying logic. I wondered with some desperation if I were going to have to write the poems *all over again*? How could I

say, more irrefutably, that which I had already said in the truthful complexity of poetry? (Pratt 1991, 231–32)

Pratt's writing had helped create a "public space where we could live as lesbian and gay people" by "turning inside out the lying logic" of the very crime-against-nature ideology that Helms was intent on reinstating. Despite Helms's attack, Pratt remained committed to doing this work of writing toward lesbian/gay reclamation of social/natural environments of the nation. She describes this work as

[t]he struggle for a country where lesbians and gay men are not despised for having sex for pleasure, nonprocreative, "nonreproductive" sex. I have learned in this struggle that there is no "free" speech: we pay, in money or blood, time or pain, to assert our human dignity, to assert that we are even human. The power of our art, the making of a blood-and-bones representation of our lives, is the triumph of our imagination in a world that does not want us to believe that we *can* live, here, now, for ourselves. (Pratt 1991, 234)

Adrienne Rich's *Your Native Land, Your Life* and Minnie Bruce Pratt's *Crime Against Nature* exhibit the "triumph of (their) imagination" over the constricted landscape that crime-against-nature ideologies had imposed on homosexuals. By directly challenging the hostile use of agricultural analogies to stigmatize same-sex desire, their poetry goes to the root of centuries of heterosexist persecution and discrimination; writing lesbian desire into the landscape and using positive images of nature as emblems of lesbian desire, Rich and Pratt create a strategic oppositional alliance of same-sex desire with nature that counters centuries of dislocation and silencing. This is not a blind or innocent use of nature, but a canny form of talking back that overturns the foundation of Pauline doctrine and challenges the ways that dominant ideas about the natural world have grounded societal restrictions. Rich's and Pratt's poetry demonstrates the power of queering nature, making obvious the potency of our ideas about nature and our use of naturalization, for ill or for good, and the very real effects of such discourses on our social/sexual identities and relationships with natural environments. Although more than a decade after Rich and Pratt's publications on this topic the U.S. crime-against-nature statutes that criminalized homosexuality were overturned by the 2003 *Lawrence v. Texas* Supreme Court decision, many people continue to view homosexuality as unnatural and immoral and wish to drive gays and lesbians out of rural environments, as Katie Hogan's chapter in this volume on Ballot

Measure 9 in Oregon attests. Political and legal battles over the "nature" of desire and sexuality still rage in current conflicts over gay marriage, gay adoption, and abortion rights, and right-wing fundamentalists still use the language of natural/unnatural sex to curtail sexual freedoms. Rich and Pratt demonstrate the value of reclaiming the discourse of nature and staking another claim to social/natural environments as an aspect of and means to sexual justice. In so doing, they open a path for lesbians and gays to join forces with other marginalized communities whose relationships to their physical environments have also been jeopardized by national policies that grant dominant populations access to natural resources and nontoxic spaces and sacrifice other communities for the profit of those in power. By queering nature, Rich and Pratt reimagine anOther claim to native land.

NOTES

The lines from "Yom Kippur 1984," Poem 3 of "Contradictions: Tracking Poems," Poem 21 of "Contradictions: Tracking Poems," and Poem 28 of "Contradictions: Tracking Poems" are from *Your Native Land, Your Life: Poems* by Adrienne Rich. Copyright © 1986 by Adrienne Rich. Used by permission of the author and W. W. Norton & Company, Inc.

The lines from "No Place," "The Place Lost and Gone, the Place Found," "Crime Against Nature," and "Dreaming a Few Minutes in a Different Element" are from *Crime Against Nature* by Minnie Bruce Pratt, Ithaca, N.Y.: Firebrand Books, 1990. Permission for use generously granted by the author.

1. Adrienne Rich notes in her essay "Invisibility in Academe" that the death penalty was prescribed for lesbians in 1656 in New Haven, Conn. See Rich (1986a).

2. For pertinent discussions of the historical consequences of the construction of homosexuality as unnatural, see Greta Gaard (1997), and Gayle S. Rubin (1993).

3. For discussion of contemporary queer reactions against nature as foundation for sexual identities see, for example, Diane Chisholm's critique of Lee Edelman's queer manifesto *No Future* in her chapter in this volume. For discussion of previous rejections of nature as pertinent to sexual identity, see Lilian Faderman (1991), and Jonathan Katz (1976). For an example of postmodern rejection of nature as a foundational category for identity, see Judith Butler (1990).

4. Bonnie Zimmerman (1990) traces a similar tendency in fiction by a number of lesbian novelists writing in the second half of the twentieth century. Zimmerman argues that such novelists created a "green world" where lesbian romantic love was renaturalized through its pastoral location and where women were safe to engage in same-sex love, beyond the boundaries of the homophobic society. Catriona Sandilands's (2004) study of lesbian land communities in Oregon analyzes the way that the women's relationships with each other and with the land itself challenged heteropatriarchal social and ecological relations and offered an alternative lesbian ecology.

5. Rich and Pratt both identified themselves as lesbian feminist poets at the time that they wrote the volumes of poetry that I am discussing. While I am aware that a number of radical lesbians and older lesbians reject the term "queer," since they believe that it erases the particularity of lesbian oppression and identity by lumping all sexually diverse persons into one indistinct category that takes no account of gender oppression, both Rich and Pratt do use the term "queer" in their writings. They also emphasize the specificity of lesbianism, and the bulk of the poems that I discuss present lesbian speakers and experiences in particular. I refer to Rich and Pratt's writings as lesbian texts, but I do not believe I do any disservice to Rich and Pratt's self-identifications and positions when I argue that they are queering nature in these volumes of poetry.

6. Rich uses the term "native land" loosely, to include all who inhabit a nation, whether they are born there, or immigrant. She is actually often writing about immigrants, counter to nativist ideologies that would marginalize immigrants. I use "native land" in this paper in the same spirit, to include all inhabitants of a nation.

7. T. V. Reed (2002) discusses Adrienne Rich as an environmental justice poet who addresses the intersections of social/environmental issues in the poem "Trying to Talk with a Man."

8. In June of 1980 Julianne Williams and Lollie Winans were murdered during a camping trip to the Shenandoah National Park in Virginia. Their throats were slashed. For a feminist response to this incident and the attempts to have it investigated as a hate crime, see Karla Mantilla (1996). In 1988, while making love in their campsite along the Appalachian Trail in Furnace State Park, Pennsylvania, Rebecca Wright was murdered and her partner Claudia Brenner was also shot multiple times by Stephen Ray Carr. For Brenner's account of this event, see Claudia Brenner with Hannah Ashley (1995). In October 1998, gay college student Matthew Shepard was murdered by being severely beaten by Russell Henderson and Aaron McKinney and left tied to a fence outside of Laramie in rural Wyoming.

9. Gilmore and Aldrich (1992) focus upon the ways that Pratt rewrites the concept of home. They argue that "deprived of the 'natural' relations with her children, her story of home and family can only be inverted—the story of how forced separation has made her relationship with her sons 'unnatural,' conducted as it is on the premise of homewrecking. . . . Excluded, or more correctly, outlawed from the social interiors of home, Pratt meets her sons on the outside, frequently on river banks" (40).

REFERENCES

Adamson, Joni. 2001. *American Indian Literature, Environmental Justice, and Ecocriticism: The Middle Place.* Tucson: University of Arizona Press.

Brenner, Claudia, with Hannah Ashley. 1995. *Eight Bullets: Surviving Anti-Gay Violence.* Ithaca, N.Y.: Firebrand Books.

Bryant, Anita. 1977. Save Our Children, Campaign Media Appearance. Northwest Baptist Church (March).

Bullough, Vern, and Bonnie Bullough. 1977. *Sin, Sickness, and Sanity: A History of Sexual Attitudes.* New York: New American Library.

Butler, Judith. 1990. *Gender Trouble: Feminism and the Subversion of Identity.* New York: Routledge.

Evans, Mei Mei. 2002. "'Nature' and Environmental Justice." In *The Environmental Justice Reader*, ed. J. Adamson, M. Evans, and R. Stein, 181–93. Tucson: University of Arizona Press.

Faderman, Lilian. 1991. *Odd Girls and Twilight Lovers: A History of Lesbian Life in Twentieth-Century America*. New York: Columbia University Press.

Gaard, Greta. 1997. "Toward a Queer Ecofeminism." *Hypatia* 12.1 (Winter): 114–37.

Gilmore, Leigh, and Marcia Aldrich. 1992. "Writing Home: 'Home' and Lesbian Representation in Minnie Bruce Pratt." *Genre* 25 (Spring): 25–46.

Hunt, V. 1997. "An Interview with Minnie Bruce Pratt." *Southern Quarterly* 13.3 (Spring): 99.

Katz, Jonathan, ed. 1976. *Gay American History: Lesbians and Gay Men in the U.S.A.* New York: Crowell.

Mantilla, Karla. 1996. "Murder on the Appalachian Trail." *Off Our Backs*, July. http://findarticles.com/p/articles/mi_qu3693/is_199607/ai_n8749751/print.

Mariner, Joanna. 2004. "The Beauty Queen of Bigotry: Anita Bryant's Legacy." *Counterpunch*, February 6. http://counterpunch.org/mariner02062004.html.

Moral Majority Timeline. http://www.moralmajority.us/index2.php?option+com.

Pratt, Minnie Bruce. 1990. *Crime against Nature*. Ithaca, N.Y.: Firebrand.

———. 1991. *Rebellion: Essays 1980–1991*. Ithaca, N.Y.: Firebrand.

Reed, T. V. 2002. "Toward an Environmental Justice Ecocriticism." In *The Environmental Justice Reader: Politics, Poetics, and Pedagogy*, ed. J. Adamson, M. Evans, and R. Stein, 145–62. Tucson: University of Arizona Press.

Rich, Adrienne. 1986a. *Blood, Bread, and Poetry: Selected Prose, 1979–1985*. New York: Norton.

———. 1986b. *Your Native Land, Your Life: Poems*. New York: W. W. Norton.

Rubin, Gayle S. 1993. "Thinking Sex: Notes for a Radical Theory of the Politics of Sexuality." In *The Lesbian and Gay Studies Reader*, ed. H. Abelove, M. Barale, and D. Halperin, 3–44. New York: Routledge.

Sandilands, Catriona. 1994. "Lavender's Green? Some Thoughts on Queer(y)ing Environmental Politics." *Undercurrents* 6.1: 20–24.

———. 2004. "Sexual Politics and Environmental Justice: Lesbian Separatists in Rural Oregon." In *New Perspectives on Environmental Justice: Gender, Sexuality, and Activism*, ed. R. Stein, 109–26. New Brunswick, N.J.: Rutgers University Press.

Stein, Rachel. 2000. "'To Make the Visible World Your Conscience': Adrienne Rich as Revolutionary Nature Writer." In *Reading under the Sign of Nature: New Essays in Ecocriticism*, ed. J. Tallmadge and H. Harrington, 198–207. Salt Lake City: University of Utah Press.

———. 2004. *New Perspectives on Environmental Justice: Gender, Sexuality and Activism*. New Brunswick, N.J.: Rutgers University Press.

Townsley, Ben. 2005. "Pope: Fighting Gay Marriage Is a Priority." Gay.com, January 11. http://www.gay.com/content/tools/print.html.

Zimmerman, Bonnie. 1990. *The Safe Sea of Women: Lesbian Fiction 1969–1989*. Boston, Mass.: Beacon Press.

CHAPTER 11

"fucking close to water": Queering the Production of the Nation

BRUCE ERICKSON

Although I have been for the last twenty years, credited with the quote you use, "A Canadian is someone who knows how to make love in a canoe," it is not actually my own—at least I don't think so.

—Pierre Berton

And somewhere in that self-consciousness, which knows it is fundamentally incompatible with itself, the nation acknowledges that its strategies of self-consciousness are inadequate to their task, and it silently confesses that its existence is also a crime.

—Chris Bracken

Failure

In order to start with honesty, I should inform the reader that my title, and my subject, is an absolute cliché for a novel take on the canoe in Canada. One of the first collections on canoeing in Canada (Raffan and Horwood 1988) contained two articles that started with the proposition, credited to Pierre Berton, that, "a Canadian is one who can make love in a canoe" (Raffan 1999b, 255). Bruce Hodgins (1988), in his contribution to the anthology, reaffirms Berton's statement by saying that "making love in a canoe is the most Canadian act that two people can do" (45). Philip Chester adds a qualifier, stating, "while this may or may not be true, I would add that, unlike his American cousin, the true Canadian knows enough to take out the centre thwart" (1988, 93). The list of authors who use this quotable quote as an introduction to canoeing in Canada is enough to leave the phrase behind (Benidickson 1997, Chester 1988, Hodgins 1988, Raffan 1999a, Raffan 1999b) and the "bad joke" twist that

I have added is less than heroic, taken from a Monty Python sketch as it is. However, there is, I believe, more to this—something highlighted by my use of a joke in the title, somewhat along the lines of flogging a dead horse—a talent for making jokes useful even after they have failed. Indeed, my suggestion is that it is failure itself that is captured so effectively by the statement attributed to Pierre Berton.

If we continue to follow the use of the equation in Canadian canoeing discourses, we find that it is almost always paired with failure. Raffan, in the prologue to his book on the canoe in Canadian culture, says that his failure is in finding a place in his book for all of the information he collected. One such piece of knowledge is that "it is impossible to make Love in a canoe because this small Saskatchewan town is not on a navigable waterway" (Raffan 1999a, xiii). Ferguson also points to the failure: "Pierre Berton once defined a Canadian as 'someone who knows how to make love in a canoe.' But John Robert Colombo was quick to correct him: 'A Canadian is someone who *thinks* he knows how to make love in a canoe'" (Ferguson 1997, 158). Benidickson is more methodical in his approach to contemplating the failure:

> One of the more intriguing examples of collaborative canoe management must centre on the author Pierre Berton's proposition that a Canadian is someone who knows how to make love in a canoe (not illustrated). The hypothesis is difficult to substantiate on the basis of conventional research methodology. According to survey results from the late 1980's, only 18 per cent of the population indicated that they had engaged in sex in moving vehicle "such as a car, boat, train or bus." (1997, 13)

Benidickson proceeds in the next two pages to examine the failure of different historical and fictional characters to succeed in the act. At the end of his book he returns to the action, only to dismiss it through a quotation from a Calgary-based journalist: "'Canadians do make love in a canoe, but ... this is not considered romantic outside of Shawinigan'" (Lee, quoted in Benidickson 1997, 255).[1] Raffan, not satisfied with declaring the act impossible due to geography, returns to the subject in an article, and has the final word on the failure of the statement:

> In an attempt to settle the attribution of this quote once and for all, I wrote to Pierre Berton to ask when and where he made this quip. In a letter dated 7 March 1996, he replied: "Although I have been for

the last twenty years, credited with the quote you use, 'A Canadian is someone who knows how to make love in a canoe,' it is not actually my own—at least I don't think so, it's been so long. It seems to me I saw it somewhere else and used it with attribution, but the attribution has long since been lost and I'm tired of telling people I didn't actually think of it. So I'm afraid I can't help you much. I notice I'm even in the Canadian Book of Quotations as having said that; so at this late stage it's difficult for me to say I didn't. Maybe I did, but I don't think so." (1999b, 255)

The failure of the act, and the failure of attribution, is present within these texts, and try as they might, nowhere is the problem of failure solved.

Given the popularity of the canoe as a symbol of the Canadian nation—it adorns the twenty-dollar bill, sits in the Canadian Embassy in Washington, has been an official gift from the state to foreign dignitaries, and is part of a multimillion-dollar nature tourism industry in Canada—it is this failure, and the iteration and action surrounding the failure, that spurs me to return to this topic, my cliché, one more time and find out the investment behind such a failed signification. Canadian nationalism has a long history of failures,[2] and as Kieran Keohane (1997) argues, this is often seen as part of the identity of Canadians, where the inability to define oneself acts as a form of identification. Yet, the failure of nationalism is not so much out of the lack of iteration of national identity, but may have something more to do with the structure of nationalism. As Homi Bhabha (1994) reminds us, the construction of nationalism requires a narration of national identity that attempts to override the experiences of the national citizens. There will always be a gap between the ideal image of the nation and the actual performance of the nation in the lives of the subjects within the nation, and the dissemination of nationalism occurs in the processes by which that gap is overcome (Bhabha 1994). Canadian failures mandate a continual interruption into the lives of the subjects living inside the nation, such that our lives are constantly concerned with the achievement of the national dream (for a similar analysis in terms of multiculturalism in Canada, see Day 2002). The observation of a failure in the present allows for a continual investment by the nation in the future, such that we are always looking to the time when the nation will have been.

The failure of canoe-sex within Canadian nationalism suggests a failure that connects sexuality, nature, and race to the future existence of the state. In my exploration of these connections, I move through three modes of understanding Berton's statement: the modes of Nation, Land, and Possibility. It is these modes that illustrate the discursive work that relates leisure, landscape, sexuality, and canoeing to the production of the nation. Starting with the question of the investment in nationalism, I take up Michel Foucault's notion of biopower to show how the construction of identity in modern capitalism is intimately a part of the production of capitalism. Identity, specifically national identity, is made into an active part of the biopolitical frame of the nation, such that identity becomes another form of labor that is focused upon normalizing and controlling bodies and pleasures. As Foucault reminds us, sexuality stands at the heart of modern power, and its discourse arose along with imperialism and the power of the modern nation-state. In Canada, such a consideration of sexuality is intimately connected, as a part of the imperial project of nation building, to ideas of race and citizenship.

From a consideration of biopower I move into an examination of the construction of the discourse of land within canoeing. The myth of the canoe in Canada celebrates an image of landscape as the justification for the establishment of the nation. This discourse argues that prior to its inception, Canada existed in the land itself and it was up to European subjects, through the use of the canoe, an indigenous cultural artifact made into a tool of colonization, to extract the nation from the landscape. This myth establishes canoeing under the banner of the nation as part of the biopolitical frame that relies upon both race and sexuality to establish a naturalized colonial nation-state. My final section, on Possibility, returns to Berton's claim and suggests some possibilities for queering the production of the nation through the landscape of the canoe. In the modern world, our quest for identity is inherently productive, as late capitalism relies upon the desires of identity to fuel patterns of consumption. My paper concludes with ways that we could reconceptualize the pleasures of canoeing outside of the desire for identity, outside of the demands of the nation. Queering in this frame, as Shannon Winnubst (2006) suggests, means moving outside the frame of history that is necessary for the biopolitics of utility to grab hold of identity. The nation relies upon the linear movement of history to deny the ultimate failure that it holds at the moment of inception, as the pedagogical work of history hides the cracks in the myth of the nation itself. Outlining the violent history of sex in the name of landscape (like the history of residential school abuse) as well as the subversive ecstatic forms of erotic landscapes (like the Lesbian National Park Rangers[3]), we can glimpse a view of the Queer landscape that could have been.

Nation

> Put another way, nations require particular sentiments of attach-
> ment, ones that often rest at least in part on the erotic.
> —Steven Maynard

Steven Maynard's (2001) statement that sentiments of nationalism require a form of attachment that is often operated through the erotic, while written about hockey, comes close to describing the ideal relationship between the canoeist and the nation in Canada. If mobilized properly, the attachment is generated at the level of landscape, creating powerful feelings for spaces of wilderness and the people that are in it, and then generalized outward to the state and myth that protects the land of canoeing. While many canoeists may agree with the connection between activity and nation (and this sentiment is a large part of the contemporary writing on canoeing in Canada, see Jennings 1999, Raffan 1999a, Whipper 1988), the assumption of an erotic attachment to nation may come as a surprise. Indeed, the ideal relationship of connection to landscape held by the canoe, as I will show, is about hiding the actual form of the relationship with the landscape, whether racist colonialism or the production of heterosexuality, to accomplish a fetishizing of the leisured, supposed innocent connection to the land of the new world.

Take, as I often insist when talking about the canoe in North America, the story of Columbus, which is the starting point of this myth if there ever needs to be one. As Anne McClintock clearly shows, Columbus's image of the new world was eroticized from the start:

> In 1492, Christopher Columbus, blundering about the Caribbean in search of India, wrote home to say that the ancient mariners had erred thinking the earth was round. Rather, he said, it was shaped like a woman's breast, with a protuberance upon its summit in the unmistakable shape of a nipple—toward which he was slowly sailing. (1995, 21)

Similarly, Jan van der Straet famously painted the founding of America as a land that is presented to Vespucci in the form of an inviting naked woman, to be rendered by the flag and finally take his name (McClintock 1995, 25). Europeans have often eroticized the land of America from the moment of its naming and "discovery," yet the common interpretation of this myth as a form of *amor patriae* hides the heterosexuality implicit within such genealogies. By normalizing the erotics held within landscape, the images of nature in modern nation building attempt to naturalize the subject position held within the project of nationalism.

Despite the popularity of the statement, the ability to have sex in a canoe, which is less categorically "Canadian" than exotic and slightly ironic, is not an exclusive club, nor is it particularly inclusive. The ironic claim to identity makes explicit the repetitive performance of recognizable activities that structure an identity, and through this process calls into question the degree of naturalness that identity holds. As Jay Prosser explains, this natural sense is a result of the performance; speaking in terms of sexuality, he states "It is not that heterosexuality is natural and queer denaturalizing; rather, heterosexuality is naturalizing, concealing the masquerade of the natural that queer makes manifest" (1998, 44). This naturalization has productive effects in the material world, effects that are caused by more than a simple action (for instance, canoeing). For Judith Butler, "performativity must be understood not as a singular or deliberate 'act,' but, rather, as the reiterative and citational practice by which discourse produces the effects that it names" (1993, 2). These effects are found in what has become natural. Thus in the claim to having sex in a canoe, the relationship between the heterosexual image of the nation and the landscape in which the performances take place is naturalized. The failure of the performance, illustrated by the repetition of the ways that sex does not happen in canoes in Canada, makes the quotable quote work at the level of metaphor. As such, it is not the mere ability to canoe, or even to have sex in a canoe, that embodies Canadian-ness, but rather the reiteration of desire to canoe in Canada—a desire for Canadian canoeing—that embodies the Canadian-ness expressed through the canoe. This desire, naturalized through a history of landscape, privileges heterosexual white desire over any different, non-national, or perverse forms of canoeing pleasure. Before I move to show the reduction of the landscape in the specific myth of the canoe, I want to take some time to explain the conflation of sexuality and landscape within the colonial imaginary that has become Canadian nationalism.

The end of Michel Foucault's *History of Sexuality,* volume 1, has become, as David Halperin and Ladelle McWhorter show, a vital text in radical queer politics, such that it is hard to practice queer theory without having read it (Halperin 1995; McWhorter 1999). For both Halperin and McWhorter, one of the strengths of Foucault's reading of sexuality in modern life is that whatever one's place within discourses of sexuality, one is always just that, placed within discourses of sexuality. "There was no outside to the sexual identification system, no place for me to be a human being without any sexual identity at all" (McWhorter 1999, 100). The experience of living within the realm of sexuality, while just as real for those who identified successfully as heterosexual, was made manifest for anyone attempting to live outside of the heterosexual label. Gay men, lesbians, bisexuals and, as McWhorter illustrates, people outside of identification were always exposed to the fact that sexuality is not about the truth of the matter, but about the power of truth. The expansion of power into the minute folds of sexuality, argued Foucault, takes place in the cooperation between two regimes of power. First, disciplinary power focused upon the control of individual bodies, increasing capabilities to fuel efficiency, aligning mechanic repetitions toward efficiency. Second was a politics that focused upon the control of populations, what Foucault described as the "species body" (1978, 139). The regulatory controls of the population focused upon the reproduction of life, the control of birth and death in the larger realm of society. The combination of the regulatory and disciplinary powers produced a mode of biopower that sought to "invest life through and through" (ibid.). Foucault's articulation of the myth of the repressive hypothesis, that Victorian society and its legacy was sexually repressed, flows from this understanding of biopower: that sexuality was so strictly policed is not a sign of repression, or lack of sexuality, but rather shows an intensification in the deployment of sexuality within a newly developing regime of biopower. As Foucault explains, sexuality fits at the axes of the two forms of power: "On the one hand it was tied to the disciplines of the body: the harnessing, intensification, and distribution of forces, the adjustment and economy of energies. On the other hand, it was applied to the regulations of populations, through all the far-reaching effects of its activities" (145).

The role that sexuality plays within the development of biopower shows how the politics of the species body was fulfilling a demand brought upon by the emergent capitalist economic system. Capitalism "would not have been possible without the controlled insertion of bodies into the machinery of production to economic processes" (Foucault 1978, 141). The ability to manipulate bodies in such a way that they could endure the work regime of the factory and office was facilitated by the creation of bodies and "the joining of the growth of human groups to the expansion of productive forces and the differential allocation of profit" (141). The deployment of sexuality was not simply because of a repressive morality of the prevailing classes, but rather the repressive morality of the prevailing classes fulfilled a utility within the economic system of capitalism. It is biopower, and the conditions of capitalism that developed along with it, that Foucault credits with the "entry of life into history" (141). The dual-pronged approach of biopower is bent upon taking control of life, of making life itself fit within the utility of its service. History, the present, and the future become areas of production that are amenable to modes of power. Michael Hardt and Antonio Negri illustrate the consequences of the development of biopower in the relation between life and production: "The relationship between production and life has thus been altered such that it is now completely inverted with respect to how the discipline of political economy understands it. Life is no longer produced in cycles of reproduction that are subordinated to the working day; on the contrary, life is what infuses and dominates all production" (2000, 365). Life becomes the reproduction of production, not merely through biological production of more workers, but by continual work in the realm of the commodity. Sexual identity, as Foucault shows, is made to be part of that production, an argument only proven more and more correct by the increasing power of the "pink" dollar under capitalism.

It is easy to assume that the moral of *The History of Sexuality*, volume 1, pertains to the regulation of sexual identity above all else. However, as Ann Laura Stoler illustrates, the connection between race and sexuality is made explicit in the last sections of the book, and, as she clearly points out, Foucault's theory of modern bourgeois identity is only enhanced by reading sexuality through the colonial scene. Doing such a reading connects our understanding of sexual identity and capitalism as being tacitly coded by race, and by extension, nation. Stoler (2002) extends the reading of biopower through Foucault's 1976 lectures on race, recently published in English as *Society Must Be Defended*. By elaborating on Foucault's notion of state racism, where the hierarchies of racial classification work through a normalizing power entrenched within statist institutions, Stoler argues that racism is not "an aberrant, pathological development of state authority in crisis but a fundamental 'indispensable' technology of rule— as biopower's operating mechanism" (Stoler 2002, 159). The same logistics that operated through a deployment of sexuality, in terms of the regulation of bodies and the species body, occur at the level of race, specifically as a part of a national dream.

In Canada, the question of race is central to understanding the role of landscape in national imagery. As I will show, race anchors a distinction in the use of the land that justifies the colonial existence of the nation-state. It was the productive use of the land in North America that allowed European subjects to justify their acquisition of all the fertile and useful land occupied by First Nations peoples. Perhaps most famous proponent of this view is John Locke, but Chris Bracken (1997) provides a Canadian. Gilbert Sproat used such an argument for the possession of Aht land on Vancouver Island. "Sproat gives himself the right to seize 'the soil' around Alberni because the Aht do not 'use' it *and* because 'their general behavior as a nation' annuls their claim to it. Labor for Sproat, is more than the source of the right to private property. It is a sign of what he considers a superior culture—his own" (Bracken 1997, 21, original emphasis). The failure of the race allowed for, as Stoler (2002) shows in the East Indies, the deployment of sexuality to work in tandem with the techniques of state racism such that populations and bodies, of both the colonized and the colonizer, were subject to the regulations of race and sexuality.

The reservation system seems to be the most obvious conflation of sexuality, race, and landscape in Canada. By establishing a space in which to monitor the reproduction (and in many cases, the hoped-for death; see Francis 1992 and Bracken 1997) of First Nations communities, the Canadian government looked to invest in the life of First Nations through and through. Census data, marriage regulations, and identity papers were utilized to fence in populations that stood in the way of the general claim of the state to the landscape. But reserves are only the most entrenched mingling of sexuality and race in the Canadian landscape. Indeed, Gary Kinsman states unequivocally, "[a] crucial part of the subjugation of . . . Native peoples was the destruction of their erotic, gender and social life and the imposition of European social and sexual organization. . . . This story of extreme cultural, social, and physical violence lies at the root of the Canadian state" (Kinsman 1996, 92). As Stoler argues, in considering the deployment of sexuality in western states, it is necessary to follow a "circuitous imperial route" (1995, 7) and illustrate how modern notions of national subjectivity are based upon the prohibitions and regulations of colonial sexuality.

Land

Consider . . . the following rather imperfect syllogism:
"where is here?"
"We're here, we're queer, get used to it!"
"Here is queer."
—Peter Dickinson

In Canada, the first official contact between Europeans and what we now call the canoe happened with Jacques Cartier in the Gulf of St. Lawrence. The boats he encountered on the shores of the Bay of Chaleur were Mi'kmaq *gwitnn*, birchbark boats designed for both ocean and river travel. As with others of the multitude of indigenous designs that have been classified under the label of "canoe,"[4] the form of the *gwitnn* is directly related to Mi'kmaq interpretations of their geography. Cartier, it is said, saw the value of the canoe to the colonial endeavor: "To go inland into Canada, Cartier realized that he needed the boat derived of the landscape realities of the new world. Cartier realized he needed a canoe" (Raffan 1999a, 24). The canoe's first European contact and use in Canada, then, was a monetary encounter, a desire for transportation that would present the bounty of the land to the traveler (Jennings 2002b). John Jennings, a canoe historian, performing a pedagogical moment for the canoe in Canada, constructs this history as one that differed from the previous encounters of Europe with the limit of itself: "While it lasted, the canoe frontier set itself apart from all the others in the western world . . . the frontier of the canoe did not covet the land, only its bounty" (29). According to Jennings, the French style of colonial relations in North America was unique because of the respect and partnership with Native peoples, not just a desire to acquire land and labor. This French style "had partly to do with an acceptance of Native culture. It was also based on the unique social dynamics of the canoe" (Jennings 2002b, 30). These unique social dynamics, conceived through the freshwater river system of the area to which the canoe was the answer, forced diplomacy between the two groups (a diplomacy that Jennings credits to the French). It is this relationship, for Jennings and others, that allows Canada to become a unique nation in the future. The canoe frontier becomes a frontier of respect that foreshadows Canada's unique leadership as a multicultural nation. "The officials of New France established policies of racial tolerance and respect on this frontier that were later adopted by the English and Scottish traders of the Hudson's Bay and North West companies and eventually by the North West Mounted Police, when they brought law and order to the Plains region of the new Canadian state" (Jennings 2002b, 32).[5] In Jennings's history, the economic function of the canoe takes a back seat to the social function of producing a European state that is founded upon racial tolerance and a respect for diversity.

Jennings's assertion that the relations among French, English, and First Nations peoples in what was to become Canada were indicative of the nation that was to be works as a normalizing power in two ways. First, it relates a benevolent view of the current nation-state and idealizes the application and vision of the current policy of multiculturalism. One need not look far for critiques of Canada's multiculturalism as a policy that is not effective in its attempt to create "racial and ethnic harmony and cross-cultural understanding" (Government of Canada 2009). For example, Himani Bannerji argues that the language of diversity in official multiculturalism ignores the power relationships of the nation. Instead, it is a mode of presenting difference in relation to the pre-existing white Canadian identity, making the language of diversity "a coping mechanism for dealing with an actually conflicting heterogeneity, seeking to incorporate it into an ideological binary which is predicated upon the existence of a homogenous national, that is, a Canadian cultural self with its multiple and different others" (Bannerji 2000, 37). Richard Day (2002), similarly, illustrates how this discourse of managing diversity demands that diversity itself is always seen as a problem.

Second, and perhaps more deleterious, is the way such a view of history establishes a certain nation subject as the natural outcome of the land of the nation, as it was explored by the canoe. If a yet to be established policy of multiculturalism was the modus operandi of the new world, then the nation that was established, after continual conflict (and, it should be added, persistent conflict to this day), gets naturalized through the interactions between nature, citizen, and activity. Yet these are not truly the only experiences of landscape in Canada. As Peter Dickinson suggests, the accounts of "here" in Canada extend beyond the singular vision of the land. In response to Northrop Frye's question that haunts Canadian identity, "where is here?" Dickinson responds, "here is queer" (1999, 3). He elaborates: "this is not to say that 'here' is only or ever 'queer,' nor that resistance to a heteronormative nationalism is always or exclusively homosexual; what . . . this . . . does suggest, however, is that 'queer,' as a . . . category of an almost inevitably definitional elasticity, one whose inventory of sexual meanings has yet to be exhausted, challenges and upsets certain received national orthodoxies" (5). In queering "here," Dickinson wants to illustrate that the question of the land, as it becomes normalized, regulates a plurality of encounters, including sexual encounters, that form our understanding of landscape. The myth of the canoe, I suggest, is one such mode of regulation that ties a normalized view of the land to a privileged national subjectivity.

In the discourse of the canoe in Canada, as a "symbol unique to Canada," (Jennings 1999, 1), which reworks essentialized aspects of indigenous cultures into a symbol of national health and success, the material being of the canoe is often placed ahead of the construction of the nation. For example, Jennings describes the relationship between the canoe and Canada: "To paraphrase somewhat the words of Bill Mason, one of Canada's greatest paddlers: God first created the canoe and then thought up the ideal country to go with it. Thus did Canada come into being" (ibid.).

The mythological creation of Canada (following Mason's Christian beliefs) is also related to the way the canoe is seen as a "gift" from Aboriginal people to the European settlers.[6] For Jennings, "The canoe is perhaps one of the greatest gifts of the Native Peoples to later cultures" (1999, 3). Moreover, from this gift, the canoe has become the historical reason for the being of Canada; "Canada is not an artificial creation; she exists, not in spite of history, but because of it. The essential shape of Canada was determined, above all, by canoe exploration and the fur trade" (6). The nation becomes, because of the exploration by canoe, a unique entity in a sea of countries and identities, and the canoe is the guard that maintains the boundary of that identity.

This connection to the land is promoted as unique to Canada, something that might be equaled in the symbol of the cowboy to the American West (Jennings 1999). However, in the discourse of the canoe as national subject, the cowboy is less authentic because it is viewed as a Western import, unlike the Aboriginal canoe. The uniqueness of the canoe in Canada is further substantiated by its use in colonization, a use not lost in many writings on the canoe. As Jennings shows, unlike canoes in other parts of the world, from Japan to the Congo, "only in North America did the bark canoe reach near perfection and play an important role in the development of later European craft" (2002a, 20). For even though canoe-like boats, in some form or another, have existed on all six inhabited continents (and were one of the earliest links between them), the canoe in Canada, according to the national myth, has achieved perfection, and has thus brought forth a nation to invoke its symbolic potential. Because it is the specific nation that flows out of this connection, it is important to make the note that the perfect canoe is made perfect only by its ability to be incorporated into European expansion. While Jennings compares the North American birchbark canoe to canoes from the Amur Valley in Manchuria, and follows canoe historian Tappan Adney in describing the similarities between such a canoe and ones found in the British Columbia interior, he maintains that the canoe of the Amur Valley, "had no continuing historical importance" (2002a, 20). The perfection of the bark canoes of North America, opposed to the similar craft in Asia, is because the vehicle was adopted by European paddlers.

The connection of the land to the canoe as a discourse of inevitability illustrates the privileging of the European subject as the natural inheritor (indeed, the rightful inheritor) of First Nations land. It is not merely, as Dickinson will be quick to remind us, a European subject, but also a heterosexual (and implicitly patriarchal) subject as well. Dickinson gives us a clue to this encounter by using Eve Sedgwick's (1985) theory of male homosocial desire. While he uses Sedgwick's theory to illustrate a pattern in Canadian literature, it is clear that the myth of the canoe follows a pattern of homosocial activity from its European roots to its firm entrenchment as a leisure activity to befit the nation. For Dickinson, the analysis of the homosocial becomes relevant for Canadian nationalism because "Canadian literature, or at the very least *English*-Canadian literature, is riddled with male couples who displace their love for each other—and frequently their nation . . . onto a mythically feminized region or landscape, which they symbolically exploit" (Dickinson 1999, 5, original emphasis). For Sedgwick, the relationship between male homosocial desire and male homoeroticism is a matter of degrees, with the key difference being that homosocial desire mediates its desired object through a secondary item, which for Sedgwick often is figured through a woman.

Sedgwick's (1985) book *Between Men* examines the triangular structure that enables male bonding within English literature. Deflecting this desire through another object, usually the heterosexually acceptable object of a woman both men are connected to, the men can build relations between themselves without fear of any homosexual reproach, although the underlying desire within this structure is toward the other man. By symbolically possessing the other as a passive object within the triangle, the men promote an active relationship between themselves, maintaining their role as dominant subjects. By remaining the active subjects, along with the distance the triangle provides from accusations of homosexuality, male homosocial desire functions as both heteronormative and sexist. Dickinson's (1999) use of male homosocial desire in his reflections on the possibility of queering the Canadian literary landscape shows that in Canada the triangle works through landscape, gender, and race. Homosociality in the Canadian canon often figures through the complex relationship that nationalism has to both the landscape and its imperial position. Thus, in reading the queer of here, Dickinson shows the role that sexuality plays in constructing some images of landscape within the national imaginary.

The European history of the canoe in Canada, in many ways, is a history of these same homosocial patterns. The canoe as a vehicle of the fur trade had European men fight and collaborate over the prize of land and animals. The triangle works in several ways here—such as that between Samuel Hearn and Chief Matonabbee over Matonabbee's daughter and the knowledge of the land that Matonabbee has, or the relationship between French and English traders fighting over the animal pelts being drained from western Canada. As the canoe became less relevant to the fur trade, the leisured use of the canoe developed, especially in the burgeoning tourist industry of hunting and fishing. Predominantly male hunters employed First Nations guides to ensure a successful catch of fish, moose, deer, wolf, or waterfowl. The interracial homosocial promoted an active masculinity by absorbing the exoticized other of the guide. This relationship is only thinly veiled in the title of the predominant magazine of the hunting and fishing culture of the turn of the century, *Rod and Gun,* which my colleague Jocelyn Thorpe mockingly calls "Penis and Penis." The culture of masculinity promoted by such encounters with wilderness and savagery was soon incorporated into the education of boys through summer camps, where canoe trips and native masquerade allowed boys to develop the skills needed to lead the nation (a literal goal, in the case of Pierre Elliot Trudeau). In the development of leisure canoeing, the connection between nation and masculinity was always made overt, yet even in contemporary articulations of canoeing, the national homosocial exists. We can look to Jennings's triangular position of French/English explorers' diplomacy with First Nations in their quest for bounty. The desire, in Jennings's position, for Canadian canoeing follows a pattern of male homosocial desire, where the land becomes the desired object of relations between men. In rethinking the possibility of canoeing desire, we need to reach beyond the bounds of these relationships.

Possibility

To call for a politics without a future, therefore, must also be to call for the politics of the past, the lost pasts that were silenced and erased by the forward march of progress.
—Shannon Winnubst

So far, I have charted the role that biopower plays in establishing utility at the heart of modern power regimes. Looking at the politics surrounding the connection between landscape and nation in Canada, I argued that landscape not only provides a symbol for Canadian nationalism, but also naturalizes the claims of the nation. Focusing specifically on the case of the canoe in Canada, we can see that our leisure patterns are held within a desire for the nation that ultimately reproduces a heterosexist and masculinist naturalization of the nation. The need for utility required by biopolitical regimes of the state has established a homosocial interaction between nation, gender, race, and sexuality in the idealized image of the canoe. Yet, it is precisely the demand for utility that we might be able to exploit in attempts to resist the nationalist regime of landscape and sexuality.

Shannon Winnubst offers a possibility of resisting the totalizing regime of utility by demanding a "politics without a future" (2006, 190). Queer, as a category that defies articulation of the specific identity claims that normalize behavior, offers a pivotal space in which the already existing future of the nation can be contested. For Winnubst, "to queer things is to transform them, in ways that we cannot anticipate: to queer is to foil anticipation and its temporality of a future-anterior" (139). The establishment of the regime of utility that permeates late capitalism requires a predictable view of the future, identified by Winnubst as the future anterior; the space where things "will have been." I participate in activities, purchase goods, and engage in civic politics in order to have been a good citizen, in order to have performed my identity as a Canadian. Such thinking ascribes meaning only as it should be; thus, Jennings can ascribe multicultural intent to the diplomacy of the French during the establishment of New France. Attending summer camps is to ensure that boys will have been made into men. The future is always anticipated and dictated to a function of the nation. A queer politics, argues Winnubst, will move away from a concept of the future.

Quick to clarify her suggestion, Winnubst tells us that it is not about leaving things to happen unpredictably, adopting a nihilistic "anything goes" attitude, but about being careful about how we look upon our history. The future anterior demands a vision forward, while selectively taking what is needed from the past, in a way that often promotes specific acts of amnesia. The answer lies in turning ourselves away from the linear idea of future and opens possibilities for the past to contribute to the ethics of our time.

> To call for a politics without a future, therefore, must also be to call for the politics of the past, the lost pasts that were silenced and erased by the forward march of progress. It is to frame experience through a temporality of "what might have been," rather than the dominant one of "what will have been." Such a call, if they/we can hear it at all, will render the masterful, free "I" of white bourgeois Christian subjectivity vulnerable to the violences of the past. (Winnubst 2006, 190)

In thinking about the violence of slavery and the continued regime of whiteness in the United States, Winnubst suggests that "we cannot possibly anticipate what might happen, if we were really to consider the ten million bodies at the bottom of the Atlantic Ocean" (190). The possibilities of such a dialogue are eclipsed by the totalizing connection of biopower to utility.

Thinking through a politics of nature without a future means rethinking nature such that it is not bent toward the utility of power. Opening ourselves to the possibilities of history means addressing the ways in which the ideologies and concrete practices that have formed our current understanding of nature represent more about the desired human outcomes than they do the about anything nonhuman. It means reconceiving the nation to understand that its supposed unifying function is built upon the exclusion of certain targeted parts of the nation. In short, this would call for a politics of the canoe that addresses the failure of nation and nature to be exactly what we desired. So then, if the ability to make love in a canoe is not about being Canadian, what can we do with the desire for canoeing?

To conclude, I will give two short possibilities that attempt to open our desire to the possibility of "what could have been." First, thinking through canoeing desire means that we need to understand the connection between the theft of land performed by the slow and determined entry of the European into the landscape and the attempt to eliminate the First Nations presence on the land. Similar to really considering 10 million dead bodies in the Atlantic Ocean, this would mean really considering (as a broad list) the malicious wars over land and fur, the forced conversions, the repeated exposure to flu epidemics, the establishment of reservations and classification of First Nations as wards of the state, and the widespread physical and sexual abuse in residential schools designed to assimilate and civilize a supposed "savage" population. Second, we could also do well to take Dickinson (1999) seriously to consider the queer habitations of Canadian space and nation. If the short history of homosocial bonding in the canoe presents anything, it shows that there are a variety of ways in which the canoe spreads desire across networks of power. Reading a history of queer desire through the canoe, from the relationships between fur traders to the serendipity celebrated by many women-only canoe trips, would firmly place the sexual role of the nation within the politics of wilderness in Canada. The task at hand is to find a politics that addresses both race and sexuality.

Tomson Highway, the Cree playwright and novelist, gives us a glimpse of the possibilities of this politics in his novel *The Kiss of the Fur Queen*. His story is about two Cree brothers, born in Northern

Manitoba to a champion dog musher and his wife. Champion/Jeremiah and Ooneemeetoo/Gabriel Okimasis are blessed with the gifts of music and dance respectively, gifts that are incubated living with their parents amongst the forest and lakes, traveling by canoe and dogsled from summer retreat to the reserve and back again. Taken to a residential school several hundred miles south at the age of six, Champion and Ooneemeetoo are baptized into the Catholic Church, have their names changed, and are forbidden to speak the language of their parents. Abused by the priests at the school, Jeremiah and Gabriel struggle with their parents' admiration for the priests who have inflicted this upon them. Returning home one summer from the residential school, they canoe past an island that had housed a shaman woman, Chachagathoo, with whom the priest of the reserve had constantly fought. Gabriel, the younger, curious about the island and the reason his family has always avoided looking at it, is told that Chachagathoo is an evil woman, who had *machipoowamoowin,* which is translated for the reader as "'bad blood' or 'bad dream power'" (Highway 1998, 91). Gabriel, still unsure of what is wrong with Chachagathoo, jokes in English (so his mother won't understand) to his brother, "Do *'machipoowamoowin'* mean what Father Lafleur do to the boys at school?" (91). Jeremiah's response solidifies the gap between younger and elder caused by the residential school system:

> Jeremiah's words, in English, were as cold as drops from a melting block of ice.
> "Even if we told them, they would side with Father Lafleur."
> Selecting one of the three Native languages that she knew—English would remain, for life, beyond her reach and that of her husband's—Mariesis turned to Jeremiah. "What are you saying, my sons?"
> If moments can be counted as minutes can, or hours or days or years, one thousand of them trickled by before Jeremiah was absolutely sure Gabriel's silence would remain until the day they died. And then he said, his voice flat, *"Maw keegway."* Nothing. (Highway 1998, 92)

The distance between Mariesis and her sons was established that day in the canoe by Jeremiah's shame, and it is not just his parents that he is alienated from by the education and sexual predation of the school priests, but also the land, language, and culture of his people. It is not surprising that this discussion happens in a canoe. Understanding that their time at school has made them different, both sons soon end up at high school in the city, one looking forward to a career as a concert pianist and the other as a dancer. As their relationship develops in the city, Jeremiah's shame starts to encompass his identity as Cree, the aching knowledge in the back of his head of the murders of aboriginal women in the city's downtown core, and his brother's sexual relationships with men. After high school the boys split up, Gabriel taking off across the world as a dancer with his lover, and Jeremiah, abandoning his dreams of the piano in large part due to his shame, working as a social worker in Winnipeg's north end.

Translation provides a key problem to both boys; looking for an explanation of why he is not staying on the reserve after high school, Jeremiah thinks to himself, "how for God's sake, did one say 'concert Pianist' in Cree?" (Highway 1998, 189). Gabriel, whose experience of abuse is marked by an erotic ambivalence embodied later in life through his continual sexual conquests of priests, finds that it is his desire that excludes him from the (newly) heterosexualized landscape of his family. Afraid of "this most catholic of men," his father, and the Catholic Church's fear of his sexuality, Gabriel avoids the reserve, knowing that there is little way to bridge his life in this small town. After his father's death, confronting the possibility of his own, he mimics Jeremiah's earlier question to his face, saying "how do you say AIDS in Cree, huh? Tell me, what's the word for HIV?" (296). While he is alienated from his hometown by Catholicism's homophobia (even despite Father Lafleur's enculturation of his homoerotic desire), Gabriel finds continual inspiration from traditional Cree culture. At a powwow on Manitoulin Island, north of Toronto, Gabriel recognizes his need to know the cultures that were suppressed by the residential school. As the crowd dances to the *migisoo,* the eagle, Gabriel realizes its power: "Gabriel saw people talking to the sky, the sky replying. And he knew he had to learn this dance. Someday soon, he may need it" (Highway 1998, 244–45). Indeed, it is through this reclamation of traditional culture, re-invented in the city by a gay Cree dancer and the collaboration he brings to his brother, that they find the strength they had as children in their parents' care. Collaborating on the play, *Chachagathoo the Shaman,* they re-narrate the past of their lives in order to understand the real effect of colonial imposition on Native lives. As Gabriel lies dying in his bed, the end of the novel presents his journey into death as the mixture of tradition and novelty, symbolized by his brother and sister-in-law's attempts to burn sweet grass in the hospital while Gabriel dreams of the Fur Queen his father once won a dogsledding crown from.

Highway's semi-autobiographical novel suggests an understanding of the politics of making love in a canoe by asking us to consider the possibilities of leaving the future open in such a way that we can always turn to the past. The lives of Gabriel/Ooneemeetoo and Jeremiah/Champion float between their assigned names, from the determined biblical references chosen by the priests to the more specific and historical paths of their parent's visions (Ooneemeetoo translates as "dancer" in Cree). And while my reading of this novel is necessarily brief despite its complexity, what comes to the reader at the end is the fact that the movement between tradition and innovation is always fluid and uncharted. As such, Highway's novel enacts a politics that leaves the future undetermined and pays close attention to the details of past experiences. Showing the sexualization of space through colonialism, illustrated by Gabriel's need for, yet alienation from, his land and culture, Highway forces us to remember the possibility of a less determined sexual identity of nature. Thus, while, as a quirky national joke, the idea of making love in a canoe surely belongs to the post–sexual revolution of the later twentieth century, we need to remember that as a national symbol, the connection it strives to make between the canoe, nature, and nation signals a sexual politic that was born of the age of imperialism. As Foucault reminds us, the legacy of the Victorian repression of sexuality is held within the resistance of the sexual revolution that fails to move outside the biopower networks of modern sexuality. This is perhaps illustrated by the failure of Berton's statement; it appears that Canadians do not want to connect sex and nature literally. But it is precisely this that we must do if we are to engage with history, and look toward a politics of nature that we can possibly call Queer.

NOTES

1. Shawinigan is the home town of long-time Liberal Prime Minister Jean Chrétien.

2. Several important observations of the failure of Canadian national identity have served as pivotal points in Canadian nationalism. First, Goldwin Smith's *Canada and the Canadian Question* (1971) argued, shortly after the creation of the nation in 1867, for the unification of Canada with the United States since Canada would no longer be able to maintain the British identity that kept it as a dominion. George Grant's *Lament for a Nation: The Defeat of Canadian Nationalism* (1965) was a second key commentary on Canadian nationalism. Arguing that the end that Smith sought almost a century earlier was now an inevitable (although unwanted) conclusion, Grant's book was incorporated (somewhat tentatively due to Grant's social conservatism) into a resurgence in a left-leaning national politics as a response to American dominance. Currently, despite the vast array of Canadian nation institutions and cultural currency of "Canadian," there is a feeling that Canadians have an identity as a result of their lack of identity (Keohane 1997).

3. Shawna Dempsey and Lorri Millan founded the Lesbian National Parks and Services in 1997 as a way of inserting a lesbian presence into the natural landscape. In full uniform, the performance artists interact with the public, and point out potential hazards to the flourishing of lesbian flora and fauna in natural settings, including sexism and the naturalization of heterosexuality in human and nonhuman contexts (Dempsey and Millan 2002).

4. It was Columbus who adopted the Arawak word for "boat" to describe the dugout boats of the Arawak and Caribs that he met on his voyages. The use of this label for other indigenous boats in America ignores the diversity in use and material construction of these boats. It also sutures together all the indigenous peoples of America under the discourse of "primitive" that surrounded Columbus's first use of the word.

5. This is obviously a very romantic image of the French colonial relationship. As Day (2002) shows, it is the preferred view within Canadian history. "There is no doubt, however, that the French attempted to exterminate the Iroquois nations many times, and the only thing that stopped these people from being wiped out was their own ability to bend with and redirect the tide of death flowing their way" (84).

6. The idea of gift facilitates the colonial guilt over the actual disappearance of First Nations communities throughout Canada, and is therefore related quite closely to the belief that First Nations peoples are dying out. See Bracken (1997) for a detailed analysis of both gift and death in Canadian colonialism.

REFERENCES

Bannerji, Himani. 2000. *The Dark Side of the Nation: Essays on Multiculturalism, Nationalism and Gender*. Toronto, Ontario: Canadian Scholars Press.

Benidickson, Jamie. 1997. *Idleness, Water and a Canoe: Reflections on Paddling for Pleasure*. Toronto, Ontario: University of Toronto Press.

Bhabha, Homi. 1994. *The Location of Culture*. New York: Routledge.

Bracken, Chris. 1997. *The Potlatch Papers: A Colonial Case History*. Chicago: University of Chicago.

Butler, Judith. 1993. *Bodies That Matter: On the Discursive Limits of "Sex."* New York: Routledge.

Chester, Phillip. 1988. Motives for Mr. Canoehead. In *Canexus: The Canoe in Canadian Culture*, ed. J. Raffan and B. Horwood, 93–106. Toronto, Ontario: Betelgeuse Books.

Day, Richard. 2002. *Multiculturalism and the History of Diversity in Canada*. Toronto, Ontario: University of Toronto Press.

Dempsey, Shawna, and Lorri Millan. 2002. Video. *Lesbian National Parks and Services: A Force of Nature*. Winnipeg, Manitoba: Video Pool Media Arts Centre.

Dickinson, Peter. 1999. *Here Is Queer: Nationalisms, Sexualities, and the Literatures of Canada*. Toronto, Ontario: University of Toronto Press.

Ferguson, Will. 1997. *Why I Hate Canadians*. Vancouver, B.C.: Douglas and McIntyre.

Foucault, Michel. 1978. *The History of Sexuality, Volume 1: An Introduction*. Trans. R. Hurley. New York: Vintage.

Francis, Daniel. 1992. *The Imaginary Indian: The Image of the Indian in Canadian Culture*. Vancouver, B.C.: Arsenal Pulp Press.

———. 1997. *National Dreams: Myth, Memory and Canadian History*. Vancouver, B.C.: Arsenal Pulp Press.

Government of Canada. 2009. http://www.pch.gc.ca/progs/multi/ inclusive_e.cfm.

Grant, George. 1965. *Lament for a Nation: The Defeat of Canadian Nationalism*. Toronto, Ontario: McClelland and Stewart.

Halperin, David. 1995. *Saint Foucault: Towards a Gay Hagiography*. Oxford, U.K.: Oxford University Press.

Hardt, Michael, and Antonio Negri. 2000. *Empire*. Cambridge, Mass.: Harvard University Press.

Henderson, Bob. 1988. Reflections of a Bannock Baker. In *Canexus: The Canoe in Canadian Culture*, ed. J. Raffan and B. Horwood, 83–91. Toronto, Ontario: Betelgeuse Books.

Highway, Tomson. 1998. *The Kiss of the Fur Queen*. Toronto, ON: Doubleday Canada.

Hodgins, Bruce. 1988. Canoe Irony: Symbol and Harbinger. In *Canexus: The Canoe in Canadian Culture*, ed. J. Raffan and B. Horwood, 45–58. Toronto, Ontario: Betelgeuse Books.

———. 1999. The Canoe as Chapeau: Reflections on the Role of the Portage in Canoe Culture. In *The Canoe in Canadian Cultures*, ed. J. Jennings, B. Hodgins, and D. Small, 239–46. Winnipeg, Manitoba: Natural Heritage.

Jennings, John. 1999. The Canadian Canoe Museum and Canada's National Symbol. In *The Canoe in Canadian Cultures*, ed. J. Jennings, B. Hodgins, and D. Small, 1–14. Winnipeg, Manitoba: Natural Heritage.

———. 2002a. The Realm of the Birch Bark Canoe. In *The Canoe: A Living Tradition*, ed. J. Jennings, 1–25. Toronto, Ontario: Firefly.

———. 2002b. The Canoe Frontier. In *The Canoe: A Living Tradition*, ed. J. Jennings, 26–45. Toronto, Ontario: Firefly.

Keohane, Kieran. 1997. *Symptoms of Canada: An Essay on the Canadian Identity*. Toronto, Ontario: University of Toronto Press.

Kinsman, Gary. 1996. *The Regulation of Desire: Homo and Hetero Sexualities*. Montreal, Quebec: Black Rose Books.

Mackey, Eva. 2000. "Death by Landscape": Race, Nature and Gender in Canadian Nationalist Mythology. *Canadian Woman Studies/Les Cahiers de la Femme* 20.2: 125–30.

Maynard, Steven. 2001. The Maple Leaf (Gardens) Forever: Sex, Canadian Historians and National History. *Journal of Canadian Studies* 36.2: 70–105.

McClintock, Anne. 1995. *Imperial Leather: Race, Gender and Sexuality in the Colonial Context*. New York: Routledge.

McGuffin, Gary, and Joannie McGuffin. 1988. *Canoeing Across Canada*. London: Didem.

McWhorter, Ladelle. 1999. *Bodies and Pleasures*. Bloomington: Indiana University Press.

Prosser, Jay. 1998. *A Skin of One's Own: The Body Narratives of Transsexuality*. New York: Columbia University.

Raffan, James. 1999a. *Bark, Skin and Cedar: Exploring the Canoe in Canadian Experience*. Toronto, Ontario: HarperCollins.

———. 1999b. Being There: Bill Mason and the Canadian Canoeing Tradition. In *The Canoe in Canadian Cultures*, ed. J. Jennings, B. Hodgins, and D. Small, 15–27. Winnipeg, Manitoba: Natural Heritage.

Raffan, James, and Bert Horwood, eds. 1988. *Canexus: The Canoe in Canadian Culture*. Toronto, Ontario: Betelgeuse Books.

Sedgwick, Eve. 1985. *Between Men: English Literature and Male Homosocial Desire.* New York: Columbia.

Smith, Goldwin. 1971. *Canada and the Canadian Question.* Toronto, Ontario: University of Toronto Press.

Stoler, Ann Laura. 1995. *Race and the Education of Desire: Foucault's History of Sexuality and the Colonial Order of Things.* Durham, N.C.: Duke University Press.

———. 2002. *Carnal Knowledge and Imperial Power: Race and the Intimate in Colonial Rule.* Berkeley and Los Angeles: University of California Press.

Whipper, Kurt. 1988. Foreword. In *Canexus: The Canoe in Canadian Culture,* ed. J. Raffan and B. Horwood, ix–xi. Toronto, Ontario: Betelgeuse Books

Winnubst, Shannon. 2006. *Queering Freedom.* Bloomington: Indiana University Press.

CHAPTER 12

Melancholy Natures, Queer Ecologies

CATRIONA MORTIMER-SANDILANDS

One of the penalties of an ecological education is that one lives
alone in a world of wounds.
—Aldo Leopold

It is as if the land secretes pheromones testifying to its abuse,
detectable only by those who are themselves damaged.
—Jan Zita Grover

Sandy rang to say Paul is now very ill. I feel furious and impotent,
why should this happen? Lovers shriveled and parched like the
landscape.
—Derek Jarman

A contemporary echo of Aldo Leopold's famous comment about environmental awareness as a "world of wounds" is currently reverberating
around assorted blogs, Web pages, and other internet conversations. Entitled "The World is Dying—and So Are You," the short piece (originally
a 2001 op-ed commentary in the *LA Times*) begins with the following
diagnosis:

> At the heart of the modern age is a core of grief. At some level, we're
> aware that something terrible is happening, that we humans are
> laying waste to our natural inheritance. A great sorrow arises as we
> witness the changes in the atmosphere, the waste of resources and
> the consequent pollution, the ongoing deforestation and destruction
> of fisheries, the rapidly spreading deserts, and the mass extinction
> of species. (Anderson 2001)

The article goes on to use (loosely) Elisabeth Kübler-Ross's popular theory
of grief (1969) to suggest a series of stages through which this "ecological

grieving" might proceed both societally and individually.[1] Kübler-Ross notwithstanding, it is the imperative that ends the article that is worth considering. Anderson writes: "It's necessary to face our fear and our pain, and to go through the process of grieving, because the alternative is a sorrow deeper still: the loss of meaning. To live authentically in this time, we must allow ourselves to feel the magnitude of our human predicament" (Anderson 2001).

While I have some discomfort with Anderson's chosen language of "authenticity," the idea that there is a relationship between an engagement with environmental loss and environmental responsibility, and that meaning is gained in negotiation with something that can be seriously considered grief over the condition of the world, suggests a dimension of environmental thought that has not been particularly well explored even if the fact of that loss seems, as Anderson himself describes, an all-pervasive condition of modernity. There are exceptions: SueEllen Campbell, for example, in an elegant narrative nonfiction account of coming to understand the many layers of meaning of a part of the New Mexico desert that contains, at once, millennia of geological and biological history and the apocalyptic legacy of Los Alamos, confronts that lack, the absence of a societal and personal story of loss and grief in which to place environmental understanding:

> Was this [place] just the same old sad story, the one about human violence, the endless damage we do, may always have done, to ourselves, everything around us? Yes, I thought, but that didn't make it simple. I couldn't even tell myself that if humans are violent and destructive, the natural world, at least, is peaceful and enduring, not while I lay with my back pressed tightly against the remnants of enormous volcanic explosions and the cold winter earth stole my own body's warmth. (Campbell 2003, 5)[2]

Campbell's response to human destructiveness is both emotional and sophisticated. Her increasing awareness of environmental fragility is cause for profound sadness and, indeed, her own prolonged depression. She does not, however, respond to her sadness by romanticizing a pure and everlasting nature to oppose to anthropogenic destruction, but instead develops a complex and meaningful position in which destruction and loss are always already part of the character of the place where she lies: "transience was and always had been everything" (40).

But Campbell is a rarity: by and large, as this essay will explore, there is in late capitalist nature relations a patina of nature-*nostalgia* in place of any kind of active negotiation of environmental mourning. Specifically, I will argue that Anderson is right—at the heart of the modern age is indeed a core of grief—but that that "core" is more accurately conceived as a condition of *melancholia,* a state of suspended mourning in which the object of loss is very real but psychically "ungrievable" within the confines of a society that cannot acknowledge nonhuman beings, natural environments, and ecological processes as appropriate objects for genuine grief. In such conditions, loss becomes displacement: the object that cannot be lost also cannot be let go, and as a psychoanalytic perspective reveals, such disavowed objects are preserved within the psyche in the form of identifications and incorporations. In late capitalism, I would argue, nature-nostalgia—ecotourist pilgrimages to endangered wildernesses, documentaries of dying peoples and places, even environmentalist campaigns to "save" particular habitats or species against the onslaught of development—are exactly a form of melancholy nature, in that they incorporate environmental destruction into the ongoing workings of commodity capitalism.[3]

Recent queer scholarship on melancholia, however, much of it propelled by the enormity of AIDS and the omnipresence of personal and overwhelming death and loss—in the midst, as Judith Butler points out, of a homophobic culture that barely tolerates, let alone values, homosexual attachments—is focused exactly on the condition of grieving the ungrievable: how does one mourn in the midst of a culture that finds it almost impossible to recognize the value of what has been lost? As this scholarship has pointed out, melancholia is not only a denial of the loss of a beloved object but also a potentially politicized way of preserving that object in the midst of a culture that fails to recognize its significance. Melancholia, here, is not a failed or inadequate mourning. Rather, it is a form of socially located embodied memory in which the loss of the beloved constitutes the self, the persistence of which identification acts as an ongoing psychic reminder of the fact of death in the midst of creation. In a context in which there are no adequate cultural relations to acknowledge death, melancholia is a form of preservation of life—a life, unlike the one offered for sale in ecotourist spectacle, that is already gone, but whose ghost propels a *changed* understanding of the present.

Following expanded discussions of both the capitalist present of melancholy natures and the political potential of a queer rewriting of loss and melancholia, this essay will consider two literary works that specifically engage a politicized melancholic sensibility drawn from lesbian and gay experiences of AIDS to rethink commodified late capitalist nature relations.[4] Jan Zita Grover's *North Enough: AIDS and Other Clear-Cuts* (1997) and Derek Jarman's *Modern Nature* (1991), both first-person accounts/memoirs of intimate and world-changing relationships with AIDS and death (Grover was a caregiver in San Francisco in the late 1980s and early 1990s; Jarman died from AIDS-related illness in 1994), are also active engagements with and meditations on the natural world. As a result of their (acknowledged) melancholia, I will argue, both Grover and Jarman come to write about and act in nature in ways that develop exactly the kind of political, embodied understanding of death and mourning that is missing from the romantic portrayals of loss and salvation emphasized in contemporary environmental spectacle. In particular, both Grover and Jarman come to love and understand *devastated* landscapes: Grover (and her cutover Minnesota and Wisconsin north woods) and Jarman (and his stark Dungeness garden overlooking a nuclear power plant) transform their melancholic attachments into a principled and public recognition of the ongoing loss of nature, and also of the ways in which that loss is constitutive of their environmental relationships on a daily basis. In so doing, I would argue, both authors point us toward a queer ecology that both emerges from and politicizes melancholy natures, incorporating the experience of a "world of wounds" into an ethical stance that resists, rather than fostering, fetish.

Mourning and Melancholia

In his 1915 essay "Mourning and Melancholia," Sigmund Freud offers that both mourning and melancholia are reactions to the loss of a beloved object: both are "grave departures from the normal attitude to life" (1984, 252), but where in mourning "we rely on its being overcome after a certain lapse of time" (252) in that the bereaved ego becomes able to transfer attachment to new objects ("is free and uninhibited again," 253), in melancholia the ego will not let go. Instead of transferring attachment outward to a new object-cathexis, the melancholic internalizes the lost object as a way of preserving it. That internalization, for Freud, takes the form of an unconscious ego-identification: the ego holds on to the object by devouring it and making it part of itself, substituting narcissistic for cathectic energy. In this way, melancholia "borrows some of its features from mourning, and the others from the process of regression from narcissistic object-choice to narcissism" (259). In addition, as Freud continues, the process of identification includes *ambivalence* about the lost object (i.e., the fact that love relationships include both attachment and hostility); this ambivalence creates a turning inward not only of loss but of *anger,* creating in the melancholic a critical hostility toward itself, "an extraordinary diminution in his [*sic*] self-regard, an impoverishment of his ego on a grand scale. In mourning, it is the world which has become poor and empty; in melancholia it is the ego itself" (254).[5]

In this essay, at the same time as Freud overtly contrasts a "normal" process of mourning with a more problematic melancholy (which some continue to portray as an "incomplete" mourning, see Ruti 2005), one can see that even here he is wavering on the question of the latter's actual *pathology.* At one point, for example—echoing older conceptions of melancholia as an affective state bound to self-reflectiveness and genius[6]— Freud writes that the relentless inner criticism of the melancholic (he offers Hamlet) contains a certain quality of truthfulness: "We only wonder why a man has to be ill before he can be accessible to a truth of this kind" (1984, 255). Further, despite the self-directed pain of melancholy, it is fundamentally the same process as mourning save for the fact that it occurs internally and unconsciously. Indeed, as Butler points out, in his revised thinking on melancholia in *The Ego and the Id* (1923), Freud goes so far as to suggest that melancholic identification may be a *prerequisite* for letting the object go, and that

> by claiming this, he changes what it means to "let an object go," for there is no final breaking of the attachment. There is, rather, the incorporation of the attachment *as* identification, where identification becomes magical, a psychic form of preserving the object. . . . [O]ne might conclude that melancholic identification permits the loss of the object in the external world precisely because it provides a way to *preserve* the object as part of the ego and, hence, to avert the loss as a complete loss. (Butler 1997, 134, original emphasis)

A further important point in Freud's account is that he clearly indicates that the *losses* leading to melancholy may not be "ordinary." Specifically, he notes that, although melancholia can certainly "be the reaction to the loss of a loved object" it can also occur in response to losses of "a more ideal kind" (1984, 253). In fact, he writes, in yet other cases the nature of the loss may not be at all clear in melancholia: a loss has occurred, "but one cannot see clearly what it is that has been lost, *and it is all the more reasonable to suppose that the patient cannot consciously perceive what he has lost either*" (254, my emphases). The conflict over loss is withdrawn from consciousness (into the ego): indeed, one might reasonably argue not only that a lack of clarity about the nature of the loss is part and parcel of its movement into subterranean, melancholic conflict (e.g., the patient "knows *whom* he has lost but not *what* he has lost in him," 254, emphases in original), but even that the inability of the melancholic to register consciously the nature of the loss might have roots in the *social* relations that allow only certain *kinds* of loss to appear as loss, in other words, as legible and grievable.[7]

Interestingly, as Matthew von Unwerth argues, Freud developed his early thinking on mourning and melancholia with the natural world very much present in his mind. In a lesser-known essay entitled "On Transience" (also 1915), Freud narrates a "summer walk through a smiling countryside in the company of a taciturn friend [probably Lou Andreas-Salomé] and of a young but already famous poet [probably Rainer Maria Rilke]" and, along with the walk, a conversation about the ephemeral quality of nature:

> The idea that all this beauty was transient was giving these two sensitive minds a foretaste of mourning over its decease; and, since the mind instinctively recoils from anything that is painful, they felt their enjoyment of beauty interfered with by thoughts of its transience. (Freud, quoted in von Unwerth 2005, 215, 217)[8]

Freud disagrees with his companions' refusal to acknowledge beauty because it is so easily lost, not least because he is surrounded by tremendous loss himself. The war "robbed us of very much that we had loved, and showed us how ephemeral were many things that we had regarded as changeless" (218); this devastation underscored, for Freud, the importance of love (and nature) because, not in spite, of its fragility. Although he is clearly thinking about a "normal" process of mourning when he speaks of the necessary passage of libidinal energies from a lost object to a new one, he is also clear that a recognition of fragility—an active remembrance of loss—might be part of an ethical relationship to the devastation of the First World War: "When once mourning is over, it will be found that our high opinion of the riches of civilization has lost nothing from our discovery of their fragility. We shall build up again all that was has destroyed, and perhaps on firmer ground and more lastingly than before" (219). For Freud, the devastation of the war underscored the importance of the things lost to that war; mourning was thus a process of *recognition* of beauty as well as an acknowledgment of its extinguishment (things are beautiful *because* they die), and there was no greater example of this recognition than in the natural losses of seasonal cycles.

Melancholy Natures

The above passage shows that Freud was, in 1915, still an optimist and a champion of modernity: the fact of overwhelming loss, through mourning (not melancholy), was to propel a greater achievement, rather than an ethical diminishment, of civilization. Indeed in this account, Freud clearly indicates that loss should confirm progress rather than interrupt it: mourning involves the transference of libidinal attachment from one object to another one, a movement forward involving an appropriate leaving-behind of the past, however beautiful it may have been, in favor of a present that offers like riches. In this respect, it is interesting to note the similarities between Freud's account and Bruce Braun's argument about contemporary ecotourism in his book *The Intemperate Rainforest*. Briefly, Braun argues that mourning the loss of nature is a constitutive condition of capitalist modernity. Specifically, he argues that wilderness tourist practices (he is writing about ecotourism in Clayoquot Sound on Vancouver Island, BC) are a form of ecosocial ritual by which consumers of "vanishing" nature confirm their own transcendence of nature in the moment of mourning its loss: by understanding nature as something "lost" at the hands of modernity, and by witnessing its demise in the fetishized chunks that are offered up to spectacular consumption *by* modernity, the victory of the modernity *responsible* for that loss is confirmed. The temporal logic of this (bourgeois) progressivist narrative is very akin to Freud's: the position of the present as "better" than the past is achieved through an understanding of loss that assumes the libido will simply "move on," and that also, in this case, assumes that modernity will simply move on from nature even as it memorializes its legacy in parks and monuments.

Braun's analysis of the fetishization and commodification of a lost, romanticized nature—"unspoiled" wilderness—is extremely important for this analysis; it is the very quality of nature's impending extinguishment (buy now or you'll miss it) that fuels much ecotourism. The quality of nature as "lost" is, in fact, *exaggerated* by ecotourism in its insistence that the nature we are to mourn (and through which we are to confirm ourselves through mourning) is a mythic, idyllic one; as a commodity, then, nature becomes a fantasy, a fetish that can be bought to extend the reach of capital rather than prompt a criticism of the relationships that produced the loss in the first place. The idea of a pristine nature on the perpetual verge of destruction is not only a violent rationale for the dispossession of peoples and livelihoods but a seductive fantasy that keeps consumers poised to *watch* that destruction (the more exotic and the more at-risk the better). Nature as a fantastic, watchable, visitable commodity is a *part* of modernity, a projection onto the world (qua Braun, of the nature that modernity is always already able to overcome) of a very particular fantasy; the consumption of nature as wilderness is an imposition of one hegemonic relationship—capitalist exchange—into a landscape of many other relationships and intimacies, relationships that are often destroyed in the process of consumption itself. Crucially, the fantasy of wilderness is not only infinitely consumable, but infinitely replaceable.

Perhaps this "mourning" is not, then, all that sad? Perhaps a grief that can only confirm the ongoing ability of the libido to attach to another object (consumption) and not be profoundly transformed by what it has lost is not what Freud had in mind at all when he wrote about the importance of the recognition of the ephemeral as part of the lesson of grief? What Braun's analysis suggests is that mourning can be easily commodified (perhaps even that the insistence on libidinal movement "forward" is part of the social organization of mourning in commodity capitalism), and indeed, that the marketing of environmental loss can be a positive boon for the unfettered progress of capital despite appearances to the contrary. But, as blogs and Web sites such as Anderson's demonstrate, perhaps this fetishized loss is not all there is to say about environmental grief in late capitalism. I would argue that experiences of environmental loss—a species of butterfly rendered extinct for a housing development, a salmon stream destroyed for clear-cut logging, a frog-filled swamp silenced due to climate change—are present, tangible, and everyday aspects of living in the world, both on a small and intimate scale and piled up to the level of planetary crisis. Spectacularizing them in ecotourist pilgrimage makes them palatable, but it does not make them meaningful except as part of a logic of substitution and consumption.

In between the personal experience of an environmental loss and ecotourist and other spectacles, there is something of an emotional void, even if there may be a simultaneous informational glut, when it comes to the mass destruction of the natural world. There are few if any public rituals of environmental mourning (which are different from public announcements of environmental catastrophe, of which there are plenty), little keening and wailing for extinct species or decimated places (which are different from lists or maps of them, of which there are also plenty). In short, there is lots of evidence of environmental loss, but few places in which to experience it *as* loss, to even begin to consider that the diminishment of life that surrounds us on a daily basis is something to be really *sad* about, and on a personal level. Nonhuman beings and particular, life-filled places are, here, *ungrievable* in the same moment that their loss (or impending loss) propels their value on the market.[9] In what seems to be a vicious cycle, the sale of vanishing nature might both emerge from and allow one to evade an incoherent sense of having lost something in a social context in which there is no language to express that loss, no collection of shared symbols or rituals to acknowledge the significance of that loss, and certainly no systemic recognition that that loss might be (literally) earth-shattering for many people, akin to the death of a lover, a parent, a child. The power of wilderness-as-fetish in modernity, then, may be related to the fact that the everyday relations we have with the more-than-human world are unmarked, unnamed, and ungrievable.

I would argue, then, that ecotourist nature-spectacles and the like signal a collection of *melancholy* natures, in that they are losses in which we cannot "recognize what has been lost" and, relatedly, in that they allow us to preserve the lost object in the present and thereby *avert* its complete loss. As the following section will explore, queer theorists who grapple with questions of mourning and melancholia are faced with a similar set of conditions: how does one grieve in a context in which the significance, the density, and even the existence of loss is unrecognized? For many, queer melancholia is thus not so much a "failed" mourning as a psychic and potentially political response to homophobia: a preservation of both the beloved and the fact of love itself in the face of a culture that barely allows, let alone recognizes, intimate queer attachments. Melancholia is pressed, here, into the service of memory, and this insight is vital in order to develop the conditions in which environmental loss becomes something recognizable and meaningful—and grievable.

Queer Melancholia

Judith Butler has investigated the significance of melancholia for queer attachments and politics in several ways. Although her most well known discussion of melancholia concerns the ways in which compulsory heterosexuality institutes gender itself as a melancholic condition,[10] she has also devoted a broader attention to the question of "what makes a grievable life" in the context of conditions of massive global violence, and to the social and political consequences of the demarcation of particular contemporary boundaries around the recognition of grief. Although "loss and vulnerability seem to follow from our being socially constituted bodies, attached to others, at risk of violence by virtue of that exposure" (2004, 20)—in other words, although we are constituted as social beings by loss and its continual possibility—not all losses are created equal, and only some attachments and relationships are considered "real" enough to merit public consideration. For Butler, compulsory heterosexuality and homophobia are exemplary of the social relations by which only certain attachments are "real" and thus grievable; queer melancholia is thus revelatory of a much broader set of cultural phenomena. She writes:

> When certain kinds of losses are compelled by a set of culturally prevalent prohibitions, we might expect a culturally prevalent form of melancholia, one which signals the internalization of the ungrieved homosexual cathexis. And where there is no public recognition or discourse through which such a loss might be named and mourned, then melancholia takes on cultural dimensions of contemporary consequence. (1997, 139)

For Butler, mourning is a process of "accept[ing] that by the loss one undergoes one will be changed, possibly for ever" (2004, 21), and she makes interesting use of Freud to support this view. In her interpretation, Freud moved, in his later writing, from a position of ideal libidinal substitutability toward one in which the subject had to "go through" a process of melancholic incorporation as part of mourning: One has to be transformed by loss through melancholic attachment in order to truly mourn. Here, then, Butler underscores the political quality of melancholia: In what conditions is the enormity of that transformative incorporation recognized? Under what circumstances is it clear that the subject will not, simply, "substitute" one object for another, thus insisting on incorporation as an active engagement with loss and memory? Thus, in a similar vein, David Eng and David Kazanjian (2003) argue that melancholia is a productive response to the twentieth century's "catastrophic losses of bodies, spaces, and ideals, [and that] psychic and material practices of loss and its remains are productive for history and for politics" (5). Rather than renounce loss as *past* in an ongoing search for new cathexes, melancholia suggests a present that is not only haunted but *constituted* by the past: literally built of ruins and rejections.[11] Indeed, as they note, melancholia suggests not only a complex process in which the multiple traumas, losses, and systematic violences of contemporary life are made corporeally and temporally present, but also an *ethical* relationship to the past that acknowledges its perpetual incompletion and contingency. For precisely the reasons Butler outlines, melancholia sits at the intersection of a set of relationships that is at once somatic and social, psychic and regulatory, personal and political. In particular, I would argue that melancholia suggests a non-normalizing relationship to the past and the world, in which the *recognition* of the identificatory persistence of loss in the present—loss *as* self, the fact that we are constituted by prohibition, power. and violence—is central to our ethical and political relationships with others. Or, as Butler writes, grief "furnishes a sense of political community . . . by bringing to the fore the relational ties that have implications for theorizing fundamental dependency and ethical responsibility" (2004, 22).

Queer theorists Douglas Crimp and Ann Cvetkovich have both written eloquently about the social, corporeal, and political conditions in which these ethical relationships have been revealed with particular force and clarity to gay and lesbian communities in the midst of the catastrophic losses that are AIDS. Crimp's mourning begins in ambivalence and takes place in the midst of a pressing exhortation to substitute anger for grief: "Don't mourn, organize!" Particularly, he explores the idea that mourning, for many gay readers of Freud, "promises a return to normalcy that we were never granted in the first place" (1989, 6); in that context, militancy seems the far greater political imperative, and mourning a form of normalizing capitulation. Arguing, however, like Butler, for a more complex Freud, Crimp insists that "for many gay men dealing with AIDS deaths, militancy might arise from conscious conflicts within mourning itself, the consequence, on the one hand, of 'inadvisable and even harmful interference' with grief and, on the other, of the impossibility of deciding whether the mourner will share the fate of the mourned" (10, quoting Freud). But the point, Crimp insists, is not to psychoanalyze AIDS activism: it is to insist that, for gay men, the terrain of traumatic losses that is AIDS is both the genesis and the object of politics, both the ground giving rise to activism and a goal of activist recognition. "The numbers of deaths are unthinkable" but "the rest of society offers little or no acknowledgment" (15); it is not surprising that gay men feel "frustration, anger, rage, outrage, anxiety, fear and terror, shame and guilt, sadness and despair" but rather that "we often don't" (16). For Crimp, the failure of activism to acknowledge the fact that AIDS is bound up with internal violence as well as external is itself a form of disavowal; "by making all violence external, pushing it to the outside and objectifying it in 'enemy' institutions and individuals, we deny its psychic articulation, deny that we are effected, as well as affected, by it" (16). In other words, for Crimp, melancholia is a part of the politics of AIDS, and mourning a vital companion to organizing.

For Cvetkovich, it is exactly the melancholic insistence on engagement with the past in the present that spells the importance of melancholy for queer politics. For her, trauma is an important element of lesbian public culture; "thinking about trauma from the same depathologizing perspective that has animated queer understandings of sexuality opens up possibilities for understanding traumatic feelings . . . as felt experiences that can be mobilized in a range of directions, including the construction of cultures and publics" (2003, 47). Recognizing the constitutive nature of loss is, for lesbian and gay communities prevented from *having* loss (or being lost), an important political goal; recognizing that these losses constitute lesbian relationships, politics, and understandings of self and community further indicates the political qualities of melancholia as a concept and experience. Thus, for Cvetkovich, the collective *preservation* of loss as an "archive of trauma"—which is an important animating thread for many of the creative works of lesbian literature, film, and politics she documents—suggests the acknowledgment of melancholia as a public activity: for lesbians, public melancholy is a form of survival.

Although I think it is clearly not the case that gay men and lesbians have some unrivalled access to a language in which to remark or remake ungrievable environmental losses by virtue of an intersecting experience of queer melancholia, it is still interesting to consider the two threads in juxtaposition. How can the overtly politicized understanding of melancholia located in the midst of AIDS illuminate unrecognized losses in the midst of environmental destruction? What might it mean to consider the preservation of a public record of environmental loss, an "archive of ecological trauma"—made up of the kinds of art, literature, film, ritual, performance, and other memorials and interrogations that have characterized so many cultural responses to AIDS—as part of an environmental ethics or politics? What would it mean to consider seriously the environmental present, in explicit contrast to dominant discourses of ecological modernization, as a pile of environmental wreckage, constituted and haunted by multiple, personal, and deeply traumatic losses rather than as a position from which to celebrate their demise by consuming them (and moving on to something else)? In short, what might it look like to take seriously the fact that nature is currently ungrievable, and that the melancholy natures with which we are surrounded are a desperate attempt to hold onto something that we don't even know how to talk about grieving? Here, queer culture has a lot to teach.

Queer Ecologies

The two works of literature I would like to use to explore these queer contributions to environmental understanding are personal memoirs drawn directly from experiences of dying and living with AIDS. They are both, to use Cvetkovich's terms, part of the archive of trauma of AIDS[12] and, to use Crimp's, self-conscious demonstrations of the generative and creative relationships involved in recognizing the intimate encounters between mourning and militancy. In addition, both works significantly engage the natural world: although very differently, Grover and Jarman stage intense and direct conversations between landscape and death, between environment and AIDS, between places and bodies. Several other works of AIDS memoir have included an active focus on the natural world: Mark Doty's intense and intimate account of his lover's death in *Heaven's Coast* (1996), for example, is firmly emplaced in Provincetown, and includes many poignant references to its landscapes woven through the memoir's accounts of love, illness, friendship, and death. But Grover and Jarman are quite unique in their insistence on holding nature and AIDS up to one another in a reflective conversation in which both sets of issues are changed as a result. For both authors, AIDS does not and cannot propel a retreat into nature in order to find solace and harmony, even if that may have been what Grover at least wanted at the outset of her journey, as if nature could heal the trauma of their experience. Rather, the fact of being corporeally vulnerable in a specifically damaged landscape—*wounded* in a world of wounds—offers both Grover and Jarman acute insight into the historical, multiple, and daily losses that surround them in the natural world, into the fragility of human life in the midst of these losses, and especially into their own constitution by them. In short, both Grover's and Jarman's memoirs are melancholic, in that they hold on tenaciously to the dead for whom they grieve, but that holding-on offers a perspective with which to appreciate and mourn the particular natures around them in a way that challenges dominant commodity substitutability and that offers a sense of what it might mean to inhabit the natural world having been transformed by the experience of its loss. In Jarman's case in particular, nature, in the form of his garden, is also a site for specifically *queer* acts of memory, in which environmental histories and knowledges are rewritten as part of a memorial project. For both Grover and Jarman, their natures are not saved wildernesses; they are wrecks, barrens, cutovers, nuclear power plants: unlikely refuges and impossible gardens. But they are also sites for extraordinary reflection on life, beauty, and community.

AIDS and Other Clear-Cuts

Jan Zita Grover's *North Enough* opens in the process of her movement from San Francisco, where she has worked as a personal caregiver to many individuals who were dying, and died, of AIDS, eventually to the woods of Northern Wisconsin and Minnesota. She is suffering from extreme burnout, and seeks a "geographic cure," "a place where I might be at peace, where suburbs didn't metastasize weekly across the foothills, mile after mile, . . . where AIDS [is] still a background noise, albeit a growing one—something one might anticipate and plan against instead of react to in furious desperation" (1997, 3). She sought an oasis but, of course, could find no such refuge; her problems, her rage, her guilt moved with her into the north woods, where she finds herself "still heavy with mourning, thick with sorrow" (5) as she continues to watch old and new friends die, continues to wrestle with dimensions of loss that are deeply ingrained in her. She has not mourned any of her losses; they are unspeakable and unacknowledged. As she writes in retrospect, however, in their persistence they generate a form of imagination—an awareness of the persistence of loss—that allows her to conceive of the natural world around her in ways that challenge the logic of commodity substitution characterizing contemporary relations of nature consumption. "The north woods," she writes:

> did not provide me with a geographic cure. But they did something much finer. Instead of ready-made solutions, they offered me an unanticipated challenge, a spiritual discipline: to appreciate them, I needed to learn how to see their scars, defacement, and artificiality and then beyond those to their strengths—their historicity, the difficult beauties that underlay their deformity. AIDS, I believe, prepared me to perform these imaginative feats. In learning to know and love the north woods, not as they are fancied but as they are, I discovered the lessons that AIDS had taught me and became grateful for them. (6)

As Grover discovers even on her first trip to the woods in a real estate agent's ragtop Jeep, the landscape of her dreams "looks more like a candidate for reclamation than the stately northern retreat I am seeking" (12). We learn with Grover in her research on the social and ecological history of the region that this place is one that has been systematically abused: logged several times, drained, subjected to failed attempts at agriculture, depleted, abandoned, eroded, invaded, neglected. But even in her first reflections on the jack pines that predominate in the region, she pulls from their gnarled and "modest architecture" a sense of admiration for their tenacity: they are "the first conifers to reestablish themselves after a fire" (16), in their own way remarkable even as they are useless for timber, short-lived, and not at all the sorts of trees about which adjectives like "breathtaking" circulate. These trees in this landscape are not easy to love; indeed, they are a loud testament to the violences that have generated them. "The diminishment of this landscape mortified and disciplines me. Its scars will outlast me, bearing witness for decades beyond my death to the damage done here" (20). But still: the love emerges, painfully, gradually, intimately.

Grover is, by her own admission, "deeply suspicious of metaphor" (21). She does not go into the ravaged woods seeking out a sort of ecological mirror for her experiences with death and dying: that equivalence would be too easy, too prone to abstraction, and it is clear that neither the place nor her past can be understood abstractly. She is intensely conscious of the fact that the meanings she chooses to pull from her environmental observations are neither given in the landscape itself nor directly inherited from her past, but instead emerge from a conscious, laborious process of reflection grounded in intimate experiences and local histories, in the precise ways in which pain and loss are manifest in lives and events. Still, the persistence of pain and loss in her body, the weight of her relationships to the dead, conditions her seeing; her melancholic attachment to the men for whom she cared, her unresolved grief for each one of them, propels her to experience the landscape in terms of loss and change, rather than idyll and replacement. It is all personal; it is all about developing a way of making meaning that recognizes the singularities of the past and takes responsibility for the future in the midst of intimate devastation.

Thus the stories of human loss that Grover tells are deeply particular, not about AIDS in general but of the livings and dyings of named, individual men. There is Darryl, who craves and orchestrates but cannot eat the fried chicken dinner that reminds him of his mother's cooking; there is James with the terraced L.A. garden, whose life (much to his partner Stan's annoyance) comes to revolve around daytime television; there is Eric, whose father seems to have forgotten the horrific sexual abuses he committed against his son and who now as his son dies visits with his new wife—Eric with the dragon tattooed around the base of his penis, Eric who buys a memorial brick at the Golden Gate Bridge Plaza for himself and his beloved scarlet macaw Murphy; and there is Perry, Grover's friend in Minneapolis, with whom she fantasizes about California flowers in the middle of the bitter northern winter and whose "purple-and-black cotton sweater," now worn by Grover as she is writing, "matched his KS lesions exactly" (17). Her writing and thinking in the woods is of them, and also to them: "My dearest dead, it is here to the north of you that I now enter the fullness of my loss" (76).

Thus, not surprisingly, the stories she tells about the north woods are also deeply particular. For example, she devotes an entire chapter to a meditation on nativity that begins with fly fishing in the Whitewater River in Minnesota;[13] the chapter situates her pleasure in the movements and rituals of casting in a discussion of both the destructive legacy written on the river by poor farming practices in the nineteenth century and more recent attempts to restore the area's indigenous hardwood forest. She writes about the (continuing) practice of stocking rivers with large, sports-fishery-friendly species of trout (rainbow, brown) and the generally destructive effects of these introductions on native species such as the smaller brook trout. She writes about the changing temperatures of rivers caused by logging and diversion (warmer waters benefit the introduced trout species); she writes about the specific policies, politics, and technologies that have also had effects on the rivers, the fish, and the other species with whom the fish cohabit in the variety of habitats that the north woods' waters support. For Grover, "fishing proved to be my way into thinking about what it meant to be native to a place—and not just a native human but a native fish" (84). As the chapter demonstrates, in the particular place of the Minnesota north woods and in specific ways that are tied to both the social and the ecological history of the place, environmental hubris has caused enormous losses. Grover's writing is a detailed documentation of some of those particular losses—including a list of specific regional species that are "designated to undergo . . . death by suffocation in order to produce fisheries worthy of human anglers" (92)—but it refuses both to romanticize a sort of pure and pre-lapsarian northern river system and to demonize the "invasive" species that are edging out so many of the area's prior inhabitants. For Grover is, of course, herself an invasive, both culturally (white settlers having displaced the Ojibway) and personally (in her recent choice to move to the region from California). Thus, her ethical claim is not for purity but for an active and thoughtful remembering of historical violences in the midst of the ongoing necessity of movement and change:

It is in the name of a radiant diversity that I claim room and right for us, and this does not always shake out in favor of the preferences of the purist or the displaced. . . . This argument acknowledges the violence that we humans, as well as other sources of natural perturbations (a retrovirus, a bark beetle, a forest fire) can do and have done, the shifts in damage and adjustment that occur as one population declines and opens opportunity for others. It assumes that pain and displacement are also engines of change, of new designs. (94)

For Grover, then, pain and displacement are things to be specifically remembered in reflections on nature, ecology, and landscape. She carries her dead with her, and the pain of their passing becomes epistemic possibility. Important histories of a place are to be found in the specific details of its change and emergence, and those processes include arrogance, failure, death, and loss. Here, environmental value inheres in places in something other than appearance: "The appearance of a body of water does not necessarily tell me if it is healthy or not" (95). Indeed, Grover actively courts relationships with waste-spaces such as landfills and clear-cuts (excellent sites for viewing wildlife and/or witnessing rapid ecological succession) in order to bring to the foreground the massive weight of human devastation of the natural world that is so much a part of her new home: "A discerning eye can see how unstewarded most of this land has been. The charm lies in finding ways to love with such loss and pull from it what beauties remain" (81).

In her own understanding, AIDS gave her that determined trajectory of ecological vision. The text thus juxtaposes one set of losses with the other, and finds in their intersection a richness of vision and a cultivated ability to "pull beauties" from destruction. Grover's refusal to abstract meaning from landscapes and relationships is particularly important to this project. She does not romanticize the dying even as she might mourn their loss to the world, and neither does she understand herself as a bearer of some transcendent meaning that is to be gathered from the collection of losses she lists. Instead, through Grover, we witness each loss as particular, irrevocable, and concrete: she is their witness. Comparison between the deaths of her friends and clients and those of species and places remain specific, even if their juxtaposition allows for a bleeding together of social and ecological meaning and mourning. One of the most beautiful passages in this regard places the north woods directly inside an AIDS-ravaged body. On a dawn walk in the woods, Grover notes that a small meadow has appeared where last year there was water. "This," writes Grover, "is what I see: a former beaver pond, perfectly round and silted up, wind- and animal-seeded, moving slowly through the ordinations of succession. It is on its way to becoming a forest clearing, then a patch of forest" (22). Rather than mourn the loss of the pond "as it was," she greets the emergence of the meadow with a recognition of the in-process character of all that she sees, the fact that the landscape is *formed* through the death of some things en route to others. Then, on the next page, she describes changing the dressing on a sick friend's leg that has been macerated by Kaposi's sarcoma. Unwinding the reeking bandage, she wonders "how much of the world could I wind in something that was dying . . . returning to orderless matter?" Indeed, the leg is already fast becoming something else: "It did not look like a leg. It looked like freshly turned soil, dark and ruptured." She is forced, in this comparison, to ask of the leg the same question she asked of the meadow: could she learn to see it "as creation as well as destruction" (23)?

For Grover, then, acknowledging environmental loss and grieving the deaths of so many of her friends and clients allow a mutual recognition. Her melancholic refusal to "get over" the traumas and losses of her work as a caregiver forces her to consider the multiple presences of loss and death in the natural landscape around her, beyond the easy movements of substitution that would allow her to move her grief beyond the one attachment into another. In turn, Grover's acknowledgment of her landscape as a palpable collection, rather than a forgetting, of ongoing and devastating losses, allows her to consider the ways in which ruins have constituted *her* not as a "whole" being who has moved beyond death to a different sort of life, but rather as a being who is made of, must live amidst, and must mourn daily, the multiple deaths that surround us both environmentally and socially. For Grover, this position is hard-won and profoundly ethical: Rather than mourn the loss of the pristine, she carefully cultivates an attitude of appreciation of what lies before her, beyond the aesthetic wilderness to the intricate details of human interactions with the species and landscapes of the region. In this manner, she comes to be able to find the beauty in, for example, landfills and clear-cuts; far from naïveté or technophilia, this ability is grounded in a commitment to recognizing the simultaneity of death and life in these landscapes, the glut of aspen-loving birds in the clear-cut, the swallows, turkey vultures, and bald eagles near the landfill. Writing against a bland relativism that would fail to distinguish at all among landscapes, however,[14] she insists on a dialectics of loss that recognizes dying, and also beginning that is born, unpredictable and fragilely, from death.

Modern Nature

Derek Jarman's *Modern Nature* (1991) is written as a journal; its composition is, in contrast to *North Enough*'s carefully reflective essays, immediate, sensuous, and largely centered on the descriptive present of empirical experiences as they unfold. Beginning on January 1, 1989, the journal opens with Jarman's description of Prospect Cottage, his home on the remote shingle of Dungeness, and his intentions of planting a "wilderness" garden in the barren, exposed landscape: "There are no walls or fences. My garden's boundaries are the horizon. In this desolate landscape the silence is only broken by the wind, and the gulls squabbling round the fishermen bringing in the afternoon catch" (3). The text ends on September 3, 1990, with a brief entry describing his recent acute illness, his pain, a hospitalization, an appendectomy, dark morphine-induced nightmares, and more pain: "it's six months since I became ill. I've lost a stone and a half and the razor bumps across my face again" (314). In between, and in different depths and combinations, are stories about the gardens of Jarman's past and his varied relationships to them (and their gardeners), botanical lore and poetry quoted from a variety of historical sources, details about what Jarman has planted at Prospect (and what the rabbits, salt, and weather have or have not destroyed), and descriptions of the daily and seasonal changes to the garden and to the Dungeness landscape (including the day Jarman thought there had been an explosion at the nearby nuclear power plant). Increasingly as the text continues into later 1989 and 1990, there are homages to the friends and colleagues Jarman is losing to AIDS, in addition to painful descriptions of Jarman's own experiences as he begins to experience some of the acute illnesses related to his HIV infection.[15] And throughout, there is sex: passages of erotic play and longing as Jarman encounters a group of pretty young men on a film shoot; passages of fond memory as he recounts sexual experiences at his boarding school and in his young adulthood in London; and passages of frustration and anger as he considers the ways AIDS had affected not only his personal sexual possibilities ("my whole being has changed; my wild nights on the vodka are now only an aggravating memory, an itch before turning in," 25) but the sexual culture of his generation ("I walk in this garden/ Holding the hands of dead friends/ Old age came quickly for my frosted generation," 69). Sex, for Jarman, was a remarkable, wonderful freedom that gay men both had won and were in danger of losing (not just in the middle of AIDS, but also in the middle of an increasingly conservative Thatcherite Britain); the violent insinuations of death and homophobia into sex—through AIDS and Thatcher both—have brought into Jarman's being an uneasy requirement to rethink gay male sexuality away from a sort of pastoral embrace of innocent erotic abundance and toward a new respect for survival, tenacity, struggle, and small pleasures gathered in unlikely places. Jarman's garden is both an embodiment of this sexual trajectory—as his own body turns toward a more immediate dying, as his friends die, and as his generation's abundant sexual culture withers in a homophobic Britain, his hardy rosemary, sages, and marigolds survive and flourish despite all odds—and also a testament to the survival of the erotic-ecologic possibilities that, for Jarman, were integral to the gay male culture of his generation, including especially his own friends and lovers: "Before I finish, I intend to celebrate our corner of Paradise, the part of the garden the Lord forgot to mention" (23).

Daniel O'Quinn (1999) argues that Jarman's *Modern Nature* uses the figure of the garden—the "sacred sodomitical space" that the Lord forgot to mention and that Jarman is cultivating in Dungeness—as a way of inserting an alternative, queer temporality into dominant and monumental understandings of history and knowledge characteristic of Thatcherite Britain. Against sanitizing and naturalizing accounts of the British nation (and with it, British nature), both Jarman's garden and his journal consist of fragments of queer possibility lent political sharpness as disruptions of the homophobic and (I would add) increasingly naturalizing rhetorics of 1980s and 1990s state (sexual, national) conservatism. Gardens are figures of both monumental and (in Jarman's terms) also "modern" nature: where formal English gardens and parks speak of a sanitized, Masterpiece Theater–esque nostalgia for class privilege brought to the service of ongoing paternalism,[16] Jarman's garden deploys found objects and survivor-species (from rescued plants to recycled World War II anti-tank fencing) as a way of queering natural space, of (in O'Quinn's reading) creating a site of "holy" queerness for the dispossessed whose history is written out of conservative national heritage-natures, and especially for those whose erotic possibilities are eradicated by homophobia and surveillance: "Two young men holding hands on the street court ridicule, kissing they court arrest, so the worthy politicians, their collaborators, the priests, and the general public push them into corners where they can betray them in the dark. Judases in the garden of Gethsemane" (Jarman 1991, 15).

Importantly, O'Quinn also points to the parallel between Jarman's botanical assemblage and his literary one, noting that as his garden is a form of unlikely being-in-common deployed against univocal, conservative understandings of nation, nature, and heritage, so too is his collection of quotations and recounted memories an embodiment of resistant queer community in which sex, death, and nature manage to cohabit with some political force. Thinking in particular about the sensual immediacy of Jarman's juxtapositions of nature, sex, illness, and politics, I would thus suggest that *Modern Nature* is itself a sort of queer garden, one that cultivates an ethical practice of remembering as part of a queer ecological response to loss. Specifically, Jarman's choice to create his unlikely garden at Dungeness, and also to write about the process of doing so in the form of a collection of cohabiting experiences, expositions, and quotations, suggests a practice of queer memorialization that both politicizes AIDS by (melancholically) refusing to forget the lives and experiences and deaths of his friends and lovers (and, we know, eventually his own) and also establishes that memory in a sensuous, sensual world of plants, shingle, wind, salt—and a nuclear power plant. The garden is a metaphor for queer possibility in the midst of AIDS and homophobia, to be sure; Dungeness is, as Martine Delvaux writes, "Jarman's body, a garden in front of a nuclear power plant, a garden of shingle, rocks and pieces of metal in which rare, beautiful, luscious flowers grow" (2001, 137). But his queer ecology is also quite literal; his garden, alongside and in intersection with his writing, is a putting-together of forms of knowledge, experience, and plant life that are grounded and grown in a history and present of distinctly gay sexual and botanical experience (including, but not limited to, his own). For Jarman, his journals and his gardens are a writing of *natural* history in a queer vein, a deeply politicized insistence on understanding the garden as an ongoing legacy of queer lives and possibilities that thrive despite hostile conditions.

Jarman's nature is definitely queer. In the one sense, he clearly rejects any view of gardens and gardening that relies on an overarching systematization of gardening practice, be it based on application of horticultural science, quest for aesthetic harmony, or even adherence to ecological principle. His journals are a true pastiche of fragments, loosely collected into an almanac of occasionally clashing elements without movement toward resolution or ending; the journals disrupt the unity of the very *idea* of the garden as an element in progressivist history.[17] But in another, even more powerful sense, Jarman's nature is also distinctly *homosexual.* In mixing together fragments of historical plant-knowledge, literary quotations, and gardening experiences with his own often erotically charged memories of gardens, he insists that we read each species he considers—primrose, rosemary, narcissus, dill, daffodil, bugloss—in light of its role in sexual histories as well as the botanical ones with which sex has been historically intertwined. These sexual histories are sometimes mythical, sometimes medical, sometimes personal, and sometimes all of the above. For example, Jarman has a lot to say about violets. His entry for Wednesday, March 22, 1989, begins by quoting Gerard, who notes that the flowers "stirre up a man to that which is comely and honest" (37). It goes on by invoking Culpeper, Pindar, and Goethe, who "carried violet seeds on his country walks and scattered them" (37). And then:

> The violet held a secret. Along the hedgerow that ran down to the cliffs at Hordle deep purple violets grew—perhaps no more than a dozen plants. I stumbled across them late one sunny March afternoon as I came up the cliff path from the sea. They were hidden in a small recess. I stood for some moments dazzled by them.
>
> Day after day I returned from the dull regimental existence of an English boarding school to my secret garden—the first of many that blossomed in my dreams. It was here that I brought him, sworn to secrecy, and then watched him slip out of his grey flannel suit and lie naked in the spring sunlight. Here our hands first touched. . . . Bliss that he turned and lay naked on his stomach, laughing as my hand ran down his back and disappeared into the warm darkness between his thighs. . . .
>
> Obsessive violets drawing the evening shadows to themselves, our fingers touching in the purple. (37–38)

The gay eroticism of violets is thus *part* of their history and lore: Jarman entwines sexual biography back into botanical history by pointing out that, despite his grandmother's disapproval of the memorial violets on his bedside table as "flowers of death," they are "the third in the trinity of symbolic flowers, flower of purity" (38). Their sexual texture is integral to their existence in the journals and in the garden; each flower brings with it not only a complex web of knowledges and possibilities, but a distinctly *queer* legacy that is both opened by Jarman's biography and sustained by the enmeshment of its distinctly sexual textures in the middle of that web. For Jarman, the garden has always been queer; the point of *Modern Nature* is to remember it.

In addition, of course, Jarman insists that we remember in other ways. Noting the particular dead with whom he walks, hand in hand, in the garden, he demands we speak with his dead friends, lovers, and colleagues because they are here, planted in *this* queer garden, their fragments literally and figuratively set among the rosemary (herb of remembering) and borage: "To whom it may concern/ in the dead stones of a planet/ no longer remembered as earth/ may he decipher this opaque hieroglyph/ perform an archaeology of the soul/ on these previous fragments/ all that remains of our vanished days . . ." (16). The "our" is specific: Jarman's garden is a memorial for his generation, for the sense of open sexual and political possibility on which it thrived; included among his plants are also parties, anonymous blow jobs on Hampstead Heath, old queers in Rolls Royces with young boys in tight pants. "Each stone has a life to tell" (178). He is not nostalgic for an imagined gay London golden age, as if there were not repression and violence then as well as now; rather, he tells of the 1960s and 1970s through particular stories, encounters, clothes, happenings, and aspirations, and ties each one firmly to the present by inserting it into the particular days of his almanac. This present moment leads me to *this* past fragment; this plant or motion or event reminds me of *him* on *this* day. The sexual, political past thus remains inside the melancholic present, and the journals extend that remaining; Jarman insists not only on interrupting a blanketing logic of conservative forgetting, but also on keeping particular people, particular sensations, particular experiences and possibilities alive in his gardens.

Particularly as 1989 moves into 1990, his journals are increasingly taken up with descriptions of his own experiences of illness. Jarman is most definitely alive in 1990 and is not about to confirm the British media's premature dispatch of him to the grave (his last film, *Blue,* was released in 1994). But it is clear that his present is marked by his death, and it is often the garden that allows him to imagine a world beyond fevered delirium, drugs, and hospital wards: "I'm feeling much clearer this morning, planting the garden in my mind, sowing fennel and calendula" (258). Or again, past gardens: "childhood flowers, dew-boned peonies, dark red, along the paths at Curry Malet. . . . Syringia in the vases. A cream white rose climbing through the old apples. . . . My cacti gardens. Beans for salting: scarlet, french and broad. Never a cauliflower. . . . All this I remember at 12:30 after a night sweat" (278). After an extended stay in the hospital in London, Jarman returns to Dungeness and revels in a series of small observations: bees, sunshine, a butterfly. He is moved to tears: "I weep for the garden so lonely in the shingle desert" (281). The journals become more compressed as the physical realities of Jarman's illness impact his ability to write. He moves between quickly sketched, imagistic renderings of the landscape and its varied inhabitants and frustrated confessions of the various failures of his body. "I'm as breathless as an octogenarian. A red admiral flew newly minted, fluttering against the kitchen window" (290). It is as if he is concentrating on placing his memories into the garden that will clearly outlast him, that will bear his memories alongside the other dead for whom he created it: "Collected stones for the garden along the beach. Cut back the curry plants. Dark clouds and suffocating heat. . . . Mrs. Richardson, who was born in this house four years after it was built, came to look at the garden. She was pleased that Prospect Cottage is loved" (311).

Modern Nature was not Jarman's final word. It was, however, a particular kind of textual-botanical memorial to the queer past, to his generation, and indeed to himself. Even more than Grover, perhaps, Jarman politicizes remembering by insisting on the queerness of writing and gardening as parallel memorial practices. His garden embodies the sensuous and erotic present of his writing; his writing joyfully cultivates a queer botanical mélange; and both carefully plant a specifically queer memory that links sexual fullness with natural history in refusal of conservative national, sexual, and historical rhetorics. His melancholic garden is, then, a very queer nature indeed.

Conclusions

As I have argued throughout this chapter, melancholia is a psychic state of being that holds the possibility for memory's transformation into ethical and political environmental reflection. Particularly in a context in which certain lives are considered ungrievable—here, including both non-heterosexual and more-than-human relationships—melancholia represents a holding-on to loss in defiance of bourgeois (and capitalist) imperatives to forget, move on, transfer attention to a new relationship/commodity. Both Grover and Jarman have grieved magnificently, and have held on to their beloveds (individually, collectively, culturally) by bringing them to nature, both literally, as in Jarman's politicized memorial planting of queer sexual histories in his gardens, and metaphorically, as in Grover's growing understanding of her landscape as a site of death and transformation to which she has ongoing ethical obligations. Although, again, I would not want to make an argument that gay men and lesbians—or bisexual, transgender, intersex, or any other queer-identified folks—have a special, experiential relationship to nature or to environmental issues by virtue of their identities or experiences, it is still worth noting that for both Grover and Jarman, an emotionally charged practice of melancholic remembering took them from a gay-focused experience of AIDS to a distinctly queer appreciation of nature in deeply moving and ethically/politically sophisticated ways.

But one might ask: What, after all, is especially "ecological" about any of this queer remembering? Despite a couple of passing references in *Modern Nature* to global warming, it is hard to claim Jarman's journals as a work informed by overtly "environmental" sentiments, and even Grover's more obvious engagement with environmental ethics might be said to owe as much to Aldo Leopold as it does to any specifically queer origins. In response, I would answer: their queerness *as* ecologies is key. Both Grover and Jarman refused dominant understandings of nature (as substitutable commodity, to be sure, but also as wilderness, as park, as "ecological integrity," as national heritage, as linear unfolding of biological events, and as origin and reflection of natural law and morality) in order to allow their memories to take hold and to influence their material and epistemic landscapes. By allowing the natural world to be a field of intimately mourned lives and possibilities, both Grover and Jarman developed a principled understanding of the relationships between non-heterosexual lives in the midst of homophobia and the more-than-human world in the midst of environmental devastation. To return to Anderson's opening imperative—"it is necessary to face our fear and our pain"—both Grover and Jarman underscore that we have to make room in our relationships with the natural world, queer and otherwise, for the recognition that that is what we might be feeling in the first place.

NOTES

Small portions of the section "AIDS and Other Clear-Cuts" were previously published, in an earlier version, in Mortimer-Sandilands (2008).

1. In her 1969 book *On Death and Dying,* Kübler-Ross outlined a five-stage theory of grief that has had an enormous impact on contemporary thinking about so-called normal processes of grief despite profoundly mixed clinical evidence—and also the tremendous problems, as I will discuss below, with normalizing understandings of proper responses to loss. Her stages are: denial, anger, bargaining, depression, and acceptance. In his article, Anderson substitutes "despair" for depression and omits bargaining altogether.

2. There are other exceptions. The final chapter of Andy Fisher's *Radical Ecopsychology,* for example, is focused on the suffering inherent in modernity and the need for its acknowledgment, in addition to the development of conditions to allow suffering to be borne meaningfully. Indeed, the phrase "environmental grief" ap-

pears to have been trademarked (!) by thanatologist Kriss Kevorkian (2006), whose research explores the experiences of animal scientists for whom the loss of individual animals, families of animals, and even species of animals is felt as the personal loss of a loved one.

3. The rhetoric of "saving" one special place may be effective in preserving that one place for a particular set of uses, but it seldom has the effect of challenging the relations that made it necessary to save it in the first place. See Sandilands 2003.

4. In this chapter, I use the term "queer" not as an equivalent to "lesbian and gay," or to the acronym "lgbttq." I understand that Grover's and Jarman's experiences of death and loss certainly emerge from their particular experiences in the context of particular gay and lesbian communities and politics, but I also insist that their choices to politicize grieving in and through reflection on landscapes is part of a queer sensibility, a choice to *trouble* prevailing sexual and, in this case, environmental ideas and practices.

5. Freud amplifies this idea in *The Ego and the Id,* in which he argues that these highly critical melancholic identifications (including guilt) are a process by which the "character" of the ego is built violently in the super-ego's relentless criticism of the ego in relation to its ideal.

6. This chapter does not address the history of melancholia, including its classical origins, its humoral attributions, its association with aestheticism and literary work, and its most recent associations with clinical depression. Suffice it to say that the understanding of melancholia as associated with mourning is historically recent (Freud is attempting to *establish* this connection in "Mourning and Melancholia") and that the condition has carried with it considerable ambivalence—e.g., it has been conceived as both illness and creative source—across a variety of historically specific understandings. For an excellent rendering of that history, see Radden 2000.

7. In *Black Sun* (1987), Julia Kristeva argues that the subject compensates for loss by identifying with the *sign,* in other words, by rendering melancholia nameable and meaningful. Although this essay will not pursue Kristeva's analysis of melancholia, it is worth noting that the absence of a sign, in her argument—a loss that cannot be named—would prevent meaning.

8. Von Unwerth notes that this walk never took place: Freud did have a meeting with Rilke in 1913, but it was at the Fourth Annual Psycho-analytical Congress in Munich (45). Freud's literary choice to locate the discussion of transience in nature *in nature* (and in the summer, not autumn) is thus interesting.

9. By "life-filled places" I do not mean wilderness, but rather rich and deeply particular experiences of being surrounded by creatures that are not all human. If anything, I am privileging a personal experience of something like biodiversity, but I would be willing to argue that even the loss of a monocultural stretch of suburban grass on which one once played cricket would qualify. The only place in which there appears to be any recognition at all of loss of a nonhuman being as an allowable grief is in the loss of a pet, and even that is far from universal ("you should get another cat" is a clear indication of the fact that animals are often considered substitutable).

10. Briefly, her argument (Butler 1997) is that masculinity and femininity are precarious achievements that are socially and psychically produced, in the context of a prohibition against homosexuality, through the *compulsory loss* of homosexual attachments. Prior to the Oedipal relation (in which heterosexual desire is already assumed) children of both (all?) sexes are forced to reject a primary homosexual attachment, and loss of that attachment is—in the identificatory "resolution" of the Oedipal relation—essentially melancholy in character. The lost (homosexual) desire is

eventually incorporated into the ego in the form of an ego-*identification* with the lost object, namely, gender identity. The key to the melancholic quality of this relationship lies, of course, in the fact that the primary homosexual attachment is not only lost but ungrievable: the (demanded) loss of the homosexual attachment is disavowed, and the impossibility of grieving it is what propels it into unconscious conflict, and toward ego-identification (in the course of which process the gendered "character" of the ego is established).

11. The resemblance to Walter Benjamin's "Theses on the Philosophy of History" (1968) is not accidental. Write Eng and Kazanjian, "According to Benjamin, to mourn the remains of the past—rather as one might imagine Klee's *Angelus Novus* doing in his backward-moving gaze on the *ruins of a history of ruins*—is to establish an active and open relationship with history" (1, original emphasis).

12. Cvetkovich also discusses Grover's book (212–18).

13. Grover has written extensively about fly fishing, and is (according to the cover of *North Enough*) an editor of *Midwest Fly Fishing*. She casts without a hook: "I love trout streams, I love to be where fish are, I love to cast, but I don't want to play fish for my pleasure" (83). She weights her tippit with "Day-Glo acrylic" wool instead.

14. Grover has no place for sentimentality. Upon seeing a robin feeding from a puddle of human vomit, she notes: "Both deprived and blessed by no longer needing to mine other creatures' offcasts for our own sustenance, we have gone so far as to lose touch with what such substances as shit and vomit actually are" (116). For Grover, the sentimental separation of nature and human does neither any intrinsic good; the ethical art, for her, is to greet the complex interactions between and among them with intelligence (including ecological intelligence), wonder, and gratitude.

15. There are also narrative passages about some of the film projects on which Jarman was working at the time, including *The Garden* (1990) and *Edward II* (1991). Although many of the themes raised in *Modern Nature* are echoed in Jarman's films—*The Garden* was filmed in Dungeness and clearly overlaps in both formally and thematically important ways with the diaries—this chapter sticks to the written memoir. For an interesting review of Jarman's filmic oeuvre that includes a description of *The Garden* as "a pastoral paean to England's shingly, majestic, luminously changeable shoreline," see Kennedy (1993, 34).

16. O'Quinn focuses on Jarman's treatment of Sissinghurst and the Borghese Gardens. Sissinghurst is especially interesting: its previous incarnation as the erotic botanical playground of the Sackville-Wests has been "'heritized' in the institutional hands of the National Trust" (Jarman 1991, 15).

17. The resemblance to Walter Benjamin's thinking is again worth noting, here concerning the montage as a way of shattering bourgeois, linear historical unities.

REFERENCES

Anderson, Richard B. 2001. The World Is Dying—and So Are You, orig. Commentary. *Los Angeles Times*, January 7. www.forthefuture.org /assets/articles/col_grief .htm.

Benjamin, Walter. 1968. *Illuminations*. Trans. Harry Zohn. New York: Schocken Books.

Braun, Bruce. 2002. *The Intemperate Rainforest: Nature, Culture and Power on Canada's West Coast*. Minneapolis: University of Minnesota Press.

Butler, Judith. 1997. *The Psychic Life of Power: Theories in Subjection.* Stanford, Calif.: Stanford University Press.

————. 2004. *Precarious Life: The Powers of Mourning and Violence.* London: Verso.

Campbell, SueEllen. 2003. *Even Mountains Vanish: Searching for Solace in an Age of Extinction.* Salt Lake City: University of Utah Press.

Crimp, Douglas. 1989. Mourning and Militancy. *October* 5 (Winter): 3–18.

Cvetkovich, Ann. 2003. *An Archive of Feelings: Trauma, Sexuality, and Lesbian Public Cultures.* Durham, N.C.: Duke University Press.

Delvaux, Martine. 2001. The Garden as Memento Mori: Derek Jarman and Jamaica Kincaid. *Canadian Woman Studies* 21.2: 135–38.

Doty, Mark. 1996. *Heaven's Coast: A Memoir.* New York: HarperCollins.

Eng, David L., and David Kazanjian, eds. 2003. *Loss: The Politics of Mourning.* Berkeley and Los Angeles: University of California Press.

Fisher, Andy. 2002. *Radical Ecopsychology: Psychology in the Service of Life.* New York: State University of New York Press.

Freud, Sigmund. 1984. *On Metapsychology: The Theory of Psychoanalysis.* Trans. and ed. James Strachey and Angela Richards. Penguin Freud Library, vol. 11. London: Penguin Books.

Grover, Jan Zita. 1997. *North Enough: AIDS and Other Clear-Cuts.* Saint Paul, Minn.: Graywolf Press.

Jarman, Derek. 1991. *Modern Nature: The Journals of Derek Jarman.* London: Vintage Books.

Kennedy, Harlan. 1993. The Two Gardens of Derek Jarman. *Film Commentary* (November/December): 28–35.

Kevorkian, Kriss A. 2006. Environmental Grief: Hope and Healing. Proceedings of Environmental Justice and Global Citizenship: 5th Global Conference, July 3–6, 2006, Mansfield College, Oxford. http://www.cybercultures.net/ptb/ejgc/ejgc5/s13.html.

Kristeva, Julia. 1987. *Black Sun: Depression and Melancholia.* New York: Columbia University Press.

Kübler-Ross, Elisabeth. 1969. *On Death and Dying.* New York: MacMillan.

Leopold, Aldo. 1949. *Sand County Almanac: And Sketches Here and There.* New York: Oxford University Press.

Mortimer-Sandilands, Catriona. 2008. "I Still Need the Revolution": Cultivating Ecofeminist Readers. In *Teaching North American Environmental Literature,* ed. Laird Christensen, Mark C. Long, and Frederick Waage, 58–71. New York: Modern Languages Association of America.

O'Quinn, Daniel. 1999. Gardening, History, and the Escape from Time: Derek Jarman's *Modern Nature. October* 89: 113–26.

Radden, Jennifer. 2000. *The Nature of Melancholy: From Aristotle to Kristeva.* New York: Oxford University Press.

Ruti, Mari. 2005. From Melancholia to Meaning: How to Live the Past in the Present. *Psychoanalytic Dialogues* 15.5: 637–60.

Sandilands, Catriona. 2003. Between the Local and the Global: Clayoquot Sound and Simulacral Politics. In *A Political Space: Reading the Global Through Clayoquot Sound,* ed. Warren Magnusson and Karena Shaw, 139–67. Minneapolis: University of Minnesota Press.

von Unwerth, Matthew. 2005. *Freud's Requiem: Mourning, Memory, and the Invisible History of a Summer Walk.* New York: Riverhead Books.

CHAPTER 13

Biophilia, Creative Involution, and the Ecological Future of Queer Desire

DIANNE CHISHOLM

Our essence as a species binds us to explore and affiliate with all life. We are lovers who can add up glucose, amino acids, water, fragrant oils, pigments, and other tissue and call it both a flower and a mystical gesture. We can also decimate pollinators with an unloving tonnage of pesticides, precipitating the extinction of entire populations of those mystical gestures, once and forever. . . . Lives without access to sensation are lives that edge out the earth's raw, pervasive sweetness, that deeply biophilic connection to all life.

—Ellen Meloy

Somehow I am able to cross species lines without a single lesion in self-respect.

—Ellen Meloy

In Ellen Meloy's seriously quirky writing of the desert southwest, the linking of affections and affiliations across species lines are more than idiosyncratically queer.[1] Meloy uses ecologist Edward O. Wilson's "biophilia" hypothesis as a method of cognitive adventuring into the frontiers of symbiosis.[2] Her explorations of bio-erotic-diversity map flows of desire that escape classical biology and exceed even the "biological exuberance" with which nonhuman animals embrace homosexuality.[3] She is more likely to track creative, nonprocreative interspecies crossings and the molecular heterogenesis between radically differing (animal, vegetable, mineral, other) life forms, than to wonder, as Wilson does, at the elaborate organization of reproductive sex between individuals of the same species. If, for Wilson, biophilia is a mindful reverence for the infinity of organic sexual-social order, for Meloy, it is an earthy curiosity for the erotic vitality with which life—especially desert life—affects fidelity to extreme geography. She senses a *philia* more physical than ideal, one that stirs and connects her cognitive desires (epistemo-bio-philia) to the evolving endemism of desert species.[4] With a field scientist's fidelity to nature's experimentality, her writing conjugates the elements of survival and vitality in variations too perverse to be classified. And with an eye for the exotic in her own backyard, she enters voyeuristically into the multifarious sex comedy of her desert cohabitants. Such involvement allows her to see beyond the set schemata of natural selection to whatever queer couplings enable life to thrive in the desert's volatile landscape.

E. O. Wilson's biophilia, then, becomes something else in Meloy's reworking of the concept. For Wilson, it is a love for the diversity of non-human life that stirs the mind to infinity for the beneficial enlightenment of humanity; for Meloy, it is an erotic-ethical affiliation between human and nonhuman life in experimental symbioses whose ecological benefits are sensed and desired, if not fully cognizable. What makes Meloy's nature writing queer is not an express allegiance to minority sexuality but a creative and attentive naturalism that tracks interspecies couplings across the desert's vital landscape on a map of co-adaptation, which standard ecosite grids and biological taxonomies fail to chart.

The language, thought, and perception with which Meloy explores the queer nature of survival on the Colorado Plateau are more innovative than her sources in ecological and biological science. A more radical philosophy might illuminate her revision of biophilia. French philosophers Gilles Deleuze and Félix Guattari have invented a conceptual "plan/e of nature" for rethinking desire on and for earth that abandons the conceits of anthropocentric humanism. Their monument to geophilosophy, *A Thousand Plateaus* (1987) presents Meloy's reader with a pluralist empiricism with which to analyze the queer conjugations of affect and affiliation in her nature writing.[5] Meloy, I contend, shares with Deleuze and Guattari various philosophical sources in theoretical biology, quantum physics, and chaos and complexity theory. She, like them, prefers Darwinian to Freudian conceptualizations of evolutionary processes, and, like them, she describes a vitalism in which nonreproductive sex is a primary force of nature. Meloy maps her Plateau as a nonlinear experiment in symbiotic couplings and heterogenesis that calls to mind what Deleuze and Guattari describe as the "creative involution" of germinal life.

The aims of this chapter, then, are to: (1) introduce readers to Ellen Meloy's new concept and practice of nature writing; (2) investigate the conjugations of affect in this writing that surpass both biophilia and biological exuberance in their capacity to que(e)ry adaptive interspecies cohabitation and coevolution; and (3) illuminate the radical, ethical, and philosophical implications of this writing by reading it alongside Deleuze and Guattari's geophilosophy. Finally, this chapter will show how Meloy poses an ecological future for queer desire in place of a popular form of queer nihilism that fails to imagine life beyond pro-life conservatism and its critical deconstruction.

Biophilia, Epistemophilia, Cognitive Adventuring

To Dana Phillips's (2003) skeptical question "What Do Nature Writers Want?" at the end of his book on *The Truth of Ecology*,[6] we can find in Meloy's work an ironic answer: nature writers desire to know what nature desires. Her investigation of nature places less emphasis on the writer's desiring self than on the desiring (plant or animal) other, and on writing as a way to explore the desiring nature of desert life—of desiring life in extremis. What, she asks, does a prickly pear cactus desire that couples it so tenaciously to bare basalt sandstone with a sexual rhythm that erratically keeps pace with drought and flash flood? What conjugation of organic and inorganic elements add up to such a thriving, if exotic, symbiotic assemblage? As a committed "biophiliac" (Meloy 2002, 244), Meloy artfully pursues the flow of desert desire by mapping its (un)folding ero-eco-logical entanglements in first-person narratives of queer affection.

For instance, the prologue to her desert journal *Eating Stone: Imagination and the Loss of the Wild* (2005) places the reader with the narrator in the zone of proximity where human and wild animal "meet," and where the border of difference is both most intense and most porous. The "intercourse" that ensues is neither zoophilic bestiality nor anthropomorphic romancing; rather, it is a transmutation of human being into something other, prompted by the closeness of the human body to the vibrating heat and rhythms of the animal pack. After months of tracking a wild band of desert bighorn sheep through their seasonal cataclysms of rutting, lambing, and survival canyoneering at intensifying close range, Meloy describes undergoing a schizoidal shift in self-consciousness. More precisely, self-consciousness becomes other-consciousness, through the conduit of affective proximity:

> On one of my last winter days with the desert bighorns, they no longer kept me out of their world. With motions I had come to know as an exquisite union of liturgy and physics, they closed the

distance between us and herded me toward a threshold, a place best described as a hairsbreadth. . . . They moved serenely among themselves, brushing flanks warm with blood, weaving me toward that breach of transmutation. . . . I wanted to leap into that wild side—their side—then bring back their startling news from the other-than-human world. (Meloy 2005, xi)

Encountering the wild animal at so close a range as to enter the other's bodily orbit, her own biorhythms seem to pulse to the beat of the beast. Stirred by the movements of the pack to a threshold of becoming-other-than-human, she desires to sense what the bighorn senses, to know the bighorn's world. This is not to say that she desires to metamorphose into a bighorn or to transcend being human in an animistic leap of faith. Instead, by being so intensely proximal to the pack, she becomes caught up in its migrations and affections in an other dimension of belonging to place. She senses an otherworld with defamiliarized, or deterritorialized, human sensibility—a sensibility pushed to the limit of being human on the threshold of becoming other, alert to how bighorn world the earth, and how they attune and attach themselves to a homeland. But if she imagines crossing species lines, it is only to "bring back their startling news" to the human side, where human knowledge of the nonhuman can be put to mutually beneficial work. Such a transmutation of being human could have ramifications for becoming wiser about cohabiting the wild symbiotically, instead of approaching it unilaterally with ideas of human progress and development.

Referring to recent evolutionary theory, Meloy interprets her threshold experience of becoming-bighorn as "cognitive adventuring" (Meloy 2005, 160). She is careful to distinguish the imagination it entails from psychoanalytic fantasy and/or romantic phantasmagoria. Evolutionary cognition stresses the fluidity of human, and especially childhood, imagination, as well as the imagination of paleo-peoples who once lived side by side with packs of wild animals; it does not locate imagination in the interior domain of the human psyche or limit its cultivation to fantasmatic structuration and cultural transmission. The human mind, Meloy believes, evolves in contact with animal life. Children's playacting the animal is an elementary act of becoming human, of animating the senses, and of connecting and communicating with other animals and other animal territories. Children are drawn to animals, and to "explore and affiliate" with nonhuman life forms more easily than are "stodgy adults" (161). Biophilia, then, should not be mistaken for "epistemophilia"—Freud's "instinct for knowledge" that expresses an unattainable desire for sexual satisfaction in more or less sublimated fantasies of phallic self-mastery and self-possession.[7] *"Arrivederci,* Sigmund. Hello, Charles Darwin" (160), Meloy announces, affirming neo-Darwinian theory that human cognition evolves through a capacity to connect with and imagine other/animal life.

Meloy's nature writing experiments in cognitive adventuring and crossing species lines evoke Deleuze and Guattari's neo-evolutionary ontology of "becoming-animal." In their "anti-Oedipal" revision of Freudian/Lacanian theories of desire, these philosophers consider flows of attraction and sensation that escape the intra-psychic dynamics of the ego and hook the sensory body into its external affective environment in multiplicities of sense. In a paradigmatic case of radical revision, they reinterpret the horse phobia of Freud's famous client "Little Hans" to be less a masochistic fixation with the paternal phallus than an expression of compound affect. Accordingly, Little Hans does not so much fear the horse's phallus onto which he projects an inflated and terrifying paternal imago (against an image of his own small "pee-pee-maker"), as he is struck by the horse's affective body—or by affects that radiate from the horse when it pisses voluminously after falling under too-heavy loads and being whipped by an infuriated driver. Accordingly, the child enters into an affective assemblage of "becoming-horse," composed of real sensations and virtual affiliations between the human and the animal. It is not that the child identifies with the horse as possessor of a pee-pee maker, or that he projects paranoiac homosexual fantasies of a paternal beating out of desire for recognition of his own phallus-bearing potency. Rather, proximity to the flailing horse affects the child's body with the vibrating anguish of the animal body. The child senses he is part of a complex. He becomes virtually attached to the body that is being lashed and made to piss, and through which the other's pain is conducted to the boy's own vulnerable body with powerful affection (Deleuze and Guattari 1987, 257).

"Disguised as an adult" (Meloy 2005, 162), Meloy goes into the field to study desert bighorn who live in the canyon near her home in southeastern Utah, and who mysteriously disappear in summer drought to secret waterholes. She wants to know where they go and how they adapt so tenaciously to such severely parched territory. With her she takes "friends"—a childhood teddy bear and a stuffed toy bighorn (named "Nelson" after the subspecies *Ovid canadensis nelsoni,* 163–64). These toys are not symptoms of infantile regression but playful attendants to long hours in the field that wildlife observation demands. More importantly, they are talismanic cues to cognitive adventuring that a child is best equipped to undertake. Meloy primes herself to enter bighorn territory by placing herself in contact with these animal simulacra, which in turn, induce a "becoming-child" of the adult, or a re-engagement of the child's proclivity to undergo, like Little Hans, a "becoming-animal." As Deleuze and Guattari explain,

> it is as though, independent of the evolution carrying them toward adulthood, there were room in the child for other becomings, "other contemporaneous possibilities" that are not regressions but creative involutions bearing witness to *"an inhumanity immediately experienced in the body as such,"* unnatural nuptials "outside the programmed body." (Deleuze and Guattari 1987, 273, original emphasis)

Lusting after Linnaeus

Meloy's "A Field Guide to Brazen Harlotry" expresses a graphic form of biophilia. Drawn from her still-wintering home in Montana to desert latitudes where spring blooms prodigiously, Meloy uproots her domestic life for the Southwest's vernal heat. She maps her vagrancy in a hybrid language attuned to the biologic, edaphic, and chromatic machinery of wildflower sex. In purple passages of cognitive adventuring she imagines "leaping into bed" with desert flora to satiate a craving to know their seduction of color. With spring wildflowers she is readily "able to cross species lines." The intensity with which flora inflame her perceptive and cognitive lusts can be attributed to molecular attractions between light and pigment, especially in conjugations of red:

> Red flowers sear retinas made weary by winter, by snow or the season's low, angular light. . . . There are physical reasons for the boldness of red. Light waves are longer at the red end of the spectrum of visible light. During a lurid desert sunset, layers of dust close to the horizon absorb the short wavelengths while the long red waves reach the eye. . . . The eye bears three pigments—blue, green, and red—that absorb light and signal the brain to read colors. . . . In plant and human worlds, in mountain and desert, red flowers like the snow plant and paintbrush are visual aphrodisiacs, they signal the seasonal shift from dormancy to reproductive frenzy, from the cerebral to the carnal. . . . Red is the color of martyrs, blood, hell, and desire. It quickens the heart and desire. It quickens the heart and releases adrenaline. (Meloy 2002, 226)[8]

The "searing" red of desert blooms, made especially luscious "against blond rock," arouses an attraction that is brazenly sexual and peculiarly female—given the chromosomal variation in pigmentation that marks sexual difference: "Some women have two different red pigments in their eyes. They see subtle differences in color that men and other women cannot see" (ibid.). It is not the blond but the red against the blond, and it is not the other sex but chromatic difference and intensity that "quickens" Meloy's affection.

The volatility of desert spring inflames Meloy's desire to explore the secrets of terrestrial life. As the first color to spring from dormant buds, red allures her eye for seasonal change; "red is common to early bloomers," she observes, "as if nature wished to jump-start spring" (225). The speed and intensity with which bone-dry vegetation turns lush with hydration stirs her senses into palpitating attention: "Desert flora are sparse and ephemeral. There are spines, thorns, uncertain seeds, long periods of dormancy, and, when, moisture comes, a passion so accelerated, you feel their demands on your heart, the mounting pleasure, the sweet exhaustion" (221).

Meloy's heart literally beats to the desert's pulse, prompting a rhythm of thought that moves in synch with the accelerated speed of germinal life. For example, a profusion of flowering globemallow erupting across the slickrock stirs her to imagine "How Flowers Changed the World":

> The globemallow fields of spring could, in a reckless descent into the deep past, recall the burst of flora into the raw dust-and-basalt monotone of a primordial planet. . . . For several million years— the crashing reptile, lizard bird, wimpy mammal ancestor, swamp years—plant life held little in its palette beyond a "slowly growing green." . . . At the eclipse of the dinosaur age, "there occurred a soundless, violent explosion. It lasted millions of years, but it was an explosion nevertheless. It marked the emergence of angiosperms— the flowering plants." (2002, 227, citing Loren Eiseley)

Thinking contiguously with the blooming landscape, Meloy's observation leaps from the contemporary to the evolutionary. At the sight of flaming globemallow on monochrome basalt, she virtually beholds the first "explosion" of plant sex, "the emergence of angiosperms [that] even the great evolutionist, Charles Darwin, called . . . 'an abominable mystery,' because they appeared so suddenly and spread so fast" (227–28, citing Eiseley).

Understanding the physical reasons for why she feels such allure to the reds of claret-cup cactus and red-rock strata, Meloy explains and confirms her attachment to place. "I cannot put the desert at my back. I cannot leave the red" (Meloy 1994, 253), she confesses, explaining the homesickness she feels on return to her Montana abode. Despite being happily married and at home on the Montana range, Meloy tracks desert "harlotry" with an affiliate vagabondage. She follows the "edaphic endemism" of desert paintbrush with a queer fidelity to the plant's rootless lust for red-rock soil: "Paintbrush genera spread themselves from Wyoming to New Mexico and eastern California to Colorado. But many of them slip their lives into bare-boned sandstone. The paintbrush becomes attached to its homestead. I interpret this as affective as well as physical and take them on as allies. I admire their loyalty to dirt" (Meloy 2002, 225). Such sensation of alliance surpasses any aesthetic appreciation or phenomenology of taste; it expresses an ecological affection for earth and a nomadic territoriality.

Meloy confesses her wildflower passions in prose more vivid than the "botanical pornography" of Carolus Linnaeus (Meloy 2002, 239). She follows standard field guide practice by "counting petals, defining shapes and symmetries, sorting the petiole from the pappus, the basal rosettes from the pinnately compounded," but she also invents a pornologia that strays from classical taxonomy. Linnaeus scandalized the scientific community by "naming a genus of pea plant *Clitorida*," but he also coded his erotic onomastics in sexual legitimacy: He "acknowledged nothing premarital or illicit. All was 'husbands' and 'wives' or *polygamia* and *polyandria* when male (stamens) or female organs (pistils) were multiple. . . . He edged into plant lust in descriptions of nuptial beds with perfumes and petal curtains for privacy" (239). In contrast, Meloy invents a "slickrotica" (224) that names the thousand tiny sexes that more complexly compose desert flower seductiveness. In passages of cognitive adventuring, she enters zones of proximity with the flower where her floraphilia becomes most intensely aroused by the multiple colors, shapes, and touch of sex:

> I climb and curl up inside the bloom of a prickly pear cactus and think that the sex life of plants is not a simple affair. So many delicate body parts for seduction and consummation—filament, anther, pistil, ovary, stigma, style, a corolla of silky petals to enclose the cusp of love. In this blossom the corolla is a warm bath of golden light. Although some prickly pear bloom in magenta, and a rare coral pink, I have chosen one with bright cadmium-yellow flowers that blush rose on their backsides, outside the cup. The thick petals shimmer with a heated luminosity; they feel like satin against my lips. (239)

Flower sex, she intimates, escapes containment by the conjugal relations ordained by Linnaeus. There are "so many delicate body parts for seduction and consummation," so many body parts that commingle promiscuously with part-bodies of other plants, and insect and animal bodies. She imagines conjugations of color, light, and touch in compound symbiotic molecularities that may or may not aid sexual reproduction and filiation. Her expression of botanical eroticism practices a kind of empiricism that escapes categorical thinking and engages the senses of the naturalist in erotic acts of cognition. "There was," she writes, "little doubt in my mind what all these plants were up to, their wild, palpable surge of seduction best absorbed by the undermind—no categories, no labels, no conscious grasping but a kind of sideways knowing. Spring in the desert grew beyond the reach of intellect and became a blinding ache for intimacy, not unlike beauty, not unlike physical love" (224).

Rhizome Sex and Creative Involution

"Sideways knowing" implies a perception of oblique affections and couplings that Meloy entertains whenever she crosses species lines. She shares with Deleuze and Guattari a focus on the transversality of life processes. *A Thousand Plateaus* conceptualizes desire as a force that is ontologically immanent to all life on earth, and that propels "earth moves" across and between geological strata and biological orders. By mapping the transversality of symbiogenesis across the vertical lines of genealogi-cal descent,[9] Deleuze and Guattari ask us to think *rhizomatically* like an earthbound desert nomad, and to not (or not only) think *arborescently* (transcendentally, linearly) like a European metaphysician. Thinking, they say, should look to

> the wisdom of the plants; even when they have roots, there is al-ways an outside where they form a rhizome with something else— with wind, an animal, human beings (and there is also an aspect under which animals themselves form rhizomes, as do people, etc.). "Drunkenness as a triumphant irruption of the plant in us." Always follow the rhizome by rupture; lengthen, prolong, and relay the line of flight; make it vary, until you have produced the most abstract and tortuous lines of *n* dimensions and broken directions. Conjugate the deterritorialized flows. Follow the plants. . . . Write, form a rhizome. (Deleuze and Guattari 1987, 11)

"A Field Guide to Brazen Harlotry" literally and literarily *follows the plants* by writing a rhizome of plant proliferation across the desert, entangling her own sensations and affections in the weave of parasitic and symbiotic connections. Parodying Victorian *scientia sexualis* and discourses on deviance, she observes:

> You can tell [desert paintbrush] by its fiery scarlet and early bloom, as if it wants these curvaceous sweeps of sandstone to itself before the wildflower season's full Baroque. Paintbrush is usually parasitic on the roots of other plants. Underground, it invades the vascular tissue of another plant and absorbs its nutrients. Sometimes paintbrush nudges up seductively close to the host, a flashy scarlet starlet in pickpocket position. (Meloy 2002, 224–25)

Paintbrush "harlotry" is rhizomatic. It messes with the properly arboreal model of unitary phallic root, binary sex, and proper family relations by attaching itself to "curvaceous sweeps of sandstone" with edaphic lasciviousness and by sucking promiscuously on the tendrils of other plants.[10]

Reveling in the profligate seductions and philandering entanglements of another desert harlot, Meloy observes:

> Cliffrose prefers slickrock and shallow dry washes, where the embrace of low-slung rims on either side provides not so much shelter as a degree of difficulty, perhaps, to match the cracks and soil pockets in which they grow. . . . Bees in the cliffrose fill the quiet parts of the gust rhythm. They are delirious and so am I. The cliffrose fragrance envelopes us in a spicy musk. . . . It incites blatant acts of sensuality. Other plants prompt reactions that are aesthetic, intelligent, or herbal. Not cliffrose. . . . Sit by one and your heart will open and desire will flood into the emptiness created for it. (251–52)

Between cliffrose and its desert habitat emanates a myriad of affective communications, the concatenation of which defines the fidelity with which the plant "loves" its geography. As a voyeur of this love, Meloy succumbs to a delirium of sensation that allows her to feel how the cliffrose "prefers" slickrock soil and geomorphology, or how it "embraces" territory "in conspiracy" with juniper—"the omnipresent tree that grows atop mesas and in folds of wind-smooth sandstone across the Colorado Plateau" (251). She trails the cliffrose closely until its linear and collateral attachments break into lines of escape:

> From this tree other cliffrose follow fissures in the rock in a somewhat orderly direction—the creases offer more moisture and soil

than the acres of bare sandstone—but four or five more pale torches escape the line and erupt in different places, so there are cliffrose everywhere until the land drops off into the sheer space above a deep, green canyon, and, below my high perch, meets the emerald-green crowns of a cottonwood bosque in the canyon bottom. (252)

In other words, she follows the rhizome "by rupture" and she "conjugates its deterritorialized flows," mapping its flight, as Deleuze and Guattari advise, "in *n* dimensions and broken directions" (Deleuze and Guattari 1987, 11),[11] and she foregrounds "transversal communications between different lines [that] scramble the genealogical tree" (10–11). Such conjugations of paintbrush + pinyon + sandstone, and cliffrose + juniper + bee, produce no new being, but they do relay a transmutation of being—a "becoming"—whereby heterogeneous beings conjoin in *aparallel evolution* (11). "Becoming is always of a different order than filiation"; Deleuze and Guattari explain:

It concerns alliance. If evolution includes any veritable becomings, it is in the domain of *symbioses* that bring into play beings of totally different scales and kingdoms. There is a block of becoming that snaps up the wasp and the orchid, but from which no wasp-orchid can ever descend. . . . There is a block of becoming between young roots and certain microorganisms, the alliance between which is effected by the materials synthesized in the leaves (rhizosphere). (238)

In place of evolution, understood as mobilized by sexual selection for reproducing and developing species perfection in transcending succession, Deleuze and Guattari coin the term *involution*. "Becoming is involutionary, involution is creative" (238) if not *procreative*. What *becomes* in creative involution is a rhizome (239);[12] a rhizome *involves* creative—adaptive, symbiotic or parasitic, evolutionary—entanglement of heterogeneous elements across species/specific lines of filiation and descent. It involves other beings in micro-couplings of becoming-other that may invade and compound genetic and genealogical transmission in life's virtually ongoing experiment. "Always look for the molecular, or even submolecular particle with which we are allied" (11), Deleuze and Guattari instruct their readers in neo-evolutionism. Neither progressive nor regressive, creative involution affects bodies of different kinds with the change of time.

A Becoming–Prickly Pear

Among the illustrations that figure in "A Field Guide to Brazen Harlotry," one stands out with its florid floraphilia and the sensational proximity with which the naturalist comes into contact with the seductiveness of the plant. Meloy draws a prickly pear cactus flower (Meloy 2002, 236) in springtime profile, outlining fleshy and spiny jointed pads with multi-foliated blooms. Color is missing from the black-and-white text, but the mutual attraction is clearly rendered. Over the lips of one bloom droop human limbs, presumably those of the succulent-satiated narrator, prompting us to imagine another ontological "breach of transmutation." Here is a flower power that can caress, seduce, and intoxicate human sense into sexual delirium. We see before us a becoming–prickly pear of the woman, as the acephalic human gives herself over to unnatural nuptials with a species from another kingdom of life. At the same time, the plant exhibits a voracious affection for the human, sucking on succulent female parts in a becoming-woman of the prickly pear. Discussion surrounding the image maps the spread of prickly pear desire and its varying conjugations onto an expansive narrative terrain. As she sinks more deeply into the plant's erotic body, she touches upon part-bodies and other bodies that couple the plant to its ecology and territory. Less interested in searching for the root, she follows the organs of connection, and she drifts into a "sideways knowing" that relays a rhizome-tale of bio-geo-history:

> Languishing in the deep-butter sex glow of the prickly pear flower, I let an arm drop to a pad, avoiding the spines' sharp white daggers. My hand reaches a dense mass that feels like rolled-up cobwebs attached to the cactus's waxy green pad. The wad is slightly powdery and the whitest white. I touch it and rub my fingers together. The white disappears, leaving stains of gorgeous carmine. . . . I am wearing the fluids of cochineal. . . . Female cochineal insects (*Dactylopius coccus*), a type of scale insect, reside on the pads. . . . She [the female cochineal insect] spends her life sucking on a cactus. She is a tiny factory of pigment. . . . In pre-Hispanic Mexico the Mixtec Indians farmed cochineal by farming the prickly pear cactus. . . . The color drove the conquering Spaniards wild with desire. . . . For over two centuries they monopolized all trade in the cochineal dye between Mexico and European royalty until, in 1777, a French naturalist smuggled cactus pads from Mexico to Haiti. Cochineal textiles soon appeared in India, South America, Portugal, and the Canary Islands. In the 1800s cochineal-dyed *bayetas,* blankets of red flannel reached

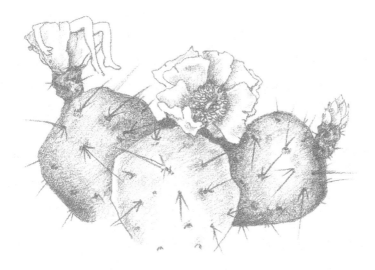

FIGURE 13.1. Prickly pear cactus flower (Meloy 2002, 236).

trading posts in the American Southwest. Navajo weavers, who had
no such bold red dye in their traditional rugs and blankets, eagerly
traded for the *bayetas,* which they unraveled thread by thread. . . .
Then they wove the red yarn into their own rugs. (241–42)

The passage tracks the volatile desirability of cochineal red across a weave
of deterritorializing and reterritorializing trajectories. After the floraphil-
iac rubs her fingers over the cactus body they become stained with "gorgeous carmine," the sight of which pricks her historical memory of how
the Mixtecs cultivated cochineal and venerated the dye. "Indigo, carmine
and other shades of bright red were the colors of the highest social status,"
she relays. "A wealthy Mixtec who wore red wore power" (241). Stained
fingers recall the stain of conquest by power-lusting Spaniards, whom
"the color drove wild with desire" and who "monopolized all trade for
two centuries." Not until cochineal dye enters global markets does it wind
its way home to the Southwest, where Navajo reweave the red thread of
traded *bayetas* into rugs of their own. There is a kind of biophilic justice to
this dilatory narrative of desire, whereby the thread of connection winds
its way back home from colonial exploitation in a creative involution of
becoming native.

In sum, Meloy writes a rhizome whose ecology interweaves desire across species lines, linking the attractions of prickly pear cactus and cochineal insect with human affection and aspiration. If the rapport between cactus and cochineal is local, the farming of cochineal is transportable, as well as transmutable into various forms of colonization and globalization. Touched by life indigenous to the desert heartland, Meloy allies herself with native nature/culture, and she foregrounds and reconnects pre- and postcolonial territorial practices. Against major history, she outlines a "minor literature" of autochthonic peoples who engage closely with the desert where they find themselves living.[13] Her mapping of Mixtec cultivation of cochineal, followed by its deterritorialization by Spanish invaders, and, again, by its reterritorialization by Navajo weavers interweaves her own desire "to explore and affiliate" with life that is native to the desert Southwest. Immanent to the molecular processes of her becoming–prickly pear is a micropolitics of affect, or more precisely, a biophilic ethics of alliance.

"To Touch an Otherworld": Biophilic Ethics

Species interdependence is the name of the worlding game on earth, and that game must be one of response and respect. . . . Queer messmates in mortal play, indeed.
—Donna J. Haraway

In *Eating Stone,* Meloy weaves an elaborate rhizome of interspecies crossing that involves herself and other naturalists, a red-rock canyon, and desert bighorn sheep. She narrates a nomadic quest to know this wild animal, so threatened by urban encroachment, yet so fervently territorial that it faces relocation or extinction. She chronicles the territorial refrains of a local herd that she names "the Blue Door Band" after a relic of human settlement found on bighorn turf in a canyon near her new homestead in southeast Utah. Above all, she desires to know what desert bighorn desire and to relay to her own species what might be done to aid its survival. With aroused biophilia, she observes rampant rutting and miraculous lambing, though her focus of attention falls on conjugations of sheep and plant and rock. In a signature passage, she ruminates on a meal of bighorn meat she has the mixed blessing to enjoy. As she consumes the animal, she senses a carnal consummation of earth and home: "the taste of the meat lingers on my tongue. Rain and river. Bedrock to soil to plant to milk to bone, muscle, and sinew. I am eating my canyon. Eating stone" (Meloy 2005, 296).

Over the course of her ovine adventures, Meloy evokes a becoming-bighorn of the human and, vice versa, a becoming-human of the bighorn. The first transmutation is a natural hazard of field work: "Given time you will eventually match your own habits, at home and afield, to the animal you study. . . . Desert bighorn people eat, move, stand, ruminate. They are vigilant. They nap" (182). Conversely, the second transmutation is a coercive, intrusive, and paradoxical affair—especially when wildlife management must counter a bighorn instinct to migrate to areas of gene-pool-diminishing niche habitats in an effort to escape encroaching urbanization. "With sheep confined to cliffy atolls in a sea of human activity, management of these animals has a tendency, and often an urgency, to intensify," Meloy explains, citing biologists' fears that "cultural selection will wholly displace natural selection" (181). The "anthropogenic factor" plays a powerful role in bighorn ecology, including threatening the wild with extinction; but the reverse, she urges us to consider, is also true. For humans to aid bighorn survival, it is crucial to understand the zoogenic factor (or the autopoiesis of animal life) in coevolutionary ecology. She regards the puzzle of how the Blue Door Band perennially embarks on an untrackable migration to secret watering holes in the canyon's labyrinthine depths at the onset of winter drought, as the kind of puzzle we humans must learn to solve and respect if we want to ensure the vitality of desert life (including our own).

Meloy's affiliation with the bighorn is put to the supreme test when the time comes for her to partake in a relocation operation. Scheduled to help conduct an experimental transplantation of twenty-four of the remaining eighty-six-member herd, she foresees the unfolding of ecological mysteries at close range:

> To watch these twenty-four sheep stake out their place, establishing their fidelity to it, for the first time would be to witness everything that makes this animal what it is, its evolution and its hunger, its seamless, nearly molecular bond to landscape. To see how they map the stone would be to know this canyon with extraordinary intimacy. To see how they do it would be truly to learn something. (315)

The event reaches a climax when Meloy helps the wildlife management team restrain a wild ewe to be prepared for transport, and, incredibly, contact is made across alien worlds, forming a liturgical refrain in her brain: "Her nose rests in the palm of my hand" (313), and again, "her nose is in my hand" (315), and again, "the palm of the hand is a most sensitive human organ. On it, the warmth of a breathing animal is pure solace"

(316). For a moment, the haptic is a conduit to the cosmic. To sense the wild ewe's nose in the palm of her hand is "to touch an otherworld with more than one sense" (319). Synesthesia weds symbiosis in a post-anthropocentric recovery of the wild—a becoming-animal of wildlife management that "runs contrary to the historical imperative to press everything alive, dead, or otherwise into human service" (307).

Meloy's bighorn biophilia implies an ethic that Deleuze and Guattari's ethology can elaborate. Paraphrasing Spinoza, Deleuze writes: "We know nothing about a body until we know what it can do, in other words, what its affects are, how they can enter into composition with other affects, with the affects of another body, either to destroy that body or to be destroyed by it, either to exchange actions and passions with it or to join with it in composing a more powerful body" (Deleuze and Guattari 1987, 257). Such ethology clarifies the ethics of Meloy's situation. Meloy questions the "affectability" of an experiment that brings two different animal bodies together in a queer composition by conveying the mortal terror of the wild ewe that touch conducts from one body to the other: "she shakes uncontrollably from head to tail. . . . Her mute trembling bears a message of fear so profound, it borders on grief, and I am not certain that I can move beyond it" (Meloy 2005, 313). The climax of *Eating Stone* relays an affect that cannot be reduced to sentiment, or to romance, or to any emotion at all. Meloy is moved not to tears but to immobility: only those affects that have been habituated, domesticated, and humanized are immoblized. On the frontier of knowledge and perception, at the border of animal and human worlds, she communicates the affective, asignifying, existential tension between survival and extinction where she/we and the wild bighorn meet.

This experimental relocation implies practical questions of the highest ethical stakes. How will this animal-human assemblage work? Will it compose a more powerful body, or will many bighorn bodies be destroyed in the exchange? How will the transplants recompose their connection to the land? (Meloy notes that, in the lambing season after relocation, the transplants do, in fact, show a healthy adaptation to their new canyon, 322–23.) These are questions that concern not just the well-being of a pet favorite. They concern the vitality of a whole population and its ability to form a powerful attachment to their new canyon: "To survive," she observes, "this is what the band would have to do: make this perfect match of flesh to earth" (322).

Deleuze emphasizes the anti-utilitarian, communal ethics of becoming-animal. "It is no longer a matter of utilizations or captures, but of sociabilities and communities," he declares (1988, 126). Likewise, Meloy rejects any initiatives of conservation that aim to reterritorialize wildlife without respecting the range of desire that is vital to its survival. Instead, she advocates human alliances with wild animals that do not just protect animal territoriality but also promote animal-earth symbioses. Wary of past management practices, and fearful of the ethological and ecological ignorance that current recovery experiments entail, she asks how human interference in bighorn territorialization can proceed while, as Deleuze would say, "preserving or respecting the other's own relations and world?" (1988, 126) The ethics of bighorn recovery entails a biophilia that moves us humans to become sufficiently acquainted and allied with bighorn life as to know how to benefit the animal's capacity to thrive in its changing "otherworld."

The Ecological Future of Queer Desire

Opponents to native fish recovery programs . . . measur[e] worth as most of us do, by human ego. What good are these fish? You can't eat them, they appear to have no medical, economic, sport, or industrial value. . . . Even their file drawer in the wildlife management bureaucracy—"nongame"—assigns them not their own innate something but that which they are not: not sport, not food. These fish, many people believe, are dead-end. Tertiary detritus with strange humps and weird lips. *They are just too queer. . . .* What does a humpback chub want?

—Ellen Meloy

The biophilia that moves Meloy "to explore and affiliate with all life" is pronouncedly queer. For her, "all life" includes queer life. Thus, she can envision a future where creatures deemed unproductive by utilitarian standards are valued for their own nature, as well as for their part in determining a healthy local ecology. Her political strategy as a nature writer is to compose a rhizome of connectivity that foregrounds devalued desert species and that illuminates their coevoluntionary prospects.

As her conjugation of rare bighorn band + wildlife management team + high-tech science shows, Meloy overlooks the survival of the fittest in favor of cyborg syntheses and unnatural symbioses (survival of the queerest?). Her bighorn love commits her to espouse "creative involution," symbiogenesis, and other maverick versions of evolutionary ecology in favor of the theory of sexual selection that refines and perfects the family tree. As Deleuze and Guattari explain, "sexuality . . . is badly explained by the binary organization of the sexes, and just as badly by a bisexual organization within each sex. Sexuality brings into play too great a diversity of conjugated becomings; they are like *n* sexes, an entire war machine through which love passes" (Deleuze and Guattari 1987, 278).

Does Meloy's nature writing function as a war machine? We might think so, if we take literally her ironic claim that "we nature buffs, when we were not too busy trying to decide what sex to be, had brought mining, logging, ranching, and the military-industrial complex to their knees (Meloy 1994, 200–201). Mocking the exaggerated fears of western rednecks, Meloy gleefully imagines a scene wherein sexually ambivalent "nature buffs" triumph over the phallocratic "military-industrial complex." If she does not explicitly side with minority sexuality, she satirizes reactionary stereotypes of "gays" and "tree huggers" (291), and she critically lampoons the popular media's polarization of factions: "youthful, pampered, overeducated, gorp-propelled urban androgynes on foot versus petro-propelled, overweight, manly men who cry that taking away access for snowmobiles, Jet Skis, ATVs, and other motorized toys is taking away their freedom" (290).[14] At the same time, she adamantly allies herself with desert lovers of all freak sorts, including the queer chub, in a concerted minoritarian struggle to outlive and defeat the State machine and its unsustainable logging, ranching, and mining.

We might best describe Meloy's biophilia as "an entire war machine through which love passes" (Deleuze and Guattari 1987, 278), given how rampantly it wreaks havoc on social order and domestic life:

> The attraction to this landscape also resembled an outlaw coupling, the wild anarchy of a love affair whose heated obsession betrayed and unraveled some other, weaker, fidelity. I risked social and professional obligations, and my loved one's patience, simply to submit to an involuntary hunger for light, rock, and air. (Meloy 1997, 200)

In addition, Meloy's conjugations of desert sex "[bring] into play too great a diversity of conjugated becomings" to be contained by conjugal propriety and natural selection. Her floraphilia, zoophilia, piscophilia, and so on "are like *n* sexes" that trouble not only binary sexuality but also evolutionary certainty through the survival of the straightest. With desert bighorn, humpback chub, and other cyborg and/or transgenic species, Meloy offers a queer paradigm of desire that replaces the apparatus of heterosexual genealogy, while embracing other, creative variations of becoming-life. Does her ethics of becoming-bighorn not challenge the most radical platform of queer activism, no less than the "save-the-whale" (and other select-species versus companion-species) campaigns of animal rights?

Take, for instance, Lee Edelman's (2004) provocatively irreverent and perversely logical anti-(pro)life argument and manifesto. In *No Future,* Edelman calls for queer insurgency against the dominant culture of "the Child" and its moral imperative to breed for the future. Only queers, he claims, can battle an imperative that unites Left and Right, thereby neutralizing domestic politics.[15] Edelman inspires dissent in queers who resent the social complicity of breeders and futurists, and he instructs queer nihilists how to wither the symbolic vitality of pro-life morality. Specifically, he advocates an overthrow of popular media (especially film), and he demonstrates to his readers gleeful ways of monkey-wrenching the aesthetic technology of social/sexual reproductive machinery. For Edelman, "life" is the ideological enemy that queer desire ought to, critically and clinically, annihilate. Despite the potential of his approach to assemble a new queer coalition of negation, it fails to engage those queers who despise pro-life fascism yet desire to have children. Moreover, in its single-minded attack on pro-life, it offers nothing toward re-imagining queer involvement with life's creative and multiple becoming.

If *No Future* benefits queer desire by giving it an easy target and a sado-aesthetic armature of deployment, it disdains any attempt to rethink queer desire with respect to ecology's larger-than-pro-life crises. Alternatively, Ellen Meloy (married, no children, untimely dead at fifty-seven of a brain aneurysm), presents a paradigm of queer—nonreproductive, nonfiliative, anti-sexist, thoroughly perverse, and wildly anarchic—desire that conjugates the beneficial "affectability" of radically different bodies. Her biophilic compositions demonstrate the ecological future of queer desire, while obliquely challenging the biophobic moralizing that often passes for a love of life.

.   .   .

So, then, what *does* a humpback chub want? What piscine desires must humans desire to know so as to help recover native populations and the health of the desert overall? What unclassifiable cross-breeding and hybridization enable the (sub)species to survive so far, or does the growing presence of "intergrades" signify evolutionary failure to surmount rapid ecological change and degradation? Following the chub to one of few remaining habitats with a crew of fisheries biologists, Meloy becomes involved in exploring chub biology. What they want, she hazards, is:

High-walled sandstone chasms, fast water, steep gradients, spring floods. Humpback cubs thrive in whitewater—the swift, turbulent currents that race against big boulders and sheer rock walls, pause for deep pools, and bulge into eddy fences, the shear zone between the main current and slower water. In their thirty-year life span, they move less than a mile from their home waters except to spawn. They feed in eddies in morning and evening and rest in pools during the day. They eat aquatic organisms, seeds, algae, plant bits, Mormon crickets, and mayflies, food they rake inward and tear with pharyngeal teeth common to cyprinids.(Meloy 1994, 208–209)

Beyond these tidbits of knowledge, she must join the scientists in biospeculation. "The acutest minds still struggle to undo a taxonomic muddle among *Gila* manifested by a curious mix of their physical features in a single fish," she notes. "We cannot identify the life needs of this fish until we identify the fish" (209). But chub identification defies regular taxonomic practice and calls for a "sideways knowing" that can see across (sub)species lines and imagine hybridization beyond genealogical paradigms. A "better science and monitoring" is required if variants are to be identified as sympatric (species that cohabit the same region, which do not usually interbreed but which do hybridize naturally, if rarely) or extrinsic (hybridization due to human civilization "changing environmental features important for reproductive isolation or reducing fish numbers to a point so law contacts among individuals of the same species are less likely than contacts among conspecifics," 214–15). More than improved technology, it takes "devotion" (213) to distinguish variations that signal either adaptive evolution or "the last-ditch, high-pitched shriek of preextinction" (215). For life's sake—or more precisely, for life for life's sake—our biophilia is put to the ultimate test.

NOTES

1. Ellen Meloy is the author of four books on the American desert southwest for which she has won national and international acclaim: *Raven's Exile: A Season on the Green River* (1994), *The Last Cheater's Waltz: Beauty and Violence in the Desert Southwest* (1999), *The Anthropology of Turquoise: Reflections on Desert, Sea, Stone, and Sky* (2002, Pulitzer Prize finalist); *Eating Stone: Imagination and the Loss of the Wild* (2005, National Book Critics' Circle Award finalist).

2. The citation from "A Field Guide to Brazen Harlotry" (Meloy 2002, 221–55, 244, 252) that heads this chapter paraphrases the hypothesis that Edward O. Wilson propounds in *Biophilia: The Human Bond with Other Species* (1984). Meloy uses and adapts Wilson's "biophilia" throughout her writing. The term "biophiliac" is her invention (2002, 244).

3. See Bagemihl (1999). Stacy Alaimo's chapter in this collection refers to the surprising abundance and diversity with which Bagemihl documents the occurrence of homosexuality in nonhuman animals as support for a queer approach to ecology studies. My chapter reinforces Alaimo's call for a queer ecology by foregrounding Ellen Meloy's narrative documentary of symbiotic interspecies (including human and nonhuman) desire that is even more queerly exuberant than nonhuman homosexuality, and that, despite its ubiquity, has been no less marginalized than homosexuality by majoritarian models of the family tree.

4. As an ally of all life that is native to her desert homeland, Meloy often refers to "endemic" species. The desert's endemic plants, she explains, are erotically "edaphic": "Edaphic endemism is rampant on the Plateau. In other words, the range of certain endemics, or flora limited to specific localities, is often determined by soil conditions" (Meloy 2002, 225). Her emphasis on the *lushness* of desert life expressly counters the tendency in American political geography to represent the desert as barren, and thus supposedly open to inconsequential toxic and destructive land-use by the State's industrial-military machine, including nuclear testing. For more on this, see Meloy (1999) and Chisholm (2006).

5. For studies in culture, ecology, and the environment that use Deleuze and Guattari, see Bonta and Protevi (2004), Halsey (2006), Hayden (1998), and Muecke, Roe, and Bentarrak (1996). See also these recent collections: Chisholm (2007) and Herzogenrath (2009).

6. Phillips echoes Freud's "What Do Women Want?" with a similar rhetorical skepticism.

7. Freud's speculations on epistemophilia or "instinct of knowledge" are most extensively entertained in "Three Essays on Sexuality" and "On the Sexual Theories of Children." See Freud (1977).

8. Meloy's desert writing combines ecology with phenomenology, biophysics, and physiology. She describes seeing red as more than a matter of "retinas and wavelengths," and as involving "sensual, aesthetic, and cultural, as well as biological cues" (Meloy 2002, 230). She refers to Goethe's *Theory of Colours,* as does Gilles Deleuze in his analyzes of T. E. Lawrence's desert writing (see Deleuze 1997).

9. Symbiosis and autopoiesis are primary concepts in Deleuze and Guattari's elaboration of neo-evolutionism (or "creative involution"). They help to clarify and elaborate what these authors mean by "becoming." "Becoming is not an evolution, at least not an evolution by descent and filiation. Becoming . . . concerns alliance. If evolution includes any veritable becomings, it is in the domain of *symbioses* that bring into play totally different scales and kingdoms, with no possible filiation" (Meloy 2002, 238). "Autopoiesis" explains how "living beings and environments stand in relation to one another through the activity of 'mutual specification' and codetermination'" (Pearson 1999, 147, citing Francisco Varela). In other words, "'life is not DNA but a 'rich network of facilitating relationships'" (Pearson 1999, 147, citing Robert Rosen). Guattari develops the concept along with "transversality" in *The Three Ecologies* (2001).

10. Plant ecology, however, persistently interprets such parasitic and promiscuous entanglements between different species in terms of family relations. For example, scientists recently report that "'plants have a secret social life'" with evidence that "the sea rocket is able to . . . distinguish between plants that are related to it and those that are not. And not only does this plant recognize its kin, but it also gives them preferential treatment." Accordingly, kinship rules in the plant, no less than the animal, kingdom. "If the sea rocket detects unrelated plants growing in the ground with it, the plant aggressively sprouts nutrient-grabbing roots. But if it detects family, it politely

restrains itself. . . . If an individual can identify kin, it can help them, an evolutionarily sensible act because relatives share some genes. The same discriminating organism could likewise ramp up nasty behavior against unrelated individuals with which it is most sensible to be in claws- or perhaps thorns-bared competition" (Yoon 2008). If such reporting suggests a turn to social Darwinism in plant ecology, Meloy avoids such a turn by mapping the invasive spread of desert paintbrush in terms of "brazen harlotry." She emphasizes the plant's promiscuous, parasitic, and/or possessive couplings with non-kin (other plant species) and non-kind (sandstone), foregrounding a desire that is flagrantly wayward and composing a deterritorializing rhizome, instead of a declaration of loyalty to family roots.

11. In Deleuze and Guattari's terms, the plant deterritorializes the cliff whose cracks and angles it hooks into and overflows, just as the cliff deterritorializes the plant by pressing upon its direction of growth with its geomorphology and soil conditions. The condensation of terms in the name "cliffrose" suggestively signifies symbiosis or heterogenesis: the becoming-cliff of the rose and the becoming-rose of the cliff. As Deleuze and Guattari explain, "a becoming is neither one nor two, nor the relation of the two; it is the in-between, the border or line of flight or descent running perpendicular to both. . . . The line or block of becoming that unites the wasp and the orchid produces a shared deterritorialization: of the wasp, in that it becomes a liberated piece of the orchid's reproductive system, but also of the orchid, in that it becomes the object of an orgasm in the wasp, also liberated from its own reproduction" (1987, 293).

12. "The term we would prefer for this form of evolution between heterogeneous terms is 'involution'. . . . To involve is to form a block that runs its own line 'between' the terms in play and beneath assignable relations. . . . Movement occurs not only, or not primarily, by filiative productions but also by transversal communications between heterogeneous populations. Becoming is a rhizome, not a classificatory or genealogical tree (Deleuze and Guattari 1987, 238–39).

13. Deleuze and Guattari (1986) coin the term "minor literature" to name writing that invades the language and narrative (including historical narrative) of dominant and/or colonizing culture with the foreign accents and affects of dominated and/or subaltern culture.

14. Meloy's parody of the stereotyping of green activists is not exaggerated. A writer for the *New York Times Magazine* reports: "One thing that always struck me about the term 'green' was the degree to which, for so many years, it was defined by its opponents—by the people who wanted to disparage it. And they defined it as 'liberal,' 'tree-hugging,' 'sissy,' 'girlie-man,' 'unpatriotic,' 'vaguely French'" (Friedman 2007, 42).

15. "For the Child, whose mere possibility is enough to spirit away the naked truth of heterosexual sex—impregnating heterosexuality, as it were, with the future of signification by conferring upon it the cultural burden of signifying futurity—figures our identification with an always-about-to-be-realized identity. . . . The consequences of such an identification both of and with the Child as the preeminent emblem of the motivating end, though one endlessly postponed, of every political vision as a *vision of futurity* must weigh on any delineation of a queer oppositional politics. . . . The queerness we propose . . . delights in [civilization's] mortality as the negation of everything that would define itself, moralistically, as pro-life. . . . What is queerest about us, queerest within us, and queerest despite us is this willingness to insist intransitively—to insist that the future stop here" (Edelman 2004, 13, 31).

REFERENCES

Bagemihl, Bruce. 1999. *Biological Exuberance: Animal Homosexuality and Natural Diversity*. New York: St. Martin's Press.

Bonta, Mark, and John Protevi. 2004. *Deleuze and Geophilosophy*. Edinburgh, U.K.: Edinburgh University Press.

Chisholm, Dianne. 2006. Ellen Meloy's Deep Nomadology (How to Map the Heartland of a Post-Nuclear Desert). *Rhizomes: Cultural Studies in Emerging Knowledge* 13. http://rhizomes.net/issue13/chisholm/chisholm.html.

———, ed. 2007. Deleuze and Guattari's Ecophilosophy. Special issue of *Rhizomes: Cultural Studies in Emerging Knowledge* 15. http://rhizomes.net/issue15/index.html.

Deleuze, Gilles. 1988. *Spinoza: Practical Philosophy*. Trans. Robert Hurley. San Francisco: City Lights.

———. 1997. The Shame and the Glory: T. E. Lawrence. In *Essays Critical and Clinical*, trans. Daniel W. Smith and Michael A. Greco, 115–25. Minneapolis: University of Minnesota Press.

Deleuze, Gilles, and Félix Guattari. 1986. *Kafka: Toward a Minor Literature*. Trans. Dana Polan. Minneapolis: University of Minnesota Press.

———. 1987. *A Thousand Plateaus*. Trans. Brian Massumi. Minneapolis: University of Minnesota Press.

Edelman, Lee. 2004. *No Future: Queer Theory and the Death Drive*. Durham, N.C.: Duke University Press.

Freud, Sigmund. 1977. *On Sexuality*. Vol. 7 of *The Pelican Freud Library*, trans. James Strachey. New York: Penguin.

Friedman, Thomas L. 2007. The Power of Green. *New York Times Magazine*, April 15.

Guattari, Félix. 2001. *The Three Ecologies*. Trans. Ian Pindar and Paul Sutton. New Brunswick, N.J.: Athlone.

Halsey, Mark. 2006. *Deleuze and Environmental Damage*. London: Ashgate.

Haraway, Donna J. 2008. *When Species Meet*. Minneapolis: University of Minnesota Press.

Hayden, Patrick. 1998. *Multiplicity and Becomings: The Pluralist Empiricism of Gilles Deleuze*. New York: Peter Lang.

Herzogenrath, Bernd, ed. 2009. *Deleuze/Guattari and Ecology*. London: Palgrave Macmillan.

Meloy, Ellen. 1994. *Raven's Exile: A Season on the Green River*. Tucson: University of Arizona Press.

———. 1999. *The Last Cheater's Waltz: Beauty and Violence in the Desert Southwest*. Tucson: University of Arizona Press.

———. 2002. *The Anthropology of Turquoise: Reflections on Desert, Sea, Stone, and Sky*. New York: Random House.

———. 2005. *Eating Stone: Imagination and the Loss of the Wild*. New York: Random House.

Muecke, Steven, Paddy Roe, and Kim Bentarrak. 1996. *Reading the Country: An Introduction to Nomadology*. Liverpool, U.K.: Liverpool University Press.

Pearson, Keith Ansell. 1999. *Germinal Life: The Difference and Repetition of Deleuze*. New York: Routledge.

Phillips, Dana. 2003. *The Truth of Ecology: Nature, Culture, and Literature in America*. New York: Oxford University Press.

Wilson, Edward O. 1984. *Biophilia: The Human Bond with Other Species*. Cambridge, Mass.: Harvard University Press.

Yoon, Carol Kaesuk. 2008. Loyal to Its Roots. *New York Times,* June 10.

CONTRIBUTORS

STACY ALAIMO is Associate Professor of English at the University of Texas at Arlington. Her books include *Undomesticated Ground: Recasting Nature as Feminist Space* and (edited with Susan Hekman) *Material Feminisms* (Indiana University Press, 2007).

DAVID BELL is Senior Lecturer in Critical Human Geography in the School of Geography, University of Leeds. He is editor of *Mapping Desire: Geographies of Sexualities* (with Gill Valentine) and (with Jon Binnie) *The Sexual Citizen: Queer Politics and Beyond.*

DIANNE CHISHOLM is Professor of English and Film Studies at the University of Alberta. She is author of *Queer Constellations: Fictions of Space in the Wake of the City.*

GIOVANNA DI CHIRO is an independent scholar and environmental activist. Her publications include the article "Living Environmentalisms: Coalition Politics, Social Reproduction, and Environmental Justice" in the journal *Environmental Politics* and the book (edited with Ron Eglash, Jennifer Croissant, and Rayvon Fouché) *Appropriating Technology: Vernacular Science and Social Power.*

BRUCE ERICKSON is a postdoctoral fellow in environmental history at Nipissing University. His articles include "Colonial Climbs of Mount Trudeau: Thinking Masculinity through the Homosocial" in the journal *TOPIA: Canadian Journal of Cultural Studies.*

Andil Gosine is Associate Professor of Sociology at York University.

Katie Hogan is Professor of English and Director of Women's Studies at Carlow University. She is author of *Women Take Care: Gender, Race, and the Culture of AIDS* and editor (with Nancy Roth) of *Gendered Epidemic: Representations of Women in the Age of AIDS.*

Gordon Brent Ingram is Associate Dean for Environmental Projects and Associate Professor in the Department of Environmental Sciences and Policy, George Mason University. He is co-editor, with Anne-Marie Bouthillette and the late Yolanda Retter, of the 1997 survey anthology *Queers in Space: Communities\Public Spaces\Sites of Resistance.*

Ladelle McWhorter is James Thomas Professor of Philosophy and Women, Gender, and Sexuality Studies at the University of Richmond. Her books include *Bodies and Pleasures: Foucault and the Politics of Sexual Normalization* (Indiana University Press, 1999); *Heidegger and the Earth: Essays in Environmental Philosophy;* and *Racism and Sexual Oppression in Anglo-America: A Genealogy* (Indiana University Press, 2009).

Catriona Mortimer-Sandilands is Professor of Environmental Studies and Canada Research Chair in Sustainability and Culture at York University. She is author of *The Good-Natured Feminist: Ecofeminism and the Quest for Democracy* and editor (with Melody Hessing and Rebecca Raglon) of *This Elusive Land: Women and the Canadian Environment.*

Rachel Stein is Professor of English and Director of Women's and Multicultural Studies at Siena College. Her books include *Shifting the Ground: American Women Writers' Revisions of Nature, Gender and Race* and *New Perspectives on Environmental Justice: Gender/Sexuality/Activism.* She is editor, with Joni Adamson and Mei Mei Evans, of *The Environmental Justice Reader: Politics, Poetics and Pedagogy.*

Noël Sturgeon is Chair and Professor of Women's Studies and graduate faculty in American Studies at Washington State University. Her books include *Ecofeminist Natures: Race, Gender, Feminist Theory and Political Action* and *Environmentalism in Popular Culture: Gender, Race, Sexuality, and the Politics of the Natural.*

Nancy C. Unger is Associate Professor of History in Women's and Gender Studies at Santa Clara University. She is author of *Fighting Bob La Follette: The Righteous Reformer*. Her other work includes a forthcoming book, *Beyond "Nature's Housekeepers": Turning Points for American Women in Environmental History*.

INDEX

Note: Page numbers in *italics* refer to illustrations.

Cuonzo, Margaret, 54, 69n3
custody rights, 290
Cuvier, Georges, 80, 97n8
Cvetkovich, Ann, 341, 342, 343
"Cyborg unities," 31

Dade County, Fla., 289
dance, 326
Daniels, Cynthia, 210
Darwin, Charles: on angiosperms, 365; and
    Meloy, 361, 363; and neo-Darwinian
    theory, 363; and sexual selection, 7–8;
    and species debate, 75, 81–82; and tele-
    ology, 11
Davenport, Charles, 86
Davis, Angela, 174
Dayton, Ohio, 155
DDE, 206
DDT, 178, 204, 205–206, 221, 225n2
de Waal, Franz, 70n10
death, 164, 315, 350
Decandole, Augustin Pyramus, 80, 97n8
decolonization, 276
decriminalization of homosexuality, 272,
    273, 274
Deephaven (Jewett), 24
deforestation, 154, 345, 346–47
degeneracy view of homosexuality, 9, 11,
    13–15
Del Mar, Ennis (fictional character), 1–2,
    37, 40nn3,5
Delany, Samuel, 25
Deleuze, Gilles: on autopoiesis, 379n9; on
    becoming child, 364; and biophilia, 39,
    374; and creative involution, 360–61;
    on deterritorialization, 380n11; on in-
    volution, 380n12; on minor literature,
    380n13; on transversality of life, 367,
    369
Delvaux, Martine, 351
demasculinization, 212, 213, 214
D'Emilio, John, 244, 245
democracy and democratization, 26,
    136–37, 277
demographic shifts, 258, 262, 269
Dempsey, Shawna, 41n14, 328n3
Denmark, 86
depression, 218
DES (diethylstilbestrol), 208
The Descent of Man (Darwin), 7
desert bighorn sheep, 65–66, 361–64,
    372–75, 376
desert environment: and cochineal dyes,
    370–72; and edaphic endemism, 379n4;
    and Meloy's work, 359–60, 376; and
    nature writing, 361; and wildflowers,
    364–67

Desert of the Heart (Rule), 25
desire, 150, 157, 207, 356n10, 375–78
deterritorialization, 380n11
Devall, Bill, 169n8
devastated landscapes, 38–39, 334
developing countries, 124–25
developmental disorders, 210
deviance and deviation: and eugenics,
    90–91; McWhorter on, 69n4; and non-
    reproductive sexualities, 7; and sexual
    politics, 30; and "species" concept, 75
DeVine, Phillip, 251n2
Di Chiro, Giovanna, 27, 35–36, 54–55, 103
diabetes, 202, 218
dibutyl phthalates, 222
Dickinson, Peter, 317–22, 324
dicophol, 206
Dicum, Gregory, 136
dieldrin, 225n2
diethylstilbestrol (DES), 208
Dillard, Annie, 37
dimorphism, sexual: and environmental
    damage, 11, 40–41n11, 209, 216; and
    eugenics, 88, 90–91; and sexual diver-
    sity, 12
Dinan, Frank J., 203
dioxins, 225n2
disabilities and disabled people: and con-
    servationists, 83; disability theory, 202,
    224; and endocrine-disrupting toxins,
    201; as an environmental problem, 202;
    and eugenics, 233; and immigration,
    84–85; lgbtq associated with, 202; and
    race hygiene/betterment movements, 76;
    work-related injuries, 200
disciplinary power, 18, 315
Discovery Channel, 144
discrimination, 75, 138, 140, 274
diversity: biodiversity, 55, 59, 356n9; as
    biological asset, 32, 96; and body as
    home/ecology, 200; and Canadian
    identity, 318–19; and evolution, 74–75;
    at Michigan Womyn's Music Festival,
    187; as species strength, 32, 76, 91; at UC
    Berkeley, 213; variety of animal sexual
    behaviors, 32, 54–55, 56–60; in the
    workplace, 73–74
Dixon, Alan F., 62
DNA, 92
Dobzhansky, Theodosius, 90, 92–94
documentaries, 70n11, 139, 144, 333
"dogging," 135
dogs, 58, 77
Dogwood Monarchist Society, 274
Dollimore, Jonathan, 24
dolphins, 70n12
domestic animals, 31, 139

citizenship, 21; and environmental justice, 126–29; and eugenics, 234–36, 238; and green consumerism, 34; and indigenous populations, 122, 152; and melancholia, 333; and mourning for lost nature, 38–39; and nationalism, 155–59; and non-white reproduction, 152–54; and overpopulation, 149, 152–54, 159–60, 169n7; and penguins as symbol, 114–18; and public sex, 154–55, 158–59, 160–63; and queer skepticism, 251; and reproductive justice, 104; and same-sex eroticism, 154–55; and sexual politics, 29

environments, alternative. *See* alternative lesbian environments

ephemeral quality of nature, 336

epidemiologic evidence from wildlife, 207

epistemophilia, 361–64

Ereshefsky, Marc, 94

Erickson, Bruce, 38

erotic landscapes, 312

eroticism, 64, 141, 313

erotophobia, 29, 63–64, 165–66, 169n11

Essay On Population (Malthus), 152

"Essay on the Equality of Races" (Gobineau), 157

Essex Chronicle, 159

estradiol, 212

estrogen, 201, 208, 212, 226n9

The Estrogen Effect: Assault on the Male (1994), 205

ethics: biophilic ethics, 372–75; communal ethics, 374–75; environmental ethics, 23, 60, 355; ethical hedonism, 53, 62; and queer melancholia, 341

Ethiopia, 151, 169n8

ethno-nationalism, 152

ethology, 374

eugenics: and anti-toxics discourse, 202; and *Ballot Measure 9,* 240; defenses of, 153; and environmentalism, 233–36, 238; and euthanasia, 86; familial eugenics, 98n20; and immigration, 84–85, 90, 93, 97nn13,14, 233, 234, 235; and Measure 9 in Oregon, 241; and "profamily" movement, 98n20; and queer ecocritique, 250–51; and the species debate, 83–89, 93–94; and sterilization, 18, 20–21, 85–88, 93, 98nn15,18,20,21, 153, 234

Euroamerican context of queer ecology, 166

evangelical Christians, 109, 290

Evans, Mei Mei, 240, 287

"Everyday Eugenics" (Hartman), 233–34

evolution: adaptive evolution, 378; and cognitive adventuring, 362; evolutionary ecology, 375–76; and genetic diversity, 74–75; and human reproduction, 129–30n1; and nature/culture divide, 33; neo-evolutionism, 369; and nonreproductive sex, 360; and pleasure seeking, 61; and promiscuous entanglements, 379–80n10; and sexual selection, 7–10; and sovereign bodies, 30; and species concept, 75; and variety of animal sexual behaviors, 31

Evolution's Rainbow: Diversity, Gender, and Sexuality in Nature and People (Roughgarden), 12, 52, 137, 139

exhibitionism, 136

Exile and Pride: Disability, Queerness, and Liberation (Clare), 25–26, 243

extinctions, 209, 359

extremism, 118

Exxon Mobile, 123

"faggot separatism," 28–29, 41n21, 42n22

"The Falling Age of Puberty in U.S. Girls: What We Know, What We Need to Know" (Steingraber), 217

families and family structure: and camping, 4; and capitalism, 13–14; and climate change, 123; and environmental justice, 126–29; familial eugenics, 98n20; family planning, 125; family units, 33–34; heterosexual families, 166; and overpopulation, 125; and penguins, 108–14, 116; and reproductive politics, 105–108; and urbanization, 15; U.S. nuclear family, 114

Federal Drug Administration (FDA), 222

Federation for American Immigration Reform, 125

fellatio, 158

The Feminine Mystique (Friedan), 178

femininity, 356–57n10

feminism: ecofeminism, 179–80, 203; and endocrine-disrupting toxins, 208, 210, 215–16; and environmental reproductive justice, 103; and feminization of men, 210; and "flight from nature," 56; and lesbian festival attendance, 191; and lesbianism, 259, 264, 272, 286; and materiality, 215–16; and reproductive rights, 164–65; and sex/gender distinction, 65

feminization: of males, 210, 212; of nature, 201

femme lesbians, 177, 271

Fenholloway River, 219

fertility motif, 296–97

festivals, 34, 35, 186–89, 191–92

fetishism, 334, 337–39

Field, Kristin, 60

"A Field Guide to Brazen Harlotry" (Meloy), 364–68, 369–72
Fierstein, Harvey, 111
Finland, 86
Fire Island, 28, 175–76
First Nations: and Canadian national identity, 316–18, 320–21, 322, 324; and canoes, 320; disappearance of, 328n6; and overpopulation, 149; and Stanley Park, 266, 268. *See also* indigenous peoples; Native Americans
fish and fishing: and environmental damage, 203, 204, 346, 376–78; fly fishing, 346, 357n13; intersex fish, 35, 201, 219; native fish recovery efforts, 375, 376–78; transsexual fish, 66
Fisher, Andy, 355n2
Fisher, R. A., 95
flooding, 124
floraphilia, 364–67, 369–72
Florida, 183
flow, 277
flowers, *371*
Folks, Wash., 154
follicles, 206
Fone, Byrne, 23
Foreman, Dave, 153, 169n8
forestry, industrial, 137
Forman, Richard T. T., 262
Forster, E. M., 27–28
Fort Worth, Tex., 162
Foucault, Michel: and biopower concept, 312, 314–16; Halperin on, 36–37; and *scientia sexualis*, 7; and sexual "deviation," 30; and species debate, 75, 81; on Victorianism, 8, 327
Fox-Keller, Evelyn, 69n6
fragments, 262, 277
Frank, Thomas, 104
Freeman, Dorothy, 37
Fresno, Calif., 162
Freud, Sigmund: and epistemophilia, 362–64; and melancholia, 38, 334–36, 337, 356nn5,6; and mourning, 341; and Rilke meeting, 356n8
Friedan, Betty, 178, 179
frogs: and endocrine-disrupting toxins, 203, 211–12, 213; intersex frogs, 201, 223, 226n12
"From Silent Spring to Silent Night" (Hayes), 211, 214
Frye, Northrop, 319
Fuck For Forests (FFF), 33, 135–37, 142–43
Fugate, J. C., 231
"The 'Fun Gay Ladies': Lesbians in Cherry Grove, 1936–1960" (Newton), 175
fundamentalism: and anti-gay campaigns, 289–90, 306; and HIV/AIDS, 118; and penguins, 102, 109, 110; and reproductive politics, 165; and rural areas, 244; and woman-centered spiritual practices, 188. *See also* Christianity; right-wing politics
fur trade, 320, 321–22, 324
furans, 225n2
"future-anterior," 323
The Future of Human Heredity (Osborn), 90

Gaard, Greta, 29, 63, 165, 167, 169n11, 236–37
Gaian principles, 137
Gainesville, Fla., 189–90
The Garden (1990), 357n15
gardens and gardening, 192–93, 295–97, 343–44, 349–54
Garland-Thomson, Rosemarie, 224
Gaskell, George Arthur, 168n3
Gastown, 275, 279n11
gay bars, 290
"gay brain" research, 140
The Gay Games, 34
gay liberation, 258, 272
"A Gay Manifesto" (Wittman), 264–65, 278–79n1
gay marriage conflict, 306
"Gay Pride" events, 274, 279n10
gay rights movement, 272
Geelong, Australia, 163
Geist, Valerius, 54
gender and gender identity: and access to nature, 241; determinants of, 214; and ego-identification, 356–57n10; and eugenics, 85–86, 90–91; and gay pride events, 279n10; gender essentialism, 64; gender inverts, 8–9, 16, 24, 84; gender oppression, 234; and marginalization of women, 287; and nonreproductive sex, 137; and power relations, 105; and "queer" term, 307n5; and sex/gender distinction, 65; and stereotypes, 113–14; transgender people, 11, 137, 189, 220; variation in, 65
"Gender Transformed: Endocrine Disruptors in the Environment" (Langston), 214–16
genealogy of queer ecology, 6
genetics, 89–96; and animal sexuality, 58–59; and gay gene, 235; genetic determinism, 55–56, 60, 69n6, 113, 129–30n1; genetic diversity, 74–75; genome research, 75; and human reproduction, 129–30n1; and "promiscuous entanglements," 379–80n10; and species definition, 92
genitals, deformed, 202, 207, 208

Haraway, Donna: and animal sexuality, 31; on companion species, 67; and feminist science, 40n8; and illegitimate natures, 32; on interdependence, 372; and "naturecultures," 128, 134, 143; and queer animals, 52; on Rooseveltian masculinity, 14; and scientific study of animals, 57–58

Hardaway, Tim, 231

Hardin, Garrett, 153

Hardt, Michael, 316

Harlem, 35, 174, 176, 195

Harrison, Gary, 119

Hartman, Betsy, 233–34

hate crimes, 233, 242, 292–93

Having Faith: An Ecologist's Journey to Motherhood (Steingraber), 216

Hawkins, Ronnie Zoe, 69n6

Hayes, Tyrone, 211–14, 226nn12,13

health issues, 202, 209

Hearn, Samuel, 321–22

heart disease, 202

Heaven's Coast (Doty), 343

hedgehogs, 55

Hegelian historical materialism, 260

hegemonic culture, 286

Hekman, Susan, 69n5

Helms, Jesse, 304–305

Henderson, Russell, 307n8

heptachlor, 225n2

herbicides, 211

Herdt, Gilbert, 137

hermaphrodites, 203, 209, 210–11, 212, 214

Herring, Scott, 28

Herzog, Werner, 60

heterogenesis, 380n11

heteronormativity: and *Ballot Measure 9,* 238–39; and Canadian identity, 319; challenges to, 23, 232; and ecocriticism, 233; and endocrine-disruptor thesis, 216; and explanations of queer sex, 63–64; and *Happy Feet,* 117–18; and hegemonic culture, 286; Lancaster on, 59; and landscape ecology, 254, 260; and lesbian feminist poetry, 285; and oppression, 301; and penguin sexuality, 112; and public sex, 162; and the religious right, 290; and reproduction, 9–11, 57–60, 129–30n1; and research, 54, 57–60; and social structure, 104–108; and variety of animal sexual behaviors, 54–56, 64–65; and wildlife films, 58–59

heteropatriarchy: challenges to, 151, 306n4; and criminalization of homosexuality, 304; and lesbian feminist poetry, 299, 301; as product of capitalism-national-

ism, 167–68; and the religious right, 289, 290; and violence against gays, 292; *See also* patriarchy and patriarchal family relations

heterosexuals and heterosexism: agricultural metaphors, 296–97; as environmentally destructive, 246–51; and founding of America, 313–14; and homophobia, 202; and lesbian feminist poetry, 285; and nationalism, 313; and the parks movement, 13–14, 18–19; and pastoral tradition, 24; and public sex, 168n2; and queer melancholia, 340; and settlement of the west, 19–20; and urban environments, 19; *See also* heteronormativity

hexachlorobenzene, 225n2

hierarchical social relationships, 38, 298, 304, 316

Highway, Tomson, 38, 324–25, 326–27

Hird, Myra J.: on animal culture, 60–61, 142–44; on new materialism in science, 69–70n9; on normative views of nature, 138–39; on sexual diversity, 12; on variety of animal sexual behaviors, 52, 54, 56, 64

historical materialism, 260

The History of Sexuality (Foucault), 7, 314–15, 316

Hitler, Adolf, 86, 88–89

HIV/AIDS: and Christian fundamentalists, 118; and cultural assimilation, 326; and ecological damage, 39; and ethical relationships, 341; and Grover's *North Enough,* 334, 344–49; and Jarman's *Modern Nature,* 349–54; and landscape ecology, 262; and melancholia, 333–34, 341–42; and pathologics of sexual diversity, 166; and public sex, 161; and queer ecologies, 343–44; and sexual pleasure, 164, 165; and the West End, Vancouver, 274, 275–76

Hogan, Katie, 27, 36, 173, 305

Hogan's Alley, 271

Holmes, Oliver Wendell, 86

home, bodies as, 200

Homo sapiens, 82

homoeroticism, 4, 296–97, 302–303, 321–22

homogeneity, 73

"homophile pastoralism," 23

homophobia: absence of, in non-human animals, 143–44; and anti-toxics discourse, 202; and "back to the land" movement, 180; and *Ballot Measure 9,* 238; and criminalization of homosexuality, 297, 300–301; and effects of endocrine-disrupting toxins, 211, 214; and environmental damage, 355; and environmental politics, 34, 36; and eugenics, 241, 326; and gay ghettos, 264–65; and Hegelian historical materialism, 261; and heteronormativity, 4; and lesbian feminist poetry, 302; and melancholia, 339, 340; and pastoralism, 23; and penguin sexuality, 111; and queer animals, 137; and racism, 241; and religion, 17, 117–18, 241, 326; and reproductive politics, 111, 113, 117; resistance to, 272–77; and Rich's poetry, 294; and rural environments, 17; and Stanley Park, 257; and strategic essentialism, 140; and Thatcherite Britain, 350–51; and the West End, Vancouver, 275–76; and women's music festivals, 189. *See also* violence

Homosexual Behavior in Animals: An Evolutionary Perspective (Vasey and Sommer), 12, 67

homosocial desire and bonding, 15, 321–23, 324

Hormonally Active Agents in the Environment committee, 207

Hotel Vancouver, 270

House Subcommittee on Health and the Environment, 206

"How Flowers Changed the World" (Meloy), 364–67

How Green Were the Nazis: Nature, Environment, and the Nation in the Third Reich (Bruggemeier, Cioc and Zeller), 235, 238

Hudson's Bay Company, 318

Human Betterment Foundation, 86

human exceptionalism, 64

human rights, 257, 273, 276, 289

Humboldt penguins, 53, 112–13

humpback chub, 376–78

Huntington, Orville, 120–21

Hurricane Katrina, 124

Hutchinson, Brian, 158

hybridization, 80, 378

hyenas, 66

hypospadias, 208, 209, 226n10

identity politics, 265

Idylls (Theocritus), 4

IES (Integrated Environmental Systems), 222

Illicit Sexual Activity in Public Places (Johnson), 160

immigrants and immigration: and beauty/nail salon workers, 222; and environmentalists, 157, 169n8, 235; and eugenics, 84–85, 90, 93, 97nn13,14, 233, 234, 235; immigration law, 13, 97nn13,14, 98n15; and "native land" term, 307n6;

and racialized sexual attitudes, 157; and reproductive politics, 125; and the West End, Vancouver, 269, 276

Immigration Restriction Act, 85

Immigration Restriction League, 84

immune system, 202, 208

imperialism, 150, 152, 311–12. *See also* colonialism and colonization

In Timber Country: Working People's Stories of Environmental Conflict and Urban Flight (Brown), 244

in utero exposure to toxins, 208

inclusion, 73–74, 96, 117

An Inconvenient Truth (2006), 34, 115, 122, 125, 153

India, 160

Indiana, 155

indigenous peoples: and aboriginal cosmologies, 139; Arctic indigenous peoples, 118–23, 130nn8,9; and Canadian identity, 312, 316–18, 319; and canoes, 38, 328n4; and climate change, 102, 122, 130n9; and crime-against-nature discourse, 51; and eco-tourism, 20; endangered cultures, 118–23; and environmental damage, 118–23, 128, 130n9; and eugenics, 83–84; and global warming, 102, 119–23, 130n9; and landscape ecology, 262; and nature/culture divide, 33; and species concept, 82; as threat to pristine nature, 152; and variety of animal sexual behaviors, 66. *See also* First Nations; Native Americans

industrialism and industrialization: emergence of, 244; environmental effects of, 153; and "homosexual degeneracy," 9; industrial forestry, 137; industrial waste, 178; and overpopulation, 123, 124; and the parks movement, 13; and racialized sexual attitudes, 150; and urbanization, 154; and Vancouver, 266

infertility, 201, 208, 221, 226n10

infrastructural projects, 20

Ingram, Gordon Brent, 18, 19, 36

injustice, 199–200

innatist theory, 113, 140

insects, 10, 370–72

intelligent design, 114

The Intemperate Rainforest (Braun), 337

Inter-American Human Rights Commission, 130n9

interdependence, 200, 372

interdisciplinary sciences, 134, 254

"intergrades," 377

international development, 152

interracial relationships, 157, 237

intersex individuals: breeding for intersex

expressions, 66; definition of, 219; and endocrine-disrupting toxins, 207, 209, 212, 219–21; fish, 35, 219; frogs, 201, 223, 226n12; gulls, 207; and perceived instability of maleness, 201
interspecies crossing, 372–75
Inuit, 120, 130nn8,9
Inupiaq, 130n8
Inuvialit, 130n8
inverts, 8–9, 16, 24, 84
involution, 360, 369, 375, 380n12
IQ tests, 85, 90, 98n16
Iroquois Nation, 328n5
Iverson, Ed, 117–18

Jacquet, Luc, 102, 115
Jameson, Fredric, 261
Japanese macaques, 57, 63–65
Jarman, Derek: and AIDS memoirs, 331, 343; background, 334; and devastated landscapes, 39; film projects, 357n15; and grief, 354–55; and *Modern Nature,* 349–54
Jeffery, Duane, 67
Jeffers, Robinson, 291
Jennings, John, 318, 319, 320, 322
Jeunet, Jean-Pierre, 37
Jewett, Sarah Orne, 24
Jewish community, 83–84, 274
Jim Crow racism, 93
Johansson, Leona, 135
John Paul II, Pope, 290
Johnson, Christine, 220
jook joints, 174, 175
Judeo-Christian beliefs, 180, 286. *See also* Christianity
juniper, 368–69

Kalaaiit, 130n8
Kaposi's sarcoma, 348
Katz, Jonathan, 7
Katz, L. S., 63
Katz, Ned, 156
Kazanjian, David, 340
Keohane, Kieran, 311
Kevorkian, Kriss, 355–56n2
Kew Gardens, 27
Keyes, Steven, 73
Keynes, John Maynard, 169n6
Kimmel, David, 14
Kincaid, Jamaica, 25
Kinsey, Alfred, 15
Kinsman, Gary, 317
The Kiss of the Fur Queen (Highway), 38, 324–27
Kokomo Reservoir Park in Indiana, 155
Kooyman, Gerald, 130n5

Krafft-Ebing, Richard von, 7, 9, 84
Kristeva, Julia, 356n7
Kristiansand, Norway, 135
Ku Klux Klan, 240–41
Kübler-Ross, Elisabeth, 331–32, 355n1
Kueke, Heike, 53, 112
Kushner, Tony, 22

LA Times, 331
laborers, unskilled, 213
Lake Ontario, 207
Lake Quinsigamond, 155
Lambert, Lisa, 251n2
Lament for a Nation: The Defeat of Canadian Nationalism (Grant), 327n2
Lancaster, Roger N., 59–60, 62, 106–107, 113
landfills, 347, 348–49
landscape and landscape ecology: and Canadian identity, 320, 322; and cultural dimensions, 263–66; death and transformation in, 354–55; described, 254–57; devastated landscapes, 38–39, 334; erotic landscapes, 312; and heteronormativity, 254, 260; and "New Materialism," 261; and queer theory, 36; and sexuality, 314; and social justice struggles, 260; and spatial vocabulary, 261–63, 273, 277; and urban activism, 277–78; and urban setting, 258; and the West End, Vancouver, 36, 266–72, 279n10
Langston, Nancy, 41n11, 214–16
language, 61, 94
Larson, Edward, 88
Latour, Bruno, 51, 68
Laughlin, Harry, 86
Lavender Menace, 179
Lawrence v. Texas, 287, 290, 305
LEAP (Lesbians for Empowerment, Action, and Politics), 189–90, 192
Lee, Wendy Lynne, 29
legal rights, 287, 298
leisure patterns, 322
Lemagie, Sarah, 158
Leo Africanus, 151
Leopold, Aldo, 331, 355
Lesbian Communities: Festivals, RVs, and the Internet (Rothblum and Sablove), 195
Lesbian National Parks and Services (Lesbian Rangers), 41n14, 312, 328n3
lesbianism: and activism, 289; and athletics, 269–70; butch lesbians, 177, 271–72; "dyke" (term), 191; and environmental movement, 35; and eroticism, 37–38, 288, 306n4; and feminism, 259, 264, 272, 286; femme lesbians, 177, 271; and gay ghettos, 264, 271–72; in gulls, 54, 207;

and heteronormativity, 290–91; history of, 16; homelessness of, 299–300; lesbian novelists, 306n4; lesbian pastoralism, 24; lesbophobic discourses, 41n14; and penguin sexuality, 112; and Pratt's poetry, 297–306; "queer" (term), 191, 307n5; and Rich's poetry, 291–97; separatist communes, 135; and Victorianism, 8; and the West End, Vancouver, 258–59, 273, 276, 278. *See also* alternative lesbian environments

LeVay, Simon, 137, 140

lgbtq (lesbian, gay, bisexual, transgender, queer), 21

lgbtqqi (lesbian, gay, bisexual, transgender, queer, questioning, and intersex), 251n1

liberation activism, 289

lifestyle consumerism, 21–22

Linné, Carl von (Linnaeus), 76, 366–67

literature: ecological writing, 37; lesbian novelists, 306n4; and queer animals, 33; and resistance discourses, 22

littering, 158–59, 161

"Little Hans," 363–64

Little Sister's (bookstore), 276

Living Downstream: An Ecologist Looks at Cancer and the Environment (Steingraber), 216–19

lizards, 66

Locke, John, 317

logging, 266, 268, 345, 346–47

Lorde, Audre, 168

Los Angles, Calif., 244

low-income workers, 213

The L-Word, 21, 34

Lynch, Kevin, 261

Mabon, Lon, 240

macaques, 57, 61–62, 63–65

MacDonald, Heather, 36, 236, 238–43, 245

MacNeice, Louis, 68

MacVicar, Morgana, 183, 184

Magubane, Zine, 9

Maize, 28

Malthus, Thomas, 152, 153

Malthusianism: and homophobia, 34; and morality concerns, 159–60; and non-white reproduction, 152–54; and same-sex eroticism, 154; sociopolitical-conditions, emphasis on, 164

mammals, 203. *See also specific species*

manifest destiny ideology, 234

Maple Grove, Minn., 163

Mapping Desire (Bell and Valentine), 19

The March of the Penguins (2005): described, 102; and environmental marketing, 127; and global warming, 115; and the religious right, 33, 109–10, 117–18

marginalization, 255, 298

marketing of nature, 34, 70n12, 115–16

Marks, Jonathan, 56–57

marriage rights, 306

Marxist theory, 260

masculinity, 2–3, 356–57n10

Mason, Bill, 319–20

Massachusetts, 155

Massumi, Brian, 67

masturbation, 61–62, 159

material feminisms, 69–70n9

Material Feminisms (Alaimo and Hekman), 69n5

materialism, 180, 195

Matonabbee, Chief, 321–22

matriarchies, 189

matrix, 263, 267, 273, 276, 277

Maurice (Forster), 23, 28

Maynard, Steven, 313

Mayr, Ernst, 76–77, 82, 90–94, 97n2

McCarthyism, 270

McClintock, Anne, 313

McKinney, Aaron, 307n8

McLaren, Angus, 98n15

McWhorter, Ladelle, 29, 32, 69n4, 314–15

media, 155, 207–208, 377

medical discourses, 15

medical view of homosexuality, 13

Medved, Michael, 109

Megalli, Michael, 116

melancholia: and AIDS memoirs, 343–44; Butler on, 339–42; and eco-tourism, 339; and environmental context, 354; and environmental damage, 331–34, 342, 344–49; and Freud, 38, 334–36, 337, 356nn5,6; and grief, 38–39; and Grover's *North Enough,* 344–49; and Jarman's *Modern Nature,* 349–54; melancholic remembering, 355; melancholy natures, 337–39; and mourning, 334–36; and Oedipal relations, 356–57n10

Meloy, Ellen: and biophilia, 39, 361–64, 372–75; and Dillard, 37; and floraphilia, 369–72; on native fish recovery efforts, 375; and prickly pear biology, 370–72; publications, 378n1; and queer desire, 375–78; and rhizome sex, 367–69; on stereotyping, 376, 380n14; and wildflower sex, 364–67; work described, 5, 359–61

memorialization, 350

menstruation (menarche), 217, 226n14

mental illnesses view of homosexuality, 289

Merced, Calif., 155

metabolic diseases, 208

naturalization of sexuality, 8, 13
"Naturally Queer" (Hird), 12, 69–70n9
nature writing, 22
naturecultures: described, 134; and queer desire, 60; and reproductive politics, 128; and sexual culture in animals, 143; and sexual pleasure, 61; and variety of animal sexual behaviors, 64
nature-nostalgia, 333
Naturhistorisk Museum, 52
naturism and naturists, 33, 134, 140–42, 143
Nava, Michael, 245
Navajo, 371–72
Naveh, Zev, 261–62
Nazis and Nazism, 86–87, 90, 235
Nebraska, 244, 251n2
Negri, Antonio, 316
neo-Darwinian theory, 363
neo-evolutionism, 369, 379n9
neoliberalism, 262
networks, 257–61, 274, 277
neurological and neurobehavioral problems, 202, 207–208
neurotoxins, 210
New Atlantis (Bacon), 151
New England, 294
New France, 318
"New Materialism," 261
New Perspectives on Environmental Justice (Stein), 27
New York, 174–75, 244, 258
New York Times, 109, 115–16, 194, 203, 242
New York Times Magazine, 380n14
Newton, Esther, 28, 175
Nightline, 139
Nightwork: A Dave Brandstetter Mystery (Hansen), 36, 236–37, 246–51
nihilism, 361
No Future (Edelman), 377
"No Place" (Pratt), 299
Noble, Bobby, 41n17
non-native species, 346
nonreproductive sex, 154; and degeneracy theory, 11; and deviance, 7; and evolution, 360; and gender identity, 137; and heteronormativity, 254; and natural selection, 360; and queer nature, 360; and social relations, 10
non-Western cultures, 66
non-whites and non-white reproduction: and African sexuality, 151–52; and agency, 164; and colonialism, 151–52; and denial of erotic pleasure, 163–64, 166; homosexual non-whites, 156–57, 167; and morality concerns, 159–60, 167; and nationalism, 155–58; and over-

population, 149, 152–54; as queer sex, 150, 166; as threat to nature, 157–58; as threat to the nation, 155–57
Nordics, 83
"normate," 224
North Carolina, 298
North Enough: AIDS and Other Clear-Cuts (Grover), 334, 344–49
North West Company, 318
North West Mounted Police, 318
north woods, Minnesota and Wisconsin, 334, 344–49
Nott, Josiah, 79–81
Novartis, 211
nuclear family structure, 114, 125, 143
nuclear power and weapons, 332, 349, 379n4
nudity: at LEAP, 190; nudist movement, 33, 140–42 (*see also* naturism and naturists); at Pagoda, 183; public nudity, 140–42

obesity, 202, 217, 218
Oedipal relations, 356–57n10
Office of Community Oriented Policing Services, 160
Ohio, 155
Ojibway, 346
Olley, Brian, 159
Olmsted, Frederick Law, 18
"On Transience" (Freud), 336
Opar, Alisa, 51
oppression, 234
O'Quinn, Daniel, 350–51, 357n16
Ordover, Nancy, 233, 234–35, 241
Oregon: alternative lesbian environments in, 28, 35, 42n22, 181, 182, 183, 306n4; and Ballot Measure 9, 17, 236–43, 245–46, 250–51, 251n3, 305–306; and criminalization of homosexuality, 306; and the Donation Land Act, 19–20; and homophobia, 17
Oregon Citizens' Alliance, 36, 237–43, 251n3
Oregon Women's Land Trust, 182, 234
The Origin of Species (Darwin), 81–82
Osborn, Frederick, 88–89, 98n20
Osborn, Torie, 186
"other minds" problem, 69n3
"Others," 151, 321
Our Stolen Future (Colborn, Dumanoski, and Myers), 205, 207, 216
Out Front Blog, 195
outdoor pursuits, 3–4
ovaries: abnormalities in, 206; ovarian cancer, 202, 208
overpopulation: and agency, 164; as bad science, 153; and environmental justice,

126–29; and environmentalism, 149, 152–54, 159–60, 169n7; and homophobia, 34; and morality concerns, 159–60; and non-whites, 149, 152–54; in popular culture, 108; and reproductive justice, 123–26; and sterilization, 150, 165; and the United States, 123, 124–25

Pacific Northwest, 15
Pagoda womynspace in Florida, 35, 182–86, 192
paintbrush genera, 366, 368
pancreatic cancer, 216
paradigm shifts, 69n5
parasitism, 368, 379–80n10
Park Slope, N.Y., 17
parks: arrests in, 155, 161; Central Park Zoo penguins, 110–12; and democratization of natural space, 26; and environmentalism, 127, 355; and "everyday eugenics," 245; and gardens, 350; and hate crimes, 307n8; and heteronormativity, 12–14; and heterosexism, 19; and lesbophobic discourses, 41n14; and mourning the loss of nature, 337; national parks, 150, 152, 235, 240–41; and Nazi environmentalism, 235; and public campground design, 19; and public sex, 17–19, 26–27, 149–52, 155, 158–59, 160–63; and racial exclusivity, 240–41; and urban parks movement, 17–19; and white nation building, 159. *See also specific parks, including* Stanley Park, Vancouver
Participatory Research, Organizing, and Leadership Initiative for Safety and Health, 222–23
parties, private, 175
Partlow, William, 86, 88
partnership with nature, 180, 182, 187, 190, 195–96
pastoralism: and attitudes toward sexuality, 135; and eco-tourism, 20; and heteronormativity, 4; homophile pastoralism, 23–27, 40n5, 41n17; and Jarman's *The Garden* (1990), 357n15; and lesbian feminist poetry, 27, 306n4; and Pratt's poetry, 301; and public parks, 26; and Rich's poetry, 294; Shuttleton on, 41n17; and women-centered separatism, 41–42n21
patches, 262, 277
paternalism, 178
Paterson, Hugh E. H., 92–93, 94–95
pathological view of homosexuality, 10–11
patriarchy and patriarchal family relations: and "back to the land" movement, 181;

and capitalism, 13–14; and criminalization of homosexuality, 299; and *The Feminine Mystique,* 178; and gendered environments, 16; and oppression, 301; and overpopulation, 125–26, 149; and reproductive politics, 105–108, 109–14; and "romantic friendships," 41n13; and Stanley Park, 257; and women's political workshops, 191. *See also* heteropatriarchy
Pauline doctrine, 286–89, 293, 295–98, 305
PCBs, 204, 205–206, 225n2
pedophilia, 289
penguins: and anthropomorphism, 110–12, 130n5; Chinstrap, 116–18; Emperor, 114–18; and family structure, 108–14; homosexuality among, 53, 102, 110–14; Humboldt, 53, 112–13; and *The March of the Penguins* (2005), 33, 102, 109–10, 115, 117–18, 127; and reproduction, 103–108; and sexuality in nature, 108–14
penises, size of, 206
Pennsylvania, 187, 192, 233
Pennsylvania's Campfest, 187, 192
Perry, Adele, 267
Persky, Stan, 266
pesticides, 178, 206, 208, 213
Petchesky, Rosalind, 164–65
Peterman, Frank, 240–41
phenotypic racism, 89
Phillips, Dana, 361
Phillips Electronics, 127, 128
phthalates, 218
physical ability and access to nature, 241
Pickering, Andrew, 67
pigs, 66
Pilgrim at Tinker Creek (Dillard), 37
Pivot of Civilization (Sanger), 168n4
"The Place Lost and Gone, the Place Found" (Pratt), 301
plant ecology, 364–67, 370–72, 379–80n10
plastics, 208
Platonic view of species, 76
pleasure, 32, 37, 60–64, 150, 164–65
Pocono Mountains, 189
police: harassment of gays, 155, 161, 270–71, 273, 290; and pollution of natural spaces, 158; and public sex, 160–61, 162–63
POLISH (Participatory Research, Organizing, and Leadership Initiative for Safety and Health), 222–23
politics and political activism: and animal culture, 60; and Arctic indigenous peoples, 130n9; and biophilia, 375; and biopower, 323–24; and Carson's *Silent Spring,* 178; at Cherry Grove, 176, 177; and the Cold War, 271; and criminaliza-

tion of homosexuality, 304; and culture of "the Child," 377, 380n15; Foucault on, 315; and HIV/AIDS, 341; and indigenous arctic peoples, 119–20; and lesbian feminist poetry, 304; and overpopulation, 124; political resistance, 167–68; political workshops, 189–90; politicizing grief, 356n4; polluted politics, 224; and public sex, 143; and queer landscape ecology, 257; represented in film and fiction, 238, 243, 246; and resistance discourses, 23; and the West End, Vancouver, 258, 273–74. See also environmentalism and environmental activism

pollution: air pollution, 218; and Arctic indigenous peoples, 102; and environmental justice groups, 35; and gender dimorphism, 11; lgbtq associated with, 241; public sex equated with, 158–59, 160, 162

polychlorinated biphenyls (PCBs), 204, 205–206, 225n2

polycystic ovary syndrome, 218

polygeny, 79–81

Popenoe, Paul, 86

POPs (persistent organic pollutants), 202, 225n2

popular culture: and animal sexuality, 113; Edelman on, 377; and environmental justice, 27; and environmental threats, 119; and human reproduction, 129–30n1; Meloy on, 376; and patriarchal family structure, 107–108; penguins in, 114–18

Population Action International, 169n7

The Population Bomb (Ehrlich), 149, 153

population control, 9, 315. See also overpopulation

population growth: and environmental documentaries, 33; as environmental threat, 169n7; and Malthusianism, 34, 152–54, 159–60, 164; and reproductive justice, 123–26. See also overpopulation

Population-Environment Balance, 125

pornography, 134, 136, 143

port cities, 15, 244

postcolonial theory, 21

postindustrial global capitalism, 110

poverty, 149, 153

Pratt, Minnie Bruce: on homophobia, 285; and lesbian feminist poetry, 37–38, 288–89; and oppression, 301; and pastoral imagery, 302; poetry of, 297–306; and "queer" term, 307n5; and queering nature, 305

Preface to Eugenics (Osborn), 89

premature births, 217, 218

prenatal development, 201, 218

preservationist movement, 3, 14

Prichard, James Cowles, 79

prickly pears, 370–72, *371*

Pride events, 34, 279n10

priests and sexual abuse, 325–27

Primal Tears (Wilson), 68–69n2

Primate Sexuality (Dixon), 62

Primate Visions (Haraway), 58

primates, 58

primitivism, 51

production politics, 104, 121–22

pro-family movement, 98n20

pro-life movement, 106, 361, 377

"promiscuous entanglements," 379–80n10

property law, 19–20, 42n22

Prospect Cottage, 349–54

Prosser, Jay, 314

prostate cancer, 202, 207–208, 214

prostitution, 152, 159, 274, 275, 289–90

pseudohomosexuality, 40n9

psychoanalytic theory, 333

Psychopathia Sexualis (Krafft-Ebing), 84

puberty, early onset of, 216, 217–19, 226n14

pubic hair growth (pubarche), 226n14

public nudity, 140–42

public opinion, 267

public safety, 150, 159–63

public sex: attempts to curtail, 163, 268, 270–71; and citizenship, 17–18; criminalization of, 150, 155, 160–61, 162; and Fuck For Forests, 33, 135–37, 142–43; and homophobia, 272–73; and landscape ecology, 262; and morality concerns, 150, 160–63; nature's role in, 144; and public opinion, 267; as threat to nature, 27, 149–50, 155, 158–59, 160, 163; of women or heterosexuals, 168n2. See also Stanley Park, Vancouver

public spaces, 261, 277–78

punishments for queer sex, 286–87

purity, premium placed on, 235

Queen's Park, 26

queer animals: Alaimo on, 379n3; and homophobia, 137; and naturalism, 142; and naturecultures, 33, 134, 137–40; and sexual culture in animals, 142–44; and variety of animal sexual behaviors, 64. See also queer nature

Queer as Folk, 16, 21–22, 34

queer ecology, 5, 22, 166–68; geneology of, 6

queer nature: and Canadian identity, 312; Clare on, 25; and Haraway, 40n8; and heteronormativity, 4; and Jarman's *Modern Nature*, 350, 354; and lesbian feminist poetry, 288, 299, 302; and nonreproductive sex, 360; and scope of book, 6; and variety of animal sexual behaviors, 64. *See also* queer animals

"queer" term, 191, 307n5

queer theory: and anti-essentialism, 139–40; and ecocriticism, 236; and ecocultural relations, 22–23; green queer theory, 32; and interdisciplinary sciences, 134; and material conditions, 254–55; and queer animals, 64–65; and queer ecology, 260

queerbashing, 290

Queering the Non/Human (Hird), 134

Queers in Space (Ingram, Bouthillette, and Retter), 19

queerscapes, 278

Quigley, Peter, 232, 233

Race Hygiene/Race Betterment movements, 76

racial identity and racism: and access to nature, 240–41; and anti-immigration sentiments, 157, 169n8; at Cherry Grove, 177; and Christian conservatism, 117–18; and degeneracy view of homosexuality, 13–14; and discrimination, 287; and endangered cultures, 119; and environmental politics, 34, 234; and eugenics, 83–89, 89–91, 98n21, 241; and field of queer ecology, 166–67; and health issues, 218; and homophobia, 241; and indigenous peoples, 123; and morality concerns, 160; and nationalism, 15, 312, 313, 316–17, 318–19; and overpopulation, 125, 149, 152, 169n6; and phenotypes, 91; and polygeny, 81; and popular culture, 27; and queer theory, 51; and race riots, 266; and racial development, 83; and reproductive rights, 106; and segregation, 81, 93, 269; and "species" concept, 75–76; "state racism," 316; and sterilization campaigns, 80, 83; and the West End, Vancouver, 276; and women's music festivals, 189

Racism and Sexual Oppression in Anglo-America (McWhorter), 98n20

Radical Ecopsychology (Fisher), 355n2

radical faeries, 135

radical public naturism, 142

Raffan, James, 310–11

rainbow trout, 346

rainforest destruction, 137

Ramsey, Sandy, 188

Ray, Janisse, 219–21

Reagan, Ronald, 290

reality porn ethic, 136

Recognition Concept, 94–95

refugees, 265

religion: and access to nature, 241; and crime-against-nature ideology, 297; and forced conversions, 324; and homophobia, 17, 117–18, 241, 326; Judeo-Christian beliefs, 180, 286; the religious right, 33, 109–10, 117–18, 289–90; and reproductive isolation, 94; and Save Our Children campaign, 289–90. *See also* Christianity; Pauline doctrine

relocation of wildlife, 373–75

"Remapping Same-Sex Desire: Queer Writing and Culture in the American Heartland" (Spurlin), 244

repression, 257, 315, 353

reproduction: capacity for, 206, 207, 221; and Christian beliefs, 286, 295–97, 298; and culture of "the Child," 377, 380n15; and environmental damage, 108, 118; and environmental justice, 128; Foucault on, 315; and genetics, 129–30n1; and heteronormativity, 9–11, 57–60, 129–30n1; and indigenous peoples, 121–22; and nature/culture divide, 32–33; and naturism, 143; of non-whites, *see* non-whites and non-white reproduction; and normative views of nature, 138; and overpopulation, 119; and Pauline doctrine, 286; and primate sexuality, 56; and reproductive imperative, 156; and reproductive justice, 123–26, 221–22; and reproductive politics, 34, 103–108; and sexual selection, 7–8

"Reproductive and Sexual Rights" (Correa and Petchesky), 164–65

Republic of Haiti, 154

reservation system, 317

resort experiences, 192

resource scarcity, 124

Retter, Yolanda, 19

RFD (Radical Faerie Digest), 28

Rhea County, Tenn., 231

rheas, 66

rhizomes, 367–69, 370

Rich, Adrienne: on geographic identity, 285; and lesbian feminist poetry, 37–38, 288; poetry of, 291–97; and queer ecology genre, 25; and "queer" term, 307n5; and queering nature, 305; and the religious right, 289–91

right-wing politics, 102, 103–108, 110–14, 306

Rilke, Rainer Maria, 336, 356n8

rivers, 303, 346

Robson, Craig, 162

Roche Pharmaceuticals, 118, 128

Rod and Gun, 322

Rodonia, Brazil, 154
Roman culture, 4
romantic relationships, 41n13, 306n4
Rome, Adam, 178
Roosevelt, Theodore, 4, 14, 20, 40n6
Rothblum, Esther, 195
Rothenberg, Tamar Roth, 17
Roughgarden, Joan: and evolutionary
  thought, 12; and new materialism in sci-
  ence, 69–70n9; on variety in nature, 31,
  52, 54–56, 65–66, 68, 137–38
Roundup (glyphosate), 211
Rowbotham, Sheila, 41n17
Rubin, Gayle, 290
Ruff (birds), 66
Rugoff, Ralph, 143
Rule, Jane, 25
rural environments: and back-to-the-land
  movements, 28, 35, 180–82, 242; in
  Brokeback Mountain, 40n3; and Carpenter, 27–28; Clare on, 25–26; and heterosexism, 19; as heterosexual domain,
  243; and homophobia, 305–306; and
  identity production, 16–17; and lesbianism, 174; and pastoral tradition, 23; and
  queer theory, 243–46; queers in, 28–29,
  243, 244–45; and Rich's poetry, 294;
  urban environments compared to, 175;
  and violence against gays, 17, 287. *See
  also* parks; wilderness areas
Russo, Vito, 177

Sablove, Penny, 195
SAFIRE (Sisters in Action for Issues of Reproductive Empowerment), 222, 223
Sakao, 66
salpingectomy, 86, 88
*Same-Sex Affairs: Constructing and Control-
  ling Homosexuality in the Pacific Northwest* (Boag), 234
Sami, 130n8
San Francisco, Calif., 17, 244, 258, 344
Sandilands, Catriona: and "back to the
  land" movement, 173, 181, 182, 242; on
  ecological citizenship, 160; on erotophobia, 63, 165–66, 169n11; on lesbian gulls,
  54; on lesbian land communities, 306n4;
  and melancholy, 38–39; and "queer ecology" term, 200; and "queering nature,"
  288; on relationship of humans to nature, 163–64; on "romantic friendships,"
  41n13
Sanger, Margaret, 168n4
Savage-Rumbaugh, Susan, 61
Save Our Children campaign, 289–90,
  298–99
Scauzillo, Retts, 191, 192

Schill, Michael, 248
Science, 153
scientia sexualis, 7, 368
scientific racism, 75–76
sea rockets, 379–80n10
Sea World/Busch Gardens Conservation
  Fund, 127–28
seagulls, 11, 54, 207
Section 28, 140
Sedgwick, Eve, 56, 321
segregation, 81, 93, 269
Seibert, Scott, 242–43
Seitler, Dana, 9
sentimentality, 357n14
separatism, 22, 28–29, 41n21, 135, 180–81
serial monogamy, 113
sex panics, 202, 210, 221
sex ratios, 207, 208, 209
sex tourism, 20
sexism: and "back to the land" movement,
  180; and Christian conservatism, 117–
  18; and human reproduction, 129–30n1;
  and innatism, 113
sexology, 30, 75–76, 141
sexual abuse, 25
sexual arousal, 141
sexual differentiation, 214–16
sexual dimorphism: and environmental
  damage, 11, 40–41n11, 209, 216; and
  eugenics, 88, 90–91; and sexual diversity, 12
sexual health education, 164
sexual histories, 352
sexual identities, 8, 314–15, 316
sexual instability, 201, 202
sexual inversion, 8–9, 16, 24, 84
sexual justice, 286, 293
sexual minorities, 257–61, 262
sexual oppression, 234. *See also* homophobia
sexual politics, 5, 12–21, 27
sexual selection, 7–8, 9–10, 375–76
sexual subcultures, 264, 279n10
sexually transmitted disease, 161. *See also*
  HIV/AIDS
Shakopee, Minn., 162
"Shame the Johns" campaign, 275
Shearer, M. K., 63
sheep, bighorn, 65–66, 361–64, 372–75, 376
Shen, Eveline, 222, 223
Shenandoah National Park, 307n8
Shepard, Matthew, 292–93, 307n8
Shuttleton, David, 23–24, 41nn16,17
"sideways knowing," 367
Sierra Club, 125, 153, 157, 169n7, 235
Sierra Youth Coalition of Canada, 250
Signorile, Michelangelo, 242

World War I, 336
World War II, 20, 244
World Wide Fund for Nature, 137
Worth, Peter, 177
Wright, Rebecca, 307n8

xenophobia, 13, 84–85, 157. *See also* racial
  identity and racism

"Yom Kippur 1984" (Rich), 291, 292, 300
Young, Robert J. C., 157
Your Native Land, Your Life (Rich), 289–91,
  291–97, 305
Yu'pik (or Yupiit), 120–21, 130n8

Zeller, Thomas, 235
Zimmerman, Bonnie, 306n4

CPSIA information can be obtained
at www.ICGtesting.com
Printed in the USA
BVHW040259290520
580463BV00002B/24

9 780253 222039